CHANGING THE GAME

A HISTORY OF *NHL* EXPANSION

STEPHEN LAROCHE
FOREWORD BY JOHN GARRETT

ECW PRESS

Published by ECW Press
2120 Queen Street East, Suite 200
Toronto, Ontario, Canada M4E 1E2
416-694-3348 / info@ecwpress.com

Printing: Norecob 5 4 3 2 1
PRINTED AND BOUND IN CANADA

Library and Archives Canada
Cataloguing in Publication

Laroche, Stephen, author
Changing the game : a history of NHL expansion /
Stephen Laroche ; foreword by John Garrett.

Issued in print and electronic formats.
ISBN 978-1-77041-079-4 (pbk.)
978-1-77090-577-1 (PDF);
978-1-77090-578-8 (ePUB)

' 1. National Hockey League—History. I. Title.

GV847.8.N3L37 2014   796.962'64
C2014-902560-2   C2014-902561-0

Editor for the press: Michael Holmes
Cover design: Patrick Gray
Type: Troy Cunningham
All photos from the collection of Doug McLatchy

The publication of Changing the Game has been generously supported by the Canada Council for the Arts which last year invested $157 million to bring the arts to Canadians throughout the country, and by the Ontario Arts Council (OAC), an agency of the Government of Ontario, which last year funded 1,793 individual artists and 1,076 organizations in 232 communities across Ontario, for a total of $52.1 million. We also acknowledge the financial support of the Government of Canada through the Canada Book Fund for our publishing activities, and the contribution of the Government of Ontario through the Ontario Book Publishing Tax Credit and the Ontario Media Development Corporation.

To my wife, Michelle, and my stepdaughter, Guenevere. This book has long been a dream of mine and I wholeheartedly thank you both for your support.

This book is also dedicated to all the players, coaches and management staff who were ever involved with an NHL expansion team. Hockey fans will forever remember your amazing experiences and all that you contributed to making the sport the greatest one in the world.

FOREWORD
by JOHN GARRETT

I was playing midget hockey in 1965 when the National Hockey League announced that they were going expand by adding six teams to form another division that would begin play in the 1967–68 season. The NHL had applications from 14 cities that wanted to get into the league. That meant there would be more opportunities for me, but being a professional hockey player was not at the top of my wish list until I started playing junior hockey in Peterborough. Then in my first year in junior I won a Memorial Cup and made the All-Star Team.

I was drafted by the St. Louis Blues a year before the World Hockey Association (WHA) started up and was soon traded from the Blues to Chicago as a future consideration to complete an earlier deal for Danny O'Shea. The WHA comes into the picture a bit here, because J.P. Bordeleau originally went from St. Louis to Chicago, but he then jumped to play with the Quebec Nordiques. Chicago wanted to cover their bases and needed a player to be named later if that happened — and that player was yours truly.

The WHA began play in 1972–73 as an alternative to the NHL. Players who were previously obligated to play for the NHL team that drafted them or had traded for them now had an option. To make the paying public believe that they were truly big league, the WHA had to lure some name players. Ben Hatskin and the Winnipeg Jets went after Bobby Hull and were able to entice him to leave Chicago and head for the Manitoba capital. Hull was the centrepiece; he was the key that made other players believe this brand-new league could compete and would survive. The NHL establishment had its doubts and did not try to match the WHA money that was being offered to such great players as J.C. Tremblay, Frank Mahovlich, Paul Henderson, Gerry Cheevers and Derek Sanderson. Yet even Gordie Howe came out of retirement — and was rejuvenated — in 1973–74 when he was given the opportunity to play alongside his sons, Mark and Marty.

The WHA was the new league and could afford to try to be different. The blue puck they used rarely stayed circular after a few shots and never caught on. I have one in my basement. The clear glass boards of the St. Paul Civic Center, home to the Minnesota Fighting Saints, was a good idea for the fans but a nightmare for the goaltenders. In 1969–70, the NHL put in a rule limiting the curve in sticks to one inch, but the WHA had unlimited curvature. No wonder I let in all those long shots! The NHL limited their draft to 20-year-olds and up, but the WHA let players sign on as soon as they felt they were ready. The list of Hall of Famers and future stars who cut their teeth in the WHA is impressive. We had Wayne Gretzky, Mark Messier, Ken Linseman, Rod Langway, Michel Goulet, Rick Vaive, Mike Gartner, Craig Hartsburg, Rob Ramage, Mike Rogers, Real Cloutier and many more.

Personally, I had the good fortune to play with some of the all-time greats. I signed with the Minnesota Fighting Saints in the WHA to get a chance to play with and learn my position from one of the best goaltenders in Olympic history, and one of the best people I have ever met, Jack McCartan. If I had stayed in the NHL, I would have been stuck in the Chicago organization behind Tony Esposito and Gary Smith. The kicker was that the Hawks, even if I made the big club, were offering less than half the money!

The WHA had its growing pains, some lasting longer than others. How many of today's fans remember the Michigan Stags, the Jersey Knights, the New York City Golden Blades or the Philadelphia Blazers? They were just a few of a long list of teams who fell by the wayside.

In the last year of the WHA, it became apparent that the league and the NHL would be better served if there was a merger. Or, as the NHL preferred to see it, an expansion to include the four strongest cities and four strongest teams in the WHA. I was playing in Hartford with the Whalers and we were excited about the possibility of playing in what every Canadian kid thought of as the best league in the world.

It didn't take long for people to realize that those four teams from the WHA were as good as or better than most in the NHL. Nobody thought our Whaler team, depleted by one-sided expansion rules, could ever make the playoffs. Yet led by a determined Dave Keon, we did. And once in the NHL, the Edmonton Oilers won five Stanley Cups in their first 10 years, the Quebec Nordiques became champions as the Colorado Avalanche and the Whalers won a Cup of their own as the Carolina Hurricanes. Not bad for expansion teams!

INTRODUCTION

To this day, I can vividly recall my beginnings as a hockey fan. It is a period I look back on fondly. My introduction to the world's fastest sport came to me through books, television and, of course, hockey cards.

I was five years old during the 1981–82 season. There were 21 teams and the men who played for them were larger-than-life heroes. Although I had an appreciation for players from my hometown of Trenton, Ontario, like John Garrett of the Hartford Whalers and George Ferguson of the Pittsburgh Penguins, none of them were as big as Wayne Gretzky and his teammates on the Edmonton Oilers.

I wasn't just interested in what was going on the ice at the time. I was hooked on the history of the game. I had been taught about the Original Six era and knew which teams were around during those halcyon days. I was even more fascinated by the other teams that came after them. Once I saw a picture of a player from the California Golden Seals. *Who were the Golden Seals? Why aren't they in my hockey sticker album? Why don't I have any cards of them?*

Soon enough I began to find out more about the game's vast history and learned that occasionally teams had to relocate. That concept was introduced to me when the Colorado Rockies left the NHL and moved to New Jersey to become the Devils. I was also learning about the WHA and its crazy history and knew that the Oilers, along with the Hartford Whalers, Quebec Nordiques and Winnipeg Jets, had been a part of it. Even though I was quickly discovering that a career as a hockey player was not for me, that didn't keep me from enjoying many other aspects of the game.

As I grew older, I learned more about the origins of every NHL team. I developed a keen interest in the concept of expansion in my teen years, when the league was growing by leaps and bounds. The game was heading into the Sunbelt and new teams were appearing at a rapid pace, either through expansion or relocation. The new teams all seemed to struggle out of the gate, but I knew that that was no more than could be expected from them in their first season.

As an adult, I came to truly appreciate the human side of playing for an expansion team through my interactions with retired players in my job with In The Game, a trading card manufacturer. When I called certain players to see if they were willing to sign on for our projects, the conversation occasionally turned to their experiences playing for expansion teams. Their stories of those days were often entertaining, at times shocking, and gave me a genuine appreciation for what they went through.

This book is my tribute to all the players who ever played for a first-year team. Each of the men covered here is a part of the history of the game. Even if some of them have been forgotten, their contributions are by no means insignificant. Their presence was essential to the formation of the vast majority of the NHL's clubs. Their stories can educate and entertain and may even help us, as fans, find a little sympathy for those players who had to face greater-than-usual odds against victory every time they laced up their skates.

THE ORIGINAL EXPANSION ERA

Many fans know that the National Hockey League began play in the 1917–18 season, but few realize that the league was created as a way for a group of previously established National Hockey Association teams to cleanly break away from Eddie Livingstone, the troublemaking owner of the Toronto Blueshirts. Because the other clubs could not, according to the National Hockey Association's constitution, vote him out, they did the next best thing.

The Ottawa Senators, Quebec Athletics (otherwise known as the Bulldogs) and two teams from Montreal — the Canadiens and the Wanderers — got together to form their own loop, effectively leaving Livingstone in a league by himself and causing years of headaches for both sides. The Bulldogs were unable to drum up enough capital for the first season and their players were loaned to the other clubs. However, the NHL also decided to sell a temporary franchise to the Toronto Arena Company, enticing many Blueshirts players to jump ship. Unofficially called the Arenas, the team went on to capture the Stanley Cup in its first season and became a permanent fixture after the 1918–19 campaign before eventually changing its name to the St. Patricks.

The NHL's inaugural season also saw its first franchise fold after the Montreal Arena burned down on January 2, 1918. Before and after the fire, the Wanderers asked for reinforcements from the other teams, yet none were sent their way. The team lasted just four games before the blaze. Their next two contests were forfeited and the roster players were cut loose to other clubs.

After some delay, Quebec finally came into the league in 1919–20. They were an absolute disaster despite the presence of prolific scoring legend Joe Malone, who won a scoring championship. With a 4–20 record, they were at the bottom of the standings. The league showed some pity for them and took the franchise back. It was a smart move, as the team became the Hamilton Tigers and prevented Livingstone's rumoured new league from putting down roots in the Steel City. The Tigers were not exactly competitive for most of their existence, but there was certainly community support for them.

In the early 1920s, the NHL was still stuck in eastern Canada, but an enterprising promoter named Thomas Duggan helped change the league's fortunes by purchasing options for future franchises based in the United States. He had a hand in building the Mount Royal Arena, where the Canadiens played for a brief period and eventually sold the franchises to Charles Adams of Boston and Bill Dwyer of New York. The Boston sale was fraught with controversy, and in subsequent years long lawsuits followed. Although attentive hockey historians are aware of his contributions to the game, he never received recognition from the Hockey Hall of Fame. He died in 1930 and is almost forgotten today.

Sensing an opportunity for growth, the NHL chose to add two clubs for the 1924–25 season, and with one of them finally entered the American market. The Boston Bruins had a harsh first season, but proved a hit with local crowds and within five years saw great success. The other new club was a second team in Montreal. They tried to get the rights to revive the nickname "Wanderers" but were turned down and began play without a name. When the press and fans started calling them the Maroons, inspired by the colour of their sweaters, the name stuck. By their second season, they were Stanley Cup champions and many of the game's greatest players wore their uniform.

A labour disruption marred the end of that season, however, when players for the surprising first-place Hamilton Tigers decided to hold out for more money due to the longer schedule. As a result, the league decided to suspend them and they did not compete in the playoffs. Since the New York Americans were entering the NHL the following year, a deal was struck to send the rights of Tigers players to the new club and the Tigers were folded soon after. The Amerks played out of Madison Square Garden and were the toast of Broadway — at least for the 1925–26 season. That same year also saw the arrival of the Pittsburgh Pirates, who were built out of the ashes out of the amateur Yellowjackets club.

The death of the western pro leagues was what most furthered the NHL's original expansion. Although the sport had thrived in the west a decade earlier, the Pacific Coast Hockey Association (PCHA) eventually merged with the Western Canada Hockey League (WCHL, later WHL). The WHL had some teams in major centres, but they were all losing money, and the dream of brothers Frank and Lester Patrick, founders of the PCHA, had become a nightmare. After the 1925–26 season, talent was sold off to NHL interests looking for fresh blood, and a remarkable era of hockey history came to a close.

Many members of the Victoria Cougars ended up with the new Detroit Cougars team, and the stars of the Portland Rosebuds headed to the Chicago Black Hawks. Other NHL teams were fortified with WHL talent and the Patricks made quite a bit of money in the process — even though they did not have the right to sell some of the players. By the time Lester Patrick went to New York as coach and general manager of the Rangers, the league had 10 member clubs. Within their first decade of operation, the Cougars, Black Hawks and Rangers had each won at least one Stanley Cup and survived through to the Original Six era.

The Great Depression took its toll on many aspects of sports culture, but the NHL was hit especially hard and the league saw several franchises move or shut down. The first shift took place before the 1930–31 season, after the Pittsburgh Pirates moved across the state of Pennsylvania to become the Philadelphia Quakers. That woeful club lasted just one season, winning only four games and earning a dubious spot in hockey history.

It might be assumed that pro teams should not have too many problems up north, but the Ottawa Senators simply could not draw large enough crowds to keep their doors open. They suspended operations for the 1931–32 season and came back for two more years before they shut down for good. The franchise was moved to St. Louis to become the Eagles, but lasted only on the 1934–35 season before folding. The Montreal Maroons could not compete alongside the Canadiens for the hearts of the city's hockey fans and bid the league farewell after the 1937–38 campaign. The franchise remained active for a few years afterward, but efforts to move them to Philadelphia proved fruitless.

The New York Americans attempted to hold on valiantly for several seasons in the shadow of the Rangers. Forced to sell off top talent to stay afloat, they were mired at the bottom of the standings. Team management made an attempt to attract a different crowd by changing their name to the Brooklyn Americans, but they lasted only one final season in 1941–42. Red Dutton tried to keep hope alive that a suitable location could be found for his franchise and even served as the league's president before being shuffled out for Clarence Campbell. The team was officially folded soon after.

Even though the NHL iced just six teams for the 1942–43 season, the Americans and Maroons franchises remained active on paper for the next few years. Not long after World War II, both of them were folded and the Original Six era was officially underway.

EXPANSION YEAR RECORD: 6-24-0
(12 points — sixth in NHL)
COACH: Art Ross
FIRST GAME: December 1, 1924 —
2-1 win vs. Montreal Maroons
FIRST GOAL: December 1, 1924 by Smokey Harris

BOSTON BRUINS

In its formative years, the NHL was based in eastern Canada and its clubs came from the provinces of Ontario and Quebec. But as professional sports grew by leaps and bounds in the early 1920s and amateur hockey in America came to life, it was only a matter of time before the league chose to expand into the United States.

Boston-based businessman Charles Adams, who often travelled to Montreal to catch games, was a fan of the sport and he approached the NHL intending to bring the league south of the Canadian border before purchasing one of the franchises held by Tom Duggan. When he was officially granted a franchise on November 1, 1924, he already had some players under contract, but he immediately started to acquire free agents and talent from financially troubled western pro clubs.

Adams also hired Art Ross, one of the game's true greats, to run the team, and Ross went on to spend 30 years with the organization. When he asked Ross to come up with a nickname for the club, Ross chose "Bruins," a term often used for brown bears (although there is evidence that Adams's secretary came up with the name). Funnily enough, the name worked with the brown and yellow uniforms worn in Adams's First National Stores grocery chain.

The Bruins opened their first season at the Boston Arena on December 1. Their first opponents were the Montreal Professional Hockey Club, who were also making their NHL debut. The Bruins gave up an early 1–0 lead to the Maroons, but they bounced back in the second period with goals by Smokey Harris and Carson Cooper that were enough to secure a victory. That temporary high did not last long, though, as they lost their next 11 contests and had just two wins in their first 20 outings.

Over the rest of the schedule, they managed four wins over 10 games, two of them shutouts, one against the Maroons and the other, Hamilton. The second blanking was particularly notable because the Tigers were the regular-season champions that year — and that game also gave the Bruins their first back-to-back triumphs in franchise history. Chalking up a 6–24–0 record in their first year, Boston did not have much success on the ice, but the team was a hit with local fans.

It did not take long for the Bruins to become one of the NHL's marquee clubs. During the early years, Ross brought in some prime talent that included Hall of Famers Eddie Shore, Tiny Thompson and Dit Clapper. They won their first regular-season title in 1927–28 and captured the Stanley Cup the following year. A decade later, they did it once more with such stars as American rookie goalie Frank Brimsek and the legendary Kraut Line of Milt Schmidt, Bobby Bauer and Woody Dumart, and yet again in 1940–41 with most of the same cast.

A 29-year championship drought followed as the league moved into the Original Six era. Fans in Boston were often treated to some spectacular seasons, but in those years the club never had all of the ingredients needed to win the Cup. From 1960–61 to 1966–67, they finished out of last place only once. It took the arrival of young players such as Bobby Orr and Derek Sanderson, along with a key trade that brought over Phil Esposito and Ken Hodge from the Chicago Black Hawks, to make the Bruins contenders again. The era of the "Big Bad Bruins" truly began in 1967–68. Two years later, Orr scored a memorable goal to bring home the Stanley Cup. In 1971–72, the team won another title. The Bruins ranked among the best in the league for most of the next 25 seasons. Even as their stars grew older, they wisely replaced them with good prospects, and some of them eventually became Hall of Famers, like Raymond Bourque and Cam Neely. The team's most recent Stanley Cup came in 2010–11.

(clockwise) Jimmy Herberts, Carson Cooper, Lionel Hitchman, Charles Stewart

JIMMY HERBERTS

A free agent signed by the Bruins on November 2, 1924, Herberts played for the Eveleth Rangers of the USAHA in 1923–24 and scored only three goals in 19 games. He seemingly came out of nowhere during the club's expansion year and was the undisputed leader of Boston's anemic offence.

Comfortable at both centre and right wing, he went scoreless in the team's first outing, but managed a power-play goal and an assist against Toronto on December 3, 1924. A month later, he had a pair of tallies against Clint Benedict of the Montreal Maroons, but it was not enough in a 4–3 loss. That game marked a five-game point streak, and for the rest of the season he scored at a frantic pace. At the conclusion of his rookie campaign, Herberts ranked seventh among all NHL players in goals and number 10 in points.

CARSON COOPER

The Bruins looked as if they had potential from the beginning of their first season because Carson Cooper was in the lineup. He had just ended a great senior hockey career with the Hamilton Tigers and was expected to score some goals.

Cooper started the season with a bang by assisting on the franchise's first-ever goal and ensured its first victory with a game-winning tally against Clint Benedict of the Maroons on December 1, 1924. Nine days later, however, he was forced out of action with a knee injury during Boston's 7–1 loss to the NHL's version of the Hamilton Tigers. By the time he returned, it was too late for the first-year club and he was left looking at the next season.

GEORGE REDDING

A small but versatile player who could play left wing and defence, Redding came from the same Hamilton Tigers senior club as teammate Carson Cooper and was one of Boston's most thrilling players in the team's first season.

The strange thing is that he had second thoughts about turning pro — even after signing a contract with the Bruins. When he tried to return to Hamilton, the Ontario Hockey Association turned him away and he was forced to play in the NHL. Although his offensive numbers were weak, he accomplished a rare feat when penalties forced him to take over in net after Hec Fowler let in nine goals by the Toronto St. Patricks on December 22, 1924. In the crease for 11 minutes, "Shorty" let in just one goal by Babe Dye (who had already scored four that evening) and secured a place in league history.

LIONEL HITCHMAN

Lots of talent on the blue line in Ottawa allowed the Bruins to acquire Hitchman in exchange for cash on January 10, 1925. He became one of the club's most beloved players.

A defensive specialist, Hitchman did not put up huge numbers for his new team, but there was a noticeable decline in the number of goals opposing teams scored after his arrival. His third goal of the season helped force overtime in what eventually became a 2–1 victory over the Maroons on February 24.

HEC FOWLER

Art Ross wanted a solid veteran netminder for Boston's first season in the NHL and he was able to get one of hockey's best in Fowler. But it was not exactly a match made in heaven.

Fowler was sold to the Bruins by the Victoria Cougars of the PCHA on October 29, 1924. His arrival in Beantown was heralded as a move that could provide the new club with stability between the pipes. The relationship began well with a win over Boston's expansion cousins, the Montreal Maroons, on December 1, but the next three weeks were hell on earth for the goalie as he lost six straight. The final straw came during the disheartening 10–1 loss to Toronto on December 22. He gave up nine goals before being relieved by George Redding, and that marked the end of his time with the Bruins.

After securing his release from the club, Fowler signed with the Edmonton Eskimos of the WCHL on January 28, 1925. He stuck around the game for a couple more seasons before fading into obscurity. For fans in Boston, however, he was the goalie who started a fine tradition that spawned many Hall of Famers and memorable characters over the years.

CHARLES STEWART

After Boston's failed experiment with Hec Fowler as their starting goaltender, "Doc" Stewart was called in to breathe some life into the club's woeful defence. According to the box scores after his arrival with the team, he brought the club back from the brink.

Stewart was a veteran of senior hockey in Toronto and Hamilton and was part of the Tigers team that produced a few other members of the original Bruins roster. He signed a pro contract on December 24, 1924, and made his debut in a 5–0 loss to the Canadiens the next night.

The club's early games were marked by incredibly high scores by the opposition, but Stewart cut the other teams down to a little more than three goals per game for the rest of the schedule. He was relieved by Howard Lockhart for a couple of games, but the team was beginning to slowly turn things around. His best outings during the expansion season were shutouts against the Maroons on February 7, 1925, and against the big-league version of the Hamilton Tigers a month later.

EXPANSION YEAR RECORD: 9-19-2
(20 points — fifth in NHL)
COACH: Eddie Gerard
FIRST GAME: December 1, 1924 —
2-1 loss vs. Boston Bruins
FIRST GOAL: December 1, 1924 by Charles Dinsmore

MONTREAL MAROONS

After the Montreal Wanderers shut down following an arena fire early in the NHL's first season of 1917–18, the city's Anglophone hockey fans no longer had a team to call their own. Sure, the Canadiens had some success in the early 1920s, but as they prepared to move into the new Montreal Forum in 1924, there was an opportunity for another team to come to town.

Luckily, the NHL was prepared to expand for the first time and when they admitted their first American-based team in the Boston Bruins, they also said yes to the Montreal Professional Hockey Club, headed by James F. Strachan. Strachan had owned the Wanderers nearly 20 years earlier and he intended as team president to bring back the old name but could not obtain the rights. As a result, the club had no official nickname, but the main colour of their uniforms eventually led the press and fans to dub them the Maroons.

The Canadiens received most of the $15,000 expansion fee, but the Maroons were willing to spend freely and signed several senior and amateur players and purchased a pair of stars in Punch Broadbent and veteran goaltender Clint Benedict from the Ottawa Senators. Their most intriguing acquisition was Dunc Munro, who had helped Canada to a gold medal at the 1924 Winter Olympics. The local press did a great job of getting fans excited about the new team in the weeks leading up to their debut.

The Montreal Maroons started the year on the road in Boston

against their first-year contemporaries, but they lost by a tight 2–1 margin on December 1, 1924. They jumped out to a 1–0 lead on a first period goal by Charles Dinsmore but fell behind for good in the next stanza. Two days later, they opened their home schedule against the Hamilton Tigers but were shut out by goalie Jake Forbes.

Undaunted by their rough start, the Maroons were pumped for the anticipated arrival of the Senators on December 5, and both Broadbent and Benedict starred in the 2–1 triumph. Over the first half of the season, they managed to win back-to-back games on three occasions, but a brutal month-long 10-game slump from January 24 to February 24, 1925, undid what momentum they had going. By the end of the year, they ranked second-last in the league — surpassing only the Bruins, who had a horrendous record of their own.

Regardless of their rank, the Maroons succeeded at the box office and added some prime talent before beginning their second season. Strengthened by newcomers Nels Stewart and Babe Siebert, they went all the way to the Stanley Cup in 1925–26. Over the next decade, they proved to be one of the most successful franchises in the league and missed the playoffs only once during that period. Another championship followed in 1934–35, but the financial realities of the Great Depression meant the Maroons had the lowest attendance in the league for several years running and had to sell off several star players.

By the beginning of the 1937–38 season, there were rumours that the Maroons would be relocated, and they ended up with their worst record since their first year in the NHL. The league allowed them to suspend operations for the next year. St. Louis seemed a possible destination for the struggling franchise, but unfortunately, the costs of travel weighed too heavily against relocation.

Len Peto, director of the Canadiens, offered a glimmer of hope after he got the franchise transferred to Philadelphia, but no suitable arena could be found even after several years. By 1947, the franchise was officially folded. It was another 20 years before the NHL operated with more than six teams.

(clockwise) Punch Broadbent, Sam Rothschild, Clint Benedict

PUNCH BROADBENT

Broadbent was one of the NHL's top-scoring stars during its formative years and whenever he was healthy he put up strong numbers with the Ottawa Senators. He led the league with 32 goals and 46 points during the 1921–22 campaign, establishing a still-unbroken league standard by scoring a goal in each of 16 consecutive games.

After a rough 1923–24 season, the pioneer power-forward's days in the nation's capital were numbered. Even though he had helped the Sens to a pair of Stanley Cup titles, the team deemed him expendable. The Maroons received Broadbent, along with fellow veteran Clint Benedict, in a cash deal on October 20, 1924. Their arrival gave the new club instant name recognition.

On December 5, Broadbent scored a pair of goals against his old club in a 3–1 victory. He also scored the game-winner against them 18 days later. His best performance of the year, the club's greatest highlight during the first season, came when he scored five goals against Jake Forbes of the Hamilton Tigers on January 7, 1925.

REG NOBLE

Noble's lengthy pro career began in the old National Hockey Association before he spent several seasons with the Toronto Arenas and St. Patricks, winning a pair of Stanley Cups along the way. His tenure there ended December 9, 1924, when he was sold to the Maroons for $8,000.

Arriving in Montreal for their first matchup against the Canadiens the following day, Noble instantly became one of the club's veteran leaders. On December 13, he got an assist against his old team. His biggest goal of the season led to a 2–0 victory over the Boston Bruins on January 20, 1925.

DUNC MUNRO

Munro spent several years playing senior hockey with the Toronto Granites club and was there when they won the Allan Cup and earned the right to represent Canada at the 1924 Winter Olympics. A respected defenceman and all-around athlete, he also played on the first Memorial Cup–winning squad at University of Toronto a few years earlier.

After winning the gold medal at the Olympics in Chamonix, France, Munro had a reputation as the best amateur defenceman around and was highly sought after. The new Montreal team made the offer that most appealed to him, but the press prematurely reported the signing. He addressed the matter personally in the *Montreal Gazette*: "I have signed nothing yet, but after a long-distance phone conversation with James Strachan of Montreal, yesterday, during which he raised the ante, I wired Strachan that I would accept his terms. I am getting a salary beyond anything I thought any team would go for my services, and in addition, the people behind the Montreal team, who are among the strongest men financially in Montreal, have offered me business opportunities, which I would be foolish to turn down. St. Pats made me a flattering offer yesterday, but they cannot do for me in a business way what these Montreal gentlemen are doing for me, so I have decided to go to Montreal, give them what hockey I have, and get myself established in a real business." Though Munro lacked even a lick of pro experience, the Maroons named him team captain. His first two goals of the season came in the 6–2 win over fellow expansion club, the Boston Bruins, on December 17, 1924. His second tally of the night came when the Maroons were shorthanded.

CLINT BENEDICT

Benedict revolutionized the way goalies played the game. His propensity to hit the ice to make a save, even when threatened with a fine, eventually forced rule changes that benefited netminders. A native of Ottawa, he had played for his hometown Senators for more than a decade and backstopped them to Stanley Cup glory.

But Alex Connell was vying for the starting job in Ottawa, so the team sold "Praying Benny" to the new Montreal club along with veteran Punch Broadbent. They were two of the first players the Maroons signed to contracts.

After leading the NHL in victories for six straight seasons, Benedict was in for a shock. As part of the expansion club, he ended up, for the only time in his career, losing more games than any other netminder.

He was, however, still keeping the puck out of the net, as his goals-against average rose only slightly, to 2.12. He registered the team's first shutout on January 20, 1925, against the Boston Bruins, and he blanked the league-leading Hamilton Tigers on February 28. Despite the lack of offensive power in front of him, Benedict kept the Maroons alive in many games and his future with the club remained bright even though he was in his early 30s. His understudy during the 1924–25 season, Eric Lehman, was more than a decade younger and the nephew of Hall of Fame goalie Hugh Lehman, but he never saw a second of NHL action.

EXPANSION YEAR RECORD: 12-20-4
(28 points — fifth in NHL)
COACH: Tommy Gorman
FIRST GAME: December 2, 1925 —
2-1 win vs. Pittsburgh Pirates
FIRST GOAL: December 2, 1925 by Billy Burch

NEW YORK
AMERICANS

On the advice of a newspaper writer named Bill MacBeth, who believed that big-league hockey could be a hit on Broadway, notorious bootlegger Bill Dwyer purchased an option for an NHL expansion club from Tom Duggan, the owner of the Mount Royal Arena in Montreal. The league approved the franchise on April 17, 1925, and it was set to begin play at Madison Square Garden in 1925–26.

Instead of putting their roster together from scratch, the New York club had a stroke of good fortune that ensured their team was going to be competitive. The players of the Hamilton Tigers were suspended for going on strike at the end of the 1924–25 campaign, so the future of that particular club looked bleak. Dwyer was able to come in and purchase their players for something between $75,000 and $80,000. Once the players individually apologized to the league, they were reinstated and many of them were given even higher salaries than before. The Tigers officially ceased to be a part of the NHL on September 22, 1925, but the league did not publicly acknowledge Dwyer as the owner of the New York club; their officers were named as Duggan, Tommy Gorman and Madison Square Garden's Colonel John Hammond.

The Americans are officially considered an expansion team by the NHL, even though most of their original lineup were Tigers players. The roster was loaded with some promising talent like Billy Burch, who was born locally, and brothers Red and Shorty Green. Gorman served as coach and general manager after selling his interest in the Ottawa Senators.

The Amerks, as they were known, started the season with a four-game road swing that included a 3–1 overtime victory in their debut against their expansion cousins, the Pittsburgh Pirates, on December 2, 1925. They also got a win over the Montreal Canadiens, but lost to the same club in their home opener on December 15. An opulent affair that brought out members of high society, the game was an excellent way to showcase some of the sport's top talent in Howie Morenz and Aurel Joliat and ensure that fans went home feeling they had witnessed something special.

Later in the month, New York had a three-game winning streak, but as the season moved on, the losses began to pile up. Goalie Jake Forbes was put to the test on many nights, and Burch recorded a career-best 22 goals, but even with four wins in a row from February 19 to March 2, 1926, it was not enough to make it into the playoffs.

Despite their promising beginnings, the Amerks faced direct competition in their second season in the league when Madison Square Garden brought in a team of their own called the Rangers. In their early years, the Americans didn't improve much, but at least they didn't have a problem drawing a crowd. One of their best acquisitions came in the form of diminutive Roy Worters. His strong MVP performance in 1928–29 led them to a second-place finish in the Canadian Division and to the playoffs for the first time.

For the next six seasons, the Americans had their share of decent stars, but the team was usually near the bottom of the standings and crowds began to get smaller as the Rangers won the hearts of local fans. The end of Prohibition in the United States also did not help the organization, as Dwyer's revenues dried up dramatically. At one point, the league even turned down an idea to merge the team with the Ottawa Senators.

In 1935–36, Dwyer finally decided to cut his losses and sell the team. But no buyer could be found, so he ended up abandoning the Amerks, and the NHL took control for the following season. Lawsuits ensued and eventually team executive and original member Red Dutton took over the operation. Even with some playoff appearances, the debt was tough for Dutton to manage, and many top players were sold off before the war broke out.

(clockwise) Billy Burch, Red Green, Jake Forbes, Charlie Langlois

By the start of the 1941–42 season, Dutton was at the end of his rope. He decided to change the team's name to the Brooklyn Americans in time for their first home game. While the renaming may have seemed gimmicky, he actually intended to move his club out to the borough once a suitable arena could be built. At the end of the season, however, Dutton made a request to suspend operations. The franchise remained in limbo until 1946, when the league backed away from its promise to let the team back in after the war. Dutton was justifiably miffed and held a grudge for the rest of his life.

BILLY BURCH

Burch emerged as a top star with the Hamilton Tigers in 1924-25 when he scored 20 goals for the first time in his career and, despite leading his team into a strike with Shorty Green, was voted the second-ever recipient of the Hart Trophy as the NHL's Most Valuable Player.

Burch's presence on the debuting New York Americans club went a long way toward establishing a fan base in the Big Apple. It also helped that he was born in Yonkers, New York. He grew up in Toronto, but that did not stop the crowd from cheering him on. In the season opener on December 2, 1925, he scored the first-ever NHL goal in the city of Pittsburgh. Six days later he had a three-point night, scoring the winning goal against the Montreal Canadiens.

As the season progressed, Burch became the top offensive performer for the Amerks. He had the winner against Pittsburgh on December 26 and both goals in a tie with the Boston Bruins on January 7, 1926.

RED GREEN

Fans in Hamilton cheered the arrival of Red Green and his brother, Shorty. The duo helped carry the club to regular-season glory during the 1924-25 campaign. Red Green led the NHL with 15 assists that year, but the labour disruption quelled any chance the team had at Stanley Cup glory. Still, he was not about to rest on his laurels once they relocated to New York.

After going scoreless in the first two outings for the Amerks, Green scored once and added two assists in a 6–2 win over the Montreal Canadiens on December 8, 1925. Two weeks later, his third tally of the year gave his team a big win over the Boston Bruins, and on January 15, 1926, he had a two-goal outing in a loss to Toronto. The Canadiens were victims of another mini-outburst on February 24 when he scored twice, and he made another important game-winner against Ottawa on March 2.

SHORTY GREEN

Wilfred "Shorty" Green was a hero off the ice before he made his mark as a player. Deployed overseas with the Canadian military, he survived a gas attack at the Battle of Passchendaele and returned to his home-land to embark on a senior hockey career. He turned pro with the Hamilton Tigers in 1923–24 and served as their captain the following year, when they had their greatest success at the rink.

Although he was a big part of the players' strike in Hamilton, his salary actually increased dramatically from $3,000 to $5,000 when he was transferred to New York. His second goal of the year was the first ever scored in a hockey game at Madison Square Garden, when the largely forgotten Herb Rheaume let the puck in at 11:55 of the first period. On December 30, he scored an overtime winner against the Toronto St. Pats. He was also responsible for the difference-maker in a 1–0 triumph over the Habs on February 27, 1926.

Green's best night of the year, though, came during his last game, on March 17, when he scored three goals in a 5–3 win over the Montreal Maroons, who went on to take the Stanley Cup that season. His brief NHL career ended the following year when he suffered a dislocated kidney.

RENE BOILEAU

In order to grab some headlines in the early days of NHL hockey in New York, stories occasionally bent the truth in an effort to get fans out to Madison Square Garden. The first of these tall tales was about Rainy Drinkwater, who was then called the first-ever Native Canadian player in the NHL.

The reality is that Drinkwater was really Rene Boileau, who had been playing senior hockey in his native Montreal — not on the Cauhnawaga Reserve as the Americans claimed in their shameless press release. Besides which, most hockey historians recognize Paul Jacobs, who had played for Toronto a few years earlier, as the first Native player in the NHL.

Although many were upset by this, Boileau took it in stride and was happy to play a part in the charade. The *Montreal Gazette* saw right through the fiction, but still paid attention to his debut. Boileau appeared in seven games with the Amerks in all, but could not make an impact on the scoresheet. Over the next few years, he was relegated to the minors and eventually returned to Quebec to play senior hockey again. His son Marc later played in the NHL and also coached the Pittsburgh Penguins.

JAKE FORBES

Forbes began his NHL career with Toronto, but after the club suspended him for the 1921–22 season for not agreeing on a contract, he was sold to Hamilton. He had to endure two very rough campaigns in goal before the team managed to get things rolling in 1924–25. He led the league with 19 wins that year and had the second-best goals-against average of 1.96, but the team's player strike put a damper on those totals.

After he paid his fine and apologized for his role in the labour disruption, Forbes was transferred to the New York Americans, where he was their top man in the crease. He appeared in every game of the 1925–26 season, but even though he had most of the same supporting cast in front, his numbers were not as good. He was the goalie of record in the Amerks' first game and victory over the Pittsburgh Pirates on December 2, 1925, and he thrilled the Madison Square Garden crowd at their home opener 13 days later.

As the season neared a close, Forbes proved unbeatable against the Montreal Canadiens on February 27, 1926, recording the first shutout in franchise history. He repeated the feat on March 9, when they took on the Boston Bruins.

EXPANSION YEAR RECORD: 19-16-1
(39 points — third in NHL)
COACH: Odie Cleghorn
FIRST GAME: November 26, 1925 —
2-1 win vs. Boston Bruins
FIRST GOAL: December 2, 1925 by Lionel Conacher

PITTSBURGH PIRATES

By the time the Pirates joined the NHL for the 1925–26 season, fans in the Steel City were more than familiar with hockey, as their association with the game stretched back to at least 1895. The city's first indoor artificial ice rink hosted its first hockey game in 1899 and the Duquesne Gardens hosted several clubs over the years.

In the early 1920s, the Pittsburgh Yellowjackets of the U.S. Amateur Hockey Association had tremendous success with imported players from Canada like Roy Worters and Lionel Conacher. By 1925, the owners of the Yellowjackets had financial problems, and they sold to an attorney named James F. Callahan who had partnered with prominent bootlegger and New York Americans owner William Dwyer. Despite the conflict of interest, the NHL approved a spot for an expansion club based out of Pittsburgh on November 7, 1925. In their first season, the Pirates, looking sharp in their black and gold uniforms, primarily comprised established players from the Yellowjackets.

The club hired veteran Odie Cleghorn as a player-coach and, in so doing, gained the ability to intimidate opponents. Just 19 days after the franchise was granted, the Pirates took to the ice for the first time on the road and defeated the second-year Boston Bruins 2–1. On November 28, they unexpectedly made hockey history when they faced the Canadiens in what became the final appearance for Montreal goaltender Georges Vezina, who left the game because of a high fever. He passed away less than a year later from tuberculosis.

29

After two wins on the road, the Pirates hosted the Americans for their first home game on December 2 and lost a close one in overtime. Their record after just 10 games was a respectable 5–4–1, but then they briefly spiralled into a five-game losing streak before winning four of the five that followed. Toward the end of the season, their record improved and they won seven of their last 10, including three shutouts by Worters.

Even though the NHL was now up to seven teams, only three qualified for the playoffs. The Pirates squeaked into third place by a single point over the Bruins and met the Montreal Maroons in a two-game, total-goals series. After losing the opening game 3–1 on March 20, they needed a big win three days later, but mustered only a 3–3 tie.

The next four seasons in Pittsburgh were a mixed bag and they made it to the postseason only one more time. Boxer Benny Leonard, who was a Dwyer protégé, became part of the ownership group, but fan support waned and many key players were sold or traded. In 1929–30, they played one last season and finished at the bottom of the standings with a pitiful five wins.

Frustrated with mounting losses, Callahan persuaded the NHL to allow the team to relocate to Philadelphia. The Quakers were a flop on the ice and had one of the worst records in league history with a mere four victories. Although the team never returned to the ice after that, Callahan did hold on to his franchise, hoping to build a new home for them back in Pittsburgh. They were officially put to rest on May 7, 1936, but eventually, in 1967, both Pennsylvania cities the team played in got expansion clubs.

HIB MILKS

Milks was a familiar face to fans in Pittsburgh before the Pirates arrived in the NHL thanks to his two seasons with the Yellowjackets. The smooth and effective forward was the team's top offensive performer in their inaugural year.

In his fifth NHL career game, Hib scored his first goal on December 9, 1925, and it made all the difference in a 6–3 win over Toronto. The St. Pats brought out the best in him later on in his rookie campaign when he put four pucks past John Ross Roach on March 4, 1926.

(clockwise) Hib Milks, Lionel Conacher, Odie Cleghorn, Roy Worters

HAROLD DARRAGH

A strong skater who played a clean but aggressive game, Darragh was a senior hockey teammate of Hib Milks in Ottawa, and the pair went to play for the USAHA's Pittsburgh Yellowjackets in 1924–25. His outstanding play ensured he was brought on board by the Pirates for their first NHL season.

Darragh did not wait long to demonstrate his skills to fans and scored the franchise's first game-winner when he blasted the biscuit past Doc Stewart of the Boston Bruins on November 26, 1925. Against the Montreal Maroons on January 27, 1926, he scored an overtime goal just 48 seconds into the extra period. The extra-time heroics returned on March 12 in the second-last game of the year when he victimized Stewart once more. The Bruins protested, however, claiming Pittsburgh's goalposts were not properly fastened at the time.

LIONEL CONACHER

Known to fans as the "Big Train," Conacher was a force to be reckoned with no matter what sport he played. A multi-talented athlete who didn't take up hockey until his teenage years, Conacher won championships with the Toronto Argonauts and the Toronto Maple Leafs baseball club. After amateur hockey success that included a Memorial Cup victory with the Toronto Canoe Club, he headed south to play for the Pittsburgh Yellowjackets.

Despite a love of football, Conacher finally succumbed to the lure of turning pro before the 1925–26 season and remained in Pittsburgh with the new Pirates hockey club. He made history in the team's first game against the Boston Bruins on November 26, 1925, by scoring the franchise's first goal on Doc Stewart. He also scored the opening goal in the last game of the year, against the Ottawa Senators on March 15, 1926, and it was all his team needed to roll to a 2–0 victory.

BALDY COTTON

Cotton is often remembered by old-time hockey fans as one of Toronto's most popular performers in the early 1930s, but his NHL career began with the Pirates in the 1925–26 season. As a young man, he moved to Pittsburgh to attend Duquesne University and starred for the Yellowjackets while in school.

Thanks to his name recognition with local fans, Cotton was signed by the Pirates on September 26, 1925. According to newspaper reports, he made his debut on the road against the Canadiens on November 28. His first career point was a significant one as he earned an assist on Odie Cleghorn's winning goal against Boston on December 11. He finally bulged the twine himself on January 26, 1926, flying the puck past John Ross Roach of the St. Pats. Later in his rookie season he also scored game-winners against the Habs and Maroons.

ODIE CLEGHORN

Cleghorn, one of hockey's most feared and reviled players during the sport's formative years, had the distinction of being a playing coach for the Pirates in their first NHL season in 1925–26. He also had the daunting task of helping hockey succeed in a relatively new market just warming up to the sport.

While his expertise behind the bench led the team to a playoff spot, he played in just 17 games but did manage to score the winner in a 5–3 victory over Boston on December 11, 1925. It was a contest filled with all sorts of excitement and the Bruins had Odie's brother, Sprague, in the lineup that night. He also served as the team's captain on the ice.

The face of the franchise in the Pirates' first four seasons, Cleghorn was pressed into duty for only five games after the team's inaugural season, but he did come up with an innovation that changed the game forever. He was the first coach to use set rotating-lines during games instead of letting the players leave the ice only when they required rest. It is surprising that he has not been inducted into the Hockey Hall of Fame and unfortunate that he may never receive the recognition he deserves.

ROY WORTERS

A diminutive dynamo who kept the puck out of the net for two seasons with the Pittsburgh Yellowjackets, Worters was part of the crew that formed the first Pirates roster and gave the new club credibility in the crease.

From the first game on, he was one of the team's biggest stars and he played every game except one during the 1925–26 campaign. He ranked among the league's top goaltenders in all stats and his 1.90 goals-against average is a record for an expansion club that may never be broken. In net for the team's opening victory against Boston on November 26, 1925, Worters followed it up with a shutout against the Montreal Canadiens two days later. The Ottawa Senators were his most frequent victim; he blanked them on three occasions before heading into a playoff clash with the Montreal Maroons.

EXPANSION YEAR RECORD: 19-22-3
(41 points — third in American Division)
COACH: Pete Muldoon
FIRST GAME: November 17, 1926 —
4-1 win vs. Toronto St. Pats
FIRST GOAL: November 17, 1926 by George Hay

CHICAGO BLACKHAWKS

The Chicago Blackhawks joined the NHL at an opportune time for the young league, as it was still dealing with the threat of a rival league taking over cities they considered prime future locations.

Coffee magnate Major Frederic McLaughlin, an associate of Tex Rickard and a former military man, outbid James E. Norris for the rights to an NHL franchise in the Windy City. He stocked his team with top players from the WHL's Portland Rosebuds and dubbed his team the "Blackhawks" after the 86th Infantry Division he fought with in World War I. The name also, indirectly, had a local connection because of Chief Black Hawk of the Sauk nation. McLaughlin had no real knowledge of hockey, but he was passionate about the game.

McLaughlin's wife, ballroom dancer Irene Castle, designed the club's black and white jersey and logo.

The initial logo created some confusion over the team's official name, and for nearly 60 years, until the original charter was discovered and the error was corrected, most references to the team were to "Black Hawks" instead of "Blackhawks."

Veteran coach Pete Muldoon, who was born Linton Muldoon Tracy, was brought in to serve as the team's first coach. The roster was laden with tremendous talent like Dick Irvin, Babe Dye, George Hay, Mickey McKay and aging netminder Hugh Lehman. As a group, they had a great deal of experience at the pro level and were serious contenders.

For most of the NHL's first decade, there loomed the threat of another loop being started by constant thorn-in-the-side Eddie Livingstone. Those fears became a reality in 1926. The Chicago Cardinals of the American Hockey Association were ready to start play around the same time as the Black Hawks — and share the Coliseum. McLaughlin had actually allowed this to happen, as he had no idea who Livingstone was. The move certainly did not endear him to some of the other owners.

Nevertheless, the Black Hawks held their season opener against the Toronto St. Patricks on November 17, 1926, and rolled to a 4–1 victory for more than 7,000 fans. The crowd was noticeably smaller for a win over Boston three days later, but the contest did feature the first NHL goal by Hall of Famer Eddie Shore, who had come to the Bruins from out west.

The Cardinals made their debut soon after but played to progressively smaller houses. Sensing an opportunity to cause some damage, NHL president Frank Calder asserted that Cards players Teddy Graham and Cy Wentworth belonged to his league and that the American Hockey Association had voided their working agreement with the NHL, effectively branding them outlaws. It was a bold power play, but it discredited Livingstone in the eyes of AHA owners. Livingstone was forced to dramatically cut ticket prices to draw fans.

McLaughlin responded by cutting prices as well, but he packed the house better, thanks to the growing perception that the NHL was better than the AHA. Although he had a five-year lease, Livingstone decided to sell the Cardinals to local interests at the end of the year.

At the end of the first season, Muldoon handed in his resignation to McLaughlin, fed up with the owner's insistence on controlling too many aspects of the team. Some hockey historians swear by Jim Coleman's colourful story of the Curse of Muldoon. The myth of a disgruntled coach telling the owner that his team would never win a championship during his lifetime made for a fun tale, but it was simply a fabrication that gave the Chicago team an excuse for never being at the top of the league during the regular season.

Chicago finished third in the American Division, and they made it to the playoffs but lost a total-goals series to Boston by a 10–5 margin.

Although the team led the NHL in goals scored during the regular season, they also had the worst defensive record to go along with it, so it was no surprise they folded during the playoffs. Still, their first year was somewhat of a success.

After that modest success, the Black Hawks experienced some early growing pains as the team sought to establish themselves in the 10-team NHL. The arrival of goaltender Charlie Gardiner in their second season moved the process along. In 1933–34, fans in Chicago enjoyed their first Stanley Cup championship, but tragically, Gardiner passed away mere weeks after the victory. Four years later, they won another Cup in a most improbable fashion when they squeaked into the playoffs with a losing record and defeated the heavily favoured Toronto Maple Leafs with a lineup that included a for-the-time unprecedented number of American-born players.

In the first years of the Original Six era, Chicago had more than its fair share of struggles even with some great talents like Bill Mosienko, Bill Gadsby and the Bentley brothers, Max and Doug. By the late 1950s, many players regarded the Windy City as a sort of hockey purgatory. But the team was building into a contender with some fresh faces, including Stan Mikita, Bobby Hull, Pierre Pilote, Moose Vasko, Ken Wharram and Glenn Hall, who led the charge to a Stanley Cup in 1960–61. For the rest of the decade, they were one of the league's premier clubs and finally won a regular-season title in 1966–67 to end the supposed Curse of Muldoon.

In the expansion era, the Black Hawks continued to dominate and made it to the Stanley Cup Final in 1970–71 and 1972–73 with Tony Esposito protecting the crease. Throughout the 1980s and 1990s, they enjoyed a lengthy streak of playoff seasons but were unable to bring everything together to claim another title. As a franchise, they experienced tough times in the early 2000s as a result of fan apathy brought about by the way the Wirtz brothers ran the club, but once a new generation took over, the future looked brighter. In 2009–10, Lord Stanley's Mug made its return to Chicago, and the city is once again in love with their hockey team.

(clockwise) Dick Irvin, Babe Dye, George Hay, Hugh Lehman

DICK IRVIN

Irvin was one of the greatest playmakers of his era and a genuine star in the western pro loops before the NHL began its big expansion into American markets. He made his pro debut in 1915–16 but served in World War I and afterward was granted amateur status. In 1921–22, he returned to elite-level hockey and starred for the Regina Capitals until they relocated to Portland. In 1925–26, he scored 30 goals in 30 games with the Portland Rosebuds and the newly formed Black Hawks signed him on, hoping he would bring some of that magic to NHL rinks.

The 1926–27 season saw him lead the league with 18 assists — a strong total in an era when helpers were rarely granted — and he was second in overall scoring behind Bill Cook of the Rangers by a single point. On December 15, 1926, he had a hat trick against those same Broadway Blueshirts and one of his goals was the winning tally. The prematurely greying superstar also scored a big goal to secure victory over the New York Americans on February 23, 1927. In the postseason battle with Boston, he scored two goals in the second game, but it wasn't enough to ensure a series victory.

In his second year with Chicago, Irvin's hockey career was changed forever when he fractured his skull. He subsequently retired after the 1928–29 season to take over as the club's coach. The Black Hawks excelled under his guidance the next year. Eventually the Toronto Maple Leafs brought him over, and in 1931–32, he led them to win a Stanley Cup. He later coached the Montreal Canadiens for 15 seasons and earned three more championships. In 1955–56, he returned to the Windy City for a final year behind the bench then stepped away from the game soon before dying of bone cancer. His son, Dick Irvin Jr., is a celebrated hockey broadcaster.

BABE DYE

One of the NHL's earliest superstars, Dye scored more goals than any other player in the 1920s. He was a brilliant athlete that also excelled in football and baseball. He spent most of his professional career with the Toronto St. Pats, until 1926–27 when the team chose to sell him to Chicago.

In the Windy City, Dye proved that he was nowhere near washed up. He spent most of the season as the league's top goal producer until Bill Cook surpassed him in the last few games. He had a pair of goals against the New York Americans on December 18, 1926. He had several other two-goal games, but the most significant of them had to be the 5–4 overtime victory over the Maroons on December 29, in which he also fed the puck to Mickey MacKay to complete the comeback. At the end of the year, he had a remarkable 200 career-goals to his credit.

Dye suffered a broken leg in training camp before the 1927–28 season. He was never the same after that and scored only one more time in his career. He eventually returned to Chicago to coach the Shamrocks of the American Hockey Association and remained in the area for the rest of his life

DUNCAN "MICKEY" MACKAY

Lester Patrick considered MacKay the greatest centreman to ever play hockey in the west in the early days of the professional game. He was the Pacific Coast Hockey League's all-time leading scorer. Although he is largely forgotten by many hockey fans today, MacKay is a member of the Hockey Hall of Fame. At the time, it was a big deal that he was going to be a part of the original Chicago roster for the 1926–27 NHL campaign.

His first big game for the Black Hawks came during a 3–0 shutout of the mighty Montreal Canadiens on December 11, 1926. MacKay scored the first two goals that night against George Hainsworth. Often paired on a line with Dick Irvin and Babe Dye, he got many opportunities to score and had a couple of significant game-winners over the season. One of them helped cap a huge overtime comeback from a 4–0 deficit against the Montreal Maroons on December 29. Even more amazing than that was his big difference-maker in Chicago's 5–3 defeat of the Ottawa Senators on February 9, 1927.

GEORGE HAY

Often called "The Western Wizard," Hay was a superstar in the old WCHL with the Regina Capitals and grew up alongside hockey legend

Dick Irvin. After his strong 31-point season with Portland in 1925–26, NHL fans were looking forward to seeing him play for Chicago.

Although Hay played only a single season in the Windy City, he has a permanent spot in the team's record books because he scored the first goal in franchise history when they took on the Toronto St. Pats on November 17, 1926. He put the puck past John Ross Roach at the 3:20 mark of the first period and beat him again with the game-winning tally a minute later.

One of Hay's best goals was the opening marker that sealed the fate of Detroit in a 2–0 shutout on Christmas. The Cougars also fell victim to his first NHL hat trick on February 19, 1927, when his offence was all that was needed in a 4–1 victory. In the playoffs, he led the Black Hawks with three points.

JIM RILEY

Riley is one of the most unique athletes in hockey history because he holds the distinction of being the only person to play both in the NHL and in major league baseball.

Riley spent most of his on-ice pro career with the Seattle Metropolitans in the PCHA and put up some decent numbers, but he spent his summers playing ball and stepped up to the plate for several minor league clubs. In 1921, he debuted with the St. Louis Browns, and his last big-league action came two years later with the Washington Senators. Over six games, he made 17 plate appearances but never registered a hit.

It is not clear how he became a member of the Chicago team, but Riley was with the club during the early part of the 1926–27 campaign. A former Stanley Cup champion with Seattle, he made it into just three games with the Black Hawks, did not put up any offence and was sent to the Detroit Cougars soon after.

HUGH LEHMAN

The career of one Lehman, one of hockey's greatest goaltenders, was in its twilight when the Chicago Black Hawks came into existence, but the team made the decision to put the 41-year-old ice warrior between the pipes for their first NHL season. Lehman's pro resumé stretched back 20 years. He was one of the sport's pro pioneers who made the trek west to play in the Pacific Coast loop in 1911–12 and spent 12 seasons starring for Vancouver, winning a Stanley Cup in 1914–15.

In Chicago, he was somewhat reliable in the crease but was starting to show his age. The Black Hawks surrendered the most goals among the NHL's 10 clubs in 1926–27, but he still gave some great performances, including five shutout wins. A true workhorse, Lehman led all netminders in minutes played, but that was not enough to take them past the first playoff round.

EXPANSION YEAR RECORD: 12–28–4
(28 points — fifth in American Division)
COACHES: Art Duncan and Duke Keats
FIRST GAME: November 18, 1926 —
2–0 loss vs. Boston Bruins
FIRST GOAL: November 20, 1926 by Harold Halderson

DETROIT COUGARS

With the NHL looking at expanding once again for its 10th season, there was great interest from several groups and cities eager to jump on the pro hockey bandwagon. At a league meeting on April 18, 1926, a number of applications were examined, five of them proposing a team from Detroit, and others from Chicago, New Jersey, Cleveland, Hamilton and New York.

Just two weeks later, the NHL approved new clubs for Detroit and Chicago (the New York Rangers had been previously admitted), but two of the Motor City–based applicants — Townsend and McCreath, along with Bierer — were asked by the league to amalgamate. The very next day, the Detroit group announced they had purchased the WHL's Victoria Cougars, and the Detroit Cougars were tentatively welcomed into the league on May 15 on the condition that they have an arena ready for their first season.

Unfortunately for the Cougars, there was no suitable arena for the team to play in during the 1926–27 campaign. While they waited for the Olympia to be constructed, they were based out of nearby Windsor, Ontario, and skated at the Border Cities Arena. Art Duncan of the Calgary Tigers was brought in as a playing coach, but it cost Detroit two players because the Chicago Black Hawks held his NHL rights.

Like the Black Hawks, the Cougars also faced a threat from the upstart American Hockey Association in their expansion year. The

43

menace of the Detroit Greyhounds was short lived, however, as they could not secure home ice and folded after six-straight road losses.

Detroit's home opener was a bit disappointing, as they were blanked 2–0 by the Boston Bruins on November 18. They finally made a mark on the scoresheet two nights later against Pittsburgh and bounced back to record four straight victories. They proved a bit better on the road than at home in the first half of the season, but some serious losing streaks marred any chance they had at making the playoffs. One of those bad stretches lasted for seven games after they defeated Toronto in their final outing as the St. Patricks on February 16, 1927.

This streak also saw the end of Duncan's tenure as coach when he was relieved by Duke Keats for the last 11 games of the year. By the end of the regular schedule, Detroit was in last place in the new American Division and dead last in the league, but there was at least some hope for the future.

The Cougars finally arrived in Detroit for their second season. Jack Adams was brought in to run the team and turn it into a contender. They made their first playoff appearance in 1928–29, but struggles on the ice and at the box office led them to try changing their nickname to the Falcons for two years before becoming the Red Wings in 1932–33.

The second name change did something to spark them on the ice, and they won their first regular-season title the next year with a lineup that included Larry Aurie and Ebbie Goodfellow. In 1935–36, they were Stanley Cup champions. They repeated the victory the following year. Under Adams's guidance, they were one of the sport's best franchises throughout the 1940s, boosted by a constant influx of top talent that boasted the likes of Ted Lindsay, Red Kelly, Sid Abel, Gordie Howe and many more.

From 1948–49 to 1954–55, the hockey heroes of the Motor City captured seven straight regular-season crowns and four Stanley Cups. The Original Six era was a great time to play for the Red Wings. The early years of expansion, however, were not good for the franchise and marked the beginning of their struggles on the ice. Gordie Howe's retirement was one of the first bad omens for the team. The 1970s and 1980s were often bleak.

There was a new hope for fans in 1983–84, though, with the debut

(clockwise) Johnny Sheppard, Duke Keats, Art Duncan, Hap Holmes

of Steve Yzerman. After Mike Ilitch bought the team from the Norris family, the organization had a new commitment to success on the ice. Thanks to shrewd scouting and drafting, Detroit began to add many great players to the lineup and made it to the Campbell Conference Final twice in the late 1980s. The following decade proved even better when players like Nicklas Lidstrom and Brendan Shanahan brought them two consecutive Stanley Cup championships, starting in 1996–97.

From 2000–01 to 2008–09, the Red Wings always finished first in their division and racked up two more Stanley Cup wins. The 2011–12 campaign gave them their first third-place finish since 1990–91, but with a successful track record, it is likely they will continue to dominate for many years.

JOHNNY SHEPPARD

Sheppard was regarded as a small but very effective performer. After starring for the Edmonton Eskimos at the pro level, he was sold to Detroit for the 1926-27 season and became the club's top offensive star in their first year in the NHL.

Sheppard was a fairly consistent producer for the Cougars. One of his best efforts came against Boston on December 14, 1926, when he scored two quick goals to prevent a shutout. Two days later he scored the final goal in a 5-0 win over the Ottawa Senators that handed them their first loss of the season. On January 6, 1926, he scored twice in a 3-1 win over Pittsburgh. By the end of the season, he not only led Detroit in scoring but also was their leader in penalty minutes.

FRANK FOYSTON

A dominant playmaker from hockey's early days, Foyston had incredible success in the PCHA with the Seattle Metropolitans and was a part of their Stanley Cup victory in 1916-17. For the 1924-25 campaign he joined the Victoria Cougars where, even though his offensive totals were declining, he won another Stanley Cup before his rights were transferred to the new NHL club in Detroit.

With the new Cougars, Foyston showed some spark at the age of 35 and was second on the team in scoring. Comfortable playing at centre or on the wing, he scored the winning goal against the Boston Bruins on January 13, 1926. A little more than two weeks later, he secured another victory by scoring in overtime against the Chicago Black Hawks.

DUKE KEATS

A respected playmaker who was always looking to generate offence, Keats was a superstar and a perennial All-Star in the west for many years. He began the 1926–27 campaign as a member of the Boston Bruins but did not have the best start with the club, and he was dispatched to the Cougars as part of a blockbuster trade that involved Frank Frederickson going the other way.

One of the most obvious results of the trade was that his goal production increased dramatically. After less than a week in Detroit, Keats scored the lone goal in a shutout victory over the New York Americans. He put one in two days later in a 3–2 win over the Bruins on January 13, 1927, and scored twice more against his old club on February 22, the same night that he took over as coach of the Cougars.

On March 10, he had a hat trick in a big 7–1 drubbing of the Pittsburgh Pirates, but his 2-7-2 record as bench boss did not exactly make him want to lead the team for the 1927–28 season.

FRANK FREDRICKSON

Fredrickson was one of the biggest stars in the west before the NHL expanded southward. He made history with the Canadian team at the 1920 Olympics, winning a gold medal, and turned pro soon after. He spent several years with Victoria on the Aristocrats and Cougars clubs and was an All-Star performer.

In Detroit, Fredrickson had a strong start and scored the first game-winner in franchise history when he slipped the puck past Hugh Lehman on a pass from Hobie Kitchen in a 1–0 victory over the Chicago Black Hawks on November 24, 1926. Early in 1927, he was traded to Boston and his offensive contributions were definitely missed in Detroit.

ART DUNCAN

The playing coach, manager and captain of the Cougars, Duncan was picked up in a trade with Chicago before the season began. The veteran defender had a monumental task ahead of him in 1926–27. Before then he had starred out west for many years. He was also a flying ace with the Royal Flying Corps during World War I.

Duncan led the Cougars to just 10 victories over his first 33 games and was mercifully replaced by Duke Keats — a man who had even less luck behind the bench for the final stretch of the season.

On the ice, Duncan did not put up big numbers, but he did motivate the troops. His best game in a Cougars uniform came against the Montreal Canadiens on January 18, 1927. He popped in two goals to tie the game at three goals apiece, but the Flying Frenchmen came back to win 5–3.

RUSSELL OATMAN

Russell Oatman was a promising young winger when he joined his much older brother, Ed, in the WHL in 1925–26 and remained with the Cougars as they travelled from Victoria to Detroit.

Known as a fast skater, Oatman spent some time on the team's top line early on. His most memorable moment in the Motor City came against the Montreal Canadiens on December 23, 1926, when he scored to give the club a brief 2–1 lead. Soon after, the club suspended him for insubordination under the excuse of "breaking training" and he was sold to the Montreal Maroons on January 6, 1927. The Maroons actually had his rights before the start of the season, but he was awarded to the Cougars in the big player sale. Oatman had the last laugh, however, as he scored the winning goal in overtime against his old club on January 25.

HAP HOLMES

The only goaltender in hockey history to win four Stanley Cup titles with four different teams, Holmes was an elite netminder for many years but sadly is much forgotten by fans today. After the Seattle Metropolitans folded, he joined the Victoria Cougars in 1924–25 and backstopped them to a championship. He moved to Detroit along with many of his teammates when the professional sport essentially died in the west.

The prevailing opinion was that Holmes was not the same player he'd been in previous years, but by coming to play for a new club at the age of 38 he at least demonstrated bravery — and maybe a little madness. The NHL at the time was a no scorer's paradise and, although Holmes was on the losing end for Detroit's first two games, he quickly put together a four-game winning streak that included three shutouts against the Chicago Black Hawks, Montreal Maroons and New York Rangers. From then on, it was mostly downhill as the Cougars won consecutive games on only one more occasion and endured a rough seven-game losing streak.

EXPANSION YEAR RECORD: 25-13-6
(56 points — first in American Division)
COACH: Lester Patrick
FIRST GAME: November 16, 1926 —
1-0 win vs. Montreal Maroons
FIRST GOAL: November 16, 1926 by Bill Cook

NEW YORK RANGERS

Tex Rickard, one of the greatest promoters of athletic events in the Golden Age of Sport, expressed mild interest in hockey in the early 1920s but was not convinced the game was going to take off in New York when the NHL began to expand into the United States.

Although he was originally connected to the New York Americans club that started play in 1925–26, he chose to let bootlegger Bill Dwyer and his associates take the risk on hockey. But Rickard was won over once he saw the box-office success of the star-spangled outfit. He was granted a franchise of his own for Madison Square Garden in April 1926, and the New York Rangers were born.

Dubbed "Tex's Rangers" by the press, the team was set to begin play in 1926–27. Rickard hired a Toronto sportsman named Conn Smythe to sign players. As the team's architect, he scoured the pro and amateur ranks for potential stars and it was expected that he would serve as manager. Before the season started, he was fired and replaced by Lester Patrick. The legendary player had retired before the death of pro hockey out west, but his experience as a coach, manager and team owner made him a more ideal candidate for the position.

Smythe, having been bought out (and also shorted of some of his promised funds), soon resurfaced as owner of the Toronto St. Patricks and rechristened them the Maple Leafs. He later speculated that he was let go by the Rangers because his refusal to sign Babe Dye had angered Colonel John Hammond.

Although some felt the lineup might not be successful, the Rangers made some strong acquisitions before taking to the ice, and Smythe's hard work and eye for talent ensured early success. On November 16, they made their home-ice debut against the previous year's Stanley Cup champions, the Montreal Maroons, and won 1–0. It was hardly a fluke, as they went 6–3–1 over their first 10 games and later won four in a row in early January 1927.

The freshness of the game in the Big Apple ensured early box-office success, but the Rangers justified the adulation by gelling as a team. There were attempts to make the game more attractive to local ethnic communities by changing the names of Lorne Chabot and Ollie Reinikka to Lorne Chabotsky and Ollie Rocco, but the press saw through that ruse. The presence of a top-flight line made up of Frank Boucher and brothers Bill and Bun Cook and rock-solid defenders Taffy Abel and Ching Johnson helped the Rangers finish first overall in the American Division and win five straight before dropping the final game of the year to Boston on March 26, 1927.

After earning a bye in the playoffs, they faced the Bruins in a two-game total-goals clash. The momentum their opponents had was too much to overcome. The first meeting on April 2 was a scoreless tie, but the boys from Beantown won the second game 3–1 to move on to the Stanley Cup Final.

The Rangers worked hard to make sure the rest of the NHL knew they were not a one-year wonder, and they won the Stanley Cup in 1927–28. In one of the games during the final, 44-year-old coach Patrick stepped in for injured goaltender Lorne Chabot and helped defeat the Montreal Maroons before a replacement could be found for the rest of the series. Another championship followed in 1932–33, and the club continued to bring in top talent, fast becoming the act New York's hockey fans wanted to see most.

In 1939–40, the Stanley Cup came back to Broadway once again, but the outlook was grim with the onset of World War II. The Rangers lost a great deal of talent as players took up with the various Armed Forces, and only a ragtag group of prospects remained. After making the playoffs 15 times in their first 16 seasons, there was little to celebrate at the end of the 1940s until the team's stars returned. They made it to the Stanley Cup Final again in 1949–50, but lost a tight seven-game series to the Detroit Red Wings that sent the team into another downward spiral.

Between 1950–51 and 1965–66, New York made the playoffs only four times and finished in last place on only three occasions. By the mid-1960s, the organization was looking like a contender again with bright young talent such as Jean Ratelle, Rod Gilbert, Vic Hadfield, Jim Neilson and goalie Ed Giacomin leading them back to the postseason. In 1971–72, they finally made it back to the Stanley Cup Final but lost to Boston in six games.

For the next 20 years, the Rangers were competitive and further endeared themselves to their local fan base with their hard work on the ice. It was an especially daunting task after the arrival of local competitors in the New York Islanders in 1972–73 and the New Jersey Devils a decade later. They made another return trip to the Stanley Cup Final in 1978–79 but barely avoided being swept by the Montreal Canadiens. The arrival of Mark Messier in a trade early in 1991–92 helped the team to a regular-season title, and they finally reclaimed Lord Stanley's Mug two years later in a dramatic seven-game clash with the Vancouver Canucks. Three seasons later, Wayne Gretzky joined their roster, but his presence was not enough to help them to glory, and they set a franchise record for futility by missing the playoffs for seven straight seasons from 1997–98 to 2003–04.

Following the lockout that eliminated the 2004–05 campaign, the Rangers were back among the NHL's elite and have since regularly competed for a playoff spot. The play of Henrik Lundqvist in net has given them a solid defensive backbone and the addition of top scorers like Brad Richards and Marian Gaborik helped New York celebrate an Eastern Conference crown in 2011–12.

BILL COOK

A pure goal scorer who developed into one of hockey's best in the west in the mid-1920s, Cook was a marquee player the New York Rangers

(clockwise) Bill Cook, Frank Boucher, Ching Johnson, Lorne Chabot

needed to ensure early success on Broadway. The club picked him up when the Saskatoon Crescents liquidated their assets.

On November 16, 1926, Cook secured the team's first victory, scoring the only goal in a 1–0 win over the Montreal Maroons. The goals after that came at an incredible pace as he played the right side of the Bread Line with his brother, Bun, and passing-wizard Frank Boucher. In New York's second game, he recorded the first hat trick in franchise history in a 5–1 romp over the Toronto St. Pats. On January 9, 1927, he had the winning goal against Detroit that secured the Rangers the top spot in the American Division.

Cook scored all three goals, including the overtime winner, in a battle with Pittsburgh on February 12, and the same club surrendered another hat trick to him on March 22. In the next outing against Chicago, he potted the winning goal in a 4–0 triumph for the Rangers. He finished the year as the NHL leader in both goals and points. Once the playoffs began, the team hit a scoring slump and Cook got their only offence in during the two-game total-goals series.

FRANK BOUCHER

Boucher returned to NHL action with the Rangers in their first season. He had spent his first pro season with the Ottawa Senators before heading west for four years with the Vancouver Maroons. A budding playmaker, he was sold to New York for just $15,000 and proved one of the team's superstars in their early years.

Even though he was considered a gentlemanly player by fans and peers — he later won the Lady Byng Trophy a record seven times — Boucher's debut with the Rangers saw him earn a major penalty in a melee with Bill Phillips of the Maroons. He sustained a cut above the eye and was fined $15 for the infraction. Placed on a line with the Cook brothers, he began to rack up lots of points and scored twice when New York visited the Boston Bruins on January 18, 1927. He scored the winning goal against the Pittsburgh Pirates on February 6 and repeated that feat two weeks later in a rematch with the Bruins. On March 26, he closed out the season with a hat trick in a close 4–3 loss to Boston.

BUN COOK

During his amateur days, Fred "Bun" Cook helped take the Sault Ste. Marie Greyhounds to the Allan Cup and at age 21 turned pro with the WCHL's Saskatoon Crescents, a team that already had his older brother, Bill, on the roster. Over two seasons there, he proved one of the most promising young players in the game but was sold to the Rangers, along with his sibling, before the start of the 1926–27 campaign.

Bun was a skilled playmaker and is credited by some historians as being the inventor of the slapshot. The first goal of his NHL career gave the Rangers some insurance in a 2–0 win over the Canadiens on November 27, 1926. He was also at his best in the February 10, 1927, come-from-behind victory over the Toronto St. Pats when he scored twice to make it 3–2. On February 27, he got the winning goal in a 4–1 triumph over the New York Americans.

TAFFY ABEL

Even though he was born in Canada, Clarence "Taffy" Abel rose to prominence playing amateur hockey in the United States in the early 1920s. During his time with the St. Paul Athletic Club, he was permitted to play for the American team at the 1924 Winter Olympics and scored 15 goals over just five games. He turned pro with the Minneapolis Millers in 1925–26 and signed with the Rangers as a free agent soon after.

Paired with Ching Johnson on New York's blue line, Taffy was the team's top-scoring defenceman during the Rangers' first season in the league. On December 7, 1926, he scored his team's only goal in a 1–0 triumph over the Boston Bruins, their fifth win in their first seven games. He was also New York's lone producer in a 1–1 tie with the Toronto St. Pats on January 13, 1927.

MURRAY MURDOCH

Before turning pro, Murdoch was a star with the University of Manitoba and helped take the team to the Memorial Cup in 1922–23, after scoring an incredible 30 points over eight games. He joined the Winnipeg Maroons for the 1925–26 season and there caught the attention of

Conn Smythe, who made him the first player ever signed to a contract by the New York Rangers.

Murdoch is remembered as a checking forward. He made his NHL debut in the season opener against the Montreal Maroons on November 16, 1926, and scored his first goal four days later on John Ross Roach of the Toronto St. Pats. The Madison Square Garden audience warmed up to him rather quickly when he came off the bench in overtime to score against Boston on December 12.

His best performance of the year came on January 16, 1927, when he had a hat trick in a 5–4 win over the Chicago Black Hawks, his final tally proving the winner that night. Murdoch was involved in controversy about a month later when he scored against the Maroons, but the goal judge failed to signal the marker since he was too busy talking to a woman in the crowd.

CHING JOHNSON

Johnson was unlike many of the other players who joined one of the three NHL expansion teams for 1926–27, because his previous experience came in the hockey hotbed of Minnesota. There he starred for teams in Eveleth and Minneapolis before taking a three-year contract with the Rangers.

Unafraid to play a physical game, the burly and balding defender served notice early on that he was focused on protecting New York's net. He took the first penalty in franchise history for cross-checking Babe Siebert, and his rambunctious play meant he missed some ice time early in the year with a broken collarbone. On November 27, 1926, he scored the winning goal in a shutout victory over the Canadiens. At the end of the season, he still managed to rank second on the team with 66 penalty minutes.

Johnson's nickname had roots in racist sentiment, as some felt that his face looked Asian and reportedly chanted "Ching Ching Chinaman" whenever he carried the puck. This was shortened to "Chinaman," then to the even more offensive "Chink," before becoming "Ching." Despite this, Johnson had an amazing career and is a member of the Hockey Hall of Fame.

OLLIE REINIKKA

A top amateur player in the early 1920s, Reinikka turned pro with the Vancouver Maroons in 1924–25 and had a 10-goal season as a sophomore. When he was sold to the Rangers, a publicity man thought it would be a good idea to try to attract some of New York's Italian community with a "native son" named Ollie Rocco. The stunt managed to fool a few people and some of the published game summaries list Rocco as a member of the Rangers, but the truth was quickly made public and he was able to resume playing under his real name.

What the Rangers were not counting on, however, was the distinct lack of offence they would get from Reinikka, and he was sent down to the Springfield Indians of the Can-Am League after 16 games.

HAL WINKLER

After two seasons with the Calgary Tigers, Winkler was the first goalie to step between the pipes for the New York Rangers. The team made the rare decision to start the year with two goaltenders, but he got the nod for the season opener against the Montreal Maroons and came out with a big 1–0 victory at home.

Not wanting to interrupt a hot streak, Lester Patrick let Winkler start the next game, and he came away with a win against the Toronto St. Pats. Even after Lorne Chabot got a shutout victory on November 27, 1926, Winkler returned to the crease three days later and earned his third and final win with the Rangers in overtime as the Chicago Black Hawks went down by a score of 4–3.

The Rangers sold Winkler to the Boston Bruins on January 17, 1927, and he helped his new club to the Stanley Cup Final against the Ottawa Senators. He played one more season in the NHL before heading to the minors. Strangely, the Bruins engraved his name on the Stanley Cup when they won it in 1928–29.

LORNE CHABOT

Chabot is perhaps the greatest goaltender who is not a member of the Hockey Hall of Fame. Teammates knew him best as a fun and loyal player, but that does not mean he didn't have a great deal of on-ice success. Before he joined the Rangers, he starred at the senior level for the Port Arthur Ports club and even took them to the Allan Cup one year while reportedly taping his broken hand to his stick.

After Chabot signed on with New York, a creative marketing man decided to promote him as a Jewish player with the last name of Chabotsky in an attempt to draw in some fans. This deception was quickly vetoed and he made his NHL debut on the road against his hometown Montreal Canadiens, winning the game and the adulation of the crowd for his 2–0 shutout victory. In a matter of weeks, he won the number one position in net over Hal Winkler and ended up ranking second in the league, with a goals-against average of 1.46. His 10 shutouts that season put him in fourth place among all netminders.

In the postseason, Chabot gave up just three goals to the Bruins in one contest and earned a shutout in the other, but it was not enough to take the total-goals series. The next year, he led the Blueshirts to their first Stanley Cup title.

THE ORIGINAL SIX

When the Brooklyn Americans shut down after the 1941–42 season, the NHL was reduced to a roster of clubs that will forever be known as the Original Six — the Boston Bruins, Chicago Black Hawks, Detroit Red Wings, Montreal Canadiens and Toronto Maple Leafs. For 25 years, these teams were at the pinnacle of the professional hockey world and their owners controlled the game with iron fists.

The early part of this era was marked by the fact that many players were going off to fight in World War II. But at the same time, a new generation of stars was coming to the forefront and the NHL continued to grow in popularity through radio and newspaper coverage. The league brought in Clarence Campbell as its new president in 1946.

Throughout the rest of the 1940s, the rivalry between the Canadiens and Maple Leafs intensified, and it was this rivalry that brought the game to new levels among Canadian fans. The Habs, who often featured the best players out of Quebec, had icons like Maurice Richard heading the charge, but Syl Apps (and later Teeder Kennedy) ranked among the most popular Toronto players. Once the NHL expanded to a 70-game schedule, the two teams met 14 times during the regular season. The intensity spilled off the ice as players did not even acknowledge each other outside of the rink.

The early 1950s saw the Red Wings dominate, as they won seven straight regular-season crowns, and between 1949–50 and 1954–55, they captured four Stanley Cups. Otherwise, it was Montreal controlling the decade — winning five straight championships from 1955–56 to 1959–60. The Bruins had a spotty record during this time, the Rangers rarely made the playoffs and Chicago was regularly excluded from the playoff picture.

Perhaps the most significant events of the 1950s were the Richard Riot that took place after Richard was suspended by the NHL in 1954–55 and the brief formation of a players' association created by Ted Lindsay and Doug Harvey in 1957. Team owners quickly moved to squash the association, and any players involved in unionization efforts were dispatched to other teams.

Heading into the 1960s, the hard-luck Black Hawks had several aces up their sleeves after they picked up goaltender Glenn Hall and developed two major prospects in Bobby Hull and Stan Mikita. In particular, Hull emerged as one of the game's greatest superstars, and Chicago won a Stanley Cup in 1960–61. Afterward, the resurging Maple Leafs won three more Cups of their own before the Canadiens began a quiet dynasty that carried over into the expansion years. The only interruption was Toronto's championship in 1966–67 — the final year of the Original Six, and the last time the Leafs won the Cup.

Some owners resisted the first official signs the league wanted to add to their membership, but in time, the threat of the Western Hockey League getting a national television contract in the United States changed their minds. The Americans had earlier attempted to return along with a Philadelphia-based group that owned the Montreal Maroons franchise, but they were rebuffed. Other cities had come forward at various times, but the NHL wanted to protect its own interests as much as possible. The most notable attempt to get a team was from Jim Hendy in 1951, who ran the American Hockey League's Cleveland Barons. He wanted an NHL team badly, but the team owners collaborated to keep him out.

William M. Jennings, who was a governor for the New York Rangers, proposed the idea of expansion in 1963 and pushed for the creation of teams on the west coast to battle the WHL threat. The owners balked but he persisted, and by March 1965, the NHL was officially considering doubling in size.

1967

THE YEAR THAT CHANGED
HOCKEY FOREVER

Most professional sports leagues in the United States in the 1960s grew tremendously, but the National Hockey League was comparatively slow to expand beyond its beloved Original Six teams and gain a greater market share.

One of the biggest hurdles the game faced in the early 1960s was that it lacked a national television contract in America. In Canada, there was little problem getting air time on radio and television. But at the time, the NHL was regional and simply did not appeal to audiences west of Chicago. Local minor league teams had strong followings, however, and the Western Hockey League was considered a major threat on the west coast.

Team owners were finally convinced by William M. Jennings that to head off a catastrophe, they needed to double their membership to 12 teams. Clarence Campbell announced these intentions in March 1965. Some of the cities deemed acceptable or potential sites for new clubs included Vancouver, San Francisco-Oakland, Los Angeles and St. Louis. Less than a year later, the NHL was presented with 14 different applications — five from Los Angeles, two from Pittsburgh and one each from Philadelphia, San Francisco-Oakland, Baltimore, Minneapolis-St. Paul, Buffalo and Vancouver.

Each successful applicant was expected to pay $2,000,000 for the privilege of membership. A few months later, the California Seals, Los Angeles Kings, Minnesota North Stars, Philadelphia Flyers, Pittsburgh

Penguins and St. Louis Blues were welcomed to the league. Interestingly enough, the St. Louis franchise was granted without an ownership group in place, as the location was viewed as an opportunity for the Wirtz family to sell off the city's arena and generate some cash.

Many Canadian fans were rankled that Vancouver did not receive a team, but one of the primary reasons they were blocked was that the Canadiens and Maple Leafs did not want to share their television revenues.

The six new clubs made up the new West Division and they were expected to primarily compete against one another during their early years. The teams were mostly assembled by way of the first NHL Expansion Draft on June 6, 1967, and existing clubs were permitted to protect most of their top stars. The Philadelphia and Los Angeles clubs augmented their lineups by purchasing minor league teams.

Once the new clubs hit the ice, they suffered many growing pains, but the NHL's first modern attempt to expand proved a success. In time, two of them relocated, but the remaining four have strong followings to this day and three of them have won the Stanley Cup at least once in their original cities.

EXPANSION YEAR RECORD: 15-42-17
(47 points — sixth in West Division)
COACHES: Bert Olmstead and Gord Fashoway
GENERAL MANAGER: Bert Olmstead
FIRST GAME: October 11, 1967 —
5-1 win vs. Philadelphia Flyers
FIRST GOAL: October 11, 1967 by Kent Douglas

CALIFORNIA SEALS

Throughout most of the 1960s, the WHL's San Francisco Seals were one of the most successful teams in the minors. Named after an old minor league baseball club, they played out of the Cow Palace and won league championships in 1962–63 and 1963–64. Known for their toughness, they had an intense rivalry with the Portland Buckaroos and the Los Angeles Blades and had little trouble drawing decent crowds.

When the NHL was looking to expand for the 1967–68 season, Seals owner Barry Van Gerbig bid for a new franchise. The success of the San Francisco club undoubtedly made them an appealing choice, and they were selected as one of the new NHL teams in February 1966. In their last WHL season, the team changed their name to the California Seals and moved across the Bay to play in the Oakland-Alameda County Coliseum. Several of the players on that team, including Gerry Odrowski and Charlie Burns, were on the initial NHL roster.

In preparation for NHL action, the big-league Seals originally hired veteran hockey-man Rudy Pilous, who had coached the Chicago Black Hawks to a Stanley Cup in 1960–61, to run the team. But the team fired him before the start of the 1967–68 season and replaced him with retired hockey great Bert Olmstead. Pilous launched a breach-of-contract suit against the Seals and later went on to help the WHL's Denver Spurs to great success.

Olmstead took over the team in time for the 1967 NHL Expansion Draft and with his first selection brought in a former teammate in netminder Charlie Hodge. Their goaltending was solidified, since Gary Smith, a prospect on the rise, backed up the former Vezina Trophy winner. The rest of the team started to come together with some experienced defencemen in Bob Baun, Kent Douglas and Larry Cahan and veteran forwards Bill Hicke and Billy Harris.

Once training camp began, it was evident that the Seals were going to run according to Olmstead's strict rules. A multi-time Stanley Cup champion, he knew what it took to win and was not looking for other ways of doing things. The hockey press predicted California would finish first overall in the West Division thanks to their goaltending and defence, but there remained questions about their lack of offensive power.

The biggest Seals news in the pre-season came in the form of a grizzled veteran trying to make a comeback. Jacques Plante had been retired for two years when he decided to try his luck with an expansion club. The Seals actually hired him as a goaltending coach, which was a first in the NHL, but he got a chance to play in a game against Los Angeles.

"I feel like I never left," he said. "My reflexes haven't changed a bit and my eyesight is as good as ever. But wait until next week and you will have a better story."

He left the next day, though, after the New York Rangers cried foul since they held his rights. Van Gerbig claimed that the Seals had an arrangement with the Rangers to pay them per appearance for Plante, and more if he made the team, in addition to another amount for each year he played in the NHL with them.

Luckily, the Seals inked a deal with Hodge soon after and were protected in net. In an interesting move, Van Gerbig chose to let some of the people who originally bid for the San Francisco-Oakland area franchise purchase a minority interest in the Seals. The group included Bing Crosby, among others, but their investment started to look shaky in a matter of months.

On the ice, the Seals looked good, at least in their first two games. They won their debut against the Philadelphia Flyers on October 11, 1967, and then shut out the Minnesota North Stars three days later. From that point, they embarked on a 14-game winless streak, blanked in consecutive home outings. After these struggles, the owners decided to change their name to the Oakland Seals to try to draw more local fans, as their old supporters were not crossing the bridge from San Francisco. The logo also changed slightly as the "C" became an "O."

"It was the desire of the league that we try to identify with San Francisco," said Van Gerbig. "The only way we could identify with both cities would be to play in the middle of the bridge. There should be no kidding ourselves. We're Oakland. . . . The centre of population is right where our building is. We have access to four million people within an hour's drive of our arena on freeways. . . . I don't agree that our success depends wholly on getting people to come across from San Francisco."

On the hockey side, Olmstead started to show signs of frustration with his club.

"I can't explain it. It's a mystery. I know we've got a better team than we've shown. We haven't been skating, everything suffers — passing, playmaking, defence, everything. They can't be tired, it's too early in the season. . . . We've got a pretty good team and we are in the position now of just having to ride out the low spots. But no excuses for losing, the only way we'll get better is to work harder."

There were also early rumours that Van Gerbig was going to sell the team when it was drawing fewer than 4,000 people per game. Buffalo and Vancouver apparently wanted an NHL team, but he was not quite ready to sell.

"We are going to stay here as long as we can survive and I can't set a time limit on that. We knew it was going to be rough in the first year, but frankly we are disappointed. We thought we'd do better than we did in the minors, but we know, too, that things are going to pick up. If we didn't feel that things were going to improve then I probably would have started talking business with some of the people who want to buy the Seals franchise. But here it becomes a question of motives. Some of the new owners probably are in this game strictly for the buck. Well, I'm not. I have other ideas about this sport but I'm not going to stay around and get killed either."

NHL president Clarence Campbell firmly supported their stance.

"They've got all kinds of resources. I don't consider them to be in a bad way and neither do the owners. . . . I don't know why the NHL has to apologize. The NBA went with crowds as low as 875 at times. We don't expect capacity crowds in our new division cities."

The rumour mill churned throughout the year, especially after Van Gerbig was spotted in Vancouver.

On December 15, the Seals hosted the Boston Bruins and got a surprise win, but their rematch 10 days later was a Christmas Day massacre as penalties were called and fines administered. Even Olmstead got in on the action; he had to shell out $200 after chasing a fan with a stick and lost another $50 for going out onto the ice. Although the Seals could not land a radio contract their first year, they did get some celebrity attention from *Peanuts* creator Charles M. Schulz, and he eventually built a long-standing relationship with the team. Years later, he designed their mascot, a seal named Sparky.

With losses piling up, the Seals dealt away problematic defenceman Kent Douglas to Detroit for a three-player package that included Ted Hampson, who gave Oakland some spark. The problems between Olmstead and his players intensified, though, when Billy Harris walked out during a loss to the New York Rangers. In the face of extended practices, ridiculous fines and other contentious issues, the players seemed ready for mutiny. The coach called it quits and focused solely on his GM duties with just 10 games left.

"I was sick and tired of looking at them and I'm sure they were sick and tired of looking at me," said Olmstead. "I had to get off the bench to keep my sanity but I'm getting a new perspective; maybe players and I aren't made of the same material. . . . I saw a lack of effort and a lack of trying. They are not passing, and not checking, and not skating. Ninety-nine percent of the time when you aren't skating you aren't putting out."

After Gord Fashoway got behind the bench, the Seals went 4–5–1 the rest of the way and finished in last place. Knowing that the team was troubled, the NHL gave them until May 15, 1968, to straighten out their ownership setup. It still owed the league $700,000 of the $2 million initiation fee, but Labatt Breweries wanted to buy the Seals on condition that they could be moved to Vancouver. Most insiders did not think that would happen and Campbell said there had been no application to move the franchise.

The NHL agreed to accept Labatt's offer to advance the Seals the $700,000 the NHL was owed. Campbell listed two conditions for the transfer of the franchise: nine of the 12 league governors needed to approve the move, and the Vancouver WHL franchise owner needed to agree with the transfer and also satisfy its obligations to its partners in the WHL in defecting from that league.

"Insofar as Vancouver now is equipped with a first-class rink, it is conceivable that a further expansion of two clubs could be conducted without too much difficulty, taking in Vancouver and some other new club," said Campbell.

At the end of the year, Olmstead was let go and the NHL ultimately decided to let the Seals stay put. Van Gerbig eventually launched a lawsuit claiming that the league violated the Sherman Act, but the suit was settled in the NHL's favour in 1974. And instead, Vancouver got a franchise of their own that would start play in 1970–71.

The legacy of the Seals is one of failure and futility in the eyes of many hockey fans. To be fair, it almost seemed as if they were doomed from the start. Even though the Seals rebounded and made the playoffs in their second and third years in the league, their slide back to the bottom of the standings was swift — especially once Charles O. Finley took over ownership.

Baseball fans are familiar with the exploits of Finley, who packed up the Kansas City Athletics and moved them to Oakland. He had a reputation for making some eccentric moves. When he entered the world of the NHL, he changed the team name to the California Golden Seals and changed their jerseys to a so-bad-it's-good combination of green and yellow to match the baseball club's colours. He also came up with the much-maligned idea of painting the team's skates white, provoking the laughter of fans and opponents alike.

Under Finley's oppressive thumb, the Golden Seals never did contend, even though at times they had some solid young talent. Their best season during his tenure came in 1971–72 when Gilles Meloche arrived as their number one netminder. But they were unprepared for the WHA talent raids and by the next year were a vastly different club. Finley refused to pay higher salaries to keep players happy, and they were more than ready to leave for bigger contracts. The team also gave up many high draft-picks along the way. When Finley tried to sell them to a group out of Indianapolis, the league rejected the idea and took over the franchise in 1974.

In early 1975, the press reported that the Golden Seals were heading to Denver, as that city had already been granted a conditional expansion club set to begin play in 1976–77. The NHL also said that if a sale to the Denver group was not completed, the team would be liquidated. They hung on long enough to be purchased instead by hotelier Mel Swig, but he wanted to move them from Oakland to a proposed arena in San Francisco. Unfortunately for Bay Area fans, the arena deal fell through and the Seals were on the move, as minority owners George and Gordon Gund convinced Swig that their fortunes might improve elsewhere.

For two seasons, the former California club played as the Cleveland Barons. Their time in Ohio was plagued with problems. Besides having little hope of being playoff contenders, they also had to play in the suburb of Richfield in a large arena not even close to being filled with hockey fans. Even with the most seating in the league at the time, they rarely drew more than 10,000 fans per game. The city had long supported pro hockey, but the distance to the new rink was viewed as a major inconvenience, and the club was stuck with a tight schedule for relocation and inadequate time to promote ticket sales locally.

The 1976–77 season was barely half over when Swig openly hinted that the Barons might not be able to finish the season due to a lack of revenue. They actually missed making payroll twice in the month of February. The league and the NHL Players' Association (NHLPA) made a loan to cover the shortfall and avoid the potential embarrassment of a team folding in the middle of the year. Soon after, Swig sold his stake of the Barons to the Gund brothers.

Cleveland's second season in the NHL was even worse than the first one when it came to their on-ice record, and the financial bleeding simply could not be stopped. Instead of closing shop, they merged with the Minnesota North Stars, who were also having money problems.

(clockwise) Billy Harris, Kent Douglas, Bob Baun, Charlie Hodge

That was a smart move on many levels, and the fortified club quickly became a contender, making it to the Stanley Cup Final in 1980–81 with several former Barons players on the roster.

GERRY EHMAN

Ehman is a perfect example of a talented minor league player who put up solid numbers throughout the 1960s but could not really crack an NHL lineup. He was a mainstay with the Rochester Americans for several years but never got a lot of consideration from Toronto coach and GM Punch Imlach. While he was part of a run to the Stanley Cup in 1963–64, and he averaged well over a point per game on the farm, the Leafs made him available to the Seals — a new club that was prepared to give up a pair of top young prospects for a crafty, high-scoring vet.

Coach Bert Olmstead already knew what Ehman could do on the ice because they had been teammates on the Maple Leafs several years earlier. He became linemates with Billy Harris and Bill Hicke and recorded a goal and two assists in their opening game, helping give them a major lead over the Philadelphia Flyers.

At times in the 1967–68 season, Ehman was the hottest performer in the West Division. He had a nice stretch in early January when he scored a pair against Minnesota and then a hat trick playing the Los Angeles Kings the following night. He also won West Player of the Week honours by scoring a pair, including the winner, against Pittsburgh on February 24 and potting one more in a clash with the North Stars the next day. He finished the year as Oakland's top scorer and led the team with 189 shots on net.

BILL HICKE

At one time, the media hailed Hicke as an heir apparent to Maurice Richard in Montreal. He became a solid NHL performer but didn't live up to the hype and was eventually traded to the New York Rangers. By the end of the 1966–67 season, the Broadway Blueshirts had given up on him, but the Seals knew that he had a lot more to give and picked him up in the expansion draft.

Hicke suffered a groin injury in training camp but came through with a huge performance in the season opener with three points — including the first game-winning goal in franchise history, scored against Philadelphia's Bernie Parent at 12:04 of the second period. Following a hot start, he ended up battling bronchial pneumonia, which was the result of an asthmatic condition that was discovered during a conversation with a doctor at a publicity appearance. He sat out for five games to recuperate and managed to get back to scoring, tallying four goals against Boston that included two game-winners on December 15, 1967, and February 17, 1968.

Coach Bert Olmstead was glad to have one of his top performers back in the lineup.

"He does wonders for our offence," he said. "He has a great attitude and he gives everything he's got. . . . Back in training camp and later I thought his tiredness was because he wasn't in condition, and tried to tell him how important it was that he get into shape. But since we've found out he has this bronchial condition — and has had it for a long time — a lot of things become clearer and you can understand him a lot better."

Hicke finished the year as the team's top goal scorer and put in 12 pucks in power-play situations. Had he not missed more than 20 games, he likely would have been the prime offensive performer for Oakland.

CHARLIE BURNS

From 1958–59 to 1962–63, Burns regularly played with Detroit and Boston, but after that he found himself mired in the minors for four seasons with the WHL's San Francisco Seals. When it became apparent the NHL was coming to the Bay Area, the big-league Seals got his rights and he had a good shot at coming back.

"It was an opportunity to play," he said. "I felt fortunate to get a chance to play in the NHL again."

In early November, he had back-to-back two-assist games against Chicago and Los Angeles. He topped that with consecutive three-point outings when the Seals faced the North Stars and Kings in early January. Burns often played on a line with Mike Laughton and George Swarbrick.

He also is one of the few original Seals to have positive things to say about coach Bert Olmstead.

"He was very demanding and very tough. You had to have a lot of respect for him. There wasn't much room for error as far as he was concerned. He demanded a lot, but you understood that because of the way he played the game himself."

When the Toronto Maple Leafs came to Oakland on February 11, 1968, Burns scored the game-winning goal with less than three minutes left in the third period. *The Hockey News* named him the West Division Player of the Week. As a result of his solid comeback season, the Pittsburgh Penguins picked him in the Intra-League Draft at the end of the year.

BILLY HARRIS

Although Harris was part of three Stanley Cup championships in Toronto, he was traded to Detroit before the 1965–66 season and never really caught on with the Red Wings. Instead, the AHL's Pittsburgh Hornets gave him a lot of playing time, and he had a big season with them in 1966–67, putting up 70 points and winning the Calder Cup.

As he was obviously nowhere near being washed up, the Seals acquired him in the 1967 NHL Expansion Draft. It was a bittersweet experience for the veteran forward. Although it was nice to be back at the top level of pro hockey, he was a constant victim of often-unjustified fines and benching from coach Bert Olmstead, and he actually walked out on the team during a 3–0 loss to the New York Rangers on January 20, 1968. The team demoted him to Buffalo of the AHL, but he hinted that he might just retire instead.

"I've got pride," he said. "I could have stayed on and gone through the motions and taken it all — the abuse and probably more fines, but I just didn't feel like going through the motions. I'm dissatisfied with my own play, sure. I'd get going and then I started to think that maybe they were right, that I didn't have it. When I got benched in the second period against New York, I knew I had to do something, so I walked out. I've made no final decision at what my future will be."

After eight games, he returned on Olmstead's terms but was undoubtedly relieved to see Gord Fashoway take over behind the bench.

TED HAMPSON

Hampson was an NHL regular with the New York Rangers in the early 1960s, but a trade to Detroit put his career on hold. After he spent three seasons mostly in the minors, he returned to the Red Wings in 1966–67 and made some solid contributions before he was traded to the Seals.

Hampson fit in nicely with Oakland and scored a tying goal against St. Louis during his debut. He had a positive outlook on his team's chances of making the postseason.

"I hope we don't quit now, we've got a good chance to make the playoffs. We've just got to concentrate for 60 minutes a game. We'll be okay."

The veteran forward also earned his fair share of praise from the club's second coach, Gord Fashoway.

"He's been great in every way. He's just a great team man and a good guy. He's a hard-working player who is going to get a few goals for us as well as pick up our playmaking."

All of Hampson's hard work and perseverance paid off in 1968–69 when he became the second player ever awarded the Bill Masterton Memorial Trophy.

"I love the guy . . . he wasn't afraid to go anywhere," said John Brenneman. "I remember when we were in Philadelphia and somebody knocked into the boards and he went back out there. He worked hard and was willing to take a hit."

LARRY POPEIN

After he saw his last NHL action with the New York Rangers in 1960–61, Popein remained with the organization and starred for the WHL's Vancouver Canucks for many years. When he wasn't taken in the expansion draft, the Seals traded for him in December 1967.

"In one respect, I was having a good year in Vancouver," he said. "I had sent Emile Francis a resumé and wanted to finish up the year before moving on to become a coach. Bert Olmstead joked, 'If you don't get your skates and get on that plane, you won't have that job with Emile!' I took a lot from him in my own coaching career."

The December 15, 1967, contest against Boston marked Popein's first NHL game in nearly seven years. He scored a goal to give the Seals a 3–0 lead in what turned out to be a 4–1 victory. Just 10 days later, he had a pair of assists in a rematch with the Bruins, but the celebration was marred by the death of his father.

"On Christmas Day, my father passed away. My concentration wasn't there for the rest of the year," he said.

The 1967–68 campaign was his last in the NHL, but Popein managed a couple of solid two-point performances before the end of the year. One of them saw him score a shorthanded goal and add an assist in a 4–0 win over Philadelphia on February 14, 1968.

KENT DOUGLAS

A rugged veteran who learned a lot of his defensive craft from the legendary Eddie Shore, Douglas spent five great seasons with the Toronto Maple Leafs. Bert Olmstead's former teammate, he was earning accolades for his tremendous play before the coach and general manager chose him in the expansion draft.

"Kent should be the best point man on the power play and one of the best at getting his puck out of the zone in the league," said Olmstead.

From the start of training camp, it appeared Douglas was going to move to the beat of his own drum. He made waves with management when he ripped the numbers off the shoulders of his new sweater, as he believed that was something for football players rather than ice warriors. He scored the first goal in franchise history at 3:23 of the first period against Bernie Parent of Philadelphia on October 11, 1967, and he also chipped in a pair of assists in the winning effort.

"He was a hard-nosed defenceman who didn't take shit from anybody," said Gerry Odrowski. "He'd talk back to Bert, but Bert knew better than to say anything to him. He had a heart of gold, but if he didn't like you — look out!"

By the halfway mark of the season, his welcome in Oakland had been worn out and he was dispatched to the Detroit Red Wings. Since the Seals had played more games at that point, Douglas finished the 1967–68 season with 76 games played and set a league record in the process.

BOB BAUN

Grit personified, Baun was one of hockey's best blueliners in the 1960s, in part because of his incredible checking talents, but many fans are most familiar with the story about him scoring a game-winning goal in the Stanley Cup Final on a broken leg. In 1966–67, he still played for the Toronto Maple Leafs and his clashes with coach Punch Imlach were well documented. Once the season ended, he was not surprised to find he was on his way out through the expansion draft. Whatever team acquired him was in for a real treat, thanks especially to his leadership abilities.

"I was prepared for the draft before it happened. I had Jim Blaney, my attorney, draft an announcement of my retirement if I had been taken by any other club than Bert Olmstead and the California Seals," he remarked at the time. "I'm pleased with the way things are going here. We have no abnormal problems but when you've got 20 players thrown together, having never played together as a team before, it's tough to mould them right off the bat and it's unfair to expect miracles in such a short time."

Hand-picked by Olmstead to be the team's captain, Baun worked hard in training camp by leading calisthenics and shouting out instructions to young players in scrimmages. He hesitated to sign a contract with the Seals until just a few hours before their first game.

"Expansion is much better than I thought it would be," he said at the time. "The new teams are better and that proves that enthusiasm and spirit is accomplishing something — it certainly makes up for a lack of overall ability and depth."

Baun was Oakland's lone representative in the NHL All-Star Game and missed some time that year as a result of a pinched nerve in his shoulder. Over the course of the 1967–68 campaign, he scored just three goals, but two of them came against the Philadelphia Flyers within a two-week period in February. He also had a pair of assists in a loss to Detroit on March 13, 1968.

With Olmstead out of the picture at the end of the season, the Seals dealt Baun to the Red Wings soon after.

"Bobby was always a great guy. I played junior against him," said Charlie Burns. "His desire to win overshadowed everything else."

GERRY ODROWSKI

With his bald head, Odrowski was instantly recognizable on the ice in the days before helmets were commonplace, but he was also known as a respected blueliner who focused on defence first. He got his NHL start with Detroit in the early 1960s, but after he was traded to Boston, he never played for the club and instead settled in with the California Seals of the Western League. When the team became part of the big league, his rights formed part of the package and he got another shot at the highest level of competition.

Part of a veteran defence corps, Odrowski embraced his offensive side with some occasional switches to left wing. Three of his four goals of the season came in November. He had a shorthanded tally against Montreal and two more came in a battle with the Philadelphia Flyers when he scored yet again while the Seals were down a man. On December 6, he got a pair of assists in a rematch with the Flyers.

Not long after scoring his fourth goal of the year in a January 21, 1968, win over Los Angeles, Odrowski was hit in the eye with Rod Gilbert's stick in an outing against the New York Rangers and was hospitalized for several days.

"We were in New York and his stick came up and caught me in the eye," he recalled. "I asked Larry Cahan where the hospital was and he said, 'I know where to go.' I was out for a month, but it hasn't bothered me since."

Despite some concerns about Bert Olmstead's coaching methods, he felt the experience of playing for the Seals was a positive one for the most part.

"We had a lot of laughs in Oakland. We weren't the best hockey team, but we had fun."

Once Gord Fashoway took over as coach, Odrowski had a confrontation with him that resulted in a demotion to the minors.

"We were waiting for the bus to leave, and I piped up because a couple of guys weren't there. He responded by telling me that I was going to Vancouver and to pack my bags. That's what you call an asshole. We used to call him 'Liver Lips.' I called Bert [Olmstead] about it, but he couldn't go against him.

Years later, I was playing for the San Diego Gulls and we were taking on Portland and he had his knuckles on the boards. I came by and rapped them with my stick and said, 'Take that you son of a bitch!'"

CHARLIE HODGE

Small in size but large in talent, Hodge was an established veteran in the late 1960s, but he often missed out on play in Montreal because of a goaltender glut or his injuries. He served as the understudy to Jacques Plante for many years, but once the Hall of Famer was traded to New York, he got a chance to shine and his name was carved on the Vezina Trophy twice in the last years of the Original Six era.

Faced with the dilemma of protecting only two goalies, the Habs chose Rogie Vachon and Gump Worsley and left Hodge exposed to the new clubs. The Seals happily brought him on board and he signed a contract with them after Plante chose to end his attempt at a comeback during their first training camp.

Thanks to Hodge's tremendous play early on, California started hot and he was named the West Division Player of the Week after he limited the Philadelphia Flyers to a single goal in the season opener and followed that with a shutout on the Minnesota North Stars on October 14, 1967. From then on, the wins became scarce, but he was in net for the club's first back-to-back victories, which came against Los Angeles on January 21 and 24, 1968. He also looked good sharing a shutout with Gary Smith against the Flyers on February 14 and in a big win over Boston three days later.

Although the Seals finished far out of playoff contention, it is safe to say that Hodge managed to keep the club in a lot of games. He remained there until the end of the 1969–70 campaign as Gary Smith gained a greater share of the workload.

EXPANSION YEAR RECORD: 31-33-10
(72 points — second in West Division)
COACH: Red Kelly
GENERAL MANAGER: Larry Regan
FIRST GAME: October 14, 1967 —
4-2 win vs. Philadelphia Flyers
FIRST GOAL: October 14, 1967 by Brian Kilrea

LOS ANGELES KINGS

The idea of hockey in Los Angeles may have seemed strange to the casual hockey fan in the 1960s, but the reality was the city had hosted several minor league clubs over the years. In the 1930s and 1940s, the Monarchs played in the Pacific Hockey League, and in the time leading up to NHL expansion, the WHL's Blades ran strong.

Jack Kent Cooke was a transplanted Canadian entrepreneur who had made a name for himself in sporting circles as owner of the NFL's Washington Redskins and the NBA's Los Angeles Lakers. Since hockey was close to his heart, it was natural that he pursued an NHL franchise. But his bid was opposed by the ownership group of the Blades, which had the support of the Los Angeles Memorial Coliseum Commission, and they were not about to let him use the local sports arena. Undaunted, he built an arena of his own in suburban Inglewood and the NHL gave him the expansion franchise.

Cooke named his new club the Kings and even picked their colour scheme of purple and gold, the same as the colours worn by his basketball team. That particular shade of purple was dubbed "Forum Blue" by Cooke and he chose the same crown logo used by soccer club Real Madrid.

Even before the 1967 NHL Expansion Draft, Cooke secured a minor league affiliate for the Kings following a player strike held by the AHL's Springfield Indians. Several of the players he acquired in the purchase of that club ended up playing for Los Angeles in their first few seasons and that gave them a great deal of pro experience heading into the 1967–68 season.

Once Larry Regan was hired as general manager, the Kings sought a strong coach for their first season and signed the recently retired Red Kelly to fill that role. That move was not without some controversy. Toronto Maple Leafs coach and GM Punch Imlach cried foul because he was not given a chance to protect Kelly in the 1967 expansion draft. The teams eventually struck a compromise, and the Leafs got a young defender named Ken Block as compensation.

Much to the glee of the Kings, they obtained the first selection and chose the legendary Terry Sawchuk, fresh off a Stanley Cup victory. From there, Los Angeles focused on new talent with limited NHL experience, but the team made many shrewd picks, such as Gord Labossiere, Real Lemieux, Ted Irvine and Lowell MacDonald.

"There are going to be some mighty red faces around hockey after we've been around the circuit awhile," said Cooke. "We look like we have a very fine team."

Picked by some reporters to finish last, the Kings ignored the critics, and in "home games" played at the Long Beach Arena, they won their season opener against Philadelphia on October 14, 1967, and defeated Minnesota the following night. The unique arena had yellow and red goal lights instead of green and red ones and the faceoff circles also appeared to be in a different spot each game!

Celebrities regularly frequented early Kings games, and several Canadian ex-pats such as Lorne Greene, Art Linkletter and Monty Hall were on hand for the action. Academy Award–nominated actor George Kennedy, who used to attend New York Americans games as a child, was one of the early Kings fans.

"It is the greatest sport of all. I introduced my wife to it, and she loves it, too, and we don't miss a game if we're in town," he said. "We did give up on the Blades, finally. But we're thrilled by the NHL. You see the difference in major and minor league play very quickly. The way they get the puck to one another is amazing. We also love and support pro football, but hockey is the best."

After a six-game road trip, the Kings returned to California at the end of the month and played out of the Los Angeles Memorial Sports Arena before the Great Western Forum opened on December 30. This stretch of games featured a very controversial moment when Montreal Canadiens coach Toe Blake punched a heckler when fans moved down toward the bench after a fight finished on the ice. The heckler threw the first punch and Blake retaliated. Several Montreal players swung their sticks and bloodied the troublemaker and another fan, who ended up being taken to the hospital.

"I don't mind the heckling. I can take that," said a steamed Blake. "But the price he paid for a ticket doesn't entitle him to punch me. When the fans come at us, we're going to defend ourselves."

The two fans injured in the scuffle planned a civil suit and brought criminal action, resulting in a warrant being sworn out for the arrest of Blake and Claude Provost for "assault with a deadly weapon." They were set to return on March 6, 1968, to answer the charges, which were held over until May 20. Witnesses testified that Blake hit Bernard Weisman only after he punched first and that Provost went to his aid. The case was dismissed in early August.

CBS televised the opening of the "Fabulous Forum," but Los Angeles lost to Philadelphia by a score of 2–0. At the time, the Kings were mired in what became a nine-game winless streak.

Regan was not pleased by this turn of events but remained hopeful.

"I'm not happy with our recent play, but I'm happy with our overall play so far. And, despite the recent bad stretch, I think we'll get stronger as the season goes along. For one thing, the depth we have and Philadelphia has, having purchased farm clubs, which the other expansion clubs do not have, begin to show as injuries mount.

"For another thing, we have a lot of young players who have faltered here and there, but who have shown they have the stuff and are bound to improve. And we have some older players who have disappointed me so far, who have found out the expanded NHL is a lot tougher than they thought it would be, and who now realize they're going to have to give a little extra, both on and off the ice, if they are going to play to their potential, which I think they will begin to do.

"Finally, I think we have a lot of former minor-leaguers who used to coast and shrug off a couple of bad games as long as they were high in the standings, who now realize you have to take every game seriously in the majors, who now realize you have to fight for two points every night you take to the ice if you're going to survive in the big time. Overall, I'm quite pleased with where we are at this stage."

The transition from player to coach for Kelly proved difficult at times, but he earned a fair amount of praise from Regan.

"He has done a fantastic job. I really think he's the best coach in hockey already. Watching him game after game, I'm impressed as he gets steadily stronger and sharper. I'm particularly impressed by his patience. He doesn't panic. He has the team under a firm hold. With Red, this team should wind up a winner."

Los Angeles finished the season second in the West Division and met the North Stars in their first playoff series. They won the first two games, but Minnesota came back to tie the series and it eventually went to a seventh contest. Instead of going with the hot hand in Wayne Rutledge, the Kings put Sawchuk in net, counting on his playoff experience. But it did not end well. Sawchuk was bombed with 42 shots in the 9–4 loss, and the season closed for the first-year club.

"It's sad when you see guys work their guts out as these guys have all season and then see it come to nothing at the end," said Howie Menard.

In 1968–69, Los Angeles reached the playoffs once again, but Kelly jumped to the Pittsburgh Penguins and the Kings went into a spiral that saw them finish out of the postseason four years straight. By 1973–74, they were back in contention with goalie Rogie Vachon and coach Bob Pulford among the talents making believers out of fans. Marcel Dionne, the team's first true superstar, joined the lineup in 1975–76.

The arrival of Dave Taylor and Charlie Simmer in Los Angeles gave Dionne the support he needed, and the Triple Crown Line was a force to be reckoned with for many years, but still the Kings could not break into the league's elite.

By the mid-1980s, they were a bit of a disaster, but once Bruce McNall took over as owner, things began to change. His most notable move was orchestrating the acquisition of Wayne Gretzky from the Edmonton Oilers. Suddenly hockey became extremely popular in

(clockwise) Ed Joyal, Bill White, Dale Rolfe, Terry Sawchuk

California — especially with the team's new black, silver and white colour scheme.

With Gretzky racking up points at his usual feverish pace, the Kings won their first Smythe Division title in 1990–91 and two years later went to the Stanley Cup Final. The Great One remained with the team until the 1995–96 season, but a long stretch of relative futility began even before he left, as they only made the playoffs four times between 1993–94 and 2008–09. In recent years, the Kings have enjoyed a comeback and won their first Stanley Cup title in 2011–12.

EDDIE JOYAL

Once a prospect for the Detroit Red Wings, Joyal was mired in the minor league system of the Toronto Maple Leafs in the seasons leading up to the expansion era, but a great 1966–67 season with the Rochester Americans in the AHL ensured he found a new home the next year.

Joyal had a slow start in Los Angeles thanks to a sore ankle but he soon adjusted to NHL play and scored a game-winner against the Pittsburgh Penguins on October 28, 1967. *The Hockey News* named him the West Division Player of the Week in their November 18 issue after he scored two goals against the Toronto Maple Leafs on November 9. After representing the Kings at the 1968 NHL All-Star Game, he enjoyed a hot streak that included a four-point night against the Philadelphia Flyers on February 16, 1968.

His biggest goal of the year was the winning tally against the Minnesota North Stars in Game 5 of their opening-round playoff series of April 13. At the end of the season, the Kings named him their Most Valuable Player.

BILL FLETT

"Cowboy" Flett had four pro seasons behind him when the Kings drafted him from the Toronto Maple Leafs, but he put up some decent numbers in the minors while battling injuries in the years leading up to expansion.

"Toronto goes with the older players and only breaks in a few special kids every season. I began to feel I'd never get a chance with them, so I was tickled when L.A. drafted me," he told *The Hockey News*. "I've found the skating in the NHL now isn't any faster than the Central League, which is a kids' league but is less aimless. Up here, you have to anticipate the next play. The other guys check you closer and harder and you have a lot less time to make your moves."

The 1967–68 campaign marked the first season in Flett's career that he appeared in more than 70 games. He scored his first NHL goal against the Chicago Black Hawks on October 22, 1967. He began to put pucks in the net in bunches after that and excelled in clutch situations, scoring six game-winners for the Kings. On November 5 and February 1, 1968, he had hat tricks against the Detroit Red Wings and he finished the year as the league's leader in goals among rookies. That season he received consideration for the Calder Trophy and finished fourth in voting.

LOWELL MACDONALD

MacDonald first hit the NHL with the Detroit Red Wings in 1961–62 and occasionally saw action with the club over the next three seasons. Traded to the Toronto Maple Leafs in 1965, he slid further into the minors with the Tulsa Oilers of the Central Hockey League (CHL) in the two years leading up to expansion but put up decent numbers.

The Kings took him on draft day and he scored the first power-play goal in franchise history on October 15, 1967, against Minnesota. He also had two assists in that game.

"It was kind of a shock," he said about going to the Kings. "You didn't think about going to Los Angeles, but the trade-off was that Red Kelly was going to be there. I did have a sense that he thought I was a good player. L.A. was one of the capitals of the sports industry and you thought, jeez, this is going to be an exciting thing."

Because the Kings didn't have a proper home until the Great Western Forum was built, they practiced at a rink out in Burbank. It was an interesting experience for the players.

"We had a different situation there," he said. "We used to practice in Burbank and it was a half-open rink. Sonja Henie practiced there before us. We would dress before heading there and it could get really chilly there. Wayne Rutledge, Dale Rolfe, Ted Irvine and I carpooled to practice and one day there was an accident in front of us and we got turned around. You wouldn't believe the looks on people's faces when they saw us get out of the car in the hockey equipment on in the middle of a 10-lane highway!"

MacDonald's natural hat trick and assist against the Montreal Canadiens on November 19 ensured a major victory for the Kings. He also had a three-point night against the Seals on March 7, 1968. Once the playoffs began, he had a good opening round against the Minnesota North Stars, which included his game-winning goal in Game 2.

MacDonald admittedly found the rigours of travel difficult over the course of the season. His teammates often kidded him in a good-natured way about his fear of flying and even had a flight attendant present him with toy wings once as a joke.

"The only problem with me was that I wasn't a good flyer," he said. "In my second year, I had a bad flight up to Toronto for training camp and I felt like I couldn't do it anymore."

Eventually, Kelly convinced him to come back to the NHL after almost a year away from the game. He played in Pittsburgh for only 10 games before suffering a serious knee injury that took him out of the game until 1972–73. His comeback was one of the most incredible of his era when he emerged as an All-Star and won the Masterton Trophy.

BILL WHITE

White spent most of the 1960s in the AHL and was a rising star with the Springfield Indians. "I can remember Tommy Ivan and other general managers would come to training camps and we'd hear through the grapevine that they were interested," he said. Yet despite his great potential and interest from NHL clubs, he was kept down in the minors because of the oppressive management style of Eddie Shore.

White was one of the key figures in the historic strike held by Indians players and helped force changes in the game. But he holds little animosity toward Shore today, as things were much more civil when he returned to Springfield to watch a boxing card in 1970.

"The last time I saw Eddie, we were on good terms," he said. "If you stood up to him, he respected you."

White had a feeling that the new owner of the Indians might be his ticket to the NHL, but his early impressions of team owner Jack Kent Cooke were not positive.

"I had an idea they wanted certain players from Springfield and that's why Jack bought the team. I didn't have a lot of good feelings about Jack Kent Cooke. When he built the Forum, we weren't allowed in the Forum Club like the basketball players."

Although the NHL had not established official rules on age limitations for rookies in the expansion era, White garnered attention for his play as a 28-year-old freshman. Coach Red Kelly rated him as the team's best skater and passer, and he scored his first career goal against the Pittsburgh Penguins on October 28, 1967. At mid-season, he received some All-Star votes, and his play during the second half served notice that he was on the cusp of stardom. In the February 18, 1968, game with Boston, he scored twice and on March 7, he had four assists against the Oakland Seals.

By the end of the season, White received even more All-Star votes and was considered for both the Hart Trophy and the Norris Trophy. Traded to the Chicago Black Hawks in 1969–70, he developed into one of the best defenders in hockey in the early 1970s. He also played for Canada at the 1972 Summit Series.

"He was steady as a rock and had a great shot from the point," said Lowell MacDonald. "He used his energy efficiently and it's nice that he had such a great career with the Black Hawks."

REAL LEMIEUX

Lemieux made his NHL debut with the Detroit Red Wings during the 1966–67 season, but saw action only in a single contest. Nicknamed "Frenchy," he had a great year with the farm club in Memphis and scored 62 points over 68 games. When Los Angeles claimed him during the expansion draft, he became one of the club's youngest players in their inaugural season.

On October 28, 1967, Lemieux scored a pair of goals against the Pittsburgh Penguins, one while the Kings were shorthanded. He saved his best effort of the year for his old club and racked up two goals and a pair of assists in an 8–6 win over the Red Wings on February 1, 1968. From there, he turned his game up a notch further for the rest of the month and scored 10 more points!

Teammate Dale Rolfe shared a memorable moment that is rarely mentioned today.

"I remember one interview on television and the interviewer asked him if he spoke English and he replied 'Oh, fuck yeah, I speak good!'"

Lemieux continued to play pro hockey until the end of the 1973–74 season, but tragedy struck on October 24, 1975, as he passed away at the age of 30 after developing a blood clot in his brain.

DALE ROLFE

A central figure in the strike by Springfield Indians players during the 1966–67 season, Rolfe helped change the game of hockey forever.

"We beat Quebec 4–3 and I got a couple of points, but Eddie Shore suspended me for indifferent play. We went on strike and the rest is history," he said. "I'm very proud of that and getting Eddie Shore out of hockey. That was probably my greatest moment in hockey. It was amazing that we got 23 guys together. I'm very proud."

Rolfe saw action in three games with the Boston Bruins in 1959–60 and believes he should have been back even earlier than the start of the 1967–68 campaign.

"I figure I should have been in the NHL five years earlier. Detroit had wanted me and it didn't happen because Shore wanted nine players in return."

His first goal in the big league came against the Seals on October 18, 1967. He earned a pair of assists when they battled again on November 7.

But when he looks back, his time in Los Angeles was not a great time in his career.

"It was difficult because we didn't have a home, but California isn't a place to play hockey. I like having four seasons, but when you're going to the arena in a T-shirt and jeans, it's not hockey."

The veteran defender also did not see eye-to-eye with team owner Jack Kent Cooke.

"He was indirectly a lot like Eddie Shore. He and I never got along too well. One day while the Forum was being built, he and I were talking and he asked me what I thought and I said it would hold a lot of hay!"

After he was traded to the Detroit Red Wings during the 1969–70 season, Rolfe felt relieved to be in a more hockey-friendly climate.

"As soon as I put on that sweater, I felt like I had finally made it to the NHL."

TERRY SAWCHUK

Sawchuk was nearing the end of his Hall of Fame career with the Toronto Maple Leafs in 1966–67 but was still one of the game's best. He formed a solid tandem with Johnny Bower that helped take the team to a surprising Stanley Cup victory. But since they could only protect a single goalie in the expansion draft, the Leafs stuck with Bower, and the often-moody Sawchuk went as first overall pick to Los Angeles.

Sawchuk did not debut with the Kings until October 22, 1967, in a 5–3 win over the Chicago Black Hawks. He faced his old teammates three days later in a tough 4–2 loss. Long-term problems with his elbow that began in childhood — and resulted in his right arm being several inches shorter than the left — bothered him throughout that season.

"He was a guy I used to watch in practice," said Bill White. "He used to relax in practice and his arm was almost fused in a way that was perfect for a goaltender."

At the time, Sawchuk regularly refused to do interviews and preferred to think of the game first, so he was often described by the press as a dark and brooding personality.

"He was one heck of a goalie," said Lowell MacDonald. "I know the media found him difficult. I don't know if it was because he was so focused. There wasn't much to Terry, but he took the abuse. I think if he played today, his records would never be broken."

On January 28, 1968, Sawchuk recorded the 101st shutout of his career while taking on the Philadelphia Flyers. His next shutout came in a 0–0 tie against the same club on March 14. He also made an appearance at the 1968 NHL All-Star Game.

Sawchuk was chosen to start the playoffs, and *The Hockey News* named him the West Division's Player of the Week after they won the first two games of the opening round against Minnesota, which included yet another whitewashing. He fell apart a bit in Game 3, and Wayne Rutledge took over the reins until the deciding seventh game. As Sawchuk was in net for all nine of the North Stars' goals, it was a sad end to the season and his time with the Kings. He was traded to Detroit before the 1968–69 campaign.

WAYNE RUTLEDGE

Rutledge quietly made waves in the New York farm system in the mid-1960s when he had back-to-back 30-win seasons in the Central League. But with established goalies like Ed Giacomin, Gilles Villemure and Cesare Maniago ahead of him, he would have had to wait a while to get a decent shot at NHL work had it not been for expansion. In fact, he was the only goalie at the pro level to play all of his team's games during the 1965–66 and 1966–67 campaigns.

Drafted by the Kings, he battled Jacques Caron, George Wood and Bob Perani for the backup spot to start the year and earned a win over the Philadelphia Flyers during his big-league debut on October 14, 1967. He did not have to work too hard for it, though, as he faced just 15 shots.

"I didn't expect to play right off, so I was a bit more nervous than usual, and I felt the pressure of playing in the majors, but I was ready," he said at the time.

Described as a fast goaltender, Rutledge played a stand-up style and was the only player at his position to wear contact lenses at the time. Because Terry Sawchuk had injuries, Rutledge took over as the team's number one netminder on occasion and earned his first career shutout against the St. Louis Blues on December 23. Another one came when the Kings blanked the Toronto Maple Leafs on February 12, 1968.

"I was tickled to be drafted by L.A. Even though they had Sawchuk ahead of me, I figured Terry was past the point where he could play every game and I expected to see a lot of action, though not as much as I have seen. It doesn't bother me. I want to play as much as I can. It was a break for me when Terry got hurt just before the season. It got me in quick and when I did well the other players got confidence in me."

The Kings started the playoffs with Sawchuk in net, counting on his postseason experience, but Rutledge saw action in three contests, including a Game 5 win over Minnesota before they narrowly lost the next one in overtime. Over the next two seasons, he remained in a backup role before being sent down to the minors.

Rutledge passed away from stomach cancer on October 2, 2004.

Dale Rolfe, his teammate and brother-in-law, offered his thoughts.

"Wayne put us in the playoffs the first year. A very good goaltender and a great guy. I miss him every day."

EXPANSION YEAR RECORD: 27-32-15
(69 points — fourth in West Division)
COACH: Wren Blair
GENERAL MANAGER: Wren Blair
FIRST GAME: October 11, 1967 —
2-2 tie vs. St. Louis Blues
FIRST GOAL: October 11, 1967 by Bill Masterton

MINNESOTA NORTH STARS

Cold winters made hockey a natural pursuit in the great state of Minnesota, and the sport's history there extends more than a century. By the 1920s, the college game had started to take off in the North Star State. Around the same time, the famed Minneapolis Millers formed with an array of imported players. Native son Frank Goheen was one of the best players of his generation never to turn pro, and over the years, many others followed with great careers as amateurs or professionals.

By the mid-1960s, fans in the Twin Cities had two options when it came to pro hockey, with the CHL's Minneapolis Bruins and the St. Paul Rangers (later changed to the Minnesota Rangers in 1965–66). When the NHL was looking at expanding, a nine-man group that included Walter Bush Jr. put forth a bid to get a big-league club of their own, and they were granted a franchise on February 9, 1966. Less than four months later, the team was dubbed the North Stars, and the construction of the Metropolitan Sports Center began on October 3 that year.

The North Stars brought in Wren Blair as coach and general manager. He had worked his way up in the game as coach of the Allan Cup-winning Whitby Dunlops teams and had a major role in discovering Bobby Orr for the Boston Bruins. Given the task of putting their first roster together on a limited budget, he grabbed several veteran players through the 1967 NHL Expansion Draft, including a strong goaltending tandem of Cesare Maniago and Garry Bauman.

Since the concept of a tandem was relatively new in NHL circles,

92

Blair was not sure if he would let both goalies share the workload evenly.

"Don't get me wrong," he said. "I'm not dead set against alternating in goal — but only if there happens to be two men of nearly equal ability. I think that was the case in Chicago last year . . . and in Toronto, too, where Punch Imlach was fortunate to have Johnny Bower and Terry Sawchuk complementing each other. Frankly, I've always been in favour of picking out the guy who I believe is the best and go as far as I can with him just as long as he does a reasonably good job."

After training camp, there was some speculation about which player would be named captain, and most felt the responsibility would be given to Jean-Guy Talbot. Blair had other plans, though, and ended up trading away the veteran defenceman early in the regular season. Later, he allowed Bob Woytowich to wear the "C."

Blair also showed early signs of being tight-fisted with the team's finances. Most players were making no more than the league minimum, despite whatever experience they might have had at the time. Andre Pronovost and Pete Goegan were notable early holdouts, and during one pre-season game, the short-tempered coach told Goegan to take off his sweater and leave the bench. Before the NHLPA came to exist, it was not uncommon for a player to report to training camp without a contract in place and teams attempted to sign players as quickly as possible. Unfortunately, team management would often engage in various forms of psychological warfare to ensure that holdout players signed on for as little money as possible and often fined them if they had not agreed to their terms by a certain date.

Minnesota looked upon defence as their prime strength heading into the 1967–68 campaign. While waiting for the Met Center to open, they debuted on the road against the St. Louis Blues.

The October 11, 1967, contest started half an hour late as a result of extended pre-game ceremonies and Blair was less than impressed.

"I hope we never make the mistake of having anything like that up in Minnesota," he said. "It might not have been so bad had it started earlier, but I don't believe starting a game at 9:15 helped either team. The idea as I see it is to sell hockey, not some band or singer."

The game ended in a 2–2 tie, and the North Stars' early-season road swing did not produce a single victory. Their fortunes changed, though, once they had their home opener on October 21, and they got a big 3–1 win over the California Seals. As the fans filed into the new building, workers were still busy installing some seats.

Because of limited early success, there were many rumours circulating that predicted Blair would leave the coaching duties to John Muckler, but they subsided once a winning streak began in early December.

"Some day soon I will step out. But coaching is the only way I know to find the weakness of the club," said Blair. "And when I step out and go on the road, I will find better men to replace some of those on the team now, so they should be so warned."

Around this time, Maniago had firmly grasped the number one netminder job and he put together a remarkable shutout streak that included three shutouts. It ran for more than 188 minutes and came to a close on December 21. Soon after, the team made a significant deal to get J.P. Parise from the Toronto Maple Leafs organization. That transaction proved one of the greatest in franchise history.

At the halfway point of the season, the North Stars had 14 wins to their credit, and Blair was pleased by their progress as a team.

"I'm pleased to be placed so high after half of the season. We built for the long haul, not for this first season. Maybe it would even be well [sic] if we won it all this year. Our fans are supporting us fine and maybe it would be wise to just do pretty good with the promise of doing better in the future."

That optimism quickly turned to sorrow as tragedy struck on January 13, 1968, when the now-Oakland Seals came to town. Early in the first period, the popular Bill Masterton completed a pass to teammate Wayne Connelly and was checked by Larry Cahan and Ron Harris shortly after. He fell backwards and hit his head on the ice, suffering a massive brain hemorrhage in the process.

Because the injury was so severe, doctors were unable to operate and Masterton passed away two days later. Soon after, many NHL players began to wear helmets and they eventually became mandatory for all players. At the end of the year, a trophy was created in his honour, and his number, 19, was eventually retired in 1987 — even though no one had worn it since his death.

With the team in shambles, the North Stars lost their next three outings before getting a big win over the Pittsburgh Penguins on January 21. After that, they won seven of their next nine, but they had a rough stretch approaching the playoffs and barely squeaked into fourth place. There was some hope in the form of Connelly's scoring rampage, which saw him finish the year with 35 goals.

In their first playoff series, they had their work cut out for them with the Los Angeles Kings. Terry Sawchuk was the opposing starter and Blair went into the series cautiously. He had just cause, since Sawchuk was a great money player and had helped Toronto to the Stanley Cup the year before.

After they lost the first two games, Minnesota had a small breather when the third game was postponed following the assassination of Dr. Martin Luther King Jr. They got the next two wins at home to tie the series, and Blair could not have been happier.

"That victory really meant a lot to me, because after we lost those first two games to L.A., I heard some grumbling about a sweep. I consider this season to be an unqualified success regardless what happens from here on out."

The North Stars lost Game 5, but their overtime triumph three nights later set the tone for the deciding contest. They shocked the Kings by a 9–4 margin and headed into a second-round clash with St. Louis. The Blues had just added Doug Harvey to their already-impressive lineup, but Minnesota jumped to an early 2–1 lead in the series. After losing their next two contests, they had a big 5–1 triumph in Game 6. In the next game, they fought tooth and nail to get into the Stanley Cup Final, but the contest went into double overtime before Ron Schock scored to end their year.

The 1968–69 season was a disappointment for the North Stars, and they finished last in the West Division. They bounced back soon after and were playoff contenders for the next four years while Goldsworthy, Parise and Maniago emerged as local legends.

By the mid-1970s, however, the situation for the club looked grim thanks to direct competition from the WHA's Minnesota Fighting Saints. Over a six-season span, the North Stars made the playoffs only once, and as a result of their financial woes, they merged with the even more troubled Cleveland Barons in the summer of 1978.

With this merger, the North Stars returned to playoff form and made a run to the Stanley Cup Final in 1980–81. After that, they won a pair of Norris Division titles but stumbled late in the decade. That low point allowed them to select Mike Modano with the first overall pick in the 1988 NHL Entry Draft. Poor attendance was of great concern at this time, and there were threats that they would be moved to San Francisco Bay Area. A compromise was eventually made that saw the Gund brothers get an expansion club in San Jose and a new ownership group controlled by Norman Green kept the team around for a few more years.

In 1990–91, Minnesota had another surprising run to the Stanley Cup Final, but it was not enough to ensure they avoided relocation. Seemingly in preparation for a potential move, the North Stars changed their jerseys and the logo had just the word "STARS" on it. The team was moved to Dallas after the 1992–93 season because of a combination of factors, including low attendance and the failure to make a deal for a new arena.

The move to Dallas broke the hearts of Minnesota's fans, but the sport continued to thrive in the state at the minor league, college and high school levels. By 1997, the demand for NHL hockey was too strong for the league to ignore and a new expansion team, the Minnesota Wild, began play in 2000–01. As for the original franchise, they went on to great success in Texas and won a Stanley Cup in 1998–99. In recent years, however, the club has missed the playoffs in five straight seasons and had filed for bankruptcy in 2011 before being purchased by Tom Gaglardi.

WAYNE CONNELLY

Perhaps one of the biggest surprises in the NHL in the 1967-68 season, Connelly was first a prospect in the Montreal Canadiens organization before he was traded to the Boston Bruins. He spent most of the 1960s trying to crack Boston's lineup and in 1966-67 made a good impression

(clockwise) Bill Goldsworthy, J.P. Parise, Bill Masterton, Cesare Maniago

with 30 points in 64 games with the club. Since he was still on the fringe with the team, he was made available in the expansion draft. Wren Blair chose him, likely because of their time together in the minors.

"It was great because it was the first time they kept playing me. My game was scoring goals and since Minnesota was a new team, even if I had a slump, I could still play," Connelly said.

As the 1967–68 season progressed, he emerged as one of the West Division's breakout stars. He had a pair of goals against St. Louis on December 2, 1967, and scored the winner against Chicago the next night. The Philadelphia Flyers were the victim of his first hat trick of the season on January 10, 1968, and on March 2, he scored all three of Minnesota's goals in a win over the Montreal Canadiens. Even more amazing than that were his three straight winning-goals against Oakland, Detroit and Los Angeles in late January.

Connelly's phenomenal season should have given him long-term stability with the North Stars, but he had continual battles with coach Wren Blair, and they argued in contract negotiations the following year.

"It was the best place to play, and I should have been able to continue," he recalled. "To tell you the truth, he wasn't a good coach at all. He didn't teach us anything. We never had a blackboard and never went over plays. I had the impression he was going to be happy with just fourth place."

ANDRE BOUDRIAS

Boudrias was once a promising prospect for the Montreal Canadiens. Although he got into a handful of games with the club in the years leading up to expansion, he was used primarily in the minors with the Houston Apollos and averaged around a point per game over two seasons there. The Habs were building for the future by getting first-round picks from other clubs, so they packaged him off to Minnesota in a deal that eventually allowed them to select Chuck Arnason in 1971.

Boudrias was not particularly enthused about his time in Houston and looked forward to playing in a more hockey-friendly climate.

"I walked into that rink on many a day when it was in the high 80s or low 90s outside," he said. "I lived in an apartment complex, which had a swimming pool . . . and climbing out of one of those to head for a hockey rink just didn't seem right. . . . I'm really looking forward to our morning practices. I think a cold, brisk walk in cold weather does a hockey player a lot of good.

"I'm tickled pink to have been picked up by a club this far north in the United States. It gets cold in Minnesota and I think that's great for guys like me who were born and raised in Canada."

As soon as Boudrias hit the ice with the North Stars, he stood out from the pack by wearing a helmet, and he was one of the team's top penalty killers. On December 10, 1967, he scored the winning goal and earned an assist while playing the Pittsburgh Penguins. He had a three-point night as Minnesota shut out the Los Angeles Kings a little over three weeks later. By the end of the regular season, he was first in the club in assists and had the best plus-minus ranking among regular skaters.

During the playoffs, Boudrias had a decent showing, with nine points over two rounds, including a goal and two assists against the Kings on April 18. He also helped force a seventh game in the second round with the Blues when he scored the winning goal at 10:54 of the first period.

RAY CULLEN

Cullen made his NHL debut with the New York Rangers in 1965–66, but the Detroit Red Wings grabbed his rights during the 1966 intra-league draft, and he split the following season between the club and its AHL affiliate in Pittsburgh. Realizing his potential as a goal scorer, the North Stars picked him up for their initial roster, and he became one of their key performers in their first year.

"I thought it was going to be awful cold," he said. "As it turned out, I bought a house there. My wife and I just loved it."

After making the team, Cullen scored to earn their first victory during their fifth game on October 21, 1967. The even-strength tally came against Charlie Hodge of the California Seals just 2:23 into the third period. Four days later, he scored his second goal of the year and gave Minnesota its second victory in a row, this time against St. Louis.

The winning goals kept on coming in the early part of the 1967–68 season, and he had two more in battles with the Blues. He also recorded several three-point games, which helped him remain near the top of the team's scoring parade even though he missed ice time because of a hairline fracture in his ankle.

Despite his success during his first full season in the league, Cullen did not exactly have a high opinion of Wren Blair as coach.

"He was very different. . . . He never played hockey, and in those days, all of the coaches were ex-players and he didn't earn our confidence. Alfred Hitchcock was one of the greatest directors, but he was never an actor!"

By season's end, he finished fourth among all NHL players with 11 power-play goals and placed sixth with seven game-winners. During the playoffs, he had a goal and three assists on April 9, 1968, in Game 3 of the first-round battle with the Los Angeles Kings, and notched a total of eight points over 14 postseason contests.

DAVE BALON

Balon started out with the New York Rangers, but when he went to the Montreal Canadiens through a blockbuster trade before the 1963–64 season, he was given a chance to play for a contender and won a pair of Stanley Cup championships. Since the Habs had a load of talent on the roster, Balon was made available in the expansion draft and the North Stars got a decent offensive talent for their first foray into NHL action.

A skilled penalty killer, Balon had a good start to the year and scored twice when Minnesota defeated the St. Louis Blues on November 8, 1967. Unbelievably, his first goal of the night came while the team was shorthanded, and that was the only shorthanded goal the club would score in 1967–68. It truly made a statement about the team's weaknesses while down a man as they gave up 216 power plays to opponents that year.

Balon was the only member of the North Stars selected to play in the 1968 NHL All-Star Game; it was his third appearance in the annual event. He had game-winning goals against Philadelphia and Detroit in the second half of the season and earned three assists in the March 17, 1968, game with the Red Wings.

Primed for the playoffs, he evened the opening-round series with Los Angeles with a winning tally in Game 4 and had another four-point night in Game 7 when the Kings were trounced by a score of 9–4. After the season ended, Balon was puzzlingly traded away for three players.

MIKE MCMAHON

The son of a former Stanley Cup champion, McMahon followed his father in the ice wars as a New York Ranger and was claimed by Montreal before the 1966–67 season. He spent that year in the minors with the Houston Apollos and ended up sold to the North Stars not long after the expansion draft.

McMahon was regarded as the main offensive cog on Minnesota's blue line and was twice voted the Most Valuable Player in the Central League. He instantly earned the respect of teammates for his play.

"Mike could really move," said Parker MacDonald. "At the time, he was one of the few defencemen who could lug the puck like Bobby Orr could."

Putting up points like crazy, McMahon ranked among the top-scoring defenders in the NHL in 1967–68 and had three-point games against Boston and Los Angeles. As a result, he warranted serious consideration for the 1968 NHL All-Star Team but was not chosen in favour of Dave Balon.

Goaltender Cesare Maniago felt that part of McMahon's later on-ice issues came from the way he was treated by Wren Blair while in a scoring drought in the team's second season.

"It's a sad situation. I think he could have gone on and played another 10 or 15 years. By far, he was our best defenceman during our first year. Wren just jumped all over him and Mike would back off and just sulk. It was tough for him to let go and I think he lost his con-fidence. To see the talent that he had and to just lose it was an eye-opener for me. Everyone was hoping that Wren would just lay off him."

BILL GOLDSWORTHY

A product of the Boston Bruins organization, Goldsworthy appeared in 33 regular-season games with the club before the NHL expanded. He showed signs of his potential during minor league stints with the Oklahoma City Blazers and Buffalo Bisons, and Wren Blair's decision to draft him likely came from seeing his work at the junior level. Fans in Minnesota had no idea they were in for a treat over the next few seasons.

On October 21, 1967, Goldsworthy's second goal of the season came against Charlie Hodge of the California Seals and it was the first to occur at the new Met Center.

Over the course of the 1967–68 campaign, Goldsworthy often served as a whipping boy for Blair, but there was a moment when he was inspired to bust out of a slump.

He had apparently received some letters from hockey fans saying that he should be playing in the minors and was especially discouraged by the nasty notes that arrived when he was mired in a nine-game goalless streak. On a game day, he poked his head into Blair's office and mentioned that he had instead received a letter from a group saying that they were going to name a tree after him.

"You know why they're naming a tree after you? Because a tree stands still. That's what you've been doing too much of lately," the coach gruffly responded.

Now hot under the collar, "Goldy" went out and scored his 10th goal of the season in a 6–1 win over Los Angeles.

Once the playoffs began, Goldsworthy served notice that he was on the cusp of stardom, racking up points in the opening round against the Kings and having a four-point outing in Game 3 of the second-round clash with St. Louis, including the game-winning goal. From then on, the crowd in Minnesota was firmly behind him and he was a fixture with them for many years.

"We had played together in the Boston Bruins organization and he was my buddy," said J.P. Parise. "Nobody worked harder than Bill. He was one of the first guys to work out in the summer. We would play racquetball, do weights and train. We would go to camp and just dominate. A loose cannon at times, but good to have as a teammate. He was tough and would stand up for me. A great skater and shooter and he really worked at it."

Charismatic and fun-loving, Goldsworthy lived hard for many years, but drinking and promiscuity took their toll. In 1995, he bravely became the first former NHL player to publicly announce that he had AIDS and he passed away on March 29, 1996.

J.P. PARISE

A young prospect who looked forward to cracking an NHL lineup with expansion, Parise was originally taken from the Boston Bruins by the California Seals, but he didn't last long there.

"I was a good player but not good enough to play in the Original Six," he recalled. "It was hard to get in there. Training camp with Oakland was gruelling. It was unbelievable. I remember some of the practices after losing or tying, and Bert Olmstead made us do starts and stops for an hour. He blew the whistle and told us we were halfway done. I was thinking about anything but skating. It was really tough.

"Bert was a fundamental guy. Rink-wide passes were strictly pro-hibited and Bill Masterton intercepted my pass. I hit him and got a penalty and they ended up scoring. He was mad when I got back to the bench. He called me a 'little fucking frog,' and I told him where to go. He never answered and he sent Gord Fashoway to tell me I had been traded to Rochester."

Parise did not stay in the minors for long, however, as he was traded by Rochester's parent club in Toronto to Minnesota just before Christmas. He made his debut with them at Madison Square Garden on December 27, 1967.

"It was so good," he said. "Wren played me and I killed penalties and Bernie Geoffrion was on the point. I went in there and nailed him. I had been called up earlier in the year with the Leafs, so I knew I could make it."

Three days later, he scored against the Boston Bruins, and the Los

Angeles Kings were the victim of his first game-winning tally of the year on January 3, 1968. He fit in well with his new teammates and most of his offence came in even-strength situations.

In time, Parise became a fixture with the franchise, and he remained there until the midway point of the 1974–75 season. He proudly represented Canada at the 1972 Summit Series. After stints with the New York Islanders and Cleveland Barons, he returned to Minnesota and served as their captain in 1978–79 before retiring. His son, Zach, started his NHL career with the New Jersey Devils and signed with the Minnesota Wild in 2012.

BILL MASTERTON

A hard-working player who earned his bachelor of science degree in business while starring for the University of Denver's hockey team, Masterton did not turn pro until he was 23 years old. Then in 1963, he stepped away from the game, playing only on a casual level. A few years later, he turned down an offer to work as a contract administrator for Honeywell and instead decided to join the U.S. National Team for part of the 1966–67 season.

It was during this stint he caught the attention of Wren Blair, who made a deal to obtain his rights.

"I liked what I saw, so I asked Bill if he would consider giving pro hockey another fling," he told the press early in the 1967–68 season. "When he said he'd like to try it, I bought his contract from Montreal. . . . From what I saw of Bill in training camp, I think he'll help us. He had the misfortune of getting a shoulder separation before the exhibition games started but he worked hard with Lloyd Percival, our physical fitness expert, and was able to return for our last six or seven games and get three goals and a couple of assists."

Masterton was by then a father of two and living in the Twin Cities with his wife, Carol. He earned a permanent spot in the North Stars' record book by scoring the first goal for the team while Minnesota was on the power play. The puck went past Seth Martin of the St. Louis Blues at 15:20 of the second period on October 11, 1967.

"I doubt very much that I would've considered playing any place else," said Masterton. "I went to training camp knowing it wouldn't be a picnic, especially after being out of pro hockey for four seasons. I had the opportunity to skate quite a bit last summer when I coached in a summer league, and I think that helped me quite a bit. I was in pretty good shape when I reported. When I signed a two-year contract, I more or less expected to spend this season in Memphis. I may still end up there but even if I do, I won't be disappointed because I've given two years to prove that I can play in the NHL. I realize it's going to be tough, but if I can get the opportunity to play, I'm confident that I can make it."

Things were going smoothly for him on a line with Dave Balon and Wayne Connelly through most of the season, but tragedy struck on January 13, 1968, when Minnesota hosted the Oakland Seals. Late in the first period, Masterton was checked heavily by Larry Cahan and Ron Harris after passing the puck in the Seals' zone. He flipped backwards, hitting his head.

"Billy and I drove to the rink that night," said Ray Cullen. "We were all surprised by it, and it didn't look like that bad of a hit. He was a real gentleman and quiet, studious type of guy."

Other teammates recalled the incident vividly.

"I remember him crossing the offensive blue line and one player hitting before Larry Cahan hit him," said J.P. Parise. "He got up and fell back down. I went to go see him, and his eyes were moving around in his head and he was taking deep breaths. I thought he was dying, but he was swallowing."

"Cahan never hit dirty," said Cesare Maniago. "He hit him pretty good and my wife swears that he was knocked out before he even hit the ice. She was right in that corner and it was kind of like a whiplash hitting the ice. We didn't think it was going to be that severe until we got the news in Boston the next day."

Ron Harris was the other defenceman involved in the play, and he has given only one interview on the subject. In 2003, he spoke to the *St. Paul Pioneer-Press* and expressed his feelings on the only death in NHL history to stem from an on-ice incident.

"It bothers you the rest of your life. It wasn't dirty and it wasn't meant to happen that way. Still, it's very hard because I made the play. It's always in the back of my mind."

The accident also shocked coach Blair.

"It was a momentary check and they skated right on after the puck. He hit so hard that I'm sure he was unconscious before he fell. I've never seen anybody go down that way. We heard him crash to the ice from the bench."

"We went out and played the next night and got our asses kicked," said Parise. "Wren came in after and told us that if he pulled through, he was going to be a vegetable, but he died that night."

Masterton passed away in the early hours of January 15 from a massive internal brain injury. He was taken to a Minneapolis hospital where a team of five doctors was unable to save him. He never regained consciousness.

The NHL turned over $60,000 to Masterton's estate from the league's pension fund. He was insured for $50,000 on his life and received $10,000 for accidental indemnity. Soon after, many NHL players, including Brian Conacher, Howie Young, Stan Mikita, Ken Wharram, Doug Mohns and Pierre Pilote, began to don helmets.

Masterton actually wore a helmet in college and in the minors but was discouraged from the practice when he hit the NHL. After the accident, many wondered if Blair would change his tune about helmets.

"No, not at all," said Wayne Connelly. "We players took it really hard. He tried to be the tough guy and he was yelling at us to play the game."

The mood in the dressing room also changed in the days and weeks that followed.

"When you lose a teammate, you can't say that when they drop the puck that you don't think about it. It was a sad thing in our own dressing room," said Cullen.

In March, the NHL Board of Governors announced approval for a memorial award for Bill Masterton, to be presented to the player who best demonstrates the qualities of sportsmanship, dedication and perseverance to hockey. Minnesota's players also gave Masterton's widow a full share of playoff money. To this day, he is fondly remembered by teammates.

"I can remember how kind he was," recalled Parise. "He came over to the hotel where I was staying and drove me to my first practice. The night before that game, there was a party at Bill's house. My lasting vision of him is of him playing with his two kids. Years later, I would meet them again."

"As an individual, we were very close. We played together in Hull-Ottawa," said Maniago. "Quiet, but loved a sensible good time with family and on the road. Prior to him getting hit that night, we celebrated a birthday party a couple of nights before. He had been complaining about a steady headache. In retrospect, you would think he had a concussion."

In recent years, information has come to light that suggests Masterton had likely sustained a concussion in the games leading up to the accident.

"I knew Bill was hurting before. I knew this for a fact," said Connelly.

BRONCO HORVATH

A wily veteran who toiled in the AHL for several seasons after his last NHL action in 1962–63, Horvath was property of the Toronto Maple Leafs but never made it far with the club despite some solid production in the minors.

His return to the bigs came when he was loaned to the North Stars and was offered a nice contract by the club. Things were looking up for the 37-year-old.

"I had a wonderful time in Minnesota. I loved it there," he said. "They flew me in and Johnny Mariucci took me to the rink. It was the nicest arena I had ever seen and I knew a few guys there already."

He began with an assist in each of his first four games with the North Stars and scored his only goal with them on February 11, 1968, against Philadelphia.

"We were all clicking like crazy," he recalled. "Once we were going good, I got called upstairs to see Wren and he told me that I was going back to Toronto. My father phoned Imlach and he offered him

$50,000 to let me stay in Minnesota. He wouldn't and my father really was tempted to go over and kick his ass. He was the worst thing to happen in hockey, that Imlach.

"Imlach wanted four players from Minnesota for me and they offered him cash. Blair said to him, 'How can I send you four players when I need them?'"

Upon his return, Horvath was less than cordial with Toronto's coach and general manager.

"I told him to go fuck himself," he said. "I could have stayed in Minnesota, but you ruined my life. I was going to club him, honest to God."

Needless to say, Horvath was back in the minors after that, but he made a lasting impression with at least one young star in Minnesota.

"I was traded to Rochester out of Oakland and Mr. Horvath was like a father to me," recalled J.P. Parise. "We were put on a line by Joe Crozier. The first game we played together, I had four breakaways and I missed them all. He called me over and said, 'Johnny, the way you're playing, you're going to be out of the league by Christmas.' He helped me like you wouldn't believe. I find Bronco Horvath totally responsible for my career in the National Hockey League."

CESARE MANIAGO

Maniago saw action in 28 games with the New York Rangers in 1965–66, but the rise of Ed Giacomin as the club's number one goaltender gave him just six appearances the following year. Expansion gave him the opportunity to find work elsewhere in the NHL when the North Stars made him their first pick in the draft, and he proved one of their most popular players during their early years.

"In a meeting of scouts, owners and others in our group before the draft, it was agreed upon to pick a man with NHL experience if at all possible," said Wren Blair at the time. "To be truthful, we were not very interested in Terry Sawchuk, Glenn Hall or Charlie Hodge. So after Philadelphia got the second pick and took Bernie Parent, we decided on Cesare. I felt fortunate to get him. He's not as young as, say, Parent, but at 28 he should be able to give us quite a few good years."

Maniago was initially set to share the crease with Garry Bauman. His first outing of the 1967–68 season came in the club's second game, and it was a rough one against the California Seals.

"What happened is I think Wren wanted to make an impression on some of the older guys, and he comes into the dressing and he's yelling and screaming because that was his style," said Maniago. "He laid into Parker MacDonald first and he said he was lousy and that he was going to the minors and then he went after me. It was anger like I had never seen from a coach before or after. After he was done, I asked him if I could speak with him outside and then I grabbed him by the tie and said, 'You son of a bitch, if you ever pull that again, I'll put my fist down your throat!' From then on, he never, ever said anything to me. He'd start jumping on other guys, but poor Goldsworthy was his whipping boy. If I sat down with a couple of guys from the first year, we could probably put a book together about all the stuff he pulled. It really brought the team together because it was us against him."

Early in the season, Maniago missed some time due to an eye cut and groin injury, but he was in net for the first win in franchise history in a rematch with the Seals on October 21, 1967, in what was also Minnesota's home debut.

By mid-November, he had essentially taken over the starting role. He made headlines with an incredible shutout streak of 188:36, which included two blankings of Los Angeles and another against Oakland. It was eventually broken on December 21 by Pat Hannigan of the Philadelphia Flyers, but Maniago's streak was the longest since Glenn Hall's in 1955–56.

"It was good hockey and I believe those three were out on the west coast. I remember Ray Cullen and I talking at the time and I told him that the puck seemed like a big watermelon floating at me slowly," Maniago recalled.

Solid the rest of the way, he suffered a concussion in a loss to the Flyers on March 10, 1968, but was back in net again three days later. On March 23, he helped the North Stars nail down a playoff spot with a shutout against the Pittsburgh Penguins. During the playoffs, Maniago was strong in the opening-round series with Los Angeles and went to the seven-game limit with St. Louis afterward.

"It could have gone either way. I don't know if we would have done well against Montreal but it would have been nice to be there," he said.

EXPANSION YEAR RECORD: 31-32-11
(73 points — first in West Division)
COACH: Keith Allen
GENERAL MANAGER: Bud Poile
FIRST GAME: October 11, 1967 —
5-1 loss vs. California Seals
FIRST GOAL: October 11, 1967 by Bill Sutherland

PHILADELPHIA FLYERS

Before the Flyers came to town, Philadelphia was not exactly treating the sport of hockey with brotherly love. The NHL's relationship with the city began in 1930–31 when Benny Leonard brought in the Pittsburgh Pirates and rechristened them the Quakers, but their dismal 4–36–4 record still stands as the worst in NHL history. One year was enough for them, and every year for the next few seasons they asked to suspend operations until ownership finally gave up on the franchise.

One of the other problems the Quakers faced was competition from the Can-Am League's Philadelphia Arrows, who had been around since 1927–28. They lasted only eight seasons but withstood the one-season stint of the Comets club from the Tri-State League in 1932–33 before changing their name to the Ramblers in 1935–36. They won a championship that year but eventually folded after playing the 1941–42 campaign as the Rockets. During World War II, they went on hiatus then came back in 1946–47 for a three-season run.

In 1955–56, the Eastern League brought in a new Ramblers team, and they lasted for several years before relocating to nearby Cherry Hill, New Jersey. Because of that rocky history, there was much debate over whether or not Philadelphia was meant to be a hockey town. But the NHL was looking to expand, so fate stepped in and the sport finally had an opportunity win over the hearts of local fans.

A former record executive named Ed Snider came across hockey almost by chance in the early 1960s and was amazed that a perennial last-place team like the Boston Bruins consistently sold out. At the time the NHL announced its plans for expansion, he was the vice-president of the NFL's Philadelphia Eagles and he quickly threw together a proposal that won over the league. His group included Bill Putnam, who helped Jack Kent Cooke get his franchise application together, and Eagles owner Jerry Wolman. There was some speculation Philadelphia might not make the cut among the cities that applied, but they were helped by the plans for a new arena and because the Baltimore application left much to be desired.

Although Snider had to scramble to secure the franchise fee the league demanded and almost missed the deadline due to a power outage, hockey was set to return to Philly for the 1967–68 season. A contest to name the team was held soon after and the enduring colour scheme of orange, black and white was announced early on. Design and construction of the Spectrum was also set into motion, and the club became the Flyers on July 12, 1966. The name was initially suggested by Snider's sister, but more than 100 future fans also suggested it and a local nine-year-old boy named Alec Stockard was the contest winner.

The Flyers began to assemble their management team by bringing over Bud Poile from the WHL's San Francisco Seals to serve as general manager. Their coach, Keith Allen, formerly led the Seattle Totems from the same league. Less than a month before the 1967 NHL Expansion Draft, Philadelphia got an influx of talent by purchasing the AHL's Quebec Aces, a group that included a good mix of veterans and promising young stars. On the day of the draft, the Flyers went with a pair of goaltending prospects from the Bruins system, Bernie Parent and Doug Favell, before grabbing some of the best defencemen available, including Ed Van Impe and Joe Watson.

After training camp, once they had finalized the initial roster, the team held a parade to let locals know about their arrival in town. The event was sparsely attended and some members of the community welcomed them with catcalls and obscene gestures. Regardless, the Flyers were coming together and some players had the advantage of having played together in the past.

"You've got to remember, several of the lines the Aces used have played together as complete units for one or two seasons," said Don Blackburn at the time. "This means they're accustomed to the moves of the other guy. It's my opinion that better than 50 percent of the plays that work in a hockey game are not planned. Somebody hollers and you get the puck to him. It's just a matter of playing together. In other words, we've brought six different systems to training camp because we've come together from six different clubs. So, it's extremely tough until we become familiar with each other's moves, and more importantly, with the system coach Keith Allen wants us to use.

"I'd say that, despite everything, any of the new clubs will beat any of the old clubs on a given night," he continued. "The big difference, however, will show up in the 74-game season. It's tough getting up for every game. But I still say that we — in Philadelphia — have the best club on paper. From what I've seen, we have excellent material at every position and I'm really high on our great balance."

Allen had a realistic view of things before the season began.

"We've had our share of headaches in training camp," he said. "We had those two guys [Van Impe and Watson] missing from training camp for a couple weeks due to contract problems and we had our share of minor injuries. The problem was, of course, that we just couldn't get the right people on the ice at the same time. But things really started to jell just before we opened the season in Oakland."

Confident they were strong on defence and loaded with offensive potential, Bud Poile hoped the Flyers were going to finish either first or second in the new West Division. Even with only approximately 2,500 season tickets sold, the mood was still optimistic.

"We have the utmost confidence that major league hockey will go over big in Philadelphia," said Ed Snider. "If we weren't absolutely certain of that, we surely wouldn't have sought a franchise. Philadelphia is a great sports city. The fans will support a team, any team, so long as it is major league.

"We're not expecting miracles," he added. "We know we're not going to sell every seat for every game. But we understand that and we know our big job is selling the thrills and excitement of hockey to the average sports fan who cheers for the Eagles, Phillies and 76ers....We're positive it can be done."

On October 11, 1967, the Flyers opened their first season on the road but were beaten by the Oakland Seals. They also lost their next outing against Los Angeles, but they won their next three in a row, including a shutout victory on October 19 in their at-home debut against their state rivals, the Pittsburgh Penguins. Over the first few months of play, it became apparent that Philadelphia was becoming the class act of the first-year clubs. They also shocked some of the established Original Six teams, and that pleased Allen.

"Really, I'm not sure myself why we've been doing so well against the old clubs," he said. "I just know that all along I've been saying that on any given night, any team can beat another. . . . I doubt it very much if the veteran clubs are overconfident when they're playing expansion teams, but I have to say we've been going into these games with confidence that we can win them."

The wins kept piling up through the year, and there was even speculation that the Flyers might be the one expansion team that could seriously compete for the Stanley Cup.

"When we play hungry, we do real well," said Larry Zeidel. "We get on top of the opposition and we keep the pressure on. But it doesn't seem to work unless we're hungry enough to make it work."

"I'm trying not to sound overconfident," echoed captain Lou Angotti. "But right now I feel the same as I did when I was with the Chicago Black Hawks last season, and we were close to clinching first place."

One of the highlights for Philadelphia was being the first opponent for the New York Rangers in the new Madison Square Garden on February 18, 1968. They also played in the opening game for three other rinks. Less than two weeks later, they were hit by one of the worst moments in the early years of the franchise when a section of the Spectrum's roof blew off and forced the Flyers to take their act on the road. Facing a ton of lost revenue and political hassles, they were forced to hold home games in New York, Toronto and Quebec, but still they held on to capture the West Division crown.

"It's a tough situation, being forced on the road so much," said Allen. "But we can't let that interfere with what we do on the ice. We've got to make sure we're up for every game and we play our best, no matter where we're playing. We've come too far to let first place slip through our hands now, and the guys would like nothing more than to reward our struggling owners with an NHL title."

This extended road swing also saw one of the worst moments in hockey history take place as the Flyers and Bruins faced off at Maple Leaf Gardens. After Larry Zeidel heard some anti-Semitic remarks from opposition players, he and Eddie Shack engaged in a gory stick-swinging incident that made headlines and resulted in suspensions and fines. After weeks of investigation, though, league president Clarence Campbell ruled that the spectators who overheard the remarks were "in error" and that there was no anti-religious feeling or any other form of discrimination in the NHL.

Heading into the playoffs, Poile predicted that the Flyers were going to sweep the St. Louis Blues in the first round. At the time, it may not have been too bold a thing to say, since Philadelphia had dominated them 7–1–2 in their regular-season meetings. Those words came back to bite him, however, as their opponents jumped out to a 3–1 lead in the series. They fought back to win Games 5 and 6 but went down in the seventh, and deciding, contest. Their clash was a violent one at times and it saw a horrifying incident in which Claude LaForge was knocked out by an alleged sucker punch from Noel Picard.

The Flyers received at least one consolation prize at the end of their successful first season when they were awarded the newly created Clarence S. Campbell Bowl, which was originally meant for the West Division regular-season champions.

Philadelphia's early years in the NHL were characterized by several highs and lows, but the organization was focused on building both its stable of prospects and tough customers. One of the first big young stars they picked up was Bobby Clarke, through the 1969 NHL Amateur Draft, and several trades helped them become serious contenders in the West Division.

Mainstays like Joe Watson and Ed Van Impe were later joined by

(clockwise) Gary Dornhoefer, Larry Zeidel, Bernie Parent, Doug Favell

colourful characters like Bob "Hound" Kelly, Dave "The Hammer" Schultz and Don "Big Bird" Saleski, tranforming a once-placid club into the mighty Broad Street Bullies who terrorized every other team in the league. Parent left for a time, but he was back for the 1973–74 season, and the Flyers became the first expansion club to win the Stanley Cup. Another championship followed, but for all of their might, they could not overcome the Montreal Canadiens in 1975–76.

Over the next decade, the Flyers were transformed into a much different club, but they still were committed to succeed. In the 1980s, they made it to the Stanley Cup Final three times but could not capture another title. Despite the triumphs, there was also incredible tragedy with the early deaths of Barry Ashbee in 1977 and Pelle Lindbergh in 1985.

As the 1990s arrived, it was a tough time to be a Flyers fan, but the team made more smart trades, including a blockbuster deal to get heavily hyped prospect Eric Lindros from the Quebec Nordiques. By 1994–95, they were back among the game's elite clubs and finished either first or second in their division every year until they missed the playoffs again in 2006–07. The 2009–10 season was one of the team's most memorable in recent years as they fought hard to make it to the Stanley Cup Final once again.

LOU ANGOTTI

Angotti was the first captain of the Philadelphia Flyers, and although he was heading into only his fourth NHL season in 1967–68, he had the benefit of playing college hockey at Michigan Tech before embarking on a pro career. In 1966–67, he was a part of Chicago's run to a regular-season crown and he took a great deal of confidence from that experience into the premier season in Philly.

While he never scored more than 18 points in any of his previous campaigns, Angotti made the most of his opportunity to become a major offensive cog and ended up leading the Flyers in assists and points. In fact, he battled Pittsburgh's Andy Bathgate for the West Division scoring crown for most of the season before cooling off near the end of the schedule. Late in November, he rattled off a trio of two-assist games. He also scored the winner against the St. Louis Blues on December 16, 1967.

GARY DORNHOEFER

A hard-hitting forward with loads of potential, Dornhoefer spent the early part of his pro career bouncing between the Boston Bruins and their minor league affiliates. He was one of the key picks for the Flyers roster for their first season.

The new surroundings proved the boost he needed, as he finished the 1967–68 season as the club's second-highest scorer and ranked fifth in the league with his 134 penalty minutes. He also had an uncanny ability to score game-winning goals, scoring two against the St. Louis Blues plus one each while facing Minnesota and Pittsburgh. On January 14, 1968, he had three assists in a 6–3 victory over the Oakland Seals.

Dornhoefer remained with the Flyers for more than a decade and was a heart-and-soul player who appeared in two NHL All-Star Games and skated on two Stanley Cup–winning lineups. After retiring, he had a long and successful career as a broadcaster.

LEON ROCHEFORT

Rochefort's NHL career began with the New York Rangers in 1960–61. After he failed to crack their regular lineup, he was traded to the Montreal Canadiens before the 1963–64 campaign as part of a multi-player deal in which Hall of Famers Gump Worsley and Jacques Plante switched sides. Although used only on a limited basis by the Habs in the ensuing years before expansion, he was a part of their Stanley Cup–winning squad in 1965–66 after he was called up for playoff action. He appeared in 27 regular-season games the next year.

Since Rochefort starred for several seasons with the Quebec Aces in the AHL, it was only natural that the Flyers wanted to draft him in 1967. The team had high hopes that he could become an everyday player.

"I did not know too much about Philadelphia, but I was happy to be drafted by them," Rochefort reflected. "It was all equal and we didn't have any superstars, so everybody had to work. We didn't know what to expect. It was all different guys and we had good spirit."

He assisted on the franchise's first goal by Bill Sutherland in the season opener and made headlines as the first player on the team to record a hat trick when the Flyers faced the Canadiens on November 4, 1967.

"I got a pass out of the corner from Ed Hoekstra," he said as he recalled the big moment. "Then I went around big Ted Harris and I went left of [Rogie] Vachon. I came back right and had the open net. I scored and then fished the puck out of the net."

The points kept piling up over the next few months and he even scored a game-winner against the Pittsburgh Penguins on December 17. Rochefort was the only member of the Flyers selected to play in the 1968 NHL All-Star Game.

"I missed the previous one when Montreal won the Cup in 1965–66 because I was injured at the time," he said. "It was unreal."

One of Rochefort's best outings of the year came on February 22, 1968, when he had another hat trick and chipped in an assist in a 7–3 win over the Minnesota North Stars. By the end of the season, he ranked 10th in the NHL with 237 shots on goal.

"I didn't realize that I had shot so many times. I wasn't just a shooter. I was a passer, too."

In the playoffs, Rochefort managed to secure yet another spot in the club's record book by scoring the first playoff game-winning goal in franchise history on April 6 in Game 2 of the series with the St. Louis Blues.

BILL SUTHERLAND

Sutherland was a fixture with the AHL's Quebec Aces for most of the 1960s and while he put up some decent totals, he appeared in only a pair of playoff games with the Montreal Canadiens in 1962–63. Acquired by the Flyers when the Aces were purchased, he was installed on a line with Leon Rochefort and Ed Hoekstra that had some early success during the 1967–68 season.

"It was really good because all three of us killed penalties and played on the power play," he recalled. "I thought I could fit in any-where. Most of those guys on the team I had played with in the AHL.

We knew each other pretty well. It was so exciting for us guys who had been in the minors for so many years. I thought the thrill of being lucky enough to play was enough for me."

Sutherland made history during Philadelphia's first game in the league by scoring on the power play against Charlie Hodge of the California Seals. In their next outing on the west coast swing, he potted the opener against the Los Angeles Kings as well. In back-to-back games in January 1968, he scored the game-winning goal, and he also notched a pair in a 7–2 loss to the Toronto Maple Leafs on March 6.

Even though he missed a handful of games because of injuries, Sutherland managed a solid 20-goal season to start his NHL career. He was claimed by the North Stars and then the Maple Leafs in the 1968 intra-league draft and traded back to Philadelphia a few months later.

FORBES KENNEDY

Regarded as one of the toughest players of the Original Six era, Kennedy was sent down to the minors by the Boston Bruins during the 1965–66 season and spent the following campaign with the San Francisco Seals of the WHL. His 66-point year ensured that the new expansion clubs considered him, and the Flyers ended up bringing him on board. He was not bothered by the reality of joining a new organization.

"I didn't mind it as long as I was playing in the NHL, you know what I mean?"

While his willingness to play a gritty game was welcome, he also managed to put up respectable totals. He scored game-winning goals against Chicago and Minnesota in February and had some multi-point outings against Toronto in the second half of the schedule. At the end of the season, he was third on the club in penalty minutes and tied a career mark for assists with 18.

Kennedy was one of the team's hottest players in the first-round playoff matchup with St. Louis. His best outing was in Game 5, when he chipped in a goal and got an assist in a 6–1 victory.

"We beat them every game that year. Then they brought in Harvey and Moore. I told the guys that this isn't the same team we played all year."

All in all, Kennedy was happy with the experience in Philadelphia and had praise for team owner Ed Snider.

"I thought we had a great team, especially against the older ones. We had a bunch of guys who worked hard. I always say that he's the best owner I ever met. He never forgot the first-year team. We were treated well. It was first class all the way."

Kennedy was traded to Toronto late in the 1968–69 season — a year that saw him lead the NHL in penalty minutes.

"I got in a little trouble for yappin' to the press. After that, Bud Poile sent me back to Philly and I sat for two weeks. They tried to send me to Quebec. I felt that I could still play, but my big mouth got me in trouble. I knew at least a couple of teams were interested."

CLAUDE LAFORGE

LaForge is not a name that rings a bell with most hockey fans, but his involvement in one of the most one-sided fights in hockey history helped change the game forever.

One of the players Philadelphia acquired when they bought the Quebec Aces, LaForge had NHL experience under his belt from stints with Montreal and Detroit between 1957–58 and 1964–65 and was ready to come back to big-league action. On December 8, 1967, he tallied the game-winner against Los Angeles and 20 days later he scored twice while taking on the Red Wings. He also enjoyed some productive contests against the Toronto Maple Leafs that year and got the deciding goal on January 24, 1968.

During the playoffs, he was able to chip in some offence, but he was hit by Noel Picard with what was called a sucker punch in an altercation in the third period of Game 5 of the first round against the St. Louis Blues. He hit the ice almost instantly and was cut open, causing both benches to spill out and begin a full-blown brawl.

"It was just brutal," said Andre Lacroix. "Picard was not known for doing that sort of thing."

From that point on and following a rough rematch series the next year, Flyers management began drafting and trading for players who were not afraid to take on the toughest players in the league. In time, the club became known as the Broad Street Bullies, and the game was never the same again.

JOE WATSON

A fresh-faced rookie with the Boston Bruins in 1966–67, Watson played alongside fellow freshman Bobby Orr and had a solid 15-point year that made him a prized prospect heading into the expansion draft. The Flyers took him with their third pick among skaters, and he was the youngest regular member of their defence corps once the regular season started.

When Philadelphia took on the Bruins on November 12, 1967, Watson opened the scoring at 1:12 of the first period with his first goal in a Flyers uniform. That game also marked the first time the team defeated Boston, and he commented to the press about it afterwards.

"The Flyers' performance was just great. It was so good that the Philly skaters made Bobby Orr look ordinary. It's a good thing, too. If you let him get loose, he'll murder you."

Over the course of the season, Watson's solid play from the back end earned him attention from All-Star voters. He had a two-point outing against the Chicago Black Hawks on February 3, 1968. He also scored the winning goal against the Minnesota North Stars on March 10, his final tally of the regular season.

Newspaper reports noted that his mother could actually hear telecasts in Vancouver of Flyers games from radio station WCAU 1210 thanks to its powerful signal.

"Joe was steady and a smart player," said goaltender Doug Favell. "He was reliable and a smart defenceman. He wasn't flashy and maybe sometimes you didn't notice him. As a goaltender, you noticed him the most."

Watson remained with the Flyers for most of the rest of his playing days and was a defensive anchor during two Stanley Cup championships. His younger brother, Jim, eventually made the club as well. Today, he remains active with the team's alumni association.

ED VAN IMPE

The runner-up to Bobby Orr in voting for the Calder Trophy as Rookie of the Year in 1966–67, Van Impe finally became a regular with the Chicago Black Hawks that year after spending several seasons in the minors honing his skills. Many observers were shocked to see him exposed in the expansion draft, and he was the first skater selected by the Flyers.

"Believe me, we were really surprised when we saw that Van Impe was left unprotected," said general manager Bud Poile. "This changed our plans to a degree because we simply didn't think a player of his capabilities would be let go. But it's understandable. After all, the Black Hawks were really loaded up front and they've got some outstanding kids in their organization, a few who are really good prospects. Yet there was no doubt as to our picking Van Impe if we got the opportunity. Hell, anybody who played regularly on the Black Hawks' defence, well, we just had to go after him."

Given the honour of being named an assistant captain, Van Impe scored his first goal with Philadelphia on October 22, 1967, in a 5–2 win over the California Seals. On November 19, he got the game-winner against the St. Louis Blues, and later in the season he recorded two-assist games against Los Angeles and Toronto. Because of his strong play throughout Philly's first year in the NHL, he gained some All-Star votes and his future with the club looked bright.

"There's no doubt that Van Impe has all of the qualifications of being our team leader," said coach Keith Allen. "This guy comes to play. He's going to play a big role in our first few seasons."

LARRY ZEIDEL

Zeidel bravely dealt with adversity throughout his career and could be considered one of hockey's greatest success stories. One of the few Jewish players of the Original Six era, he played for Detroit and Chicago between 1951–52 and 1953–54 and won a Stanley Cup as a rookie. After that, he spent many years in the minor leagues and played with the AHL's Cleveland Barons in 1966–67.

Not ready to give up on his pro hockey career, he felt he could offer some much-needed experience to any NHL team as the expansion era began. He drafted a 10-page pamphlet entitled, "A Resume with References and Testimonials of Larry Zeidel, Professional Hockey Player, Sales Promotion and Public Relations Executive."

"With expansion coming up, I figured I'd better let people know I was available," he said. "I never attempted anything like that before, so I talked to a lot of people and used some of their ideas. The best advice I got was from a friend who said to spend some money and make the booklet a first-class presentation."

After spending $150 of his own money to produce the booklet and sending out 200 copies to just about anyone in the hockey world, Zeidel received a great number of rejections and was even turned down by Philadelphia's Bill Putnam. Once training camp began, though, Bud Poile was interested enough to purchase his rights from Cleveland.

"The Rock was different," said Doug Favell. "He was very enthusiastic and excited to be there. A unique and neat guy. To see a guy that age and knowing he was a career minor-leaguer, it kept us on edge. We needed that at the time."

From the start, Zeidel gave the Flyers toughness. His pugnaciousness came through when he spoke to *The Hockey News* about an early-season scuffle with Noel Picard of the St. Louis Blues.

"That Picard thinks he's a tough guy, but he really isn't. He hit me with a sneak punch and only floored me for the count of five. If he was as tough as he thinks he is, he would have knocked me out for the full count."

His only goal of the 1967–68 season was only the third of his NHL career, but it gave the Flyers a victory over the Los Angeles Kings on December 31, 1967. He also earned an assist that night and felt good about the team's chances to win a championship.

"If you mention that you feel an expansion club can win the Stanley Cup, a lot of people laugh in your face," he said. "Right away, they say, 'Hell, you're a new team. Those other teams have been around for years.' If you hear too much of that kind of stuff, you start doubting yourself. But right now I feel positive that it's possible."

Throughout the year, however, Zeidel had to deal with narrow-minded taunts from opponents because of his religious background. Some members of the Boston Bruins were particularly vicious with their barbs, and the tension came to a boil when the two teams met at Maple Leaf Gardens on March 7, 1968, as anti-Semitic comments were directed at the veteran defender.

"Nearly the whole Boston team tried to intimidate me about being the only Jewish player in the league," he said to the press afterward. "They said they wouldn't be satisfied until they put me in a gas chamber."

Those comments truly hit close to home because Zeidel had lost his grandparents in World War II when they were killed at the hands of the Nazis. A nasty stick-swinging incident was triggered after Zeidel cross-checked Eddie Shack as he skated over Philly's blue line during the first period. There was a fair deal of history between the two combatants stemming back from their days in the AHL, but according to some reports Shack was not the one who made the comments — just a convenient nearby target.

Andre Lacroix disagreed with that assessment, however.

"From my perspective, it was Shack saying something like 'I'm going to get you, you fucking Jew.' With all of the reporters around, you would think that somebody would have found out who said it."

Both combatants drew blood that night, and the battle came as a bit of a surprise to the officials.

"There really wasn't a buildup to it as I recall," said referee Bruce Hood. "When it happened, I was surprised. There was nothing that jumped out at me earlier in the game. I had not heard any remarks and neither had any of the other officials. It was a bit of a shock to me. I just thought to myself, 'My God, what is going on here?'"

Teammate Bill Sutherland was on the ice when it happened and did his best to calm down the situation.

"It smartened a lot of us up. Once they stopped swinging, I went to tackle Larry. We were lucky none of them got hurt."

"Boston started pulling this kind of stuff when we played them earlier in the season," said Zeidel. "I didn't let it get to me even though it hurt me to hear it. It was bad on my part to try and ignore it then, because things only got worse and they really got bad just before the start of our last game in Boston Garden. That bit about me being a 'Jew boy' is music to my ears, but when they brought up the business of the gas chamber and extermination, well, I didn't buy it.

"When I didn't retaliate immediately, they figured I wasn't the same fellow of a few years ago. So they thought they could push me around. The first thing in hockey you learn is that you don't let anyone push you around. Let them do that and you might as well pack up and leave because they'll run you right off the ice."

Fellow tough-guy Forbes Kennedy refused to name the Bruins players who made the comments but stood up to them during the game.

"It wasn't the tough guys who were yappin' at him. I didn't like it at all. I told them that, too. They were hiding behind the tough guys. That was a bad scene. I don't blame Larry at that time."

Naturally, the NHL offices were alerted to what had happened and league president Clarence Campbell called the battle a "near disaster." Each player was fined $300, Shack received a three-game suspension and Zeidel, as the aggressor in their fight, was put on the shelf for four contests.

"This was without a doubt the most vicious episode of its type the league has experienced in many years," Campbell stated. "The force of any one of the blows could easily have produced a disaster. Both of the principals are very fortunate that their injuries were of a minor nature, but such conduct is absolutely intolerable. A realistic effort will be made to stamp out such behaviour in the future."

Campbell made his ruling after reviewing footage of the incident and reports from Bruce Hood and the game's linesmen. It was reported, however, that Campbell did not want to hear a word about the anti-Semitic remarks at the hearing. Several fans who were near the bench happened to overhear what the Bruins players said, but that evidence was also disregarded when discipline was handed out. Zeidel refused to talk about the incident later in the season.

Zeidel finished the year with Philadelphia and, after playing just nine games in 1968–69, announced his retirement. Although a single incident casts a shadow on his career, fans everywhere respect him for standing up for himself.

BERNIE PARENT

Seemingly destined to become a great goaltender, Parent grew up in Montreal and watched his idol, Jacques Plante, from afar when Plante visited his sister, who lived on the same street as the budding young star's family. By the early 1960s, Parent was part of the Boston Bruins organization and he starred for the Niagara Falls Flyers before he made his NHL debut in 1965–66. Despite his incredible potential, the club chose to protect Ed Johnston and Gerry Cheevers on draft day, and Parent was the first player selected by the Philadelphia Flyers.

In net for the team's opener against California, he did not record his first victory until November 4, 1967, but it was a big one as he thrilled his hometown crowd in a 4–1 defeat of the Canadiens. By December, he was on a hot streak and earned shutouts against St. Louis and Minnesota and was at one point named West Division Player of the Week.

At the halfway mark of the season, Parent and tandem-mate Doug Favell were awarded the prize money for the Vezina Trophy because they had the lowest combined goals-against average in the league at the time. They had let in only 77 goals over the first 37 games.

"What makes me so happy is that both Dougie and I played about the same number of games," said Parent at the time. "That means each of us can feel that we had a lot to do with winning it."

The Flyers eventually finished first in the West Division, but it was Parent who got the call to step in net once the playoffs started. At the time, he acknowledged the pressure of the postseason but told reporters that he was used to it by then.

"Sure, there's plenty of pressure in the playoffs," he remarked. "But, don't forget, we had just as much pressure on us for the last six weeks of the regular season. We beat the pressure then and wound up winning the championship. I feel we'll be able to stand up to the pressure now in the playoffs. I have never played in the Stanley Cup playoffs before, but it doesn't scare me."

He appeared in five games during the first-round battle with St. Louis and was on the losing end despite a sparkling goals-against average of 1.35, ahead of all playoff goaltenders that year. At the end of the season, he placed fourth in voting for the annual All-Star Team. Parent eventually went on to a Hall of Fame career.

DOUG FAVELL

Favell was a rising prospect in the Boston Bruins organization in the late 1960s but was stuck in limbo in many ways because there were three NHL-calibre goalies ranking ahead of him on the team. A second-year pro in 1966–67, he spent the year with the Oklahoma City Blazers along with Bernie Parent and put up a 14–13–4 record. In the expansion draft, the Philadelphia Flyers surprised many observers at the time by picking him despite his lack of big-league experience.

Once training camp began, it all started to make sense when the Flyers made him their backup goaltender to Parent after he beat out veteran Al Millar for the job.

"I played well enough for them to keep me," he said. "We didn't have much scoring, but we had a great defence."

Although the team had two talented young goalies on their roster, some members of the hockey media didn't have high hopes for Philadelphia's fate in their first year. In short fashion, however, Favell's play changed their tune. He debuted in a 4–2 loss to Los Angeles on October 14, 1967, and was understandably tense beforehand.

"I never forgot that feeling. It was the most nervous I ever felt during a game. My legs were like rubber."

Just four days later, Favell managed to earn the first victory in franchise history when the Flyers beat the St. Louis Blues and the following night he shut out the Pittsburgh Penguins. Over the rest of the first half, he racked up his fair share of wins and, along with Parent, recorded the lowest combined goals-against average in the league to win the Vezina Trophy prize money after 37 games. He also placed second in first-half voting for the Calder Trophy as Rookie of the Year.

The presence of two hot goalies on the same team led the media to buzz about a rivalry between the young stars, but there was simply no animosity between them.

"That was just the media playing it up. There was never a rivalry. We just laughed about it. We kind of helped each other. There were times where I wasn't playing and I always kidded a lot and said something kind of silly to a reporter."

At the end of the season, Favell was voted the team's most popular player by fans and also placed fifth in All-Star voting. As for the Calder Trophy, he ended up in third place as a result of a surge by Montreal's Jacques Lemaire.

EXPANSION YEAR RECORD: 27–34–13
(67 points — fifth in West Division)
COACH: Red Sullivan
GENERAL MANAGER: Jack Riley
FIRST GAME: October 11, 1967 —
2–1 loss vs. Montreal Canadiens
FIRST GOAL: October 11, 1967 by Andy Bathgate

PITTSBURGH PENGUINS

Even though the NHL's Pittsburgh Pirates left town in 1930, hockey was far from dead in the Steel City, where the AHL's Hornets began play six years later. For their first 20 seasons, the Hornets served as an affiliate for the Detroit Red Wings and Toronto Maple Leafs before shutting down temporarily when the Pittsburgh Civic Arena, otherwise known as the "Igloo," was being built.

When they returned to action in 1961 once again as a farm team for Detroit, they were a hit with fans, but their days were numbered once the NHL decided to expand into the city. They won their third Calder Cup in 1966–67 and ended their AHL tenure on the highest note possible.

The drive to bring the NHL back to Pittsburgh began in spring 1965 when state senator Jack McGregor started to seek investors in the expansion bid. The franchise was viewed in part as an urban renewal project and was awarded on February 8, 1966. Seating needed to be added to the Civic Arena and a payment was made to the Red Wings to settle up over the Hornets.

Soon after, the team was given its name and a logo was created that featured a skating penguin in front of a triangle. The significance of the triangle comes from the "Golden Triangle" in Pittsburgh, and the original logo also saw the penguin wearing a scarf, which was removed early in the team's history. Jack Riley was hired as general manager; he had previously held the same position with the Rochester Americans. He in turn

130

hired a fine coach in George "Red" Sullivan, who had been the bench boss for the New York Rangers after finishing his playing career.

The Penguins picked up a handful of players during the 1966–67 season but saved most of their energy for the 1967 NHL Expansion Draft. Both the goalies they picked that day were young talents with decent potential, but first selection Joe Daley did not end up playing for them in their first year and Roy Edwards was traded soon after to Detroit for veteran Hank Bassen. There was no mistaking Sullivan's influence on the players the Penguins chose, as many of them had played under him on the Rangers. It was obvious that many of these players were also getting on in years and had a great deal of pro experience behind them. The best pick of them all proved the second-last one, as after being cast aside by the Red Wings, Andy Bathgate staged a big comeback in 1967–68.

At first glance, the new Pittsburgh club looked effective when it came to checking, and their scoring attack drew a lot of praise. The most glaring problem in training camp was that they had too many goalies to choose from.

"It's going to be a tough job to select two goalies," said Sullivan. "I'm going to be taking a good look at all of them during the exhibition games. All four of them have looked sharp in scrimmages, but I know a few other coaches who would like to be saddled with the same problem of picking out two of these four to stay with the team."

Even before the Pens hit the ice, after the owners of the Atlanta Braves purchased a minority stake in the club, there were rumours that the club was going to be moved. The Braves' president, William C. Bartholomay, openly stated that purchasing part of the Penguins was "for the purpose of assuring Atlanta a place in the league when it expands again." At the time, the NHL had no clear plans for further expansion, so fans in Pittsburgh were concerned their new team was going to leave town before they even got a chance to enjoy them. McGregor cautiously responded to the rumours in the press and tried his best to quell those fears.

"I can't deny any such intention too strongly. We are in Pittsburgh to stay and have no such plans to move the franchise anywhere. The

Braves have bought a minority interest in the club and it is simply that. As an extra protection, our legal documents have been drafted in such a way that only the founding Pittsburgh stockholders have the power to say where the sole location of the Pittsburgh franchise will be. . . . Another known factor was this: we know Atlanta wants hockey and we want a totally owned and developed minor league team. Now, we can work something out with Atlanta. In fact there is a possibility that Atlanta will be the site of our main farm team next year, provided they get an ice arena.

"We could have made a big profit," he continued. "But most of us want to give major league hockey to Pittsburgh. We feel it can be quite successful here and we want to be part of that success."

With the pre-season over and a tandem selected featuring Bassen and minor league veteran Les Binkley, Pittsburgh was ready to open the 1967–68 campaign against the Montreal Canadiens. On October 11, 1967, the puck was dropped and, despite their best efforts, the Penguins lost the game by a 2–1 margin. While Bathgate got the team's first goal, Jean Beliveau of the Canadiens also made history by scoring the 400th of his career.

Canadiens executive Busher Curry says the reputation of the Habs may have worked against them in the historic clash between old and new teams.

"In my opinion, the pressure was on Montreal more than it was on Pittsburgh. After all, [the] Canadiens have a big reputation and they were expected to win big. It may have backfired on them in this case. Canadiens were determined to outskate them, but Pittsburgh were skating like mad. The only thing is, Pittsburgh were skating all over the ice, very scrambly, and pretty soon we were doing the same thing. In other words, we played their game.

"I think we were a bit tense. There was plenty of pre-game publicity in Pittsburgh, which I think is a very good thing for hockey, mind you, but it made the team quite conscious of their image as a top-notch squad. They all wanted to win big and it might've tightened them up."

Problems arose early in the first game as the fans began to grumble when the team sagged during the second period. In their next home outing, they lost to the visiting St. Louis Blues and there were chants of "Bring Back the Hornets" and "Go Back to the Eastern League." With their next victory, against the Chicago Black Hawks on October 21, they became the first expansion team to defeat an Original Six club. Their early record against their first-year contemporaries was not good in the early going, and Sullivan addressed the issue.

"Some of my hockey players feel the NHL's new division is not quite as good as the old division and they have taken it easy when playing the newer clubs. They haven't played well at all against the teams in our division, and this is what I've been worried about since training camp."

It was his opinion that the St. Louis win may also have caused the complacency, but he did not feel his team had an easy schedule, either.

"You know, none of the other expansion teams started off against the old clubs like we did. We played Montreal right off the bat and then played Chicago and New York within the next seven games. That's the way I wanted it. I wanted to meet the older teams to show them what we could do. . . . I know I'm looking forward to a span in our schedule when we meet the new division five or six times in a row. That's when I'll find out how good of a hockey team I have. I've been saying all along that in order to make hay in this league we'll have to beat the teams in our division, so we'll just have to go out there and do it."

It was also in the first month of the season that negotiations with the Atlanta group broke down and the Penguins remained in the hands of the original ownership group. The team was proving a mess on home ice and the pressure to win got to the players.

"We seem too tight at home," said Bathgate. "Maybe we're trying too hard to impress our fans. If we can start playing well at home, we'll be back on top of this league. If we don't, then I don't know what will happen."

In December, the team's vice-president, Pete Block, quit under what were called in the press mysterious circumstances. He stepped aside to concentrate on new business opportunities and remained the club's biggest single shareholder. Attendance also became a major problem, as there was a shortfall of 2,000 fans per game and losses mounted. A big road–losing streak in December and January did nothing to raise their spirits, but the amazing play of Binkley drew raves from anyone who was watching.

"I don't know exactly where to pinpoint the trouble, but I know some of these guys aren't taking their jobs seriously," said Sullivan. "Some guys aren't pulling their weight and I'm sick and tired of it. I know I've got a good hockey club and that's what really tees me off. We'll look good one night and sloppy the next. Some of my guys haven't come through in recent games; Stratton and McDonald, for instance. They have not been cutting it. I don't know why, but they're not skating or checking like I know they can. I don't want to put the onus on those two alone. They're just a couple of examples. There are other guys too."

Injuries were also a major problem, which was particularly evident when veterans like Earl Ingarfield and All-Star Game participant Ken Schinkel were out of the lineup for extended periods.

"I think these injuries have hurt us more than most people realize," said Bathgate at the time. "The other teams can change their men around more often, keeping everyone fresh. We've had to skate longer and work harder and thus get tired quicker. Besides, we also can't get our lines balanced. Every time one line seems set, someone gets hurt and Red has to make another change. You just can't win consistently when you have to play like that."

On the bubble for a playoff spot going into the final month of the season, the Penguins suffered a serious setback when Les Binkley broke his finger in a March 2, 1968, game against Oakland. Over the next three weeks, the team won only twice and, while they had four consecutive wins to end the regular schedule, they finished two points out of fourth place. There was, however, some consolation in that Bathgate led all expansion team players in scoring. Riley summed up his opinions on the year and was not pleased.

"To say that I'm disappointed is an understatement. We've had our injuries and they've hurt. But I think our biggest problem has been our failure to win games on our home ice. We've been playing .500 at home practically since the season started. And if anyone had told me at the first of the year that we'd just break even at home, I'd have told them they were crazy.

"I know the fans were disappointed in what we did this season," he continued. "Red and I were more disappointed than most. I could give a lot of reasons for what happened this year, but I guess most people would think I'm trying to alibi. We had our share of injuries, but that really isn't any reason to lose. You've got to have depth to take up the slack when your regulars get injured and we just simply lacked the depth. We hope to rectify this situation next year by obtaining more players."

One of the craziest stories from the first-year Pittsburgh team revolves around a live mascot that was dubbed Penguin Pete.

On loan from the Pittsburgh Zoo, he was taught to skate and CCM even developed a pair of skates to fit his tiny feet. He debuted in front of the home crowd on February 21, 1968, and made several more appearances before he died from pneumonia in November of that year. Stuffed by a taxidermist soon after, he was on display in the club's offices for a brief period before he was removed due to objection from the public.

In 1971–72, a new skating penguin was brought aboard as mascot and was fittingly dubbed Re-Pete.

The Penguins slid even further in their second season but began to show improvement once Red Kelly was hired as coach. He led them to the playoffs in 1969–70, but their on-ice success was spotty during their first decade. The team went bankrupt in 1975 and the league threatened to relocate or fold them. Luckily, they were able to remain in Pittsburgh and made the playoffs seven times over an eight-year span.

Things began to look dark again in the early 1980s when their terrible record was coupled with major financial problems. What saved the team was the selection of Mario Lemieux in the 1984 NHL Entry Draft. In 1990–91, they won the first of two consecutive Stanley Cup titles and spent the rest of that decade at the top of the NHL heap.

Lemieux had a big part in the Penguins' rise to contention, but after he retired for the first time in 1997, the team began to show signs of financial problems once again. Their free spending caught up with them and they filed for bankruptcy the next year. Sensing an opportunity, Lemieux offered to take his deferred salary that was owed and used it to buy a large part of the team. He later came back as an active player, but

(clockwise) Andy Bathgate, Ken Schinkel, Les Binkley, Keith McCreary

the financial realities the Penguins were facing meant that less money was spent on bringing in expensive talent.

By building through the draft, Pittsburgh put together an incredible nucleus of young players, but they once again had to battle the spectre of relocation. They returned to playoff action with stars such as Sidney Crosby, Evgeni Malkin and Marc-Andre Fleury leading the way and won a third Stanley Cup for the franchise in 2008–09. Now with secure ownership and a new arena, the future is hopeful and bright for hockey in the Steel City.

ANDY BATHGATE

Bathgate was still considered one of the game's star players at the end of the Original Six era, but he had a rough 1966–67 campaign with Detroit that saw him briefly sent down to the minors for the first time in well over a decade. After he was taken with Pittsburgh's second-last pick in the expansion draft, casual observers may have felt that he might be at the end of his career, but he still had a lot to prove.

Bathgate made history on October 11, 1967, by scoring the team's first goal when they hosted the Montreal Canadiens. The puck popped past Rogie Vachon at the 7:06 mark of the first period. Bathgate recalled the moment today.

"It was a good, clean goal. It went far side low, but they didn't have the equipment they use today!"

Just a week later, he recorded the first hat trick in club history with all three tallies in a 3–3 tie with the North Stars. As the year progressed, he proved himself the top scorer in the West Division and scored the 325th goal of his career against Minnesota on December 23.

"I forgot about it. I didn't remember until after they announced it," he said at the time. "I'd like to get to 350, but I don't think I'll ever get there."

Coach Red Sullivan was pleased by his comeback and spoke to the press about it at the time.

"Andy is playing like I knew he could. He may not be skating the way he was four or five years ago, but he's still got the brains and the shot."

Although he had a great year with the Pens, the team was not particularly interested in keeping him for their second season. He was loaned to the WHL's Vancouver Canucks for two seasons, even though he had been tentatively dealt to the Montreal Canadiens.

"They wanted me to retire during training camp the next year. I told them that I wouldn't be retiring. I was going to play no matter what," he said. "Then they traded me to Montreal and I couldn't speak French, let alone English! My wife was from Vancouver, so I packed us up and moved out there. I called Sam Pollock and thanked him for the opportunity."

When Red Kelly took over as coach later on, Bathgate was convinced to return to Pittsburgh in 1970–71 and he finished his NHL days with 349 goals. He went to Switzerland for a year and came back to coach the WHA's Vancouver Blazers in 1973–74. The following year, he staged a brief 11-game comeback with that club and scored once to hit the 350-goal mark for his pro career.

AB MCDONALD

In the late 1950s and early 1960s, McDonald had some strong years with the Montreal Canadiens and Chicago Black Hawks and he began his career with a Stanley Cup victory in each of his first four seasons in the NHL. After a year with Boston, he was dealt away to Detroit before the 1965–66 season. The Red Wings did not use him a lot, however, and he spent some time in the minors for the first time in nearly a decade.

"I was in Pittsburgh with the Hornets, and Sid Abel called me up to come play in Detroit at the end of the year," McDonald recalled. "I said no because I wanted to stay there, and we won the Calder Cup. With Detroit, you were always up and down. I had an idea that Pittsburgh wanted to keep me there."

That is exactly what happened, too, and the Penguins claimed him in the expansion draft. Named the first captain in franchise history, McDonald was a bit apprehensive about the honour placed on him by coach Red Sullivan.

"Red was a New Yorker and I always said he was a Phil Watson guy, who wasn't very popular with his players. Red was a little bit of that style. He picked me as his captain, but it wasn't a friendship made in heaven."

During the season opener, he earned an assist on the first goal by Andy Bathgate. Two nights later, he recorded the first power-play goal in franchise history against the St. Louis Blues. His decent start included a two-assist effort while playing Minnesota on October 18, 1967, and he notched an important game-winner in a battle with the Boston Bruins on November 22. He also had two-goal efforts against Toronto on February 3, 1968, and St. Louis a little more than a month later.

After the season was over, many fans were shocked to see him traded to the St. Louis Blues for Lou Angotti, but it was not a move that came as a shock to the veteran winger.

"It wasn't a surprise," he recalled. "I kind of had an idea beforehand. I was at a meeting for the NHLPA as a player rep and met with Scotty Bowman, who I had known since my junior days. I had a feeling they were interested in getting me."

KEN SCHINKEL

After several years with the New York Rangers, Schinkel was sent down to the Baltimore Clippers of the AHL in 1963–64 and spent four seasons there before expansion became a reality. The Rangers probably could have used his offensive skills, however, as he averaged nearly a point per game there. Since his old coach Red Sullivan was helping run the show in Pittsburgh, he had an inkling that he was coming back in the NHL.

"When I started watching the draft and saw all these New York Rangers going there, I thought there might be a chance I might go there, too."

Sullivan was pleased to get one of his former charges on the team and praised him to the press during the early stages of the season.

"Schinkel is by far the best right wing in our division and he's not far from the others in the other division. If any kids are coming into this league as right wings, they should watch Schinkel. He'll show them how this game should be played."

When the Penguins met the Chicago Black Hawks for the first time on October 21, 1967, Schinkel scored three times in the 4–2 victory and was named the West Division's Player of the Week.

"Anytime you get a hat trick, it's something good," he recalled. "They put me out to check, but I don't remember how I scored them. I guess I outscored Bobby Hull three to one, so that was a feather in my cap!"

In December, he also scored game-winners against Minnesota and Toronto, and his strong play over the first half made him the first Pittsburgh player to participate in a NHL All-Star Game.

"I was pretty nervous. It was a great honour for me. I only started playing at 15 and spent so many years in the AHL, so my hard work had paid off," he recalled.

Not long after, he suffered a major setback during the January 28, 1968, game with the Boston Bruins as a Bobby Orr slapshot caused a serious injury.

"I went out to block the shot, killing a penalty, and his shot hit me on the ankle bone. I still played the rest of the game."

Schinkel came back in time for the later stages of the season, but the Pens missed out on the playoffs. He remained with the organization for the rest of his playing days and took over as a coach before moving on to scouting.

ART STRATTON

An icon in the minor leagues in the years leading up to NHL expansion, Stratton had briefly seen action with New York, Detroit and Chicago, but he had tremendous success in the AHL and CHL. He was always considered to be on the cusp of making it to the highest level, so there was little doubt he was going to find regular work once the league doubled its membership.

"At the time, I was hoping to be drafted by St. Louis because I knew the fans and the area," he said. "St. Louis wanted to take me in the 10th round."

The Blues did not end up taking him that early, however, and he was the 12th pick for the Penguins instead. His scoring talent slowly became apparent to Pittsburgh fans, but he scored the first game-winning goal in franchise history on October 13, 1967, and, funnily enough, St. Louis took the loss that day.

"You know, the biggest thing when you get a chance to play in the NHL, they want you to start off with a bang," he said to the press at the time. "They figure you've got to score now, not after a while. If you can't do it right off the bat then you're in trouble. Well, I couldn't do it right away and I didn't get too many chances. But I knew I'd be able to do it if given a chance in the first 25 games."

As the campaign progressed, he was a top point-producer for the offensively challenged club and he received three All-Star votes during the first half. By January, he began to have problems with Red Sullivan and was benched for what the team considered poor play. Stratton does not have fond memories of the coach and received letters from fans at the time saying that he should get more playing time.

"It was really one area where I wasn't too satisfied," he said, "I felt he wasn't a good NHL coach and felt he favoured a lot of the ex-Rangers. They got a lot more ice time and were made a bigger priority."

Before that point, Sullivan was complimentary of his play.

"He's playing well and not because he has scored goals. He just seems to be strong in his skating, his checking and carrying the puck. Some people say he's not a good skater, but I think he's a deceptive skater, like Gordie Howe and Gordie's been around a long time."

The Penguins traded him away to the Philadelphia Flyers for Wayne Hicks on February 27, 1968, and he returned to the minors for good at the end of the season.

"Artie was a great playmaker and moved the puck so well," said captain Ab McDonald. "He could really handle the puck. I told him that he would have been an All-Star if he could see! His eyesight wasn't great, but he was a great playmaker."

VAL FONTEYNE

Fonteyne is regarded as perhaps the most gentlemanly player the game of hockey has ever seen. He spent most of his early NHL career as a member of the Detroit Red Wings. After years of great service to the club, he was demoted late in the 1966–67 campaign when the club began a youth movement, and he helped the Pittsburgh Hornets to a Calder Cup championship instead.

"I was sent down with a month to go to a powerful team in the American League," he recalled. "We had a great team and if they had brought that team into the NHL, it could have done well on its own."

Taken by Pittsburgh in the expansion draft, Fonteyne made his first goal as a member of the Penguins count, giving them a victory over the California Seals on October 25, 1967. He missed some time after getting hit in the ankle by a puck during practice, but he managed to establish new career marks in assists and points. In early February 1968, he had back-to-back two-assist games against St. Louis and Toronto and also managed a three-point night while facing the Seals on March 2.

Today Fonteyne is remembered mostly for his clean play, but it was not something that was on his mind at the time.

"It never even dawned on me," he said. "I played that way since I was a kid, and it was just the way it was."

Team captain Ab McDonald was pleased by his effort throughout the year.

"He had great wheels and could kill penalties. When the going got tough, you could count on him."

LEO BOIVIN

The master of the hip check, Boivin was not the biggest defender in the NHL during the Original Six era, but his play was steady and he earned both fear and respect from opponents. By 1966–67, he was patrolling the blue line for the Detroit Red Wings, but he wasn't upset about being made available in the expansion draft.

"I didn't mind," he said. "I knew that I wasn't going to be protected. They were going with younger guys."

Being drafted by the Penguins was a bit of a homecoming for him, as he had started his pro career with the AHL's Pittsburgh Hornets and won a Calder Cup there in 1951–52. Looked upon as the new club's anchor on defence, he had a goal and an assist in a loss to the Los Angeles Kings on October 28, 1967. He served as a mentor to many of the team's youngsters, including Dick Mattiussi, who spoke to *The Hockey News* about Boivin.

"If he sees something you're doing wrong, he'll tell you. When you're on the ice, you're going to learn a lot faster if you're paired with him. If you make a mistake, he makes it look like it isn't a mistake; he comes up smooth."

During the drive to the playoffs, the man teammates called "Fireplug" showed few signs of slowing down and he not only managed two goals in a win over the Seals on March 27, 1968, he also had the game-winning tally against Philadelphia three days later.

"Leo and I were good friends and he could bodycheck," said captain Ab McDonald. "One of the things I always remember is that Leo would always hit Ron Ellis when he was coming down the ice. You'd think that kid would learn!"

HANK BASSEN

A solid backup netminder from the era when most NHL teams primarily used one goaltender, Bassen was often counted upon to fill in between the pipes whenever necessary. He definitely earned the nickname of "Mr. Emergency." He served regularly as a backup to Terry Sawchuk or Roger Crozier in Detroit and was coveted by the Penguins after he led the Pittsburgh Hornets to a Calder Cup championship in 1966–67. Before the start of training camp, he was traded by the Red Wings for a solid younger goalie named Roy Edwards.

Bassen was in the net in the club's opening game against Montreal and looked good despite surrendering the 400th goal of Jean Beliveau's career. Two nights later, he was responsible for the first victory in franchise history by making 37 saves in the 3–1 win over the St. Louis Blues. Platooned with Les Binkley, he recorded a shutout against the Philadelphia Flyers on November 15, 1967, and did not shy away from the rough stuff during the next outing with St. Louis. After he received a bloody nose thanks to the errant elbow of Jim Roberts, he responded by smashing his opponent's head with his stick, and a fight broke out.

As the season wore on, Binkley emerged as the team's number

one goalie and Bassen saw less and less action on the ice. Although their goals-against averages were comparable, Binkley had a better winning percentage. At the end of the year, the 35-year-old hung up his pads for good, but his son, Bob, later had a solid NHL career.

"I played with Hank Bassen in Detroit," said Leo Boivin. "He was a jolly good guy. Sometimes goalies are a little flaky, but Hank was a good guy."

LES BINKLEY

Binkley had been a pro for more than a decade when the NHL expanded and, even though he had been one of the best goalies in the minors in the 1960s, he didn't end up going to one of the new clubs until just before the 1967–68 season started. That was when the WHL's San Diego Gulls sold him to the Pittsburgh Penguins.

At the age of 33, he won the backup role to Hank Bassen and made his long-awaited NHL debut in a 3–3 tie with the Minnesota North Stars on October 18, 1967. Three days later, he became the first West Division goaltender to beat an established club when the Pens took down the struggling Chicago Black Hawks by a score of 4–2. From that point on, he began a hot streak that saw him take over as top man in the crease after earning the confidence of coach Red Sullivan.

"I know of only one man who has the edge on Binkley and that's Bower of Toronto. There are one or two others who are Bink's equal and there are several who get more publicity. But there is no one outside of Bower who has more ability as a goaltender than Binkley. . . . He consistently plays a fantastic game. Sure, he's not infallible. I've seen him make some bad plays. But for every bad one, he'll make 10 or 15 big saves. I'll match him against anyone in the league."

Toward the end of December, he shut out Minnesota and also managed to earn a rare 0–0 tie with the Oakland Seals, earning West Division Player of the Week honours from *The Hockey News*. By the end of the season, he had six blankings to his credit, but the team narrowly missed out on the playoffs. Down the stretch, he missed several games because of a broken finger, and the club suffered without him in the crease.

"He played so well and took over as number one," said Ab McDonald. "He went out and played as hard as he could. When you came up the way Bink did, you deserve it. He came up the hard way."

Ken Schinkel also had a lot of praise for the veteran goalie.

"I played against him in junior when he played for Galt. Les took over and he was the kind of goalie that made saves. He won a lot of games for us and he probably kept us in the game 50 percent or more of the time."

At the end of the year, Binkley was voted Pittsburgh's MVP and also earned votes for the All-Star Team and the Calder Trophy.

EXPANSION YEAR RECORD: 27-31-16
(70 points — third in West Division)
COACH: Lynn Patrick and Scotty Bowman
GENERAL MANAGER: Lynn Patrick
FIRST GAME: October 11, 1967 —
2-2 tie vs. Minnesota North Stars
FIRST GOAL: October 11, 1967 by Larry Keenan

ST. LOUIS BLUES

The city of St. Louis became the new home for the troubled Ottawa Senators franchise during the 1934–35 season, but the Eagles lasted only for a single season, unable to soar out of the last-place spot in the NHL's Canadian Division and the league.

As the franchise's financial problems continued, they sold off star Syd Howe to Detroit to stay afloat. Their anemic offence and poor defence proved a recipe that kept fans away from the St. Louis Arena, and the cost of rail travel to other NHL cities was prohibitive. The team sold off more players at the end of the season and then were put up for sale. A buyer could not be found, so the league bought it back and the remaining members of the club were dispersed.

Just three years later, the Montreal Maroons attempted to move to St. Louis, but the proposal was shot down by the league, mostly because of the potential travel costs. Over the next three decades, local fans got to see some great minor league hockey instead. The St. Louis Flyers of the AHA, who were around before and while the Eagles were in town, ran until the end of the 1941–42 season and then came back as part of the American Hockey League in 1944–45. Although they were not a success on the ice, they stuck around until the end of the 1952–53 campaign.

A decade later, pro hockey returned to St. Louis when the Syracuse Braves of the Eastern Professional Hockey League (EPHL) were moved mid-season and relocated to Missouri. That league closed its doors at the end of the year and was replaced by the Central Hockey League

146

instead. The Braves soldiered on, but once the NHL was looking at expansion, their days were numbered.

After the failure of the Eagles, the NHL was not entirely keen on putting a team back in St. Louis; however, there was a lot of pressure from Chicago Black Hawks owners, the Wirtz brothers, to make use of the St. Louis Arena since they owned the aging rink. Although the arena was in a somewhat decrepit state, its sale gave them some return on their investment. Once the league announced six new expansion cities, St. Louis was included without a formal bid in place — much to the chagrin of many other worthy cities that applied.

It was only a matter of time before the league found a buyer and, after a meeting with NHL executive William Jennings, insurance mogul Sid Salomon Jr., along with his son Sid Salomon III and Robert L. Wolfson, took over the reins of ownership. Naturally, millions of dollars had to be sunk into franchise fees, but they also had to make some serious upgrades to the arena to get it ready for NHL action.

Needing an experienced hockey man to build their club, the Salomons hired Lynn Patrick, who formerly coached the New York Rangers and Boston Bruins before taking over as general manager of the Blues. He was also tapped to coach the team but got some assistance in the form of a budding hockey man named Scotty Bowman, who had great success with the Peterborough Petes of the Ontario Hockey Association (OHA).

"I was coaching in the Montreal organization, and Lynn Patrick was the GM of Boston, and I think he was out on the west coast with the L.A. Blades," Bowman reflected. "He wanted to get a young guy, but I had a year left on my contract, and Montreal let me out so I could work in the NHL."

At the 1967 NHL Expansion Draft, the Blues took quite a few established veterans who were approaching the end of their careers, as well as a handful of youngsters. Their first selection happened to be Glenn Hall, who was fresh off sharing the Vezina Trophy with Denis DeJordy in Chicago. Other vets getting an extension on their playing days included defencemen Al Arbour and Fred Hucul, plus talents like Don McKenney, who had played for Patrick in Boston. As for the youngsters, there were not a lot of them, but they included players like Terry Crisp and Ron Schock, who stuck around the league for a long time.

The Blues also selected Bill Hay from Chicago, but he retired before the team took to the ice. Patrick felt that he and his scouts basically robbed the established clubs at the expansion draft, especially when they traded Rod Seiling back to the Rangers for four young players.

"We knew we would have to play 24 games with the established clubs, and we tried to draft a team that would make a credible showing, and particular attention was placed on defence because we knew we would have to stop those old clubs to beat them," said Scotty Bowman.

"We wanted to buy ourselves some time," he continued. "So we would have a team that could keep us in contention while we were building our younger players to the point where they could move into the big time."

In pre-season action, it became apparent that the Blues were going to be very strong defensively, but there were some questions about how much offence could be expected from their forward lines. Hall was not reporting to camp until October 1, 1967, as he had to bring in the crops at his Alberta farm, but there was little doubt that he would be in playing condition soon after his arrival. There were some injuries before the season started, but those problems were secondary to the reality that there were issues in getting their arena completed in time.

Luck was on the side of the Blues, however, and their home opener took place on October 11 against the Minnesota North Stars. There was a lengthy and elaborate pre-game ceremony that featured such entertainment figures as Arthur Godfrey, Guy Lombardo and his Royal Canadians, Anna Maria Alberghetti and figure skater Aja Zanova. St. Louis sent the crowd home wanting more as they managed only a 2–2 tie.

Players like Jim Roberts were very pleased by the early efforts of the team to make the players comfortable in their new surroundings.

"I think the management of the Blues is first class," he said. "They have done everything to get us settled here, they have given us a building that ranks with the best in the league, they have done everything they could to get us started in a race to the top. Now it's up to the players."

He also predicted that the Blues would be on top at the end of the season.

"All six of the teams are freshly put together. It's going to be a big question mark for everyone until we have had a chance to play each other at least once. It's not like the usual start of a season, where all you have to do is look over the roster of the opposing club and have a pretty fair idea of what to expect from each and also what you have to do to prepare for each game. But after once around the circuit, we'll all have a pretty good notion of what it shapes up like."

As for the view from the management side, Patrick said he would be happy just to be in the thick of things.

"I'm hungry, sure, but I'm not going to kid myself," he said. "I'm disappointed with the way our club has performed in camp and in the exhibition games. After the draft I said I wouldn't trade our personnel for that of any other club. Now, I'm not so sure. We seem to have a very slow defence. The other clubs may wheel around us like hoops around a barrel. Still, we have a long way to go. And we're working very hard. I do think it will be a toss-up for honours among all six teams in the new league, and very little will separate the top club from the bottom club, so we could do better than I expect."

The Blues won their first game on the road in Pittsburgh just three days after their debut, but wins were fairly scarce early on. They got back-to-back victories over Boston and Detroit at the beginning of November, but Patrick made a major change soon after that, changing the team's fortunes.

"After 16 games I found that the general manager's job is a full-time position, so I decided to appoint Bowman immediately," he said.

At the time, Bowman was 32 and the youngest coach in the league, but he had a lot of experience coaching at the junior level in the Montreal organization. The team did not respond to the change as quickly as he hoped, since they scored just two goals in his first three games behind the bench. Instead of sticking with his lineup, he brought up Frank St. Marseille and Norm Beaudin to shake things up and add some youthful vigour. They also signed retired legend Dickie Moore and made a major trade to acquire Red Berenson from the New York Rangers.

By mid-season, the Blues had a pair of three-game winning streaks under their belt and were beginning to assert themselves as contenders.

"We may have the only old building to come into the major leagues this year but we have one of the best buildings," said Patrick. "I love the town and I'm very impressed with the interest there in sports and hockey. Our attendance isn't what I would have hoped, but neither is our record. We've been losing low-scoring games. When we pick up, so will the crowds.

"We have had more problems putting together an effective combination than some of the other expansion teams. We have five players that were amateurs last year and never played pro before. That's a lot of inexperience. But these are talented players and we'll grow with them. We have a lot of old guys, sure, like Glenn Hall, Al Arbour, Dickie Moore and Don McKenney, but I just wish we had them all the time. We've had more injuries than most clubs. McKenney missed the first nine weeks. Moore just joined us. We have good personnel, and when we settle down with everyone playing regularly we'll be tough to beat. We need scoring, which is why we signed Moore."

Although they did not set the league on fire the rest of the way, they did finish in third place among West Division clubs but had the unfortunate luck of facing Philadelphia in the first round of the playoffs.

The Flyers had dominated the Blues during the regular season and their GM, Bud Poile, predicted a sweep for his team. What he was not prepared for, though, was that St. Louis was loaded with players who were playoff performers and had Stanley Cup rings to prove it. They shut out the Flyers in the series opener on April 4, 1968, and managed victories in Games 3 and 4. Both teams were bruised and battered because of some bad blood, and that animosity came to an ugly head during Game 5 when a brawl broke out after Noel Picard allegedly sucker-punched Claude LaForge.

The Blues prevailed in seven games before taking on Minnesota in the second round. That battle went to the limit as well. Three of the team's four victories came in overtime, and the series was decided with a big goal by Ron Schock that sent St. Louis to the Stanley Cup Final.

With the odds stacked against them, the Blues faced the Canadiens, an incredibly talented club in the middle of a five-year run that featured four championships interrupted only by the Toronto Maple Leafs in 1966–67. The Habs won in four straight games, but all of them were decided by just a single goal and two went into overtime. St. Louis proved that the new expansion clubs were more competitive than originally anticipated, and Glenn Hall was awarded the Conn Smythe Trophy as the postseason's Most Valuable Player.

Salomon was extremely pleased by his team's showing and rewarded the players and their families by giving them a 10-day trip to Florida. The future looked bright for the team, and they stayed at the top of the West Division in the early part of the expansion era. They went to the Stanley Cup Final each of their first three years, a lot of that success to the credit of Scotty Bowman's coaching and a strong mix of talented veterans and youngsters.

"A lot of guys had a hard time with him, but he gave me my chance and he was a great coach," said Gary Sabourin about Bowman. "He did what he had to do to win and he hated losing. He knew what kind of guys he wanted there, and the older guys he brought in had a big impact on us young guys. Everybody was ecstatic to be there, and us young guys were thrilled to be in the NHL and to be winning playoff series. The first three years were fantastic, but once they got rid of Scotty and traded Berenson for Garry Unger, things went downhill fast."

Bowman was on the outs with team ownership early in the 1970–71 season, but he eventually resurfaced back in Montreal and took them to five Stanley Cups. The Blues remained playoff contenders for most of the 1970s before bottoming out at the end of the decade. Through the hard work of Emile Francis, the team was built into a powerhouse through the draft. They were back in the playoffs by 1979–80 and did not miss them for 25 straight seasons.

During that time, the Blues dealt with the possibility of relocating to Saskatoon in 1983. But they had on-ice success with talents like

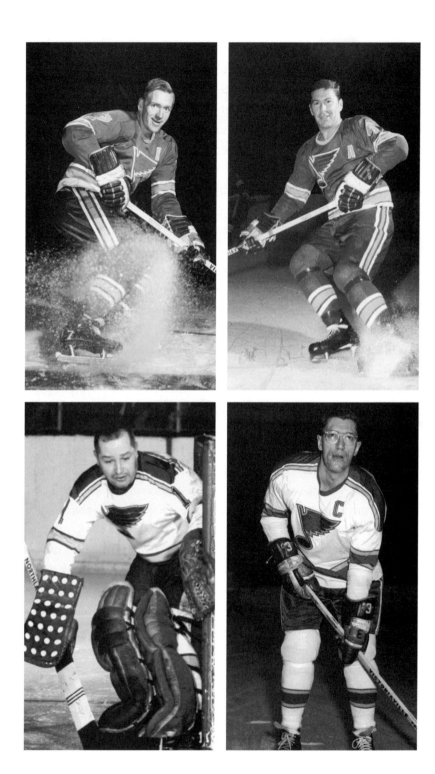

(clockwise) Red Berenson, Noel Picard, Al Arbour, Glenn Hall

Brian Sutter, Bernie Federko and Mike Liut before the arrival of even bigger stars Brett Hull, Adam Oates and Curtis Joseph, which had many wondering if the team could get back to the Stanley Cup Final in the early 1990s. Since the lockout, St. Louis had some on-ice difficulties and has made the playoffs only twice, but things look promising after a strong 2011–12 campaign that saw them finish first in the Central Division with 109 points.

RED BERENSON

Berenson was one of hockey's most interesting players in the 1960s. He had previously won an International Ice Hockey Federation (IIHF) World Championship with the Belleville McFarlands before moving on to become an All-American at the University of Michigan in the early part of the decade. From there, he went on to play for parts of five seasons with the Montreal Canadiens and won a Stanley Cup in 1964-65. Dealt away to the New York Rangers before the start of the 1966-67 campaign, he battled injuries that year but was protected in the expansion draft.

After a rough start to the 1967–68 season, he was traded to the Blues just 19 games in and instantly became a star with the first-year club.

"I was excited. I can remember when I was with the Rangers and we were all speculating where the best places to play were with expansion. Nobody really gave St. Louis a high vote. When I was traded there, it was like I had died and gone to heaven. I knew a lot of the guys there, and there was a sprinkle of former Montreal players there, and I had played for Scotty Bowman in Hull-Ottawa."

In fact, Berenson credits Bowman with helping rejuvenate his career.

"Scotty Bowman was the first coach to give me a chance to play the way I thought I could play. Scotty knew how to use players and he knew how to get the most out of them. He was good with the young players and how to use the veteran players."

His debut with St. Louis was spectacular, as he earned assists on two goals by Jim Roberts when they defeated the Los Angeles Kings 3–2 on November 29, 1967.

"I knew we got a good player in Red," said Roberts. "I was really excited when we got him because he was going to be our first big player."

Where the "Red Baron" was most noticed by statisticians was in the category of game-winning goals. He was responsible for seven victories by the Blues, one of the most notable a four-point effort against the Oakland Seals on February 3, 1968. Over 55 games with the club, he racked up 51 points, but his production dipped slightly in the postseason. His biggest playoff moments came on May 9 in Game 3 of the Stanley Cup Final, when he scored twice and helped force overtime with the mighty Canadiens.

Berenson was also impressed by the way all players on the Blues were treated by the Salomon family when they owned the club.

"There hasn't been a hockey team treated as well by the ownership as the St. Louis Blues. You felt bad if you lost, because of them."

Over the next few years, Berenson remained one of the team's marquee performers and in a battle with the Philadelphia Flyers on November 7, 1968, became the first player in league history to score six goals in a road game. He later spent some time in Detroit but came back to St. Louis to finish his career and later had success as their coach. In 1984, he returned to the University of Michigan and has led them to numerous Frozen Four appearances.

GERRY MELNYK

In Melnyk's early pro career he enjoyed some time at the NHL level with Detroit and Chicago, but in the years leading up to expansion, he was down in the minors, where he put up decent numbers and even played for the Central League's St. Louis Braves.

Seeking a familiar face for their lineup, the Blues took him in the expansion draft. Melnyk responded by being one of the club's top offensive performers in 1967–68. On October 21, 1967, he had a goal and two assists while battling the Los Angeles Kings, and on

December 27, he scored a game-winner against them. Two days later, he made all the difference in a victory over the Pittsburgh Penguins as well. The Pens also fell victim to his prowess with the puck on March 6, 1968, when he started off a three-game winning streak for St. Louis.

"Gerry had a good hockey head and very seldom gave up the puck poorly," said Ron Schock. "You knew if you threw a pass to him that he was going to get it."

Following an eight-point contribution in the run to the Stanley Cup Final, Melnyk was traded to the Philadelphia Flyers, but he retired before the start of the next season after suffering a heart attack. He took a job as a scout and his lobbying to draft Bobby Clarke forever changed the fate of the franchise.

JIM ROBERTS

An underrated and gifted defensive forward who won a pair of Stanley Cups with the Montreal Canadiens, Roberts looked to have a very bright future with the club, but with a ton of talent to protect, the Habs had to make him available in the expansion draft.

"It was an opportunity and you knew you wanted to stay in the Montreal system but it wasn't in the cards," he said. "It was exciting, though, because St. Louis drafted me with their first overall pick."

He also realized what he was in for with the team early into his time with the Blues.

"That was one of our goals as an organization. We had a number of players from Montreal by the end of the year. We wanted to be a good team in the division and we made the Stanley Cup Final the first three years I was there. I thought it was a pretty rounded team. Defence was always talked about, and goaltending, too, but outside of Red Berenson, we had guys who could contribute as well."

On October 14, 1967, Roberts scored his first goal of the season and added an assist when St. Louis got their initial win over Pittsburgh. Throughout the rest of the year, he picked on the Penguins with a game-winner on November 11 and a three-assist outing on January 31, 1968.

During the season, he was moved from left wing to defence and paired up with Barclay Plager. The two had some history together, as they had played junior hockey with the Peterborough Petes. When the playoffs began on April 4, Roberts scored the winner in the series opener with Philadelphia and his postseason experience helped the Blues get rolling toward the Stanley Cup Final.

FRANK ST. MARSEILLE

St. Marseille did not play organized hockey until late in his teen years, but he had a very solid career in the International Hockey League (IHL) with the Port Huron Flags in the mid-1960s. The 1966–67 season was a tremendous one for "The Saint" and he was named to the league's Second All-Star Team after racking up an impressive 118 points.

The expansion era gave him a chance to crack an NHL lineup, but it was a family member who caught the attention of management in St. Louis.

"His brother is an opera singer and was the one who phoned around to get Frank a tryout, and the Blues responded to his call," said teammate Terry Crisp. "He got in because his brother refused to give up, because he knew how good his brother was."

Signed as a free agent after the season began, St. Marseille made an impact early on by scoring his first big-league goal against Toronto on December 10, 1967. He had a two-goal night, including the game-winner, 10 days later against California.

"We were playing in a game in Toledo, Ohio, when Lynn [Patrick] talked to me about signing with the Blues," said St. Marseille not too long after his call-up. "I had some other chances to sign but I just liked the way Lynn talked to me and his sincerity. I'm glad I made the choices I did, because the Blues have been real good to me."

Impressive for the rest of the season, St. Marseille was one of the club's top offensive performers in the playoffs and had a goal and an assist in Game 3 of the opening round against Philadelphia on April 10, 1968. He remained with the Blues for several years and was the franchise's all-time scoring leader during their early years before he was traded to Los Angeles.

TERRY CRISP

Crisp made his NHL debut with the Boston Bruins in 1965–66 but, like many young players of his generation, grew increasingly frustrated by having success in the minors and not getting regular work with the big club.

"My modus operandi around this time was go into training camp, work like a bitch and get sent to the minors. After four years of doing that, I was about ready to quit and go into teaching," he said. "My wife told me that I was going to stick it out and play one more year in Oklahoma City, and we won another championship. That's when expansion hit and I wouldn't have played if it wasn't for her."

That season proved enough to make a good impression, since he racked up 73 points for the Oklahoma City Blazers and was taken by the Blues in the expansion draft. He made the roster out of training camp, and his first NHL goal came on October 14, 1967, against Hank Bassen of the Pittsburgh Penguins.

When Scotty Bowman took over as coach soon after, he was happy to play for the man who eventually became the league's all-time leader in wins.

"I didn't know Scotty. All we knew was that he belonged to the Montreal team and that meant winning," he said. "Right off the bat, one of the things that he brought in was that he was the boss. I loved playing for him and he was so steeped into the game. He was total hockey."

On December 9, Crisp scored a game-winning goal against the Seals; in their rematch four days later, he chipped in two assists for a 3–1 victory. With the arrival of Dickie Moore on the roster, he was able to play alongside a legend, and Crisp shared a story about a big lesson he learned from the veteran.

"I remember one time that Dickie Moore was sitting beside me on the bench and I say to him how good Beliveau looked out there. He jumped on my ass and started yelling at me about sitting on the bench and praising the other team. I thought he was going to hit me over the head with his stick! I took a big lesson from that and used that approach when I was a coach as well."

GARY SABOURIN

Sabourin was part of the New York Rangers system in the years before the NHL expanded and he was slowly working his way up to the big club. In 1966–67, he had a 23-goal season with the CHL's Omaha Knights and was initially disappointed that he was passed over on draft day. It turned out, however, that the Rangers had something in mind for him, and he became part of the package that sent Rod Seiling back to New York from St. Louis.

"I was ecstatic," he said. "I was working up at my uncle's marina. It was a nice day and they had the radio on and nobody called my name. I thought for sure that I'd get a call. After all the drafting was done, my aunt came running out and she heard about the deal between St. Louis and New York. A couple of days later, Lynn Patrick sent me a telegram saying that they were happy to have me in the organization."

Although he had a good training camp, Sabourin was sent down to Kansas City. One night, he ran into Scott Bowman in a hotel lobby in Oklahoma City and heard that there were changes coming with the Blues. Called up soon after, he was ready to make an impact.

"I got called up to go to Chicago for a game," he said. "I think Terry Crisp got hurt and I got the call. I grabbed a cab from the airport and made it just in time for the warmup. I had to go through the crowd to get to the dressing room and Lynn Patrick said he never saw anyone get dressed so fast! My line was up against Hull and Mikita, but I don't think I had the best game and was sent down afterward."

On December 13, 1967, he scored his first career goal on Charlie Hodge of the Oakland Seals and it was also the game-winner. He followed it up with another goal in the same period to ensure the victory. The next night, he had another two points in a tie with the Philadelphia Flyers. His defensive record during the 1967–68 season was solid, and he scored two shorthanded goals — tying him for fifth in the league in that category.

"He was a checker and a grinder," said occasional linemate Gary Veneruzzo. "An at-home winger. I played against him when I was with Omaha, and he was tough to play against."

During the postseason, Sabourin scored the overtime winner

against the Minnesota North Stars in the fourth game of the West Division final. He went into a small slump after that but was brought off the bench during Game 4 of the Stanley Cup Final and scored a power-play goal to give the Blues a 2–1 lead.

"You never dreamed you'd get that far the first year. Montreal was outshooting us and Glenn Hall stood on his head. Their defencemen were huge and they had good goalies. I think that first year was our best shot at the Cup."

LARRY KEENAN

Keenan first got a brief taste of NHL action as a 21-year-old with Toronto in the 1961–62 season but spent subsequent years in the minors before the days of expansion. In 1966–67, he battled an ankle injury during his time with the Victoria Maple Leafs of the WHL, but the St. Louis Blues felt that he was poised for a comeback.

"I knew [expansion] was going to give me an opportunity to play in the National Hockey League," he said. "In those days it was tough to crack the lineup of the Leafs. A lot of players, including myself, were going to be buried in the minors. They just sent you down until they needed you. Those six extra teams gave a lot of us guys an opportunity."

In training camp, Keenan was the team's top goal scorer. Once the regular season started, he was responsible for getting their first goal on October 11, 1967, against Garry Bauman of the Minnesota North Stars. In the next two games that followed, he also made an impact on the scoresheet, and in the team's third outing he had a winner against the Pittsburgh Penguins.

Soon after, his season came to a temporary halt when he broke his leg, but he returned to action in late December. Just three days later, he sustained some serious bruises and was out of the lineup for a while once again.

"Prior to expansion, I had some years that I was injured. I scored in four of the first five games and then I broke my ankle. In those days, you hid an injury because you wanted to keep your job. Players today have no idea how hard it was in the years before expansion."

Once Keenan officially returned to action, he helped the Blues clinch a playoff spot by scoring a game-winning goal against the Minnesota North Stars on March 30, 1968.

"We didn't get into the playoffs until the second-last game of the year," he recalled. "They were two men short and I scored both goals to put us into the playoffs. When you look back, it had a big bearing on the success of the Blues. When you're that close and able to come through positively, it was exciting to me."

Keenan's momentum carried over into the postseason — especially in the opening-round series with the Philadelphia Flyers. He had two points in Game 2 but made headlines with a double-overtime winning goal in the next outing. That was nothing compared to his clinching goal in Game 7, which sent the Blues into the second round against the Minnesota North Stars.

"Even in the minors, I had a lot of success in the playoffs. I attribute that to always being healthy in the playoffs and being able to rise to the occasion."

BARCLAY PLAGER

The oldest member of the Plager family to play in the NHL, Barclay came to St. Louis with Red Berenson in an early-season trade with the New York Rangers. He almost instantly helped to change the team's on-ice fortunes with his rambunctious play. Coach Scotty Bowman was pleased with his newest defenceman at the time.

"Barclay can carry that puck out of his own end real good," he said. "He gives the kind of offensive lift we need from a defenceman."

While the Blues certainly did not lack toughness before or after his arrival, Plager made some good offensive contributions, including a game-winning goal against Toronto on February 21, 1968, and a two-goal effort playing Detroit on March 16. When it came to penalty minutes, he ended up leading all NHL players in that category in 1967–68 even though he appeared in only 49 games.

"I think Barclay was just as important as Red [Berenson] to the club. He was a real competitor and kept the other teams pretty honest," said Jim Roberts.

This raw energy was truly unleashed in the playoffs, though, as Plager ran roughshod over the Philadelphia Flyers during their opening-round series. In Game 3, he timed his hit on Art Stratton perfectly for when he exited the penalty box and also went toe-to-toe with Gary Dornhoefer. Once the Stanley Cup Final rolled around, he had a goal and an assist against Montreal in the series opener.

RON SCHOCK

In 1966–67, Schock became a full-timer with the Boston Bruins following several years of trying to catch on with the club, but there were changes in the works that made his move to St. Louis a little less painful.

"I wasn't disappointed because Boston made a big trade with Chicago and got Esposito and Stanfield, so the writing was on the wall."

Schock missed the early part of the season with a charley horse and even spent some time in the minors with Kansas City. Back with the team for good after just 10 minor league games, he offered some thoughts on the coaching changes the Blues experienced in their first year.

"They had a two-coach system at the start and it didn't work out too well. When Scotty took over, he brought in a lot of players from the Montreal system and that made it work. These players knew how to have fun and they knew how to win. I knew Lynn from Boston and I liked him an awful lot, but I don't think he was as good a coach as Scotty was, but he was much better in management."

Among Schock's highlights for the year were a two-goal game against Philadelphia on November 19, 1967, and a game-winner to end a losing streak 10 days later while playing Los Angeles. Once the playoffs were in full swing, he scored a very memorable goal to seal a double-overtime victory in Game 7 of the second-round series with Minnesota.

"We got into the playoffs in the last game of the season and dug ourselves out of a hole. Scotty had a way of putting the right player out at the right time."

That goal sent the Blues to the Stanley Cup Final for the first time. Schock reflected on the experience.

"It was amazing to get out there and you're playing against a team who had been there for most of the past 20 years. You were in awe. I was very happy to be there."

NOEL PICARD

Picard was part of Montreal's farm system in the mid-1960s, but he saw some action with the Canadiens during the 1964–65 season and was a part of the Stanley Cup–winning team that year. Sent back to the minors, he split the 1966–67 campaign between the WHL's Seattle Totems and the Providence Reds of the AHL before St. Louis acquired him through the expansion draft.

Joining his older brother, Roger, in training camp, Noel Picard had little trouble securing a position with the Blues and became one of the more intimidating members of their defence corps. He recorded assists in consecutive games in early November and celebrated his 29th birthday in style when he scored his first NHL goal, the game-winner against the Minnesota North Stars on December 25, 1967.

During the playoffs, a battle between the Blues and the Philadelphia Flyers inadvertently started a revolution in hockey when Picard surprised Claude LaForge with a punch during a line brawl that escalated when both teams cleared the bench. After that, the Flyers focused on drafting and trading for tougher players, which ultimately led to the Broad Street Bullies of the 1970s.

"That's the first time I saw anybody get knocked out on the ice," recalled Ron Schock. "LaForge started to swing his stick at Picard, so he grabbed it and hit him. Ed Van Impe came over and he knocked him out cold. LaForge brought it on himself because he came off the boards swinging his stick and Noel didn't have his."

That was not Picard's only moment as a historical catalyst, as he was also the defender who tripped up Bobby Orr when he scored his famous Stanley Cup–winning goal in 1970.

AL ARBOUR

Even though he was one of the best defensive defencemen in hockey during the 1960s, Arbour spent most of the decade languishing in the minors as part of the Toronto Maple Leafs organization. After winning a Stanley Cup with Chicago in 1960–61, he won two more with the Leafs but saw only spot duty beyond the 1962–63 campaign. That changed with expansion when Lynn Patrick had his sights set on the shot-blocking blueliner he had coveted since his days running the Boston Bruins.

"I don't care how old a man is, I only care about how good he can play," said the team's general manager. "I drafted Arbour because I knew he would do the sort of job he is doing for us. . . . And I signed him to a three-year contract, too!"

Named captain of the Blues before the beginning of the 1967–68 season, Arbour scored against the Bruins on November 1, 1967, and had a pair of assists in a 3–3 tie with the Montreal Canadiens on February 28, 1968. He is one of the few players in NHL history to play while wearing glasses and he earned a lot of praise from teammate Glenn Hall.

"I don't think there's anyone I'd rather have playing in front of me than Arbour," he said. "He's the most underrated defenceman, there just isn't anyone better. Among other things, there is no one who is better at blocking pucks. Al does it with such perfect timing that it's beautiful to watch. But if I wore glasses as he does, I don't think I'd ever want to drop to my knees in front of someone with a puck on his stick."

DICKIE MOORE

Moore announced his retirement in 1965, but a little more than two years later, the Toronto Maple Leafs, who still held his rights, decided to deal him away to the Blues, who were looking for veteran experience to bolster their lineup.

"I'm very happy that he wants to play for us," said GM Lynn Patrick. "I think he can help give us the kind of lift that Bernie Geoffrion gave the Rangers last year."

Moore's return to the NHL took place on December 6, 1967, against the Los Angeles Kings. Fittingly, his first goal with his new club came against Toronto's Bruce Gamble when they met four days later, and it proved the game-winning tally. Early in the new year, he sustained a rib injury that dampened his comeback, but he was back in time for the playoffs and made important contributions on the way to the Stanley Cup Final.

Perhaps the greatest impact he made was with the team's younger players, especially those who grew up watching him play with the Montreal Canadiens. Scotty Bowman offered an appraisal of Moore's value to the team at the time.

"He's a winner. He's great for the team on the ice and he's great for us in the dressing room. . . . And when the kids see an old veteran like Dickie hustle out there, they just sort of catch the fire."

The playoffs proved to be his swan song as a pro, but Moore was certainly not washed up, as he had a goal and assist in Game 2 of the first-round battle with Philadelphia on April 6, 1968, and five days later, potted the game-winning goal in Game 4. Facing his old club in the Stanley Cup Final, he looked absolutely ageless as he scored a goal in a tight 3–2 overtime loss in Game 1.

SETH MARTIN

Hockey historians are very familiar with Martin's contributions to the game in the 1960s because he starred for the senior Trail Smoke Eaters club that won an Allan Cup on their way to a World Championship. In subsequent years, he represented Canada in international competition and won two more bronze medals at the Worlds in addition to protecting the net at the 1964 Winter Olympics.

"When we were playing in Vienna for the World Championship in 1967, Scotty Bowman joined us for the tour," recalled Martin. "He talked to me after one of the games and asked me if I was interested. He said he would contact me in the spring. I was sitting out one of the games and we talked. I later got a call from Lynn Patrick, and he ended up coming up with what I would need to go there."

To protect his pension, Martin had to plan a leave of absence from his job as a firefighter for a mining company and then he joined the Blues for their first season. Because Glenn Hall was missing the early part of the season with a hand infection, he got the call to play in the first game for St. Louis, where he looked good in the 2–2 tie with Minnesota. Three days later, he secured the first win in franchise history as they battled the Pittsburgh Penguins.

"I know I was nervous! I can't really remember much about it," he said.

That nervousness was back a few weeks later when he was about to face the Montreal Canadiens on October 28, 1967.

"Going into Montreal was a great thrill. Scotty told me that I was going to play that Saturday night game and I put my pad on the wrong leg!"

Once Hall came back, Martin's time in net decreased, but he managed a decent 8-10-7 record over 30 appearances. One of those victories was over the North Stars on December 25 and it was the only shutout of his NHL career. In the postseason, he made two appearances on the road to the Stanley Cup Final.

"That playoff run was just amazing. The excitement in the building was incredible. We weren't supposed to beat Minnesota and weren't supposed to beat Philadelphia, either."

Burnt out after more than 10 years of playing goal, Martin returned home to Trail and saw sporadic action with the Smoke Eaters before joining the Spokane Jets. In 1969–70, he helped make them the first American-based club to win the Allan Cup.

What some fans also may not know is that Martin also made his own masks.

"I started wearing a mask soon after Plante got hit, as I took a puck off the mouth while playing in Rossland, British Columbia. It wasn't the best mask in the world but it worked. I made Glenn Hall's mask in St. Louis. I had done a bit of that as an amateur and had access to the materials at work."

At the end of the year, Martin broke the masks with a rubber hammer to figure out where the weak spots were, but he does not know where his last mask is today.

CLAUDE CARDIN

Cardin was a senior hockey standout who helped the Sherbrooke

Castors to an Allan Cup championship in 1964–65, and he was on their roster when they went to the final again in 1965–66. He was unable to crack the roster of the Montreal Canadiens, and the team sold him to the Blues on June 21, 1967. He was relegated to their farm club in Kansas City, where he was fifth on the team in scoring with 52 points and showed some grit as he racked up 193 penalty minutes.

Cardin was called up for a brief one-game trial with the Blues and faced the New York Rangers. It proved to be his only NHL action, as he froze on the bench because of nerves and did not step out onto the ice when told to by coach Scotty Bowman. He was sent back to the minors almost immediately.

"I remember laughing about it after he went back to Kansas City," said Ron Schock. "I haven't seen anything like it before or since. He couldn't move his legs! On the bench, you kind of felt sorry for him, though."

Regardless of his memorable mistake, he remained in the St. Louis system with Kansas City for two more seasons. His coach in Kansas City, Fred Hucul, gave an honest appraisal of his abilities.

"He had a hard nose. He wasn't scared to hit the corners."

GLENN HALL

The man known as "Mr. Goalie" was one of the most dominant at his position in the waning years of the Original Six era. Yet even though he shared the Vezina Trophy and helped the Chicago Black Hawks to a regular-season championship in 1966–67, the team chose to protect Denis DeJordy in the expansion draft. The St. Louis Blues chose Hall as their first selection.

Hall was known to hold off on coming to training camp until the crops were in on his farm in Alberta, so he did not appear in any pre-season games. Before he could make his St. Louis debut, a hand infection kept him out of the team's opening game against Minnesota. He also had a quirk for throwing up between periods because of nerves. He realized at the time that he had even greater responsibilities with the new club.

"All goalkeepers are mental cases," he said. "I can't hold it back before the games, but I've learned to choke it back during the games. . . . I think the pressure is even greater now because Chicago owed me for a few bad games after the career I'd had there, but this is a new town, a new challenge, and I guess I have my pride and reputation to live up to."

His St. Louis debut came as relief for Seth Martin on October 21, 1967, and he put forth a solid effort during a 2–1 loss to Philadelphia. His first shutout of the season came against Oakland on December 9 and it was the first one in franchise history. Over the course of the season, he got four more shutouts, one of which was the 70th of his career on January 3, 1968. After that game, he joked around with the press.

"Not bad for an old man, one shutout for every year of my life."

Teammates were very impressed with Hall's solid play at the age of 36 and his positive attitude.

"You had the best goalie in hockey as far as I was concerned," said Ron Schock. "I remember losing one time in Boston and the score was quite high. Showering afterward, Terry Crisp said, 'Oh goalie, I'm sorry,' and he said, 'The sun will come up in the morning.' He's got a sense of humour and that was great."

The only member of the Blues selected to play in the 1968 NHL All-Star Game, Hall finished the regular season in sixth place among all netminders in goals-against average. Once the playoffs began, though, he took his play to another level and opened the first round against Philadelphia with a shutout. Brilliant the rest of the way, he went to the seven-game limit over the first two rounds and kept St. Louis within one goal in every match with the Montreal Canadiens.

Hall had to wait until a couple of days after the series ended to be awarded the Conn Smythe Trophy as the Most Valuable Player of the postseason. The award was normally given out immediately after the game, but the league decided to change the process slightly to allow voters to submit their ballots. An anonymous Canadiens player was quoted in the *Montreal Gazette* as feeling that Gump Worsley should have received the honour, and coach Toe Blake felt the same way as well.

"Who could have played better," he asked. "After all, we won the

Cup so Gump should be the logical choice. Surely they're not going to give the trophy to a loser again like when Roger Crozier got it two years ago."

Voters obviously did not agree with Blake, and Hall became the first player from an expansion club to win a major NHL award. Scotty Bowman nicely summed up the legend's contributions during the season.

"He was the franchise. He was unbelievable and was great before we got him."

DOUG HARVEY

One of the greatest players in hockey during the Original Six era, Harvey changed the game forever as a rushing defenceman with the Montreal Canadiens and he captured the Norris Trophy on seven occasions. By the early 1960s, however, he was being punished by the game's establishment for his involvement in the aborted attempt at a players' association. He played for New York and Detroit before being hired by the Blues to coach their minor league affiliate in Kansas City in 1967–68.

With the CHL's Blues, he served as a playing coach and led them to a 31-29-10 record before losing in the league's final to the Tulsa Oilers. When Harvey was called up to St. Louis as a standby, general manager Lynn Patrick said he knew early on that he would see some action with the club at some point.

"It wasn't a last-minute decision, really," he said. "Scotty [Bowman] and I had talked a couple of months ago about bringing Doug into the lineup when we got into the Stanley Cup action. We both had the feeling he would be able to give the club the kind of experience and morale lift that might be a real boost."

"Harvey steadied the club," said Bowman. "They respect him and he has actually coached a number of the youngsters on our club."

One of those youngsters was Gary Veneruzzo, who played with Harvey during the run to the Stanley Cup Final as well.

"He was a great guy," said Veneruzzo. "He gave me a lot of chances and was always pushing me to Scotty. In between periods, he wouldn't give you heck and told us stories about players he knew to keep you loose. He was a character, too!"

Brought in toward the end of the first-round series with Philadelphia, Harvey assisted on the series-winning goal by Larry Keenan in Game 7. In the next round, he assisted on a couple of early goals and chipped in another in Game 3 of the Final against Montreal.

Instead of sending him back to Kansas City the following year, the Blues kept him for one final NHL season. In retirement, Harvey stuck around the game with some coaching positions but battled alcoholism and suffered from bipolar disorder before he passed away as a result of cirrhosis of the liver in 1989.

THE EXPANSION ERA
SUCCESSES AND FAILURES

Once the first expansion season was over and the grand experiment considered a success for the most part, it was only natural that the NHL would look to the future and continue to bring big-league hockey to more North American markets.

The seeds for future expansion were sown during the 1967–68 campaign when the troubled California Seals were being shopped around by Barry Van Gerbig. A move to Vancouver or Buffalo was heavily rumoured early on but was shot down by the NHL Board of Governors. Both cities had been shut out in the first round of expansion, but their persistence meant that the league approved both locations (and avoided a potentially costly legal bill or two) when the league was ready to grow to 14 teams at the start of the 1970–71 campaign.

Both communities had a very strong minor league presence with the WHL's Canucks and the AHL's Bisons and received a great deal of support from local hockey fans from the start — even if the on-ice product needed some time to become a success. The Buffalo Sabres, who had former Toronto Maple Leafs coach and general manager Punch Imlach running the show, became a contender sooner than the Canucks and made the playoffs for the first time in 1972–73 with young stars Gilbert Perreault, Richard Martin and Rene Robert forming the legendary French Connection line.

The next round of expansion came more as a reaction to the World Hockey Association heading to the ice for the 1972–73 season. The

NHL ventured south of the Mason-Dixon line for the first time and welcomed the Atlanta Flames and at the same time created a greater presence in its largest American market by welcoming the New York Islanders. Many established and younger players jumped to the rival league, and the Islanders lost a lot of talent before even hitting the ice. As a result, their first season was a woeful one, and they won only 12 contests. The Flames, on the other hand, had a bit more on-ice success, but they lasted only seven seasons in Georgia before moving to Calgary.

With their grand plan for expansion derailed somewhat by the presence of the WHA, the NHL had to face the reality that their once-strong talent pool had been diluted. Regardless, they soldiered on with the plan to bring their membership up to 18 clubs, and the Kansas City Scouts and Washington Capitals arrived in time for the 1974–75 season. The 1974 NHL Expansion Draft was one of the worst in league history because of the lack of top-flight talent available for the picking. Existing teams scoffed at the idea that they faced any sort of challenge from the Scouts and Capitals, and most games were tough to watch. By the end of the year, Washington had set an incredible record for futility, as they won just eight games and only one of those victories came on the road. The Scouts fared slightly better, but darker times were ahead.

Around this time, the WHA began to fall into the trap of moving and shifting franchises, and some of those moves even came during the regular schedule. Their 14 teams were not all on solid ground, but some NHL teams also began experiencing difficulties of their own. The Pittsburgh Penguins, California Golden Seals and the Scouts were having trouble drawing crowds and all three were rumoured to be candidates for relocation during the 1975–76 campaign.

The NHL had actually planned another round of expansion for the fall of 1976, and the new teams were expected to play out of Denver and Seattle. Instead of giving those cities new teams, the league changed its mind and offered to move established clubs instead. Seattle Totems owner Vince Abbey struggled to secure financing in time, though, and the NHL pulled the franchise. Lawsuits were filed, but the league prevailed in court a little more than a decade later. The Penguins ended up staying in Pittsburgh, but the Golden Seals were transferred to Cleveland to become the Barons, and the Scouts headed west to Denver to begin play as the Colorado Rockies. The moves did not pan out in the long run for a variety of reasons, and Cleveland was the first to go after just two seasons, while Colorado stayed around for six campaigns.

EXPANSION YEAR RECORD: 24-39-15
(63 points — fifth in East Division)
COACH: Punch Imlach
GENERAL MANAGER: Punch Imlach
FIRST GAME: October 10, 1970 —
2-1 win vs. Pittsburgh Penguins
FIRST GOAL: October 10, 1970 by Jim Watson

BUFFALO
SABRES

Since Buffalo is so close to the Canadian border, it is only natural that hockey has been appreciated by its citizens for decades. The sport has a long history there that pre-dates the NHL's Sabres. The AHL's Buffalo Bisons were rated one of the most successful teams around and began play 30 years before big-league hockey came to town. An earlier club with the same name primarily played out of nearby Fort Erie, Ontario, as part of the International Hockey League and disbanded during the 1936–37 season.

The AHL Bisons were the first pro team to actually play out of the city, and they had lengthy affiliations with NHL clubs. The local Pepsi-Cola franchise owned the team and their colours and logo tied in with their brand. On five occasions, including their final season in 1969–70, the Bisons won the Calder Cup.

Buffalo originally sought an NHL franchise for the league's first modern expansion in 1967 but were turned down. Brothers Northrup and Seymour Knox III, who generated the bid, were not discouraged at all, and the two sportsmen even attempted to buy the troubled Oakland Seals before they were finally given a club of their own to start play in 1970–71.

The Knox brothers sought out one of the best hockey men at the time in Punch Imlach, who had already taken the Toronto Maple Leafs to four Stanley Cup championships as a coach and general manager. At the time, Imlach formed part of an ownership group for the WHL's

Vancouver Canucks, and once that team was sold to a company called Medicor, he walked away with a tidy profit and was able to come to Buffalo to get the Sabres up and running.

Unlike their expansion cousins in Vancouver, the Sabres did not start amassing talent through the purchase of minor league clubs. They began to throw together a solid group of players through the 1970 NHL Expansion Draft. Imlach picked a good mix of veterans and youngsters that included recognizable names such as Don Marshall, Phil Goyette and Reggie Fleming to go along with promising talents like Gerry Meehan and Al Hamilton. They traded Tom Webster to the Detroit Red Wings in exchange for the acrobatic Roger Crozier, but their biggest acquisition came a couple of days later.

The NHL decided to determine which expansion club was going to get the first overall pick in the 1970 NHL Amateur Draft through a spin of a roulette wheel. Imlach chose to take numbers 11–20 and, while it was initially thought that it had landed on number one, the crafty GM quietly pointed out that it had in fact landed on his lucky number, 11, just as the Canucks were celebrating. The prize pick that year was Gilbert Perreault and the Sabres built their team around him.

In the weeks leading up to the debut of the Sabres, Imlach boasted about his team's chances to the press.

"You can forget about Toronto and Vancouver. And the Red Wings didn't look like any ball of fire to me. We'll be there and you can bet on it. . . . Sure, we're a long way from being a good hockey club, but we'll get better. We made some mistakes we'll correct before camp breaks and we'll play as a unit. We'll need superior goaltending to win, and I feel we'll get it. Don't be a non-believer and count us out. We'll be there."

There was one major problem in training camp, though, because both Marshall and Goyette chose to retire. They eventually returned once the season began, but their presence was certainly missed in the early games. Defenceman Moose Vasko also announced his second retirement in camp.

The Sabres opened their first NHL season on the road and got a 2–1 win over the Pittsburgh Penguins on October 10, 1970, but their home debut was a rough one when they were shut out by the visiting Montreal Canadiens.

Perhaps the best moment for Buffalo in their first season came during their first visit to Toronto. Fans at Maple Leaf Gardens gave Imlach a standing ovation and the Sabres came through with a big 7–3 win. With a minute left in the game, there were chants of "We Want Punch!" He appreciated the efforts of his team.

"I have nothing to say. My players said it all for me and said it the way it counts. They knew how much this game meant to me. . . . This is wonderful . . . just wonderful. . . . No man ever managed and coached a team to four Stanley Cups, three in a row, and I can't see anyone topping that. I don't think I can spoil that. But I've done that. I'd like to go on winning Cups, but winning them with teams a lot of guys could win with wouldn't be so much. But, starting from scratch, taking a new team to the top, well, there's the challenge, there's something that would be worth all the sweating and cursing and suffering that comes with this job. Someone has to be the first to win a Stanley Cup with an expansion team. I say it'll be me."

Undaunted by a slow start with just four wins over 18 games, Imlach figured that he needed to make some trades to further motivate his men.

"If we can get one or two people who can do the job, we're in business. We haven't been sharp because we're going with a group of players that haven't been together before. This is par for the course with an expansion club. We're improving every time out and we'll keep getting better as we start playing as a unit."

The Sabres tried to wrangle away the rights to retired defenceman Leo Boivin from the Minnesota North Stars, but Imlach had more success in getting some of his former Maple Leafs charges through deals. Eddie Shack and Dick Duff arrived from the Los Angeles Kings, and with the return to action by Goyette and Marshall, Buffalo had the veteran leadership it was seeking.

"These guys will lend us the touch of class we need. You have to have a certain amount of experience, and these fellows have the know-how to get a club out of trouble."

(clockwise) Roger Crozier, Don Marshall, Gilbert Perreault

At the time, Imlach was also pulling double-duty, as he wrote a weekly column for the *Toronto Telegram*. Stafford Smythe complained to NHL headquarters about a column that suggested, among other claims, that the Maple Leafs were planning to dump Bruce Gamble and acquire another goalie.

"It is unfair when he can use a newspaper column to upset our team and hurt our morale when we are a club he is trying to beat out for a spot in the playoffs.... Punch always has to have a feud going. It's part of his nature and I don't object to it. I'm fair game. But I think he's wrong in attacking our club in this particular way."

NHL president Clarence Campbell was ready to put some limitations on what Imlach could say in the column in the future.

"I have had two objections to Mr. Imlach's writing. In view of the contents of the articles brought to my attention, I feel the protests were completely justified. As the general manager and coach of a team in the NHL, it is my feeling that Mr. Imlach should not comment on other general managers and coaches. That is, he should not comment in column form. If he is asked a question, he should answer it, but to comment as he has done in column form is clearly improper."

Naturally, Imlach voiced his displeasure at the decision.

"Anything I have ever put on my column is the truth. Furthermore, in no way have I ever hurt hockey, and if the time comes where I might, I would quit writing. I'm not trying to please everyone. I'm not trying to make everyone happy, and that includes the people who lodged the objections to my column."

As the season moved into its second half, the on-ice fortune of the team began to improve. Perreault began to ascend into superstardom when it looked as if he was going to set new scoring standards for a rookie performer.

"This club is coming together as a unit and that takes time," said captain Floyd Smith. "Remember, any expansion team is made up of players from a dozen different clubs. It takes time to build togetherness, and I can see where we will win a lot more games in the second half. And I'd like to think we'll be a healthier club, too."

During the final stretch of the season, the Sabres continued to compete despite being far out of a playoff spot. They ended the year with a 6–2–2 record over the last 10 games to finish in fifth place.

"I remember one guy who wrote we'd be lucky to finish the season," said Imlach. "Another said we wouldn't win 15 games. Well, with three to play, we've won 23, and we're going to finish ahead of teams which have been in this league from four to 40 years. . . . But I'll tell you this, we're in business now, and nobody, but nobody, handles us easily, anywhere. We're as established as any team in this league."

It did not take long for the Sabres to assert themselves as a contender. Once they added more talent with Richard Martin and Rene Robert to form the French Connection line with Perreault, they made the playoffs for the first time in 1972–73. Two years later, Buffalo reached the Stanley Cup Final, but lost in six games to Philadelphia. They remained a postseason regular until the mid-1980s and were a force in the following decade thanks in part to the fantastic goaltending of Dominik Hasek. In 1998–99, they made it to the final once again but lost to the Dallas Stars through a controversial overtime goal by Brett Hull that should not have counted because his skate was in the crease.

Over the past decade, the Sabres have at times dealt with uncertain ownership problems and have often struggled on the ice. Yet they have built a solid group of prospects and have loyal fans who were happy to see Terry Pegula purchase the club in 2011.

GILBERT PERREAULT

Perreault was an absolute phenomenon at the junior level with the Montreal Junior Canadiens and there was little doubt that he was going to be a high pick in the 1970 NHL Amateur Draft — especially after he scored 36 points over 12 games at the Memorial Cup that year. A spin of a wheel chose his fate before the draft; while the Vancouver Canucks thought they had won, Punch Imlach quickly pointed out that they were incorrect and walked away with the top selection.

When Perreault made his debut in Buffalo's opening game against Pittsburgh, he scored on Les Binkley at 11:36 of the first period and ensured victory for the Sabres.

"I made a move on the defenceman and was in the middle of their zone," he recalls today. "The goalie came out to get the puck and I took it and deked and made a quick move to the right side. You want to score your first goal as soon as possible and you want to prove that there was no mistake in drafting me."

After his strong start, Imlach began comparing the young star to some of the game's greatest players.

"I've been around the National Hockey League for a few years and I never saw anybody move as fast as Perreault did back of our net one shift. He can do it all. . . . It'll take a couple of years because the young man has a lot to learn, but right now at a comparable stage of his development, Perreault belongs at the same level of Gordie Howe, Bobby Hull and Jean Beliveau."

For Perreault, the respect for the boss was mutual.

"To me, the man had a big name in the NHL. I knew that he had won four Stanley Cups in Toronto. I had no problems with Punch. I believe we had good communication with each other. I was 20 years old and had a lot to learn. . . . When you look at Buffalo, it didn't take us long. In 1973, we made the playoffs and faced Montreal, and in 1975, we made the finals. Punch Imlach did a great job with the draft picks and the trades."

Many of Perreault's teammates were also impressed early on, including veteran Floyd Smith.

"We had the opportunity to watch him in practice. Imlach used to say to us, 'Get him the puck and get out of his way!' He was a really unselfish player and you knew he could have scored more than 500 goals."

For his return to the Montreal Forum, Perreault scored twice against the Canadiens on November 7, 1970, and he repeated the feat on December 26.

"I was really excited to play against the Canadiens. I knew a lot of the players and had been watching them for a couple years when I was in Montreal," he said. "You put the same effort in every city, but I was playing in front of my parents and friends. I had two goals, but we got beat. For every team, it's always special to play in Montreal."

When Perreault was selected to represent Buffalo at the 1971 NHL

All-Star Game, he had a strong showing among the game's best, and he went on to play in many more over the course of his career.

"It was a big thrill for me. I was very excited and I was trying to do my best to prove that I wasn't a mistake as the first pick."

On January 29, 1971, Perreault recorded the first hat trick of his career in a victory over the California Golden Seals. His second tally of the night was the winning goal, and the final one went into an empty net with less than 30 seconds left in the game. As the season wound down, it became obvious that he was about to set new NHL records for most goals and points in a rookie year. He had no problem accomplishing such feats, and at the end of the year, he earned the Calder Trophy and also picked up some votes for the Hart Trophy.

PHIL GOYETTE

Goyette, who had been a part of four straight Stanley Cup championships with Montreal between 1956–57 and 1959–60, joined St. Louis for the 1969–70 season. He set a new career high that year with 29 goals and 78 points, and his gentlemanly play allowed him to win the Lady Byng Trophy. Strangely, the Blues let him go through the expansion draft, and the Sabres added another veteran to their roster.

"I finished fourth in the league in scoring and was 37 years old," Goyette said. "I found it a little hard to take, because I had my best year and we went to the finals. Sometimes they don't protect you because they want to protect the young guns. I was a little perturbed, but I went to training camp. They didn't want to sign us to a contract, so Donnie Marshall and I quit. I sat out for a while, doubled my salary and came back."

He missed the first 16 games of the season, but it did not take him long to get back into form and he had three assists in a 4–4 tie with the Pittsburgh Penguins on November 25, 1970. He also had a huge night against Detroit on January 7, 1971, with a goal and four assists. A week later, he exacted some revenge on the Blues by scoring a pair that included the game-winner.

"We had a good veteran team, but a lot of the young guys had to learn," Goyette said. "With the veterans, Punch was a little different with us. He knew our capabilities, and we knew what we had to do. He was fair with me. At my age, I wasn't going to take guff from him or anyone else."

GERRY MEEHAN

After splitting his first NHL season between Toronto and Philadelphia in 1968–69, Meehan spent the following year in the minors with the WHL's Seattle Totems. He fell far enough off the radar with the Flyers organization that they barely noticed that the Sabres grabbed him in the expansion draft. That turned out to be a move that burned them later on.

"I'm sure Imlach knew about him," said Gilbert Perreault. "He was in the Toronto organization before Buffalo. He was a major part of the team. A great stickhandler and had a lot of talent."

Meehan had a great start with Buffalo that included a pair of assists in the season opener, and he also scored the first home-ice goal in franchise history in a rematch with the Pittsburgh Penguins on October 18, 1970. Four days later, he earned a pair of assists in a 4–2 loss to the Flyers, and on November 18, he was on fire in the big win over Toronto when he earned four points.

"Meehan is vastly improved from the time he was in Toronto," said Punch Imlach. "When I traded him, I felt his future in the National Hockey League was clouded. Now, he's found a natural position at centre and is playing extremely well. He is a much more aggressive player than he was, and this is the major thing. He's getting to the puck first and making big plays."

On February 20, 1971, he had a hat trick in a tight 6–5 loss to the Detroit Red Wings. At the end of the year, fans named Meehan the team's unsung hero. He spent several years with the Sabres, and his vengeance against the Flyers came during the final game of the 1971–72 campaign, when he scored with just four seconds on the clock to eliminate them from playoff contention.

EDDIE SHACK

The man known to millions of hockey fans as "The Entertainer," Shack was a part of four Stanley Cup victories with the Toronto Maple Leafs in the 1960s. At the beginning of the expansion era, he moved to the Boston Bruins and then ended up with the Los Angeles Kings for the 1969–70 season. He started the following year out west as well, but the Kings sent him and Dick Duff to Buffalo as part of a deal to get Mike McMahon.

Shack debuted with his new club when they hosted the California Golden Seals on November 29, 1970, and in his second outing four days later he registered two points against the Bruins. While some may have wondered if there were going to be problems between him and Imlach once again, Shack downplayed any sort of feud.

"I played for him for eight years and never had any more trouble with him than any other coach I've played for. When he traded me away to Boston for Murray Oliver, the Leafs also got $100,000. Punch made a lot of money for the club. That's all part of this business. I hated to leave my nice home in Los Angeles, but other than that, I'm happy to be in Buffalo and back with Punch."

Teammates also noticed the interesting dynamic between Shack and his coach.

"He was a funny guy," said Paul Andrea. "He'd be the first guy in the dressing room and the last one dressed. Punch would give him hell, and he'd say he could get dressed in six minutes — and wouldn't you know it, he'd be ready!"

From a goal-scoring perspective, the 1970–71 season was the best of Shack's career. Four of his tallies with the Sabres gave the first-year team much-needed wins. On February 4, 1971, he had a hat trick against the Kings, and one of those goals secured the victory. He had another three-goal night on March 21 as well, this time in a surprising 7–5 win over the Bruins.

"He wasn't a bad hockey player, but the way he skated and buffooned on the ice, he got a reputation as an entertainer," said Phil Goyette. "He did his job."

FLOYD SMITH

Smith had spent a little more than two seasons with the Toronto Maple Leafs and was coming off a rough year in 1969–70 when the team decided to dispatch him, along with Brent Imlach, to the Sabres in exchange for cash. Punch Imlach's decision to obtain his son's rights demonstrated nepotism at its finest, but the acquisition of Smith was something of a formality.

"I had known Punch for a long time and he asked me to come over to help put the first Sabres team together," said Smith.

Even though Smith's offensive production was waning, the Sabres looked upon him as a leader and named him their first captain. The team certainly had its share of growing pains, but he felt there was steady improvement throughout the year.

"For the first while, every guy was trying to find their way. It got much better toward the end of the season. We had a lot of good nights and a lot of bad nights."

There was probably no better night for a lot of the team than the battle with Toronto on November 18, 1970, and Smith had two assists in Imlach's heavily hyped return to Maple Leaf Gardens.

"There was no love lost between Stafford and Punch. They were in a continual fight. They weren't against having fun with each other. That was a huge, huge win for him."

Smith also had a great game when he scored twice against another one of his old clubs, the Detroit Red Wings, on December 12.

DAVE DRYDEN

Dryden spent the first two years of the expansion era as a backup to Denis DeJordy in Chicago, but the rise of Tony Esposito with that organization made him the odd man out in the Windy City. For a few months, Dryden stepped away from the game to get into teaching, but he was sold to the Pittsburgh Penguins, who then turned him around to the Sabres just before the 1970–71 season was set to begin.

Buffalo was in an interesting situation at the time, because the starting role was firmly held by Roger Crozier, but the backup job was going to be a contest between Joe Daley and Dryden.

"Punch was in the position of wanting to keep me around in case anything happened," he said. "He always showed a lot of confidence in me."

Since he saw little work in net, Dryden went to Imlach and requested a demotion to the minors to get some playing time. He played eight games with the Salt Lake Golden Eagles before being called back up. On March 14, 1971, the Sabres faced the Minnesota North Stars and he made 35 saves for a shutout victory.

Just six days later, he made NHL history when the Montreal Canadiens hosted Buffalo. The hockey world was buzzing about the possibility that he might face his younger brother, Ken, on the ice that night.

"Punch told me that he wanted to start me and was hoping that Al MacNeil would start Ken. I was out there for the opening faceoff, and Rogie Vachon started, so I got to sit on the bench. Ken and I had actually met the night before, which was unusual for me. He said that he didn't think he was going to start. We joked that if we were going to play against each other that we were going to meet at centre ice and shake hands. As soon as Ken got out there, my teammates were excited and got Punch to get me out there, too."

The Habs wound up winning the game by a score of 5–2, and Ken went on to lead the club to a Stanley Cup championship later that year. Dave remained with the Sabres until the end of the 1973–74 campaign.

JOE DALEY

Even though Pittsburgh claimed him from Detroit in the 1967 NHL Expansion Draft, Daley did not debut with the Penguins until the 1968–69 season. He spent a good chunk of the following year in the minors, and the Sabres seized the opportunity to pick him up on waivers before their first season was set to begin.

While it was nice for the Winnipeg native to get another shot at regular NHL work, he found himself in a three-way battle with Roger Crozier and Dave Dryden, both goalies who had more pro experience. Undaunted, he benefited from the tutelage of Crozier and ended up serving as the number two man in the crease over the course of the season.

One of the greatest tests of his career came on December 10, 1970, when he was sent out to protect the net from the Boston Bruins — a team arguably at its peak with big shooters like Phil Esposito and the incomparable Bobby Orr on the blue line. In all, he faced an incredible 72 shots, 30 of them in the third period! The final stanza was a goaltender's nightmare on many levels, but Daley remains proud of the game to this day.

"I played that game and it was tied after two periods," he said. "I thought we might have a shot at winning. I think Esposito had an offside goal and it just fell apart from there. There's not too many nights where you get beat that bad and have some positive memories about it."

Daley earned his third career shutout when the Sabres faced the California Golden Seals on February 12, 1971, and finished the season as the team's leader in wins with 12 triumphs. At the end of the year Buffalo dealt him away so they could bring in Don Luce and Mike Robitaille, young talent who helped them quickly rise to contention.

ROGER CROZIER

Crozier was the number one goalie for the Red Wings from 1964–65 to 1969–70. Although he helped the club to great success in the years before expansion, his success diminished after that because of an overall decline in Detroit that began in the late 1960s. He also battled pancreatitis during his last three seasons there.

After the Sabres made their picks from the established NHL teams, Detroit wanted to get Tom Webster back. When they offered up the veteran goaltender Crozier in exchange, Punch Imlach had no reservations about making the deal and was sure to let the press know about it.

"I want a major league goaltender . . . a guy with major league credentials who has proved he can do the job up here . . . and Crozier is just that man. For us to win, we must get superior goaltending."

One of Buffalo's major strengths going into their first year was the men they had to protect the crease, and Crozier became the clear-cut number one from the start. He was in net for their opening game with Pittsburgh and turned back 35 shots in the 2–1 victory.

"Any time we get the kind of goalkeeping Roger gave us in Pittsburgh, we've got a chance no matter who we're playing," said

Imlach. "Let's face it, we're an expansion team and it will take us time to come together. Goaltending can turn around a lot of games for us. Crozier was just great. A big save lifts any club and his big saves lifted us."

Over the first few weeks, he performed admirably despite the deluge of rubber being shot his way. He earned the first shutout in franchise history on December 6, 1970, in a 1-0 triumph over the Minnesota North Stars.

"Roger and I got along well, even though he was an elite goaltender," said Joe Daley. "We had a lot of conversations about all aspects of the game. There were nights early in the season when we should have lost by double digits, and he kept us in there."

Crozier's stomach woes popped up again around Christmas and he was out for a few weeks. By the end of the season, he was clearly one of the top acquisitions for the Sabres and he remained with them for several years after. In 1976–77, he made his final NHL appearance as a member of the Washington Capitals.

Crozier died on January 11, 1996. The league honours his memory with the Roger Crozier Saving Grace Award, which is given annually to the goaltender who registers the best save percentage.

"Roger was a guy with experience from Detroit. As a young kid, it was really exciting to watch him," said Gilbert Perreault. "He had a very spectacular style and was a great goalie. It's too bad his health wasn't 100 percent and I guess he was really nervous. He was a great goaltender to watch and in our first year he was our key player. You needed a key goaltender and he was one of them. We had a pretty good season because of him."

EXPANSION YEAR RECORD: 24-46-8
(56 points — sixth in East Division)
COACH: Hal Laycoe
GENERAL MANAGER: Bud Poile
FIRST GAME: October 9, 1970 —
3-1 loss vs. Los Angeles Kings
FIRST GOAL: October 9, 1970 by Barry Wilkins

VANCOUVER CANUCKS

Vancouver's rich pro hockey history dates back to 1911–12, when Lester and Frank Patrick created the Pacific Coast Hockey Association and made the Millionaires one of the new loop's marquee clubs. The team's success had a lot to do with the presence of the legendary Cyclone Taylor, and in 1914–15, they won the city's only Stanley Cup championship. The team was a perennial contender and eventually changed its name to the Maroons in 1922–23. They played their last two seasons in the WCHL and WHL before the death of western pro hockey.

For nearly 50 years, save for a rare exhibition contest, the highest level of pro hockey disappeared from British Columbia, but that did not mean the sport went away for locals. Senior hockey was always popular in smaller towns, and the Western Hockey League featured teams in Victoria and Vancouver. The Vancouver club was called the Canucks and began in the Pacific Coast Hockey League (PCHL) in 1945 before it merged with the Western Canada Senior Hockey League seven years later. The team lasted for 25 seasons and won six league championships between 1946 and 1970.

When the NHL first announced its plans for expansion in 1965, the citizens of Vancouver were chomping at the bit to finally become a part of the biggest league around. Even though they put their best foot forward during the application process, team owner Fred Hume and his group were turned down by the NHL. Speculators believe they were blocked by the Toronto Maple Leafs and Montreal Canadiens, who did not want to share television revenues. They also did not have an NHL-level arena to play in, and some reported that their overconfidence resulted in a weak proposal that made a poor impression on NHL owners.

The winds began to change during the 1967–68 season, and there was a movement afoot to transfer the financially troubled Oakland Seals north to Vancouver. Since the league wanted to avoid embarrassment, they chose to keep the team in California and made a promise that Vancouver was going to get a team the next time the NHL wished to expand. A group headed by Tom Scallen pitched the league and paid a whopping six million dollars for the right to join in 1970. They also had to first purchase the WHL club. A new era was set to begin — but not until after the Canucks won their final Lester Patrick Cup.

The Canucks had several WHL vets from the championship team already under contract and added some prime talent through the 1970 NHL Expansion Draft. Their first selection was rock-hard defender Gary Doak from the Boston Bruins, and they followed that by taking tough Orland Kurtenbach from the Rangers. From there, they picked some prime talents like Rosaire Paiement, Pat Quinn and the versatile Poul Popiel, and they also got some good goaltenders in young Dunc Wilson and former Vezina Trophy recipient Charlie Hodge. In the amateur draft, they used the second overall pick to get a promising blueliner in Dale Tallon. Kurtenbach was named their first captain and was to be assisted by Doak and veteran Ray Cullen. Overall, the Canucks drew praise from many before their first NHL season.

"This team has a lot more potential than the one I started with in Oakland," commented former Seals coach and general manager Bert Olmstead. "Not only that, it has a chance to be better right now. On paper, we looked like a pretty good club our first year in Oakland. Some of the veterans we had didn't come through for us, and by the time we got around to making some trades it was too late; and perhaps most important of all, the Canucks will play their first season in Vancouver. We had to play ours in Oakland."

The Canucks made their NHL debut against the visiting Los Angeles Kings on October 9, 1970, and the crowd roared when Cyclone Taylor made a pre-game appearance. Their first goal was scored by Barry Wilkins, but they lost the opener by a 3–1 margin. Even though they narrowly missed tallying twice in the first period when shots hit the posts, coach Hal Laycoe was not happy with the results.

"You can't really say we deserved to win, but if one of those first period shots had hit the net instead of the post, it would have given us a tremendous lift. . . . Then, who knows what might have happened?"

They didn't need to wait long for their first victory, though, as they beat the visiting Toronto Maple Leafs two days later. Although the wins were infrequent over the first month, they did get a lot of scoring from the line of Kurtenbach, Wayne Maki and Murray Hall. From November 20 to 24, they won three straight games, but the losses piled up, especially after their captain went down with torn knee ligaments, and they were out of playoff contention rather early.

After the loss of Kurtenbach, several other players tried to pick up the slack. Paiement started putting the puck in the net, and Tallon, who was often the target of jeers at home, managed to establish a new NHL rookie scoring record for defencemen. In January, GM Bud Poile lashed out at Laycoe for being too soft and at several players for not carrying their weight. Tensions began to run high and, following a 6–1 loss to Buffalo on January 31, 1971, Laycoe almost seemed resigned to what his team's fate was.

"Coaching an expansion club has to be the toughest job in the world," he said. "Because when the going gets tough, the tough don't always get going."

Sabres coach Punch Imlach also fuelled the fires by referring to the Canucks as a 4F team — fumbling, frustrated, futile and folding.

Kurtenbach's return to the lineup was a case of too little, too late. Vancouver ended the year with a strong 3–1–1 finish, in sixth place in the East Division and just a point ahead of the Detroit Red Wings in the standings. At the box office, they were a smash; 98 percent of tickets were sold. They even showed some games on closed-circuit television when there was not a seat to be had in the house. But their often insane travel schedule certainly took a toll on players throughout the year.

With one season under their belt, it was apparent the Canucks had a

(clockwise) Andre Boudrias, Rosaire Paiement, Dale Tallon, Orland Kurtenbach

long road ahead to become contenders. Over the next three years they experienced seventh-place finishes. But after they acquired Gary Smith and developed some key prospects, they enjoyed a first-place finish in the Smythe Division in 1974–75. That initial success was somewhat short lived, but eventually the club bounced back and made the post-season six straight years from 1978–79 to 1983–84. Naturally, the highlight of that period was their run to the Stanley Cup Final in 1981–82, but they were swept in four straight by the New York Islanders.

For the rest of the 1980s, Vancouver was perennially on the bubble when it came to making the playoffs. In the early part of the next decade, they finally became a powerhouse with talents like Trevor Linden, Kirk McLean and Pavel Bure leading the way. In 1993–94, they were back in the Stanley Cup Final once again but lost a close seven-game series to the New York Rangers.

Soon after, the Canucks went through a disappointing four-season playoff drought, but they rose up again in 2000–01 and have remained competitive since then thanks to stars like Todd Bertuzzi, Roberto Luongo and the Sedin brothers. In 2010–11, the Canucks came close to tasting champagne from Lord Stanley's Mug for the first time but lost to the Boston Bruins in a thrilling seven-game matchup. They took the frustration of that loss and turned it into a league championship the next year but were eliminated in the first round by the Los Angeles Kings, their quest for their first Cup once again placed on hold.

ANDRE BOUDRIAS

The 1969-70 season was one of the most frustrating of Boudrias's career, as he had an uncharacteristic 17 points over 50 games with St. Louis and was sent down to the minors. Instead of letting it get him down, though, he averaged more than a point per game on the farm and was back in time for a run to the Stanley Cup Final. Soon after, the Blues traded him to the new Vancouver Canucks for a pair of draft picks, giving Vancouver a potential first-line playmaker on the roster.

With the change of scenery, he became an instant hit and had a goal and two assists in an early-season battle with Toronto on October 11, 1970. Four days later, he was the author of the first power-play tally for the Canucks as they took on Philadelphia. As the 1970–71 campaign moved on, he had winning goals against the Golden Seals and Kings, but he was particularly impressive in a battle with Montreal on February 22, 1971, when he scored twice in a 3–3 tie.

The smallest player in the league, Boudrias was known for being a thorn in the side of opposing stars. A Vancouver disc jockey wrote a song called "Superpest" as a tribute to his play. Even Phil Esposito, who was in the midst of a then-record season in which he scored 76 goals, was held to just three in games against the Canucks. In fact, it was reported that Espo was on a salmon fishing trip and when he did not get any bites, he said, "I bet that damn Boudrias is down there!"

WAYNE MAKI

Maki followed his older brother, Chico, into a pro hockey career, but while he was with the St. Louis Blues, he was involved in a vicious stick-swinging pre-season incident with Boston's Ted Green on September 21, 1969, in which the Bruins' veteran defender sustained a fractured skull. In the aftermath, Maki split the 1969–70 campaign between the St. Louis Blues and the Buffalo Bisons of the AHL.

Maki was given a new lease on his NHL career when the Canucks called his name during the expansion draft and placed him on a line with Murray Hall and Orland Kurtenbach. The trio put up big numbers during the early stages of the 1970–71 season. He scored the first game-winning goal in franchise history on October 11, 1970, against the Toronto Maple Leafs. What many observers were watching out for, however, was the first on-ice meeting between Maki and Green a week later. The game went without incident, and while Maki found it difficult to talk about what had transpired in the past, Green considered it water under the bridge.

"It never even entered my head," he said. "It's over. It was over a long time ago."

Later on in the season, Maki began to struggle while Kurtenbach was out with an injury, but on March 28, 1971, he scored a hat trick and chipped in two assists against California. He finished the year second on the team in scoring and established career marks in goals and assists.

Maki's tale had a tragic ending, though, when he passed away on May 1, 1974, from brain cancer. The Canucks unofficially retired his number, but it was brought back into circulation when Mark Messier joined the club in 1997–98.

ROSAIRE PAIEMENT

After three frustrating seasons of minimal playing time with the Philadelphia Flyers, Paiement was ready to become an NHL regular with the second round of expansion, and the Canucks made sure to get him on draft day.

He did not have to wait long to get revenge on his old club when he tallied a goal and an assist in Vancouver's first meeting with Philadelphia on October 15, 1970. Just 12 days later, he scored his first of four game-winners of the year in a victory against Buffalo.

As the season progressed, Hal Laycoe threw Paiement on top offensive-lines. He unleashed an impressive four goals in another meeting with the Sabres on February 9, 1971. He was on fire at that point in the season, and a week later, he had a hat trick plus an assist in a big win over the Boston Bruins. When the two clubs met again on February 25, Paiement was a marked man. He scored the opening goal but also got into two fights with the legendary Bobby Orr. What the phenomenal Bruin defender was not expecting was to be dropped with two punches by the son of an arm wrestler from Northern Ontario.

"Rosie was tough and could throw them with the best. He wasn't a great skater and he found that the more he kicked the shit out of guys, the more room he got," said Bobby Schmautz.

By the end end of the 1970–71 campaign, Paiement led the Canucks with 34 goals and was third on the club in points.

DALE TALLON

In the years leading up to his arrival in the NHL, Tallon was one of the most accomplished junior golfers in Canada, but he chose hockey as a career path instead. His father, Stan, had made it to the AHL years earlier. A standout for the Toronto Marlboros, Tallon was regarded as a potential high pick for the 1970 NHL Amateur Draft, and after the

Canucks lost a spin of the wheel for the first pick, they gladly took him as the second overall selection.

In training camp, Tallon demonstrated a great deal of versatility, and it was decided that he was going to start on defence. He also battled several health issues and took some criticism for showing up 10 pounds overweight.

"I guess we have to face facts. As a junior, the kid had so much talent he could play anywhere, but in the NHL, it looks as if defence is the place he belongs," said general manager Bud Poile.

Coach Hal Laycoe believed that it was a move in the right direction for the young prospect.

"He seemed more comfortable there, though it puts more pressure on him than playing forward would. A kid can play some bad games as a forward and no one notices much and it may not hurt the team too much. Any mistakes a kid makes on defence may result in goals against and he'll be spotlighted. But this kid is tough, mentally as well as physically, and seems to be able to handle it. He's going to be a great one."

It did not take Tallon long to make an impact, as he registered his first goal and assist in October before returning to Toronto, where he had a two-point night on November 7, 1970. Even as a rookie, he demonstrated a great deal of maturity and adapted quickly to the pace of NHL play.

"I'll tell you, it's really something to be in the NHL at 20," he said. "I think when I'm 40, I'll appreciate it even more. I hope I'm still here. The big thing you notice making the jump from juniors is the accelerated pace. Everyone is making every move faster, so you have to do so, too, but without making mistakes. When you make one, you have to learn from it. Every arena has a different atmosphere. When I've played in each one, I'll know what to expect as I travel the circuit. The older players have made me feel welcome and have helped me. I can't think of anything I'd rather be doing. It's like a dream. It's rough, but I'm feeling no pain."

After he was selected to play in the 1971 NHL All-Star Game, Tallon brought his game to a new level in the second half of the year and began to challenge for the rookie scoring record for defencemen.

Bobby Orr held the mark at the time with 41 points during the 1966–67 campaign. By the end of the regular schedule Tallon had shattered that standard with assists alone. He was on fire in the final stretch and had multi-point games against Detroit, Chicago and California during the month of March. Tallon finished the year third among all defenders in scoring, behind Orr and Montreal's J.C. Tremblay, and was recognized with 12 votes for the Calder Trophy as the NHL's Rookie of the Year.

ORLAND KURTENBACH

A big and tough leader on the ice, Kurtenbach had been playing professionally for more than a decade when the Canucks snatched him away from the New York Rangers in the expansion draft. What nobody could predict, however, was the incredible impact he had as Vancouver's first captain during the 1970–71 season.

His first tally of the year came while the team was shorthanded in a surprising 5–3 win over the Toronto Maple Leafs on October 11, 1970. From then on, the points kept piling up, and he even had back-to-back winning goals against Los Angeles in November. On December 12, he recorded the first hat trick in franchise history in a battle with the California Golden Seals.

The wild ride came to a very abrupt end, however, when he missed nearly two months of action with torn knee ligaments. After such a loss to their lineup, the Canucks began to slip into the lower rungs of the standings and were unable to recover.

Kurtenbach returned to action against Toronto on March 3, 1971, and at the end of the year, was voted the team's Most Valuable Player. The recognition for his work was also apparent when voting totals for the Hart Trophy were announced and he finished in seventh place.

"He was very respected throughout the league. A real good captain and a good leader," said teammate Ray Cullen.

POUL POPIEL

Popiel spent two seasons with the Detroit Red Wings before he joined the Canucks, but he was back in the minors for part of the 1969–70 campaign. His reputation for strong defensive play made him one of the best players available in the expansion draft, and he ended up a member of the Vancouver Canucks.

"When I got to Vancouver, I knew it was an open book," he said. "When I started the year, Ted Taylor sat out, and I was told that I could play as a defenceman or at left wing. I became the anchor on a line with Andre Boudrias and Rosaire Paiement."

Popiel's rambunctious play certainly earned him a lot of attention. He had a two-goal night against the Buffalo Sabres on November 5, 1970, scoring the winning marker on Roger Crozier at 2:03 of the second period. Approximately five weeks later, he had another difference-maker for the Canucks in a 5–2 drubbing of the California Golden Seals.

The early-season success for the Canucks inspired Popiel, and he spoke about the overall mood of his teammates.

"I thought we were strong and were a tough hockey team. We felt really good in the dressing room before the game. We felt confident and like we could handle anyone."

PAT QUINN

Players throughout the league were aware of Quinn's skills as a physical defender after he had two seasons with the Toronto Maple Leafs — especially after he laid out Boston's Bobby Orr with a vicious hit in the 1968–69 playoffs. Vancouver selected him during the expansion draft to help give the team an edge during their first season.

With Vancouver, Quinn was able to get in nearly a full season at the NHL level. His first assist in a Canucks uniform was on Andre Boudrias's game-winning goal, which downed the California Golden Seals on October 20, 1970. Often partnered on the blue line with Gary Doak, he had a power-play goal and added an assist on November 4, in a tough 8–3 loss to the Pittsburgh Penguins. At the end of the year, Quinn ranked second on the team in penalty minutes.

GARY DOAK

Dependable Doak was a role player for the "Big Bad Bruins" club leading up to their Stanley Cup triumph in 1969–70. But since the team had so many great defencemen, at least one of them was going to be exposed in the NHL Expansion Draft. Drawing the short straw, he was taken with Vancouver's first selection to anchor their blue-line corps.

Often the victim of ill-timed injuries, Doak appeared in a career-high 77 games in 1970–71 and was named an alternate captain for the Canucks. His first of two goals in the season came while playing the Philadelphia Flyers on December 1, 1970, and to that point it was only the seventh tally of his career. His frustration built into a clash with coach Hal Laycoe in early February, but the matter was quickly smoothed over. At the end of the year, Doak was named the team's top defenceman because of his excellent play.

"We stayed friends ever since those days," said Ray Cullen. "He came from Boston, who had just won a Stanley Cup. He was very dedicated and couldn't wait to get on the ice."

BOBBY SCHMAUTZ

Schmautz played parts of two seasons with the Chicago Black Hawks early in the expansion era, but despite showing some promise at the minor league level, he had problems with coach Billy Reay and didn't get much chance to show what he could do on ice. At the end of the 1968–69 season, he bounced around to the St. Louis Blues and Montreal Canadiens, but he ended up back in the WHL and spent most of the next two years with the Seattle Thunderbirds.

Schmautz had a good start in 1970–71 with the Totems, but the Vancouver Canucks needed a bit more scoring talent on the roster and they sent two young players down to Seattle for the 25-year-old winger.

"When I was brought up, it was halfway through the year," he recalled. "I was very happy to be in the Western Hockey League, but when I got the chance to go into Vancouver, it was strictly a money deal. They were going to double my salary. Vancouver treated me royally when I was there."

On February 12, 1971, Schmautz had his first goal with the Canucks, assisted by Ray Cullen, against Jim Rutherford of the Detroit Red

Wings. He made some decent contributions as the season drew to a close, including a two-point night playing the Pittsburgh Penguins on March 19. He repeated the feat four days later when Vancouver hosted the St. Louis Blues.

DUNC WILSON

Wilson spent two years in the AHL with the Quebec Aces and made his NHL debut with the Philadelphia Flyers during the 1969–70 season. Stuck behind Bernie Parent and Doug Favell, however, he was not getting much chance at big-league action. The Canucks made him the first goalie they chose in the expansion draft.

"I think Wilson has a chance to become an outstanding NHL goalie," said general manager Bud Poile.

At the beginning of the season, Vancouver used a rotation of three goaltenders. Wilson debuted with the club on October 12, 1970, when they took on the St. Louis Blues. He did not get the victory, but he did register his first win against the Buffalo Sabres in the second clash between the expansion cousins on November 5. The triumphs were scarce after that (both came against California), but Wilson saw a ton of action following the retirement of Charlie Hodge and took over as the team's top man in the crease the next year.

CHARLIE HODGE

Hodge was nearly at the end of his remarkable pro career during his three-year stint with the Oakland Seals. The Canucks thought he might have at least one more good year left in him when they made him the second goaltender they selected in the expansion draft.

Hodge did not get the call for the season opener against Los Angeles (George Gardner was in net), but his experience was exactly what they needed during their second game on October 11, 1970, when he came away with a big win against the Toronto Maple Leafs. From then on, he led the team in victories and was Vancouver's best goaltender by far in their expansion year.

As the season began to wind down, however, Hodge knew that

retirement was his best option. His last NHL contest came in a loss to the Minnesota North Stars on March 21, 1971. He chose to take up an offer to work as a scout for the Canucks and later held a similar role with Winnipeg, Pittsburgh and Tampa Bay.

THE RIVAL
LEAGUE

For more than 45 years, the NHL faced no serious competition from any other professional league. But their dominance of the sport ensured that someone would eventually challenge them for hockey supremacy. In football, the NFL faced competition from the American Football League, and the two leagues eventually merged. In basketball, the NBA had the American Basketball Association (ABA) as the thorn in their side in the early 1970s.

The ABA had been the brainchild of promoting duo Dennis Murphy and Gary Davidson and it proved a modest success. The pair next set their sights on hockey, partnering up with "Wild" Bill Hunter, who owned the junior Edmonton Oil Kings, and began the process of putting together a hockey league to rival the NHL. They announced their intention for the World Hockey Association (WHA) to begin play in 1972–73.

Most hockey fans scoffed at the notion that a new loop might seriously challenge the status quo of the game, but their skepticism was quickly countered when hundreds of players signed contracts with the new teams. The world was shocked by the biggest of these signings as Bobby Hull joined the Winnipeg Jets, and other stars like J.C. Tremblay, Gerry Cheevers and Derek Sanderson followed suit.

The primary reason for this mass exodus of talent was money. NHL players were underpaid when compared with athletes from other sports, even after the formation of the NHL Players' Association a few years earlier. The WHA owners opened up their vaults and salaries rose dramatically on both sides as a result.

When the 1972–73 season began, hockey fans were treated to 12 new teams that worked hard every night to help the WHA become a long-term fixture. While there were legal challenges to Hull's status with the Jets, and small crowds in some arenas, most teams did well and came back the following year.

The WHA began to challenge the NHL head on by drafting 18-year-old players. They also scored a major coup when they brought Gordie Howe out of retirement to play alongside his sons, Mark and Marty, with the Houston Aeros. Many young prospects followed suit, and the NHL was forced to reduce its draft age.

In time, the WHA expanded to 14 teams, but the dilution of the talent pool and the rise of violence in the game proved a lethal combination in some markets. Many teams were moved or even folded, and a lot of weird and wacky stories began to pop up in the press.

The WHA lasted just seven seasons but it left an indelible mark on the game of hockey. Just four teams were admitted into the NHL, but fans, players and executives still fondly recall the league's heyday.

"The whole seven-year experience was a great experience for me," said Howard Baldwin during the 1979–80 season. "It was certainly worth the effort. It was a thrill to create something, then follow it to where it is today. . . . Sure, there were frustrations with the WHA. The most painful thing was to see three, four or even five clubs doing a major league job. The four who are in the NHL always did a good job. I thought Birmingham and Cincy didn't do a bad job. But there were some who ripped us off."

EXPANSION AND FRANCHISE SHIFTS FOR THE WORLD HOCKEY ASSOCIATION
1972-73

The World Hockey Association begins play with 12 different clubs: the Alberta Oilers, Chicago Cougars, Cleveland Crusaders (originally the Calgary Broncos), Houston Aeros (originally the Dayton Arrows), Los Angeles Sharks (originally the Aces), Minnesota Fighting Saints, New

England Whalers, New York Raiders, Ottawa Nationals, Philadelphia Blazers (originally the Miami Screaming Eagles), Quebec Nordiques (originally the San Francisco Sharks) and Winnipeg Jets.

At the end of the season, the Ottawa Nationals played their home playoff games out of Toronto's Maple Leaf Gardens.

1973-74

The Alberta Oilers change their name to the Edmonton Oilers.

The New York Raiders become the New York Golden Blades. After 20 games and playing to small home crowds, they are moved to Cherry Hill, New Jersey, and become the Jersey Knights.

The Toronto Toros begin play after spending the previous year as the Ottawa Nationals.

The Philadelphia Blazers move west to become the Vancouver Blazers.

1974-75

The WHA expands to 14 teams that are split into three divisions — Canadian, East and West. The two new expansion clubs are the Indianapolis Racers and the Phoenix Roadrunners.

The Jersey Knights relocate before the season starts and are now known as the San Diego Mariners.

After two seasons, the Los Angeles Sharks move to the Detroit area to play as the Michigan Stags. The team folds on January 18, 1975, and changes its home base to Baltimore. The Blades finish out the year and the franchise is terminated after a failure to move them to Seattle.

1975-76

Following two seasons in Vancouver, the Blazers are moved and become the Calgary Cowboys.

After the Baltimore Blades fold, the WHA adds the Denver Spurs, but it proves a disastrous move, as they last only 34 games thanks to financial woes and low attendance. The players are told of the decision to rename them the Ottawa Civics before the January 2, 1976, game against Cincinnati. As the Civics, the club did not even have an official logo. Instead, they simply wore Spurs jerseys with the crests removed! They stick around for six more games and then shut down for good. Most of the players are dispersed by the league or declared free agents.

The Spurs/Civics are not the only WHA team to shut down in 1975–76. The Minnesota Fighting Saints call it quits after 59 games. Despite a winning record, their box office struggles are too great and they officially cease operations on February 28, 1976.

1976-77

The WHA is now down to 12 teams, and they are split into East and West Divisions. After constant battles, the Toronto Toros are moved south and become the Birmingham Bulls. A new version of the Minnesota Fighting Saints is born when the Cleveland Crusaders are moved because of local competition from a new NHL club, the Barons. This time, the club lasts just 42 contests before going under.

1977-78

The loss of teams continues to be a problem when the San Diego Mariners, Calgary Cowboys and Phoenix Roadrunners do not return for another year. Now down to eight clubs in a single division, the WHA decides to count exhibition games against touring teams from the Soviet Union and Czechoslovakia in the standings.

1978-79

Now in their seventh season, the WHA is ready to merge with the NHL. Only four of the remaining seven teams make the cut. The Houston Aeros shuts their doors well before the season starts, and despite having a 17-year-old wonder named Wayne Gretzky in their line to start the year, the Indianapolis Racers fold after 25 outings.

At the end of the year, only the Edmonton Oilers, New England Whalers, Quebec Nordiques and Winnipeg Jets are admitted into the NHL.

EXPANSION YEAR RECORD: 25-38-15
(65 points — seventh in West Division)
COACH: Bernie Geoffrion
GENERAL MANAGER: Cliff Fletcher
FIRST GAME: October 7, 1972 —
3-2 win vs. New York Islanders
FIRST GOAL: October 7, 1972 by Morris Stefaniw

ATLANTA FLAMES

A little more than a century after General Sherman burned down the city of Atlanta, the city experienced an ice age in the form of its first NHL hockey team.

The roots of the Atlanta club stemmed to 1968 when Tom Cousins purchased the NBA's St. Louis Hawks and moved them to Georgia. In the team's formative years, a new arena was built and the Omni Sports Group decided to approach the NHL to obtain an expansion franchise. The league granted them one on November 9, 1971, and they hired former Philadelphia Flyers executive Bill Putnam a few weeks later to serve as the team's president.

The nameless club went on a hiring blitz over the next few months as the arena was being built. They hired former St. Louis Blues assistant general manager Cliff Fletcher as the new GM, and Don Graham was brought in as their director of scouting. On the coaching side, Hall of Famer Bernie "Boom Boom" Geoffrion was pegged as bench boss, since he had previous experience as coach of the AHL's Quebec Aces.

Just days before the 1972 NHL Expansion Draft, it was announced that the club was going to be called the Flames, even though that name was only on 198 of the 10,000 ballots submitted as part of a contest. To break the tie to determine a winner, a rationale had to be given on each entry, and the prize went to a college student named Mickey Goodman.

On draft day, the Flames took goaltenders Dan Bouchard and Phil Myre, along with a good mix of veterans and young players. In the amateur draft, they had the second selection overall and grabbed Jacques Richard from the Quebec Major Junior Hockey League's Quebec Remparts. They also announced that the team's official colours were going to be red, white and gold.

One of the advantages the Flames had over their expansion cousins in New York is that they did not lose a lot of talent to the new World Hockey Association. Only Rod Zaine and Larry Hale did not end up in Atlanta and, since both were marginal NHL players, their presence was not necessarily missed. The club was looking strong on a defensive level, but according to the pundits they were missing some depth up front, and it did not help when Lucien Grenier broke his leg during an exhibition game.

"We play New York three times during exhibition, then we open the season against them," said Geoffrion at the time. "I want to beat them all three so that when we go into New York for the opener, my boys will have the confidence that they can walk all over that team. We'll hit hard, too. I will tell my boys to go out and, ah, have a little fun with them, eh?"

Since they went 2–0–1 against the Isles in training camp, they did not have much trouble securing a road victory in their NHL debut on October 7. Morris Stefaniw scored the first goal that night and Bob Leiter got the winner. Over the first half of the season, the team looked promising, earning a whopping 41 points over 39 outings — a total that surpassed what Philadelphia and Minnesota had done five years earlier. This record is impressive considering the Flames faced more Original Six teams than the other clubs did.

Defenceman Randy Manery offered his thoughts at the time on what made the team run.

"Pride," he said. "Everybody in the whole league is waiting for us to fall. They've been calling us the worst of the expansion teams. So we've got a whole lot to prove. Something, somewhere, deep within us gets us back on the ice again. We do it individually. There's no one big holler-guy, nobody who can pick us up by himself. We've got to do it on our own. Lemme tell you this, ain't nobody on this team gonna take a fall. Tell the rest of the league that. We'll be around."

Captain Keith McCreary also had positive things to say.

"There is a great harmony on this club. We believe in ourselves, in each other, and in Bernie [Geoffrion]. We know we're not the club that Montreal or Boston or New York Rangers are. But with a few breaks and some luck, we can beat anybody. We know that because we have already."

Some key pickups, like Curt Bennett and Leon Rochefort, helped that success, but a lot of it had to do with the coaching they received. Geoffrion rarely raised his voice in practice and he offered personal instruction whenever he noticed a mistake.

Geoffrion once spoke with Vince Lombardi at a sports luncheon in New York and asked the legendary football coach for his secret in getting players to be mentally prepared for the game. Lombardi imparted seven words of wisdom, but Boomer would not reveal it to the press — only to his players — even if they didn't realize it at the time.

"Lombardi told me there were three secrets: discipline, respect, and, you'll never know the third. That's my secret and I guarantee you, I can use it to get my players higher than any other coach by a country mile. . . . I can use those seven words in many different combinations. Never the same. But the meaning is always the same and it works. Boy, does it work! I rarely use it before a game. Normally, I use it in my meeting with the players after their steak early in the afternoon. Though it is hardly ever the same, they get the message."

Where things started to fall apart for the Flames, however, was with the extended road trips, which began to take a toll on the team. Despite their geographic location, they were placed in the West Division and played in enemy arenas over five straight games while the circus was in town from February 14 to 25, 1973, managing just three points. Their second half featured just 10 wins over 39 contests, and they were eliminated from playoff contention.

The Flames made it to the postseason for the first time in 1973–74, but in the long run, they did not end up staying in Atlanta. A combination of rising operating costs and reduced ticket sales proved lethal, and they were sold to a group headed up by businessman Nelson Skalbania that moved them to Calgary after the 1979–80 campaign. In their new

(clockwise) Curt Bennett, Randy Manery, Jacques Richard, Dan Bouchard

surroundings, the club finally won a playoff series in their first year there and eventually captured a Stanley Cup in 1988–89.

BOB LEITER

Leiter began his NHL career with the Boston Bruins in the early 1960s, but he was exiled to the minors for several seasons and battled some serious injuries before he was picked up by the Pittsburgh Penguins for the 1971-72 campaign. He played a full NHL season for the first time and managed a respectable 31 points. Taken late in the expansion draft, he seemed almost an afterthought for the Flames, but the result made them seem shrewd in retrospect.

When Leiter showed up for training camp, he wore a toupée, but quickly abandoned it. He ended up using some hair tonic instead for a while, but by the end of the year, he had secured an endorsement deal for hairpieces even though he wore a helmet on the ice!

On October 7, 1972, Leiter scored the first game-winning goal for the Flames in a clash with their expansion cousins, the New York Islanders. In November, he began to show fans in Atlanta what he was capable of when he had a two-goal night against Minnesota, another game-winner while playing the Philadelphia Flyers and earned three assists in a 6–2 victory over the Pittsburgh Penguins.

"Going into camp, I only hoped our team could be respectable. We've surprised ourselves," he said. "I'm pleased at the season I'm having individually and at the season we're having collectively. We've worked hard and played as a team, and I hope it keeps paying off."

Originally, the team wanted to play up his defensive strengths on a line with Lucien Grenier and Lew Morrison, but he blossomed offensively with the Flames.

"I guess I'm more relaxed this season," he said. "Last year with Pittsburgh, I got benched when I made a mistake. Red [Kelly] is like that. He often benched me when it was somebody else's fault. So I played scared. This year, I know that I can make a mistake and still get back out there. I know Boomer's gonna give me my chance. So as a consequence, I'm more relaxed, loose on the ice.

"I try to stick around the goal and catch rebounds, maybe a tip shot or two. Heck, I'm too small to just lodge myself there in the slot and wing it like an Esposito. I get shoved out of the way if I try it. So I just rove, picking up the pieces."

Coach Bernie Geoffrion felt that playing to Leiter's strengths was the key to his success.

"Nobody ever worked with him. Nobody ever gave him the confidence to be a scorer. I knew he could be a scorer for me, though. I was sure of it. I've always liked Bobby Leiter. Everybody has tried to make him a defensive hockey player. He's not. He's a scorer and he's got to get that confidence he needs to shoot the puck."

LARRY ROMANCHYCH

Drafted by Chicago in 1969, Romanchych (pronounced Ro-man-chuck) spent the bulk of three pro seasons in the CHL with the Dallas Black Hawks and was part of the team that won the Adams Cup in 1971–72. He was the 12th pick in the expansion draft. The Flames realized he was short on NHL experience but were willing to give him a shot at making the club.

Although he was sidelined with a dislocated left kneecap early in the season, Romanchych came back quickly and earned his first point of the year when he assisted on a goal by Ernie Hicke against Pittsburgh on November 18, 1972. The next night, he scored twice in a battle with the Philadelphia Flyers and also added an assist in the 3–2 victory. He was on fire in mid-January, and *The Hockey News* named him the West Player of the Week after he scored the only goal in a 1–0 win over Toronto on January 12, 1973, and got two goals, including the winner, against the Los Angeles Kings two days later.

At the end of the year, Romanchych placed sixth among rookie scorers. He went on to spend five seasons with the Flames.

KEITH MCCREARY

Heading into their first season, the Flames knew they were going to need some veteran leadership and they found it in McCreary, whom they selected in the expansion draft. He had experience being part of a new club, as he was an original member of the Pittsburgh Penguins, but his fifth season with that team was filled with injuries and he managed just eight points.

His comeback year began when he was named Atlanta's captain, and he responded with a goal and an assist in their second game on October 8, 1972, when they took on the Buffalo Sabres. Just 17 days later, he scored twice on the power play to ensure a victory over the California Golden Seals, his winner coming at the 9:00 mark of the third period.

Perhaps McCreary's best outing of the year saw him score a hat trick that included a winning goal while facing the Sabres again on January 28, 1973. On February 9, he reached a personal milestone by scoring the 100th goal of his career against Gary Smith of the Chicago Black Hawks.

"He came to play every night," recalled Randy Manery. "He didn't have the greatest set of skills, but none of us did on that first-year team. He was a leader and a very important person for that team in those early years."

ERNIE HICKE

Hicke spent the first two seasons of his NHL career with the California Golden Seals. He scored 22 goals as a rookie in 1970–71, but his output dropped by half as a sophomore and he was made available in the expansion draft. His brother, Bill, had previously been through the experience of playing for a new team back in 1967–68 with the Oakland Seals.

Hicke earned an assist during the season opener and followed it up with a goal against Buffalo a week later. Although he started slow, he began to heat up with a three-point night against the Toronto Maple Leafs on December 20, 1972, and he was on fire in late January and early February as he scored a winning goal while facing the Minnesota North Stars and had a two-goal night when the Flames took on the Detroit Red Wings.

Less than a week later, Hicke was traded to the New York Islanders for Arnie Brown. The deal came at a strange time considering that he was in the midst of a hot streak, and he was injured in his first game with them.

CURT BENNETT

The son of a former NHL goaltender, Bennett was one of the growing number of American-born players who were making it to the highest level of pro hockey in the 1970s. After three seasons with Brown University, he turned pro in 1970–71 and saw some action with the St. Louis Blues before he joined the New York Rangers two years later.

His start with the Broadway Blueshirts was slow, as he only recorded a single assist over 16 games before they traded him to the Flames to be reunited with former Blues executive Cliff Fletcher.

"I had been traded to New York the summer of 1972 and spent three months with Emile Francis before he realized his mistake. He was playing me as a defenceman in New York. I played both forward and defence when I did play in New York. I was constantly changing my ankle guards while sitting on the bench. If I was to go out as a defenceman, I would keep the ankle guards on; if a forward, I would quickly take them off. I got traded to Atlanta after playing defence against Vancouver. We lost 3–2. Emile had the trainer call me off the bus and tell me I was going to Atlanta, where I would have a better opportunity to play. They got Ron Harris, a bona fide defenceman from Atlanta. I gave Glen Sather my chess set. I said, 'Here Glen, take my chess set. Maybe you can practice enough to beat me in the future.'"

Just two days after the deal went down, Bennett recorded a goal and an assist in a 5–5 tie with the Philadelphia Flyers on November 30, 1972. It was part of a hot start in Atlanta for him, and he scored both goals in a 2–0 shutout of Detroit on December 13. While he had success on the ice, some of his teammates were a little wary of the college grad with a degree in Russian studies who carried a dictionary with him on road trips.

"I don't know if we knew what to make of him at the start," said Lew Morrison. "He wasn't the typical Canadian guy. He handled the puck well and was big and strong. He certainly helped us, and I enjoyed playing with him. He certainly worked his butt off."

Regardless of how he was perceived, he thoroughly enjoyed playing under Atlanta coach Bernie Geoffrion.

"Boomer was like a father to me. I'd go see him when things were tough. He'd knock you down, then build you up. 'I know you are a college kid like Red Berenson,' he told me. 'But I told Red, How much you gonna make if you start teaching college instead of working on your hockey?' He wasn't an x's and o's coach. His system was if you weren't playing well, you needed to dig deeper, play from the heart and just do it. He motivated our team to play at a higher level than our ability, but he didn't have a system to learn per se. If he were a military leader you'd want him to motivate troops to kick some butt, but you wouldn't want him planning the strategy of the assault. He believed you won because you wanted to win, not because you had better tactics."

On a personal level, Bennett experienced a great tragedy during the 1972–73 season, when his younger brother, Peter, died after falling through some ice. Eventually, he pulled himself out of the doldrums in early March with a goal and a fight with Bob Stewart in a win over the California Golden Seals. He also potted a winner against Chicago on St. Patrick's Day.

RANDY MANERY

In the early 1970s, Manery was looked upon as a scrappy defender in the Detroit Red Wings farm system, but he was quickly developing into an offensive blueliner with a quick, low shot. He saw just three games with the parent club over two seasons and was looking forward to playing with the new Atlanta Flames after being selected in the expansion draft.

"I was excited because, whether to prove myself right or wrong, I deserved a chance to play in Detroit. It was nice that somebody wanted me. Having only played a few NHL games, if you read the papers and you listened to the experts, this was going to be the worst team ever. There really weren't any name players who had a consistently strong NHL career, but the older players we had were good team players. In hindsight, the scouts and writers didn't know who the heck we were."

After recording his first NHL point with an assist on Keith McCreary's goal against Buffalo on October 8, 1972, Manery scored his first goal in the next game three days later on Gary Smith of the Chicago Black

Hawks. In November, he had several multi-point games. He enjoyed playing under coach Bernie Geoffrion.

"For me it was great because Bernie was old school. If he had a problem with you, he pulled you aside. He was our best PR man as young players."

By mid-season, Manery had made a strong enough impression around the league to earn a spot with the West Division side at the 1973 NHL All-Star Game in New York's Madison Square Garden.

"It was really incredible and a tremendous opportunity. That's where being in the NHL made an impact on me. I was so excited to be there, but I wish my mom and dad had been there to see me."

By the end of the year, he was the top-scoring defender for the Flames and outpaced blue-line partner Pat Quinn by a whopping 17 points. He reflected on what the team had accomplished during their first season.

"We had done what we could and couldn't get any farther. It was disappointing but we had done better than anyone had anticipated. We beat the big clubs and when we came back for the second year, we were feeling positive."

JACQUES RICHARD

The second overall selection in the 1972 NHL Amateur Draft, Richard spent five seasons with the Quebec Remparts and scored 160 points in 1971–72. The Flames had very high hopes for the young star, but in the long run he was a major headache for the club.

The first sign of problems appeared in training camp when Richard's brashness and overconfidence started to get on the nerves of teammates. Captain Keith McCreary felt it was his duty to help protect him, however.

"There were times, many times, when several of our guys could have really clobbered the kid, really hurt him," he said. "Not because they wanted to but because of the way he'd come up the ice. If a guy's got his head down, you blast him. That's just the way the game's played. But I told the guys to lay off him at first, let him get a feel of things. He'll get better, I promise you that."

After a few exhibition games, Fletcher felt that he had drafted the best junior player available in 1972.

"No question now," said Fletcher. "Richard was by far the better player. Harris hasn't shown me much at all. Richard, however, did some good things. . . . He's only been here a week and already he's far and away the best skater in camp. I was a little worried the first few days but I'm sure not now."

Part of Richard's struggles adapting to life in Atlanta came from the fact that he did not speak English at the time. Goaltender Phil Myre felt it was just a matter of time before he adjusted.

"He's afraid somebody will make fun of him," he said. "He knows a little English but he's too bashful to speak it. He'll learn, though, especially when he gets to Atlanta and is hungry. That's when we all learn."

Richard's first NHL contest produced his first point, which was an assist on a goal by Rey Comeau against the New York Islanders, and his first goal came on October 25 against Marv Edwards of the California Golden Seals. Later on, he scored game-winners in matches with Pittsburgh and Chicago.

At one point, his youth and inexperience got him into trouble when he was benched during a win against the Minnesota North Stars. His nonchalant response to the discipline rankled a few feathers, but coach Bernie Geoffrion was not too upset.

"He's mad at me, I know. But he'll get over it. Don't be too rough on the kid. He's only played a few National Hockey League games. He's got a lot to learn."

Things got worse later when the team was in Toronto, as he left the team and went home to Quebec. There were rumours that he had quit, disappointed by his lack of production at the NHL level, but he returned to action soon after. Teammate Curt Bennett feels the Flames may have rushed the development of Richard.

"Jacques, or 'Jacks Richard' as the Atlanta telephone information girl called him, was a very successful junior player who was forced into a starring role right away. We were an expansion team, so he was the franchise. He was an example of a player who played the power player all the time but had not earned the right. If he had been sent to the minors and had to earn his way back, he would have done much better. In fact, I think he did finally end up in the minors, then after a few years he came up and scored 52 goals for Quebec. He always had the talent. I think he was handled wrong. He drove Boomer nuts. Boomer couldn't figure out why Jacques, a French wunderkind like himself, couldn't get angry and dig deeper. I think Jacques was embarrassed he got preferential treatment. It's hard to think you deserve fame and fortune when you know you don't, like a rich guy's son."

PAT QUINN

A big, tough, rock-solid defender, Quinn was with the Vancouver Canucks for their first two NHL seasons, but as a result of a rough 1971–72 campaign the team let him become available in the expansion draft. Often described by opposing players and teammates as "mean," he was set to take on the role of protecting his teammates.

"I'm not a good skater at all," he admitted at the time. "I'm tall and I don't have the good balance, so I have to do other things to make sure I keep my job. I try to prepare myself mentally for games. Keep a very sharp head. Other guys can make mistakes and cover up with quickness. I can't. But I think I play my position well. I clear the net area pretty well and I'm known as a pretty fair policeman, too. . . . I prefer to think of myself as tough. I don't play dirty, but a man has to look after his job and family. And since I'm not the good skater, I've got to compensate in other ways."

Typically good for a couple of goals a season, Quinn scored while the team was shorthanded against the Pittsburgh Penguins on November 26, 1972. Coach Bernie Geoffrion told him to move his hands down on his stick, and that helped him get the edge he needed to score that goal. On January 26, 1973, he had a pair of assists when the Flames skated to a 3–3 tie with the Los Angeles Kings.

Lew Morrison reflected on what Quinn brought to the team.

"He was a little older than I was," he said. "He seemed at home being a leader. Pat would organize team functions, and if things weren't going well, he would get us all together. He was a pretty imposing guy and didn't have to say anything."

Quinn's defence partner in the early years in Atlanta was Randy Manery, who reflected on working with the big blueliner.

"I have a world of respect for Pat. Off the ice, our families became friends, and on the ice, we played off each other's strengths. Bernie had a lot of confidence in us and we were their top defensive team those first few years. He understood the game really well and had friends all over the league. You could see that he wanted to go to that next level."

NOEL PRICE

Price was a part of the first-year Pittsburgh Penguins in 1967–68, but he ended up back in the minors for the 1969–70 season after he was claimed by Springfield in the reverse draft. He responded by winning his first Eddie Shore Award as the AHL's top defenceman and was up with the Los Angeles Kings the following year.

In 1971–72, he started the year back with Springfield but was traded to Montreal in the deal that sent Rogie Vachon out west. The Canadiens would not bring him up, however, but he excelled with the Nova Scotia Voyageurs and won the Shore once again.

"At the end of that season, Claude Ruel wanted to meet with me to see if I wanted to go to Atlanta," he said. "I said I'd love to play with Boomer again. I was certainly surprised that Montreal wanted to do that for me, but I guess they got some compensation."

With more than 15 years of pro experience, Price was a real asset to the Flames during the 1972–73 campaign, and he gave a little payback to the Habs on December 2, 1972, when he scored one goal and added an assist in a 4–4 tie. Two weeks later, he earned a pair of assists against the Penguins.

"I learned an awful lot from Noel," said Randy Manery. "He was a real classy gentleman. He taught me a lot of individual defensive drills that I could work on. He was a no-nonsense guy and he wanted everybody to realize the opportunity they had to play in the NHL."

DAN BOUCHARD

The Boston Bruins drafted Bouchard in 1970, and he had a great season with the team's AHL affiliate, the Braves, in 1971–72. He was named to the league's First All-Star Team and shared the Harry "Hap" Holmes Award after combining with Ross Brooks for the lowest team goals-against average. After a performance like that, there was little doubt he would be taken in the expansion draft, so he got a shot at big-league action with the Flames.

On October 8, 1972, Bouchard made his NHL debut in a 5–3 loss to the Buffalo Sabres. He earned his first victory 17 days later against the California Golden Seals. Over the course of the season, he proved that he was big-league material. He earned his first shutout on December 13 in a 2–0 win over Detroit, and less than a month later, he got a second one under his belt with a defeat of the Toronto Maple Leafs. Two days later, against Los Angeles, he earned an assist on the second goal of the night by Larry Romanchych.

"Danny was a unique character," said Randy Manery. "Incredibly intense. He expected the best from himself and from everybody else. That sometimes made him hard to like, but he was such a competitor."

Once the regular season was over, Bouchard placed fifth in voting for the Calder Trophy. He went on to play for the Flames all seven seasons they spent in Atlanta.

PHIL MYRE

There were a ton of goalies vying for a job in the Montreal Canadiens organization in the early 1970s, but Myre proved one of the most promising prospects under the team's control and appeared in 49 games over three seasons. He made just nine appearances in his final year with the Habs, but that did not stop the Flames from taking him with their first pick in the expansion draft.

In net for the season opener, Myre looked good in the win over the New York Islanders and later shut them out twice in the first half of the schedule. He was a big factor in the team's early success and was pleased to be playing for the Flames.

"A goaler worries about getting shell-shocked with a weak team. I only hoped we wouldn't be embarrassed so often that I'd hate to go to the games. But I've been given protection. We don't have top individual talent, but we do have hard workers and big, strong checkers, and we've been able to stay close in games and win more than we expected. It's been a thrill."

When the Flames took on the St. Louis Blues on January 19, 1973, Myre got involved in a controversial fight when he was pulled out of the crease by Steve Durbano. He responded by hitting Durbano in the neck with his stick. Once the notorious tough-guy got up off the ice, he charged the goalie and earned a misconduct penalty. When Durbano got back to the ice later in the game, he tried to get a little more revenge on the Flames' netminder and a bench-clearing brawl ensued.

As part of a young tandem with Dan Bouchard, Myre saw a greater share of action and registered a higher winning percentage, and he had a lower goals-against average. He shared the team's MVP honours and eventually spent a little more than five seasons in a Flames uniform. In retirement, he regularly found work as a respected coach and scout.

EXPANSION YEAR RECORD: 12-60-6
(30 points — eighth in East Division)
COACHES: Phil Goyette and Earl Ingarfield
GENERAL MANAGER: Bill Torrey
FIRST GAME: October 7, 1972 —
3-2 loss vs. Atlanta Flames
FIRST GOAL: October 7, 1972 by Ed Westfall

NEW YORK ISLANDERS

The New York Rangers had the local big-league hockey market to themselves for 30 seasons before the Islanders arrived on the NHL scene. If it had not been for the WHA sniffing around the Nassau Veterans Memorial Coliseum, a rival NHL team might never have come to be.

When the ownership group of the proposed New York Raiders was looking at basing themselves out of Long Island, local officials were concerned that their product was not going to be professional and wanted to find a way to legally keep them out of the rink. But by approaching William Shea and having him bend the ear of NHL president Clarence Campbell, the owners convinced the league an expansion team would be a good idea. It also proved a very costly one in the beginning, however, because Roy Boe, who owned the New York Nets of the ABA, not only had to pay the expansion fee, but also make the Rangers $4 million richer with a territorial fee.

The area was already familiar with the sport, thanks to the long-standing success of the Long Island Ducks club, which was part of the Eastern Hockey League. That team is fondly remembered for many outrageous incidents and featured one of the game's toughest players of all time in John Brophy. Once the NHL franchise was granted, there was speculation the club would take on the same name, but they settled on becoming the New York Islanders instead to build a broader appeal.

Bill Torrey, who had experience in the management of the Oakland Seals, was brought on board as the first general manager of the Islanders.

He was committed to building a contender through shrewd drafting instead of the short-term solution of trading away picks. He went into the 1972 NHL Expansion Draft with high hopes and picked up an interesting mix of cast-off players that day, including Brian Spencer, Ed Westfall and Terry Crisp to go along with goalies Gerry Desjardins and future Hall of Famer Billy Smith. At the 1972 NHL Amateur Draft, he began building the club's prospect pool with such talent as Billy Harris, Bob Nystrom, Garry Howatt and Lorne Henning, all players who would stick around until the end of the decade.

What Torrey was not likely expecting, though, was that quite a few of the players he drafted jumped to the WHA. They were unable to sign Larry Hornung, John Schella, Norm Ferguson, Ted Hampson, Bart Crashley, Gord Labossiere and Ted Taylor, but they managed to keep enough talent to have a full roster for the season opener against their expansion cousins, the Atlanta Flames.

Coach Phil Goyette was not hired until after the expansion draft. He was lucky enough to have solid goaltending and hot young rookies, but it was obvious that he also had a generally inexperienced team with a lack of offensive power and a defence corps that was largely unproven. The team's sweaters were unveiled before training camp, and it wasn't long after that Goyette realized the Isles had some potential problems brewing. Still, he remained optimistic.

"Our biggest problem when we opened camp was that no one knew each other. Now that we're working together, I feel we're getting better every game, despite what the record shows. . . . Right now I would say we'll go with 11 forwards, six defencemen and two goaltenders. There are only a few guys who are assured of making the club. Everything else is up for grabs."

The home opener on October 7, 1972, ended up a tight 3–2 loss to the Flames, and the Islanders stumbled out of the gate by not registering their first shot on goal until halfway through the first period. Billy Harris scored their first goal and he had a decent start, which is often expected out of a first overall pick. Five days later, they earned their first win against the Los Angeles Kings, but there were signs of trouble when Arnie Brown decided to leave the team and was suspended. The first month of action was rough for the team, but players like Spencer realized they were going to have some tough games.

"I think we have a much better hockey club than we've shown. Every game we've lost was because of some lapse in front of the net. True, we're a young team and going to make some mistakes, but if we can eliminate some of these, we're going to be alright."

Goyette also expressed his frustration over the team's poor start.

"I can tell them what to do but I can't play for them."

With just two wins in their first 16 outings, the players held a discussion among themselves and then went out to get a much-needed victory over the California Golden Seals. Their goalies had faced a lot of rubber already, but Goyette felt they were performing well.

"Our goaltenders keep us in the game. As long as we can stay close, you never know what will happen. Desjardins and Smith have been under tremendous pressure but have been equal to it."

Wins — or even ties — were incredibly scarce over the first few months, and the home crowd began showing their impatience during a 6–1 loss to Atlanta on January 2, 1973, and started to chant "We're number eight!" Crisp noted that the jeering was not going to get to the players, and they were out to win any way they could.

"Sure, we've been hearing the booing, but we just try to ignore it and play our game. We have pride, and we want to win just as much as they do, but we can only look at ourselves in the mirror."

For team captain and 1973 All-Star Game participant Westfall, it was nothing new.

"I think the fans as a whole have been very patient with us. I went through the same thing in Boston a number of years ago. You can't really blame them for getting on us a bit. They really want to see a winner."

Soon after, the club recorded its biggest triumph of the expansion year when they got a big 5–0 lead on the Boston Bruins and held on to win the game 9–7 to end a 12-game losing streak.

"We just caught them flat-footed," Goyette explained. "We got one, two, three goals and we just kept on coming. We charged at them from the start. That's what they usually do."

For the coach, though, the celebration did not last long, as he was let go on January 29 and replaced with scout Earl Ingarfield. Torrey did not blame Goyette for the club's poor record and saw it as a move to motivate the team out of a season-long slump.

"In making this move, I emphasize that in no way are we blaming the team's poor record on Phil, but sometimes a move of this scope is necessary and can have a definite positive effect on the team," said Torrey.

Goyette's response was simple.

"I did everything I could with these youngsters, but a man can only go with what he's got."

Ingarfield was ready to focus on getting players to commit to a positional game and work on their physical conditioning. He was expected to be a taskmaster, but it was an uphill battle.

"For a while there we were getting beat nine this and nine that. You not only lose games, you lose your pride," said Westfall. "We had a team meeting. We called on all the clichés — you know, the other team dresses just like you, they can only put six men on the ice at a time, and so forth. The thing was never giving up in games, no matter the score. Always give your best and at least you can leave with your head held high. If everyone prepares himself individually we'd do better collectively. It worked. We're in most of our games to the finish now. We win once in a while."

Down the home stretch, the Islanders did have a better record under Ingarfield and even put together a three-game winning streak at one point. They also made a couple of trades that had long-term benefits. But at the end of the season, most fans were glad that it was over. With just 12 wins to their credit, they were regarded as the worst expansion team ever, but hope was around the corner when they selected Denis Potvin with the first overall pick in the 1973 NHL Amateur Draft.

In 1973–74, Al Arbour was hired as the new bench boss for the Islanders and began to bring the team together. Torrey later added new young talent like Chico Resch and Clark Gillies, and in their third campaign they made the playoffs. Future seasons saw the arrival of Mike Bossy and Bryan Trottier. The Islanders were considered Stanley Cup contenders early on, and in 1979–80, they finally won it all, hoisting Lord Stanley's Mug for four straight years.

(clockwise) Billy Harris, Ed Westfall, Brian Spencer, Billy Smith

By 1983–84, the team's core was starting to get older. They made one last run to the Stanley Cup Final but could not defeat the rising Edmonton Oilers. The Isles slowly slid down the standings and in 1988–89 missed the playoffs for the first time in years, finishing last in the Patrick Division. The 1990s were a fairly bleak time for the Isles, but the 2000s may have been even worse, as the team made several trades and free agent signings of dubious value under the management of Mike Milbury. By this point, the team was owned by Charles Wang and Sanjay Kumar of Computer Associates, and their era has been marked with questionable decisions that have taken a once-great franchise and stomped it into the ground.

Today, the Islanders have some top young talent, but their upper management is often the brunt of ridicule by the media. Whether it is the shunning of former greats like Pat LaFontaine, the ridiculous ban placed on reporter Chris Botta, hideous alternate jerseys (including the "Fisherman" style from the mid-1990s) or asbestos in their aging arena, there are rarely positive stories about the club these days. Relocating to Brooklyn for the 2015–16 season, the team can only strive to get back to its glory days with young superstar John Tavares leading the way.

BILLY HARRIS

After a phenomenal 129-point season with the OHA's Toronto Marlboros that resulted in a league scoring championship, Harris was the front-runner for top selection in the 1972 NHL Amateur Draft. The Islanders had the pleasure of making him their first junior pick.

Impressive from the beginning, Harris scored a power-play goal in the club's first game against Atlanta and had a pair of tallies during their second outing with Los Angeles on October 12, 1972. That game also saw him take the first penalty shot in team history, but it was not successful. At the time, coach Phil Goyette commented on his strong play and felt that he met the lofty expectations held for him.

"So far he's been everything we expected. He's one of the most advanced rookies I've ever seen. He can do everything so well," he said.

Harris was a speedster who amazed observers with his great anticipation of the play. In one of his best outings, he scored two goals and added an assist in a loss to Boston on January 18, 1973. Almost three weeks later, he scored a memorable game-winning goal against the Toronto Maple Leafs. After leading the Isles with 28 goals and 50 points, he finished the season third in voting for the Calder Trophy as the league's Rookie of the Year.

"He was a wonderful player but didn't get the help he needed early on," said captain Ed Westfall. "When he was getting to the top of his career, they sent him off to Los Angeles. He and I became good friends. We roomed together and we're still friends today."

ED WESTFALL

After more than a decade with the Boston Bruins, where he won two Stanley Cup championships, Westfall was by far one of the most popular players in Beantown. Fans were disappointed and angered that the club did not protect him during the expansion draft, and he ended up becoming a member of the New York Islanders.

Although press reports at the time indicated he was pleased with the move, Westfall reveals today that he was angry about having to go to a new team.

"That's not true, I was disappointed. I went through the same pouting that other players do. A month later, you get over it. I found out about it from the customs and immigrations guys at the airport and the guy said to me, 'I can't forgive the Bruins for what they did to you.' And I said 'What?' I got a letter from John Adams, who was the son of Weston Adams, that said he was embarrassed and ashamed about what the Bruins had done. I still have that letter."

Brought in to be a leader, Westfall actually flew his own plane in from Pelham, New Hampshire, to play for the Islanders.

"I figured it was safer to fly the airplane than to drive around New York," he joked.

Westfall scored the first goal in franchise history during the season opener against the Atlanta Flames. It was a rare power-play tally for him, since he didn't get a lot of chances to play with the extra man in Boston.

"One of the jokes that Derek Sanderson and I used to have is that next to our names is that we'd never get a power-play goal," he said. "I don't really remember the details, though. It was one of the few close games we had that year!"

Over the season, he was expected to be the point man in power-play situations, play on the penalty kill and even move back to defence on occasion to help reduce the number of pucks opponents fired into the net.

"I was a defenceman when I came in and I played with Leo Boivin. It was where I was needed. People think in today's terms if a guy is a right winger, he's always a right winger. When we were a man short, Milt Schmidt used to bring me up front to kill the penalty. When I was little kid, I was a goaltender but I wasn't going back there! It was a badge of honour to be able to do all of these things."

One of Westfall's best performances of the year was when he had a goal and three assists in a 4–4 tie with the Vancouver Canucks on December 21, 1972. A little less than a month later, he scored twice against his old club in a surprising 9–7 victory, which was one of the team's brightest moments in their first season. He reflected on that victory and felt it was a true team effort.

"I think I had more goals than Orr that day! At that point, it's not an individual thing. It's a team thing. Each time I stepped out on to the ice at Boston Garden, I got a standing ovation. In fact, it caused some angst for Mr. Cherry when he was coaching. He used to send out Stan Jonathan after me years later, and I'd get a rise out of him. Years later, we were laughing and shaking hands over it."

Soon after, Westfall represented his team at the 1973 NHL All-Star Game, marking the second time in his career he was given the honour. On March 24, 1973, he gave the team its 12th victory of the season when he scored a big goal to beat the up-and-coming Philadelphia Flyers.

BRIAN SPENCER

Regarded today as one of hockey's most tragic figures, Spencer was a buzz saw out on the ice and played every game like it was his last. As a result, he had a legion of fans in every city he played for and the respect of his teammates as well.

"Very apropos that he was called Spinner," said Islanders teammate Terry Crisp. "His whole life was hockey. He was off the map because he loved being out there. He loved guns and was always showing us his rifles! When you played with the guy, you always knew he had your back or that he was going to start something. You always had the feeling, wondering if that rubber band was going to snap."

Claimed by the Islanders from the Toronto Maple Leafs, Spencer was an instant hit on Long Island. His third goal of the season gave them a rare victory over the California Golden Seals on November 21, 1972, and he had a two-point game against the Vancouver Canucks a month later. On December 23, he had another game-winner, this time against the Minnesota North Stars. Fittingly, he also had two goals and an assist while facing Toronto on January 31, 1973.

"If you told him to go through the wall, he'd do it," said Phil Goyette. "He was a team player, but unfortunately, he wasn't All-Star material."

At the end of the year, Spencer was voted the team's most popular player and he remained with the Islanders until late in the following season. After stints with Buffalo and Pittsburgh, he spent some time in the minors before retiring. It was the days after his playing career that were the most controversial, as he battled drug addiction and was later charged with murder before being acquitted in 1987. The following year he lost his life when he was shot to death in a roadside holdup in Florida.

TOM MILLER

Miller was a rookie with the Detroit Red Wings in 1970–71, but ended up being claimed by the Buffalo Sabres soon after and spent a year in the minors with the Cincinnati Swords. He was called up at one point but broke his ankle and never got to enjoy the promotion. A product of the University of Denver, he put up good numbers in the minors, and the New York Islanders called his name on draft day.

Since Miller was not interested in heading to the WHA, he joined the Isles in the fall. He earned his first point of the year with an assist against the Boston Bruins on October 14, 1972. Facing Chicago two weeks later, he scored his first two goals on Tony Esposito in a 4–4 tie. The next night, he received a cheap-shot elbow, tasted the butt end of Phil Esposito's stick and was taken to hospital with what was suspected a ruptured spleen. Tests proved negative, but team captain Ed Westfall was all over Esposito the rest of the night.

"He had no right to do what he did," said Westfall at the time. "He just stuck his stick into the kid for no reason. We weren't going to let him get away with something like that."

As the season progressed, Miller saw more playing time and his production increased. One particularly good game saw him score twice and add an assist in a 6–4 triumph over the St. Louis Blues on March 17, 1973.

"The highlight for me was the end of the year," said Miller. "I was on a line with Billy Harris and Germain Gagnon and I was beginning to score. It was my first full year in the NHL, and I was an important part of the team. All in all, it was good."

LORNE HENNING

Henning was the second amateur ever drafted by the Islanders. He was ready for NHL action after a phenomenal junior season with the New Westminster Bruins in which he scored 114 points over 60 games.

Henning made his pro debut on October 14, 1972, against the Boston Bruins, but he was sent down to New Haven shortly after for a brief conditioning stint. He returned after just four minor league games and scored his first two goals in a 5–3 loss to the Philadelphia Flyers on November 22. On December 30, he recorded a pair of assists when the Islanders faced the Vancouver Canucks.

In time, Henning developed into one of the game's top defensive specialists. He skated on two Stanley Cup–winning squads on Long Island before joining their coaching staff for two more championships.

"He and I had the same role as the Islanders got stronger. My career was winding down and he was peaking. A very dedicated guy and fun to be around. What he lacked in raw talent, he made up for in effort," remarked Ed Westfall.

TERRY CRISP

An original member of the St. Louis Blues, Crisp had five strong seasons with the club and made a reputation for himself as a hard-working forward. In 1971–72, he established a new career-high with 13 goals and 31 points, but when the season was over, he was suddenly on the outs. The New York Islanders were happy to add his talents to a thin roster.

"I went to the Island thinking that we're going to New York and that we were going to die, but we really loved it when we lived on it," he joked.

A respected grinder and penalty killer, Crisp had his first goal in an Islanders uniform in a 4–2 win over the California Golden Seals on November 21, 1972. In late December, he had multi-point games against the Minnesota North Stars and Vancouver Canucks and went on to score a key shorthanded goal to open the scoring in a 1–1 tie with the Buffalo Sabres on February 3, 1973.

Just a little more than a month later, he was traded to the Philadelphia Flyers, who were loading up for a run at the Stanley Cup. Teammate Tom Miller recalled the day of the trade.

"Terry and I were rooming together in Detroit at the trade deadline. We were out at the bar and at about 11:45, he was told to come back to the hotel. I came back there and he was dejected and sitting on the bed and told me that he had been traded to Philadelphia. It worked out well for him, though!"

Crisp feels it was a good move for the Islanders and he joked that the deal spurred the club to great success.

"I remember Al Arbour calling me at the end of the season and he asked me how I liked it, and I told him that I loved it. I was also traded for Potvin. . . . I just don't tell him it was Jean! Hey, I won the Islanders four Stanley Cups!"

GERRY HART

Hart spent years trying to become a regular with the Detroit Red Wings but, outside of a long stint with them in 1970–71, he toiled in the AHL and CHL for his first four pro seasons. The 1972 NHL Expansion

Draft was a major boost for his career, and he proved a real steal for the Islanders.

Hart was looked upon as a potential anchor for the team's defence corps, but he was out of commission before the season even began after he injured his knee in a collision with Dale Rolfe of the Rangers during pre-season action. He finally made his official Islanders debut in December 1972. Bill Torrey was aware of the impact of the young defender's absence in the early season.

"There's no question that Gerry's early injury put us in a pinch," he said. "We counted on him to be our defensive leader and his loss had an immediate effect."

His first goal of the season was the only offence New York could manage in a 6–1 loss to Montreal on January 24, 1973. Hart ended up leading the team with 158 penalty minutes during their expansion season.

BILL MIKKELSON

Mikkelson got his first taste of NHL action in a 15-game trial with the Los Angeles Kings in 1971–72. His play earned the attention of the New York Islanders, who took him in the expansion draft. He also had a hockey pedigree, as his uncle, former NHL veteran Jim McFadden, starred for Detroit and Chicago between 1947–48 and 1953–54.

"At the time, my alternative was to play with the Winnipeg Jets of the WHA, and I was close to coming to an agreement. I waited for the NHL Expansion Draft and I was selected by New York."

Considering the number of players the Islanders lost to the new league, Mikkelson easily made the team out of training camp. He earned his first assist of the season on October 24, 1972, when Billy Harris scored against the Montreal Canadiens. In the November 3 meeting with the Vancouver Canucks, he registered the first goal of his career against goalie Ed Dyck. To this day, he feels proud of his accomplishments that year, regardless of the approach management took toward on-ice success.

"Sometimes I think the bar was set too low for us. When you set the bar low, that's what you'll achieve. I'm proud of the first season. When I look back, based on what I know now, I would have done things differently. I try to pass that along to my son and daughter, that you shouldn't have any regrets. I was proud to have played there and the fact that we didn't win doesn't matter. Don't underestimate just being there, because there's a sense of achievement that sticks around for the rest of your life."

BOB NYSTROM

Nystrom was one of the earliest pieces Bill Torrey acquired in his quest to put together the championship puzzle for the Islanders and he was a third-round pick in the 1972 NHL Amateur Draft. Born in Sweden, he immigrated to Canada as a child and grew up playing hockey in Alberta. As a junior, he skated on some strong Calgary Centennials clubs and made his pro debut with the New Haven Nighthawks.

After a month in the minors, Nystrom was called up to hit NHL ice for the first time on November 8, 1972, in a 6–1 loss to the Chicago Black Hawks. On the roster for a brief trial, he did not put up huge numbers on the farm, but showed a lot of promise and toughness with 114 penalty minutes. As the season wound down, he was promoted to the lineup and earned his first point with an assist on Brian Marchinko's game-winner against the Blues on March 17, 1973. The last game of the year provided fans with a taste of things to come as Nystrom put the puck past Atlanta's Phil Myre in a 4–4 tie with the Flames on April 1.

GERRY DESJARDINS

Quick as a cat, Desjardins was often called "The Fastest Glove in the West" thanks to his strong reflexes. He played only six regular-season games for the Chicago Black Hawks in 1971–72, however, after he suffered a broken arm the previous year. The Islanders made him their first selection in the expansion draft and hoped he might bounce back enough to face the daunting task of being their number one goalie.

"I'm sure my arm is almost as good as new. Maybe I'm not quite as fast as I was when I was with the Kings, but with the new, lighter glove I'm using, you probably won't notice a difference," he said.

He was the starter for their first game against Atlanta and gave an honest appraisal of his play to the press after the game.

"I wasn't happy with the way I played. I think I should have had a couple of them, but it's a game of mistakes."

His first victory with the Islanders came on November 1, 1972, when they defeated the California Golden Seals 6–2. A week later, he stopped a penalty shot by Pit Martin in a battle with his old team in Chicago, but the Black Hawks blew them away in a 6–1 game.

Desjardins saw most of the action in the crease for the Islanders, but he earned only five of the 12 victories they had in 1972–73. He missed some time late in the season as a result of strained knee ligaments and ended the season with 35 losses, the most in the league.

BILLY SMITH

After completing his junior career with the Cornwall Royals of the Quebec Major Junior Hockey League (QMJHL), Smith turned pro with the Springfield Kings in 1970–71 and helped the club to a Calder Cup championship. The following season he enjoyed a five-game stint with the Los Angeles Kings, but since the club wanted to protect Rogie Vachon and Gary Edwards in the 1972 NHL Expansion Draft, he was made available. He was the second goaltender taken by the Islanders.

When Denis DeJordy did not meet expectations in training camp, New York knew they had a very capable backup in Smith for their first season. His debut with the club was a memorable one. He stepped into the crease in the team's second outing on October 12, 1972, as they faced the Kings. Determined to win, he outduelled Rogie Vachon and made 28 saves in a 3–2 victory.

From the start, it appeared that the young goalie was also a bit of a spitfire. He was not afraid to do whatever it took to make sure the crease was clear, and his 42 penalty minutes were a record for a player in his position during that era. Even outside of game situations, he took a serious approach to the game. Teammate Terry Crisp shared one memorable example.

"Billy Smith was amazing. He even scared me! I remember in our first couple of practices and Ed Westfall puts one up near his head and he said, 'Keep it down, boys!' After the third time, he chased Eddie around that ice and the stick was going around like a helicopter!"

EXPANSION YEAR RECORD: 15–54–11
(41 points — fifth in Smythe Division)
COACH: Bep Guidolin
GENERAL MANAGER: Sid Abel
FIRST GAME: October 9, 1974 —
6-2 loss vs. Toronto Maple Leafs
FIRST GOAL: October 9, 1974 by Simon Nolet

KANSAS CITY SCOUTS

Kansas City, Missouri, has long been a hotbed for minor league hockey action and the city has been the location of many different NHL farm clubs over the years. Whether it was the Greyhounds or Pla-Mors from the early days or the affiliate of the St. Louis Blues in the 1960s and early 1970s, there was a small but rabid local fan base for the sport.

When the WHA began making waves, the NHL decided it needed to get into new markets before the rival league could make inroads with hockey fans. The league announced two new teams on June 8, 1972, one of them to be based out of Kansas City and run by a group headed by Edwin G. Thompson.

The original plan for the team's name was to dust off the old Mohawks nickname used by minor league clubs in previous years, but the Chicago Black Hawks voiced their displeasure at league meetings and the idea was put aside. Gunzo's, a Chicago jersey and equipment supplier that worked extensively with the Black Hawks for many years, actually created a proposed sweater and it essentially looked like the Scouts final multi-coloured jersey but with the Indian head logo, which would have been an obvious trademark infringement. That potential debacle avoided, the team called themselves the Scouts after a famous statue in a Kansas City park that was represented in their final logo.

The team was set to play the 1974–75 season out of the soon-to-be-constructed Kemper Arena.

Hall of Famer Sid Abel became their general manager and he hired

Bep Guidolin to act as coach. Guidolin had taken the Boston Bruins to the Stanley Cup Final in 1973–74 and was in for a shock when he went from guiding Bobby Orr and Phil Esposito to coaching a ragtag group of castoffs from every NHL team. Kansas City added their first players through the 1974 NHL Amateur Draft and got an amazing prospect in Wilf Paiement with the second overall pick.

Later on, they made their selections in the 1974 NHL Expansion Draft and started with goalies Michel Plasse and Peter McDuffe before getting their first captain in Simon Nolet, who had just won a Stanley Cup with Philadelphia. Unlike the expansion teams from two years earlier, the Scouts got many players who ended up skating for them instead of going to the WHA. Compared to other teams in the league, it was not the most skilled set of players, but Guidolin seemed pleased with what he saw in training camp.

"These guys have been around, they know what they have to do," he said. "It's just a matter of them getting used to my methods. It is pleasing to see them play it so fast. We can't get too excited, but when I see some players it makes me feel good. I know now we can skate with anybody. Once we get our lines set, we can play with anybody in the league. We're going to be inexperienced around the net, but things will come together. But we have to skate, there's no excuse for us not to skate. . . . They're going to surprise somebody, but they're going to have to believe in themselves like I believe in them. All they've got to do is work their butts off, and they'll do it."

Unfortunately for the Scouts, a bricklayer's strike delayed construction of their home rink and they had to play their first eight games on the road. They debuted at Toronto's Maple Leaf Gardens and lost to the home team. The road trip was a true disaster, as they scraped together only one tie against seven losses, and their home debut on November 2, 1974, against Chicago was another heartbreaking defeat.

The Scouts finally got a win the next day against their expansion cousins, the Washington Capitals, and over the next two weeks got back-to-back victories against St. Louis and the New York Islanders. Many losses followed but they had a good 5–6–2 run in January 1975. One of those wins was the biggest of their expansion season, when they beat the Boston Bruins 3–2 and got a phenomenal performance in net from recent acquisition Denis Herron.

"We deserved to win," said Guidolin. "We worked our heads off out there. We have to learn how to play under that kind of pressure and we did. A victory. A moral victory."

Attendance was a big problem in Kansas City throughout their existence. NHLPA head Alan Eagleson was quoted saying there were only two teams where he had concerns about his clients getting paid, the Scouts and the Pittsburgh Penguins. This was not surprising to the players themselves, since the club was very cost-conscious and even violated league bylaws about travelling to certain cities on game days.

In the final quarter of the season, the Scouts had a brutal 17-game winless streak. Even though their record was bad, at least they were not as bad as the Capitals. Their last win of the year came against Los Angeles on April 1 and it ensured that the Kings would not be able to clinch a Norris Division title. Guidolin was pleased by how the team performed and offered an appraisal at the end of the year.

"There have been some nights when it's been discouraging. But you look at it all in all, you've got to be pretty proud of them, really. Most of the time, 95 percent of it, they've given me all they had. Look, there's a lot of clubs that have flat nights. They don't work real hard, but they have the power and depth to overcome it and win and tie on bad nights. Really, I can't complain."

The second season for the Scouts was not much better than their first, and they again finished near the bottom of the league with just 36 points. Once more, only the Capitals were worse than them, but by a mere four points. During the first half of the year, they went 11–25–4, but from that point on, won only a single game (against Washington, naturally). It looked as if NHL hockey was doomed in Kansas City.

Since the team had been playing to a barely half-full arena, and they owed a lot of money to the league and to the St. Louis Blues for territorial rights, the ownership group needed to scrape up the money to finish the season. They held a ticket drive and even attempted to bring in bigger crowds by offering free post-game concerts from popular artists like Freddie Fender and Tanya Tucker, but the plan did not stop the financial bleeding at all. By late March 1976, it was rumoured that the NBA's Kansas City Kings might purchase the team, but there was much more interest from out of town.

At the end of the 1975–76 season, the Scouts and Capitals saw a little more action despite missing the playoffs. They enjoyed a four-game exhibition series in Japan, where Washington won three of them, and that was it for Kansas City.

Although the NHL had planned to expand to 20 teams for the 1976–77 season with new clubs in Seattle and Denver, that idea was placed on hold because of the financial problems that several clubs were experiencing. The former Scouts became the Colorado Rockies and spent six years in Denver, making the playoffs only once. Team management made mistakes when it came to trading away young prospects for washed-up veterans, but at least they managed to grab some headlines once in a while. Owner Arthur Imperatore Sr. had originally planned to move the team to New Jersey in 1978, but the league turned him down because there wasn't a large enough facility there at the time. In 1979–80, they hired Don Cherry to coach the club, but he butted heads with general manager Ray Miron and was finished after a year. The Rockies could not get much momentum after that.

John McMullen purchased the Rockies in 1982 and finally moved them to the Meadowlands in East Rutherford, New Jersey. The New Jersey Devils began play in 1982–83 and, after the club shook its reputation as doormats in the Patrick Division, went on to win three Stanley Cup championships. Today, after moving to Newark and drawing smaller crowds, the team is often the subject of speculation regarding its future.

In recent years, rumours have circulated that Kansas City could still be a viable relocation site for a troubled NHL franchise. The city has a perfect location for a team in the Sprint Center and could very well have more box office success than the Scouts ever did during their dismal two-year run.

SIMON NOLET

A member of the Philadelphia Flyers' first Stanley Cup–winning squad in 1973-74, Nolet became the first skater selected by the Scouts in

(clockwise) Simon Nolet, Wilf Paiement, Denis Herron, Robin Burns

the expansion draft. In the past, he had hit the 20-goal mark on two occasions and also skated in the 1972 NHL All-Star Game. The WHA's Quebec Nordiques were also interested in bringing him in, but he chose to remain in the NHL.

Named club captain by Bep Guidolin, Nolet made an immediate impact both on the ice and in the dressing room.

"Simon was great in camp, working with the younger players, and it is obvious that he gave the whole team a lift," remarked the coach to the press.

He recorded the first goal in franchise history in the season opener against Toronto when he shot the puck past Doug Favell less than a minute into the second period. Four days later, he returned to Philadelphia and enjoyed the rare experience of being greeted by cheers from the fans as a visiting player. Buoyed by that support, he registered the team's first shorthanded goal in a close 3–2 loss.

As the season progressed, it became obvious that Nolet was also Kansas City's offensive leader. He had a big four-point night when they tied the Pittsburgh Penguins on December 19, 1974. After getting the game-winner against Detroit on January 4, 1975, he came up with three assists while playing the Minnesota North Stars two days later.

The points were piling up at the best pace of his career, so naturally he represented the Scouts at the 1975 NHL All-Star Game and suited up for the Campbell Conference. At the end of the season, he led the club in points, tying with Wilf Paiement for the most goals and Dave Hudson for most assists. He missed only a few games due to a bad bruise on his calf and was the team's nominee for the Masterton Trophy.

"Simon Nolet was the best player on our team," said Lynn Powis. "We wouldn't have won a game without him. Whatever we got was due to him."

GUY CHARRON

The Scouts may have started the season as a mostly ragtag bunch of players, but they added some interesting talent to their roster over the 1974–75 campaign that gave them a glimmer of hope for the future.

Charron was certainly among the brightest of the acquisitions. After a slow start to the year, he was packaged off to Kansas City by the Detroit Red Wings.

He rebounded quickly and was given a greater offensive role in his new surroundings, putting up three points against the Pittsburgh Penguins on December 19, 1974, and chipping in a pair of two-point efforts against St. Louis and Montreal before the new year. On January 16, 1975, he got his chance to prove the Red Wings gave up on him too quickly and scored two first-period goals in a 7–4 loss. At the end of Kansas City's inaugural campaign, he placed second among the team's scorers despite appearing in just 51 games.

WILF PAIEMENT

The youngest of 16 children, Paiement starred for the St. Catharines Black Hawks of the OHA in 1973–74, where he broke out with 123 points. As a result, there was a lot of buzz about him heading into the 1974 NHL Amateur Draft, so the Scouts took him with the second overall pick.

At the time, Paiement was the highest-paid rookie in league history thanks to agent Alan Eagleson. He quickly became one of the franchise's top talents. His first big-league point came on a goal by Randy Rota when Kansas City faced the New York Islanders on October 12, 1974, and he had his first goal six days later when he beat Phil Myre of the Atlanta Flames. Over his first 10 games, he managed an impressive six goals, but the team was not as fortunate and had a 1-8-1 record.

Although he was playing on a weak club, Paiement gave fans many glimpses of his potential with a pair of game-winning goals against California and Washington in February and in consecutive two-goal outings against Los Angeles and Pittsburgh in early March.

By the end of the season, he had tied with Simon Nolet for the team lead in goals. Paiement remained with the Scouts when they moved to Colorado. He scored 356 goals during his career and was also respected for his toughness, as attested to by his 1,757 penalty minutes.

ED GILBERT

Gilbert played his junior hockey for his hometown Hamilton Red Wings in the early 1970s, and the Montreal Canadiens took him in the third round of the 1972 NHL Amateur Draft. He had a decent rookie pro season with the AHL's Nova Scotia Voyageurs but had an even better sophomore year in 1973–74 when he scored 74 points.

"I had a pretty good minor league stint in Montreal, and Al McNeil told me to get in touch with an agent. My agent at the time told me to have a good second year and I had a good chance to get in with Washington or Kansas City."

The Scouts made him their second-last pick in the expansion draft, but there was also some interest from the WHA's Chicago Cougars. He was in the lineup to make his NHL debut in the season opener against the Toronto Maple Leafs.

"Our first game was in Toronto's Maple Leaf Gardens. I grew up in Hamilton and my mom and dad were there," he recalled. "It was late in the game and they pulled the goalie and put me on the point and the puck comes back to me and I should have shot the damned thing right away. I tried to make a move and Ron Ellis ended up taking the puck and he broke out down the ice on a breakaway. All of my buddies kidded me at the end of the year about it!"

Regardless of the rough beginning, Gilbert settled in with Kansas City quickly during their first road stretch and scored his first goal and an assist while battling the California Golden Seals on October 23, 1974. In November, he began to hit his stride, putting in a two-assist effort during the team's first victory against the Washington Capitals and scoring twice on the power play in a 7–6 loss to the Canadiens.

After the unexpected departure of Butch Deadmarsh, Kansas City named Gilbert an assistant captain. One of his most memorable games in the 1974–75 season came when the Scouts defeated the Boston Bruins on January 23, 1975. He scored once that night and also set up Gary Croteau's winning tally.

"I remember that game, and you couldn't have had a better coach for that team at that time than Bep. Boston needed to win but they were thinking it was an automatic win. That was a real physical goal and I think I ended up in the back of the net with the puck somehow. They came at us both guns blazing and it was such a huge win. My dad called me up the next day and told me that I was in the *Globe and Mail*. . . . That was pretty cool!"

BART CRASHLEY

Crashley was a rushing defender who had some success with the Los Angeles Sharks of the WHA, but he decided to return to NHL action for the 1974–75 season.

"I had re-signed with the New York Islanders, who had drafted me two years previously. Los Angeles was moving to Michigan to become the Stags. I signed a nice deal with Bill Torrey and was in training camp when I was traded for Bob Bourne."

While Bourne went on to become a four-time Stanley Cup champion, Crashley instead reunited with Sid Abel, who had coached him in Detroit nearly a decade earlier. His presence on the blue line provided big help to the team early on, but he felt there were a lot of struggles ahead.

"It was difficult for everyone," he said. "It was going to be tough. I don't think there was any sense of stability and it was a situation where we were in flux. It was a long way from what we thought an NHL team should be."

On October 25, 1974, Crashley had a pair of assists when the Scouts took on the Vancouver Canucks and later scored a goal and another helper when they met again on November 7. He continued to be a thorn in the west coast club's side when he was the author of a game-winning goal 19 days later as well.

One of his most memorable experiences with the first-year club came early in Boston on October 27. The team was down 4–0 early in the second period when a clever catcall came out of the crowd.

"That was Bep's return to Boston. A fan called out and said 'Hey, Bep! What's that Indian looking for? The first win?'"

By the middle of December, however, Crashley was on his way out of Kansas City and was moved to the Red Wings in a five-player deal.

"I was very happy and would much rather have been in Detroit," he said. "We were working on getting back to being successful."

BUTCH DEADMARSH

After Deadmarsh was selected early by the Scouts in the 1974 expansion draft, the team counted on him to be a leader because of his experience in playing with first-year clubs. As they prepared to start the year they named him an assistant captain.

It was a fairly respectable start for the veteran winger, as he scored the first power-play goal in franchise history against the New York Islanders on October 12, 1974. He was also responsible for their first game-winning tally in a match with their expansion cousins, the Washington Capitals, on November 3. The honeymoon did not last long, though, as Deadmarsh grew disenchanted with the Scouts and decided to quit the team abruptly after 20 games.

Fortunately, Kansas City knew that the WHA had been trying to get him to jump over, and a rare transaction between the two leagues took place when the Scouts sold him to the Vancouver Blazers.

DENIS HERRON

One of the most promising young goalies in hockey in the early 1970s, Herron began his career with the Pittsburgh Penguins and was the first netminder in NHL history to make his team's roster in the same year that he was drafted. He was occasionally sent down to the minors for conditioning and spent most of the early part of the 1974–75 campaign with the AHL's Hershey Bears before he was traded to Kansas City along with Jean-Guy Lagace.

"I came a lot cheaper than Michel Plasse," he said. "For me, I was very pleased because I was in Hershey. There were three goalies there and I was barely playing."

In fact, Herron did not even find out about the trade until partway through Pittsburgh's game against Atlanta on January 10, 1975, as he sat on the bench. Just 13 days later, he was in the crease for one of the most important games of his career when the Scouts took on the Boston Bruins. He stole the show that night in a 3–2 victory.

"The first shot of the game came from Bobby Orr and went right in," he said. "From there, my confidence went up. I went from a guy who wasn't playing at all and I never looked back. That was really a turning point for my career."

Over the rest of the schedule, Herron emerged as the team's top man in net, but he faced a lot of challenges in Kansas City.

"It was very rough," he said. "It was a good thing for me because I faced a lot of shots and got a lot of experience. I became a free agent after that and had the choice of going to Pittsburgh or Vancouver. I tried to work as much as possible in practice with my defencemen to let them know what I needed them to do. In that era, it was all about communication. If they have confidence in you compared to another goalie, they'll play differently with you."

MICHEL PLASSE

Plasse was the Scouts' first selection in the 1974 NHL Expansion Draft. He had spent the previous two seasons in a Montreal Canadiens uniform and performed well in a backup role. Back in 1968, he was the first overall pick in the NHL Amateur Draft and was shuffled off to the St. Louis organization for a couple of seasons. During that time, he became the first goaltender to score a goal while playing for Kansas City in the Central League.

In Kansas City, the feeling was that Plasse would be the team's number one netminder. He was in net for the club's second victory on November 13, 1974, against the Blues. Riding a hot streak, he played the next night when the Scouts took on the New York Islanders and they won by a score of 4–2. During a 2–2 tie with Vancouver on December 14, he recorded an assist on a goal by Norm Dube.

The ownership group in Kansas City was notoriously tight-fisted and, in negotiations for a long-term deal, they balked at Plasse's demand for a six-figure contract for the following season. The Pittsburgh Penguins traded for him, but he later rejoined the franchise when they became the Colorado Rockies. Sadly, he passed away from a heart attack on December 30, 2006.

EXPANSION YEAR RECORD: 8-67-5
(21 points — fifth in Norris Division)
COACHES: Jim Anderson, Red Sullivan and Milt Schmidt
GENERAL MANAGER: Milt Schmidt
FIRST GAME: October 9, 1974 —
6-3 loss vs. New York Rangers
FIRST GOAL: October 9, 1974 by Jim Hrycuik

WASHINGTON CAPITALS

Residents of the capital district had been without a pro hockey team to call their own for well over a decade, but the sport was set to return in a big way in the early 1970s to combat the spread of the WHA into new markets.

The NHL was committed to expanding to 18 teams in time for the 1974–75 season and on June 9, 1972, granted a new franchise to Abe Pollin, also the owner of the NBA's Washington Bullets. One of Pollin's first acts was to hire Hall of Famer Milt Schmidt to head up the operation, but nobody was prepared for the sheer horror that was about to ensue.

By 1974, the war between the two pro leagues had weakened NHL rosters as players left in droves to seek out more lucrative contracts. For the 1974–75 season, a whopping 32 teams were about to take to the ice across both leagues, and the talent pool was starting to seriously thin out. The NHL had already seen the result of expanding too quickly to gain a foothold in some markets, and it was about to come to an ugly culmination at the 1974 NHL Expansion Draft.

The Capitals and their expansion cousins, the Kansas City Scouts, had to pick from a talent pool that was arguably weak when compared to previous drafts, but the Capitals grabbed two promising young goalies first in Ron Low and Michel Belhumeur. After that, most of the players they chose tended to be minor-leaguers or players with limited NHL experience. Perhaps the best of the group were Denis Dupere

245

and Yvon Labre, but they were not household names. Their chances at success looked bleak, and even the addition of amateurs like first overall pick Greg Joly and rough-and-tumble Mike Marson did not inspire confidence in observers at the time.

The team's arena, the Capital Centre, was finished well before the start of the 1974–75 season, and many bumper stickers began to pop up with the phrase, "Stick it to 'em, Capitals!" Former AHL standout Jim Anderson was brought on to coach the club, and Schmidt also added a former teammate in Doug Mohns to help provide veteran leadership. Training camp was full of players who were on the bubble when it came to making it in pro hockey, but as the roster was trimmed down and they took to the ice for their first pre-season games, they actually made a good impression on some opposing clubs.

"Those guys are obviously shooting for a place on the roster," said Montreal Canadiens coach Scotty Bowman. "That's the pattern with almost all the new teams. It is amazing how deep some guys can dig."

On October 9, 1974, the Caps opened their first season on the road against the New York Rangers, and rookie Jim Hrycuik scored their first goal. They lost 6–3 that night but eventually got their first victory in their second home game when they surprised the Chicago Black Hawks eight days later. From that point on, it was a bit of a disaster — and not just because of the white pants they wore on the ice. They started a 14-game winless streak and finished with just three triumphs in the first half of the season.

The team's lack of success was blamed partly on a rash of injuries and the general inexperience of many of the players. As a result, the players held several meetings and declared Mohns their official captain. Anderson felt the pressure and opened up to the press about the problems of coaching a first-year team.

"Actually, I am satisfied as a coach," he said. "I realize the record isn't inspiring. We've been blown out at times. Other times, though, we've been in games against older teams. I know what I'm teaching. I see progress. Just about all the other teams have had some bad scores against them this year. Clubs like Minnesota, Detroit and Toronto. For some of those older clubs to get beat the way they do is terrible. We're not as bad off as they are . . . really.

"I'm certain that these guys have not given up, that they have more enthusiasm today than they did a month ago. I saw it the other night when they saw a capacity crowd at the Capital Centre. These fellows have pride and they're together as a team."

At one point, the team had 60 consecutive power plays without scoring. It just kept getting worse as they occasionally lost games by a 10-goal margin. One of the few bright spots was a 3–0 win over their expansion cousins, the Kansas City Scouts, on February 16, 1975, and attendance was actually on a bit of an upswing as the year progressed. To help shake things up they also made some trades, including a deal that saw their first All-Star Game representative, Dupere, traded away.

"We've been busting our bottoms to make it more entertaining," said Schmidt. "Our phone bills the past four days are going to put Mr. Pollin back a few more dollars, but that's the thing that has to be done. We're down in the dumps, but we're still kicking."

The Caps also faced a brief challenge when the WHA's Michigan Stags relocated to nearby Baltimore. The general manager of the Blades, Skip Feldman, shot out the first salvo on a local radio show.

"If people will pay to see the Washington Capitals, they'll pay for anything."

Schmidt probably had an inkling that the war with the Blades for the hearts of hockey fans was not going to last long and his response was much more professional.

"People in this area now have a chance to see hockey from both sides. In a way it will make them all more conscious of the sport. We'll just let the chips fall where they may."

After just five wins in his first 55 games, Anderson was let go and replaced behind the bench by chief scout Red Sullivan. Anderson was honest about his role in the team's early failures.

"I wasn't Red. I tried my best the way I thought we would build. I was in expansion hockey and they were very fair to me. Red Sullivan probably told me more of what to expect and how to handle myself more than anything else. He told me whenever I was really down that I was earning twice what they were paying me. At times maybe I was. At times maybe I wasn't. This didn't exactly jump up and hit me cold. I knew they would have to make a change if we didn't start winning. I guess I knew while we were on the west coast. I came out of the Los Angeles Forum and stared up into the dark sky. There I was standing alone and hearing things. We had lost. I was running out of time. It was a game we should have won."

The players were not necessarily gung-ho about the coaching change. One anonymous Capital was quoted about Sullivan, "He scares the hell out of me."

Sullivan felt he might be able to motivate his charges and help improve their record.

"I'm not promising I'll turn things around overnight. There are a few things that I want and I'll get them . . . respect, hard work, checking. I took it with every intention of being behind the Washington bench for 10 years. There are 26 games remaining this year, and one thing I'd like to see is that this club gets 18 or 19 more points in the standings. I don't want anyone calling it the worst team in league history."

In the end, Sullivan's winning percentage was greater than Anderson's, but it was not enough to help them improve in the standings. With just eight games left in the year, Schmidt had enough of the on-ice nightmare and took over the coaching reins.

"I have been sitting upstairs and cursing all year," he said. "I had to go down to the bench and try to do something myself. It's obvious, though, it's going to take more than coaching."

Sullivan went back to being the team's chief scout, and the Capitals finally won a road game on March 28, 1975, under Schmidt. After dispatching the California Golden Seals by a score of 5–3, they celebrated in the dressing room by taking a garbage can and parading it around as if it were the Stanley Cup, the festivities spilling out to the empty arena. They later closed out the year against Pittsburgh with their eighth win of the season. Their finish was one for the ages as it was the worst in modern NHL history.

The next seven seasons were a test of patience for Capitals fans.

(clockwise) Doug Mohns, Bill Mikkelson, Greg Joly, Ron Low

They didn't make the playoffs until Rod Langway arrived on the blue line in 1982–83. They came close to making the postseason a few times before that, but their many bad breaks did not help. For most of the 1980s and into the 1990s, they made it to the playoffs 14 straight times and finally made it to the Stanley Cup Final in 1997–98. After that, their fortunes were mixed for a few years, but they finally rose back to consistent contention after the lockout with Alexander Ovechkin in the lineup. Since 2007–08, they have earned four Southeast Division titles and even won the President's Trophy in 2009–10.

TOMMY WILLIAMS

Williams was one of the few American-born players in the NHL ranks in the 1960s. He had many successful seasons with the Boston Bruins before missing out on a Stanley Cup championship in 1969–70 after he was traded to the Minnesota North Stars. He spent some time with the California Golden Seals after that, but was sold back to the Big Bad Bruins in March 1972. Strangely, he did not end up back with the club and chose to play in the WHA for two seasons with the New England Whalers.

The summer before the 1974–75 campaign, Williams was sold once again to the Capitals and returned to NHL action. He was named one of the club's alternate captains and led them in goals, assists and points in their first season. His first goal of the season, fittingly, was scored against the Boston Bruins on November 7, 1974, and he followed that up with two-goal efforts against the Flames and North Stars later that month.

"I played with Tommy in Boston and he was good at handling the puck," said team captain Doug Mohns. "And he was better than the average player when it came to his skating ability. I think that was what kept him in the league. He took it hard when we lost, like everybody else."

On March 26, 1975, Williams became the second member of the Caps to score 20 goals in a season when he slid one past Gary Edwards in a 5-1 loss to the Los Angeles Kings. He closed the season from hell with a five-point night against the Pittsburgh Penguins on April 6 when he scored twice, including the game-winner, on Bob Johnson, who was appearing in his final NHL contest.

DENIS DUPERE

Dupere missed more than half of the 1973–74 season because of injury and so, although he was putting up points at the best pace of his career, the Toronto Maple Leafs were prepared to let him go through the expansion draft.

He surprised everyone with a decent start and had two goals during the Capitals' first victory — a 4-3 triumph over the Chicago Black Hawks on October 17, 1974. What many of his teammates remember are the "legendary" goals he had against the Boston Bruins in two early-season blowouts. He scored a late power-play goal in the 10-4 loss on November 7, and on December 14, he had their only goal in a horrifying 12-1 defeat.

Not long after he scored two goals against the Montreal Canadiens on January 12, 1975, Dupere was selected to represent the team at the 1975 NHL All-Star Game. His final goal in a Capitals uniform came in a battle with Los Angeles on January 30, and it was a shock when he was traded to the St. Louis Blues a couple of weeks later. Dupere's production decreased over the remainder of the season, and Washington got the better end of the deal with Ace Bailey and Stan Gilbertson.

MIKE MARSON

Marson had a great 1973–74 season with the OHA's Sudbury Wolves, where he scored 94 points and was named to the league's Second All-Star Team. When the Capitals made him their second pick in the 1974 NHL Amateur Draft, they made history, as he was the first African-Canadian player ever selected in the annual rite of passage for junior players. He signed a five-year deal with the club.

"I'm 19, have some money, and it's up to me now to play it all right," said Marson at the time. "If I do, I can go through life without having to work at anything but hockey. It's what I've always dreamed of doing."

Although he showed up to training camp a whopping 22 pounds overweight, he demonstrated a commitment to making Washington's roster and he hit the ice with them on October 9, 1974. No other African-Canadian player had played at the NHL level since Willie O'Ree suited up for Boston during the 1960–61 season.

On November 19, 1974, as Washington took on the California Golden Seals, he scored his first two NHL goals, and the first was the game-winner. In fact, he was the only Capital to score more than one decision-maker, as he scored another one on February 11, 1975, to upset the New York Rangers.

In the long run, Marson did not set the world on fire in the National Hockey League and he was out of the pro game by the end of the 1979–80 campaign. Although he is rarely remembered by fans today, he holds a special spot in hockey history.

YVON LABRE

Drafted by the Pittsburgh Penguins in 1969, Labre spent a lot of time in the minors honing his skills and appeared in 37 games with the club over two seasons. In 1973–74, he saw limited NHL action but had great success in the AHL with the Calder Cup champion Hershey Bears. The Capitals made him the second skater they selected in the expansion draft and he gave them instant hope on the blue line.

Voted the club's most popular player in its inaugural season, Labre scored the Caps first goal at home when he bulged the twine at 4:35 of the second period in a clash with the Los Angeles Kings on October 15, 1974. Four days later, he got a goal and an assist against the Detroit Red Wings. He was also given the honour of being one of Washington's assistant captains and had a couple of three-assist games over the course of the year.

One of his best performances was recognized by teammate Ron Low after the team shut down the Kansas City Scouts on February 16, 1975.

"Yvon was always around to help, clearing the puck and getting it down ice. The wings were backchecking, the defencemen never let them get a second chance."

Labre eventually became the longest-serving original member of the Capitals, and the team recognized his contributions by retiring his number on November 7, 1981. He is still associated with the team to this day and is a driving force behind its alumni association.

DAVE KRYSKOW

After getting a small taste of NHL action in 1972–73 with Chicago during their run to the Stanley Cup Final, Kryskow was a full-fledged rookie with the Black Hawks the following year and was extremely happy to be playing for a contender — even if it was in a somewhat limited role. That happiness was taken away at the 1974 NHL Expansion Draft when he was sent to hockey purgatory in Washington.

"I was disappointed at first," he recalled. "Chicago was a great organization and I was surprised that I was picked. I came from organizations that were well structured and I was disappointed with there being no structure or plan [in Washington]. . . . I never had a meeting with management. The whole concept of the team was building around their draft choices and that was wrong. That's all in hindsight, though.

"It was tough, especially if you came from a winning team. Here, after 20 games you were wondering how much time was left in the season. The money was immaterial. I just wanted to play, but I also wanted to win. . . . We were just happy to keep it down to a touchdown. We still scored a few goals but they were scoring seven or eight against us."

Placed on the team's top line with Tommy Williams and Denis Dupere, Kryskow had a handful of multi-point games early in the season and he also scored the first shorthanded goal in franchise history against the Los Angeles Kings on December 19, 1974. While out on the west coast, he had a conversation with coach Jim Anderson and expressed his concerns.

"We were in California and he asked my opinion and I said he should send these young bastards down to the minors and get some guys who knew how to play the game."

The frustration continually built through the season and it was only going to get worse, as he was traded to Detroit for Jack Lynch.

"I just couldn't take this shit anymore," he said. "To go to a situation in Detroit that was even worse. I wish I could have approached it differently and they should have too. . . . The first practice in Detroit, Alex Delvecchio came up to me and said they weren't going to play me much because they wanted to give the younger guys more time. I was only 23!"

Kryskow later went on to win an AVCO Cup with the WHA's Winnipeg Jets before he retired. He summed up his time with Washington.

"It was one of those times in your life that you wish you could have changed and have input in how things were done. Milt [Schmidt] was old school and it was his way or the highway."

DOUG MOHNS

Mohns was a veteran set to retire at the end of the 1973–74 season because of his back woes when he received a phone call that convinced him to spend one more year in the NHL.

"I got a call from Milt in the spring and he wanted to know if I would be interested in playing for the Washington Capitals. His offer had me thinking, and I said I will give it some thought and call him back. My wife finally agreed and the rest is history. . . . I started in the fall of 1953 when Milt was playing in his last year in Boston, and ironically we ended up on the same team 22 years later in Washington when it was my turn to retire as a player."

The Capitals purchased his contract from the Atlanta Flames and he was installed as a leader in the dressing room for a club that was not exactly brimming with NHL experience. When the team was mired in a 17-game losing streak and sliding toward a league low, Mohns called a meeting among the players early in the new year and they ended up naming him their first captain.

"Tommy Williams suggested it, and I think most of the players, if not all the players, gave me the nod. We had played a number of games at that point and I was in favour of having someone to represent the team and hold meetings among the players. I thought it would enable the players to speak their mind and share their thoughts behind closed doors. There would be no criticism allowed, only helpful suggestions that could be passed on to the coach."

The team reacted positively to their new leader and snapped the skid by defeating the Detroit Red Wings 6–3 on January 26, 1975. Throughout the year, Mohns remained in regular contact with Schmidt and, even though the club's fortunes were not good, it had no impact on the friendship they had built.

"Nothing changed. We respected one another on and off the ice," he said. "And, although we didn't express our frustrations and misery to one another, it was there. I tried to stay away from any negativism in the hope that other players would follow my example. I think it helped to some degree."

Under his leadership, the Caps won five games and benefited from the addition of some new players to the roster. At the end of the year, he retired after 22 seasons. Mohns remains one of the most under-rated players from his era.

"He was by far the most respected individual on the team," said Bill Mikkelson. "Here was a guy who had so much experience and there was nobody who could come close."

BILL LESUK

Before he was sold to the Capitals, Lesuk had been with the Los Angeles Kings since the 1971–72 season and he had an inkling he might be on the way out after refusing a three-year contract offer from general manager Larry Regan. After missing a good chunk of the 1973–74 campaign, he was ready to get some regular ice time — even with an expansion club that had limited chance for success.

"As I look back on it, you can't really fault anyone for wanting to play, which I wasn't doing on a regular basis," he said. "I remember management in Washington letting the players know from the start that there was going to be a lot of turnover and many of us weren't going to be there next year. Knowing what I know now, that's a normal occurrence, but sometimes as a player, you don't want to hear that."

Used primarily as a checker against the best players in the league,

Lesuk was out there every night plugging away. His first goal of the season came while the Caps were shorthanded during a battle with the California Golden Seals on December 20, 1974. Although some of his former teammates can be rather bitter about the 1974–75 season, Lesuk took it as a learning experience.

"In Washington, the management did the absolute best they could have done. I have a lot of respect for Milt Schmidt and his assistant, Lefty McFadden. In that turmoil, you learned a lot about your teammates. We had a meeting to find out what the problem was with the team. One player said there was a lack of talent, but that shouldn't affect how you play the game.

"Some of the players would take the games a lot more seriously than others. Some people would say things to lighten things up. It's pretty hard to remain positive through all that. I go to see my grandchildren play today and I can tell them that I've been there."

STAN GILBERTSON

Gilbertson was in his fourth NHL season in 1974–75 when he went from the California Golden Seals to the St. Louis Blues in an early-season deal. His stint with the Blues lasted a mere 25 games before he was shipped off to Washington with Garnet Bailey in a shocking trade for All-Star Denis Dupere.

Even though he had scored only two goals over his first 37 games, he picked up his production in his new surroundings. Less than a week after his arrival, he scored the game-winning goal and added an assist in a battle with Washington's expansion cousins, the Kansas City Scouts. He was also dangerous during a loss to the Toronto Maple Leafs on March 1, 1975, where he scored two goals in the 5–4 loss. His best performance of the year, however, came when he scored four goals and earned an assist in the season-ending 8–4 victory over the Pittsburgh Penguins.

Traded to the Penguins the following year, Gilbertson was forced to retire after the 1976–77 campaign when he lost part of his leg in an auto accident.

STEVE ATKINSON

His declining production with the Buffalo Sabres after their inaugural season made Atkinson fodder for the 1974 NHL Expansion Draft, but he almost didn't make it out of training camp after he hurt himself while choking on a piece of meat.

"I was too damned excited to get going," he said to the press.

Regardless, coach Jim Anderson had praise for his defensive abilities.

"He's an asset. He can play the point. At least he doesn't give up the puck," he said.

Atkinson recovered in time to start the regular season but was demoted at the end of October. Recalled from Richmond a few weeks later, he had his first goal in a Capitals uniform against Minnesota's Pete LoPresti on November 24, 1974. Over the course of the year, he was sent up and down but managed to register a pair of two-goal games against the New York Rangers.

On February 1, 1975, he scored the team's first penalty shot goal on Vancouver's Ken Lockett and the veteran winger casually joked about the big moment.

"They'll have to speed that up to play in slow motion!"

BILL MIKKELSON

Mikkelson spent the 1972–73 season with the first-year New York Islanders, but he was not on their roster the next year and skated for the AHL's Baltimore Clippers. Following a 22-point effort, he was taken by the Capitals in the expansion draft and was able to tell his new teammates about the crazy experience of playing on Long Island.

What he got was an even more horrifying year from a hockey perspective, as the Caps put together the worst record in league history. He saw a ton of action on the blue line and his first goal came on the power play when they took on the powerful Philadelphia Flyers on November 9, 1974. A little more than two weeks later, he had a two-point effort against the California Golden Seals. It was a difficult time for him as he had recently lost his brother, Warren, in an auto accident.

"That year was far less pleasant for me than the first expansion season. The death of my brother was the foremost thing on my mind. I had to be at the top of my game just to be there. There's a fine line between being a bottom-six player in the NHL and a top-four player in the AHL."

The 1974–75 season also saw the assistant captain establish a place in hockey history. For every NHL record, there is usually an opposite one. In the case of Bobby Orr's plus-minus rating of +124 in 1970–71, there is Mikkelson's standard of -82 that was established four years later with the woeful first-year Capitals. While some observers of the game do not put a lot of stock in the statistic, he offered some explanation of how the standard was achieved.

"We only really played four defencemen at the time, and that allowed us to play against the other team's top lines. When I look back on it, I was too respectful of players like Bobby Orr and Phil Esposito when I shouldn't have been. You've got to go out there and treat them like anybody else. When we went into Montreal or Boston, there was no hope. It wasn't who was going to win, but by how much. If you could get out of it at -1, that was a good night.

"Its only value may be among players on the same team for comparison, and even then, it's flawed. If I had been Bobby Orr's partner that year, I would probably have been +50. It's very much a team statistic."

Late in the season, Mikkelson was assigned to the Richmond Robins and he played in only one more NHL game. Although plus-minus records were not a big topic of discussion by fans in the 1970s, his record took on a life of its own in subsequent years.

"It started showing up as an odd blurb in the newspaper, and I would see it more and more each year. When I worked at IBM, some of my co-workers had fun with it. I told my kids that if any of the other kids gave them trouble about the record, to ask what their dad's plus-minus was. That shut them up pretty quickly! Would I trade my record for anything in the world? I would not."

His daughter, Meaghan, has had great success playing for Canada during international competitions and won a gold medal at the 2010 and 2014 Winter Olympics. His son Brendan has also followed him into the NHL and has played for Anaheim, Calgary and Tampa Bay.

JIM HRYCUIK

A second-year pro with the AHL's Hershey Bears in 1973–74, Hrycuik made a solid impression with 75 points during the regular season and was part of a Calder Cup–winning squad as well. The Capitals took notice of the undrafted youngster's efforts and grabbed him during the intra-league draft.

"I was obviously excited," said Hrycuik. "I had gone to Boston's camp as a free agent a couple of years earlier. They had too many guys under contract and I had other plans."

He knew that he was going to play on a weak team. He was responsible for their earliest highlight, scoring the first goal for Washington in their season opener against Ed Giacomin of the New York Rangers at 5:06 of the first period. He also had an assist that night.

"You never forget your first goal. I had the puck in the corner and I snuck it backhanded into the net."

Despite his decent two-point performance during a loss to the Kansas City Scouts on November 3, 1974, Hrycuik was sent down to the AHL again to play for the Richmond Robins. After he earned seven points over seven games, he was quickly brought back up and had the game-tying goal when the Caps faced the Rangers again on December 12. When the team hosted the Toronto Maple Leafs three days later, he had a goal and an assist.

Misfortune struck just three days before Christmas in a game with the Buffalo Sabres when he blew out his knee when he ran into the goalpost. That injury essentially ended his career, and Hrycuik remains critical of the management team that served during his time with Washington.

"My opinion is if we would have had a good coach, we would have won more games. We had no system. We weren't a serious hockey team and that upset me a bit. My goal was to play in the NHL and we were a bit of a party team."

GREG JOLY

Regarded as one of the biggest-ever busts in the history of the NHL draft, the Capitals placed a lot of faith in Joly after he had a phenomenal Memorial Cup tournament in 1974 while playing for the WHL's Regina Pats. In fact, he was not even rated as the top prospect coming out of the junior ranks that year, but Washington wanted to build their franchise around a defenceman — much like the Boston Bruins had less than a decade earlier with Bobby Orr.

The reality was that no matter how much general manager Milt Schmidt wanted Joly to be the next Orr, he might have had more success with other available talent such as Wilf Paiement, Clark Gillies or Pierre Larouche — all first-round picks taken in the top 10 that year who had long and productive careers.

Joly was in Washington's lineup during their opening game against the New York Rangers and recorded his first assist on a goal by Ron Anderson. He was used on the power play extensively during the early part of the season. His first career goal came against Peter McDuffe of the Kansas City Scouts on November 3, 1974, but he injured his right knee about a month later in a tilt with the Buffalo Sabres.

Team captain Doug Mohns offered an honest appraisal of the young star.

"Greg had a lot of potential and it was easy to see that he had a lot of natural talent. He was the one player I felt sorry for," he said. "Had he been on a winning team, starting out, I have no doubt that he would have had a lengthy career in the National Hockey League barring injuries. He was only 20 years old and had very little support."

JACK EGERS

After he recorded two 20-goal efforts for the St. Louis Blues, Egers was reacquired by the New York Rangers early in the 1973–74 season, but he missed time because of injury. The Rangers had originally drafted him in 1966, but he figured that his second term with the team was not going to last long with another expansion draft coming up.

His expectations proved true when the Capitals took him with their final pick. On October 17, 1974, Egers scored the goal that secured the first victory in franchise history against Mike Veisor of the Chicago Black Hawks. While that first win was an early high point for the club, many rough games followed — including an 11–1 loss to the Montreal Canadiens on November 10.

"It's hard to go into Boston or Philadelphia and know that you're not going to win," he reflected. "I have a lot of empathy for expansion teams, but I think it's fairer since then. We knew early on that we couldn't compete."

He scored their only goal in the Montreal massacre. Soon after, he began to feel a gradual shooting pain down his leg but kept on playing. A ruptured disc was the root cause, and he was expected to be out of action for three months.

After he was out for eight weeks, he came back and ruptured it again in practice and his year was over. There was at least one fringe benefit, however, as Doug Mohns let him take his place to go to Bermuda as the team's NHLPA representative. He tried to come back again the following year but did not want to head to the minors. Egers feels bitter about his time with Washington.

"You were treated like a piece of meat," he said. "I wonder if I had been given that year off if I would have had three or four more years."

MICHEL BELHUMEUR

Belhumeur got his first shot at NHL action with the Philadelphia Flyers in 1972–73, but the return of Bernie Parent to the organization sent him back to the minors. He had just finished a rough season with the AHL's Richmond Robins when the Capitals claimed him during the 1974 NHL Expansion Draft.

With a fresh opportunity to establish himself as an NHL-calibre goalie, he faced a tremendous challenge stepping into the crease for Washington. In fact, he did not win a single game for the club and ended up setting a record for most appearances in a season without a victory. The lone highlight of the team's first season was that he became the first Capitals goaltender to earn an assist after passing the puck to Mike Marson before Marson scored against the California Golden Seals on February 5, 1975.

RON LOW

The year after his 1972–73 rookie season with the Maple Leafs, Low was one of the best goaltenders in the minors, winning 23 games for the CHL's Tulsa Oilers and earning eight shutouts along the way. He was on the cusp of becoming a regular NHLer, but a glut of goaltenders in Toronto meant that he went unprotected in the expansion draft. The Capitals took him with their first pick.

Low was in the crease for the club's first outing against the New York Rangers and he earned their first victory on October 17, 1974, when they defeated the Chicago Black Hawks. The wins were infrequent after that, but he managed to maintain his status as the number one netminder. There were certainly many bleak nights over the course of the season, but he was credited with all eight of Washington's wins in 1974–75, including the first shutout in franchise history on February 16, 1975, when he blanked the Kansas City Scouts.

"I believe Ron worked harder than anyone else trying to keep the puck out of the net. He showed his stuff and never gave up — sign of a true professional," said Doug Mohns. "Ron would be my pick for the team's Most Valuable Player. I don't know how our goaltenders lasted until the end of the season. Their goals against was 446. You have to wonder how many shots, in total, they had to try and stop."

TWO LEAGUES FIND PEACE

Seven seasons of war between two rival hockey leagues helped define the sport in the 1970s, but it was a conflict that caused a great deal of collateral damage for both the NHL and the WHA. Although player salaries finally increased to a respectable level for the era, the on-ice product began to suffer and there was a frenzy of franchises shifting and going under.

There were several attempts at striking a compromise throughout the decade, but it often seemed as if they were merely talk instead of serious negotiations. The WHA's first attempt to discuss the idea came in 1977, and they proposed that six member clubs (Cincinnati, Edmonton, Houston, New England, Quebec and Winnipeg) join the NHL, bringing their membership to 24 teams. The NHL Board of Governors discussed the idea internally, but it was turned down flatly.

A year later, talks began again without the soon-to-fold Houston Aeros and the WHA faced rejection again. Out of desperation, ownership in Houston attempted to come in on their own as an expansion team and even offered to buy an existing team with the intention of relocation. Once again, the NHL balked, since they were already dealing with an internal merger of the Cleveland Barons and Minnesota North Stars.

The WHA had at least one ace up their sleeves, as they began signing underage prospects at a frantic pace to undermine the NHL Amateur Draft. Wayne Gretzky was the most prominent of these young stars, but the Birmingham Bulls went on a spree to get top talent such as

Michel Goulet, Rick Vaive and Craig Hartsburg. The 1978–79 season was bleak at best for the WHA, as the Indianapolis Racers folded after 25 games and there were only six teams remaining. It was during this campaign that merger talks picked up, and it became apparent that only Edmonton, New England, Quebec and Winnipeg were being considered for admission by the NHL.

To its credit, the WHA insisted that all three Canadian-based clubs be a part of the merger, and that caused a great deal of consternation for the Montreal Canadiens, Toronto Maple Leafs and Vancouver Canucks. When the merger was put to a vote, the Canadian teams along with the Boston Bruins and Los Angeles Kings voted against it, and it did not meet the required numbers needed to support it.

There were a variety of reasons for their votes, but the fallout was probably not anticipated by Molson Breweries, who owned the Canadiens at the time. Hockey fans in Edmonton, Quebec City and Winnipeg staged a major boycott of their products and their sales began to drop nationally as well. The Canadian teams were also not at all interested in splitting national television revenues. During a second vote on March 22, 1979, the Canucks and Canadiens chose to change their votes. Vancouver was persuaded by the promise of a balanced schedule, and the merger became official.

At that time, the WHA was still in the midst of their final season and Gretzky had moved from Indianapolis to Edmonton through a trade. At the end of the playoffs, the Jets defeated the Oilers for the last AVCO Cup. Each of the four "new" teams had to cough up $6,000,000, while Birmingham and Cincinnati received $1,500,000 parachute payments and were given the chance to join the Central Hockey League for the 1979–80 season.

It was not going to be easy for the WHA expatriates, because the NHL put forth a series of restrictive conditions on the merger. In effect, the WHA teams were basically destroyed and were practically forced to build from scratch. The NHL held a reclamation draft, which allowed the 17 existing teams to put in a claim on any players they had lost over the past seven seasons and the WHA teams did not receive any compensation. They were "graciously" allowed to protect two skaters and two goalies before the expansion draft, but the pickings were rather slim by then. The annual amateur draft became the Entry Draft, and several of the young players the WHA signed as underagers, such as Rob Ramage, Mike Gartner and Mark Messier, were made available to the established NHL clubs. The new entries got a chance to make their picks at the end of each round.

The 1979–80 campaign was a rough one for the Jets and Nordiques as a result of a combination of factors, but the Oilers and the newly rechristened Hartford Whalers squeaked into the playoffs. In time, Edmonton proved to be the most successful of the four teams and won five Stanley Cup championships.

Unfortunately for the NHL, some franchises were still in dire straits financially. The Atlanta Flames moved to Calgary for the 1980–81 season. The upside of that move was the creation of an instant rivalry. In 1981–82, the NHL realigned their divisions and based them on geographic proximity, and that move was a success. The troubled Colorado Rockies headed east to become the New Jersey Devils in 1982–83, after which the league enjoyed a decade that did not see a single franchise move or another expansion team come on the scene.

EXPANSION YEAR RECORD: 28–39–13
(69 points — fourth in Smythe Division)
COACH: Glen Sather
GENERAL MANAGER: Larry Gordon
FIRST GAME: October 10, 1979 —
4–2 loss vs. Chicago Black Hawks
FIRST GOAL: October 10, 1979 by Kevin Lowe

EDMONTON OILERS

The roots of the Edmonton Oilers go back to the 1972–73 season, when the franchise became an original member of the World Hockey Association. The team spent their first season as the Alberta Oilers before changing to their more familiar name. Over the course of seven campaigns, the Oilers were usually in the middle of the pack and made the playoffs on five occasions.

It was not until the 1978–79 season that the Oilers reached the next level, and they did it as a direct result of the coaching abilities of Glen Sather. They had a good nucleus of young talent, but the biggest addition to the roster came on November 2, 1978, when they gave up $700,000 to get Peter Driscoll, Ed Mio and a 17-year-old budding superstar named Wayne Gretzky from the floundering Indianapolis Racers. By the end of the season, Edmonton finished in first place in the league and was heavily favoured heading into the playoffs. After they eliminated the New England Whalers in seven games, they faced the Winnipeg Jets for the AVCO Cup but lost in six.

During this time, the NHL and WHA agreed to merge. The Oilers became one of four new NHL clubs in 1979–80. The rather unbalanced terms favoured the NHL greatly, but Edmonton did not lose as many players as the other teams in the now-defunct WHA because they reacquired Risto Siltanen, Stan Weir and Dave Semenko through trades. Luckily, they were permitted to protect Gretzky along with goalies Mio and Dave Dryden. In the 1979 NHL Expansion Draft, the team added some blue-line strength in Colin Campbell, Pat Price, Doug Hicks and Lee Fogolin and they got gifted grinder Dave Hunter back.

In the early years of the Edmonton Oilers, the club scoured the hockey world for the best talent. Their first NHL Entry Draft was a great one as they took Kevin Lowe with their premier selection and added Mark Messier in the third round. Both proved ready for action in time for the season opener, but they had to wait for Glenn Anderson because he was going to play for the Canadian Olympic Team instead.

"I don't think there will be too many guys over 30 on the club, not that that's exactly a sin," said Sather in a 1979 interview. "If we're going to struggle in our first year, and that's a possibility, I'd rather do it with kids than guys, say, 32 or 33 with only a few years left in their careers. I plan on building with youth . . . like teams like the New York Islanders."

On October 10, 1979, the Oilers began their NHL odyssey with a road game against the Chicago Black Hawks. Their opponents got off to a 2–0 lead in the first three minutes, but Edmonton evened it up with goals from Lowe and Hunter. Gretzky got his first NHL point with an assist on Lowe's tally, but the tie was quickly erased and the contest ended with a 4–2 win for the home team. Three days later, they began a four-game home stand but didn't earn their first victory until the Quebec Nordiques came to town on October 19. At home, the team played in front of a full house every night, and the fan support reflected how much the community supported their local heroes.

For some Oilers fans, the first month of NHL action was an exercise in frustration, since they managed only one victory against five losses and four ties. Slowly things began to turn around as they went 4–7–2 in November, two of those wins coming against the New York Islanders. As Gretzky began to pick up his offensive production, teammates Blair MacDonald and Stan Weir also generated their fair share of goals.

Over the first half of the season, Dryden and Bill Flett each announced their retirement and the youth movement began to gather steam. Goaltending became a major problem because Mio sustained injuries, so as a result Jim Corsi had more chances to play. They also used some unproven talents, but more as a stop-gap measure than as a long-term solution.

Edmonton had the opportunity to play an exhibition game against the touring Moscow Dynamo team on January 4, 1980, but lost 4–1. A little more than a month later, MacDonald and Gretzky became the team's first representatives at an NHL All-Star Game, around the same time that the Oilers' young superstar began to close the gap in the scoring race. He averaged nearly two points per game over the second half of the schedule, and while setting some of his earliest records, he began to receive serious consideration for the Hart Trophy.

At the trade deadline, the Oilers made some moves that ultimately helped them secure a playoff spot. They gave up veteran Bobby Schmautz to get more youth and strength in Don Ashby of the Colorado Rockies, and they sent tough-guy Cam Connor to the New York Rangers for the troubled but promising Don Murdoch. The best deal of them all, however, saw captain Ron Chippefield go to the Nordiques for goalie Ron Low. Over the remainder of the regular schedule, Gretzky's scoring and Low's play in net helped Edmonton go 8–2–1 and they narrowly beat out Washington by two points to qualify for postseason action.

In 1979–80, the NHL adopted a system that allowed the top 16 teams in the league to make it to the playoffs. The Oilers had to take on the Philadelphia Flyers — a team that finished first overall and went undefeated for 35 straight games that year. Most observers expected blowouts in the series, but Edmonton kept each game to a single goal and two of them went into overtime as the Flyers swept them in three straight.

For the rest of the 1980s, the Oilers proved themselves one of the best organizations in the NHL and were built into a Stanley Cup championship dynasty. They made it to the Stanley Cup Final for the first time in 1983 and went on to win it all in five of the next seven seasons. Gretzky was the team's primary superstar but his supporting cast included legends like Anderson, Messier, Lowe, Jari Kurri, Paul Coffey and Grant Fuhr. In the 1990s, the club experienced some tough times when they missed the playoffs for the first time, but they bounced back with the addition of talents such as Curtis Joseph and Ryan Smyth to the lineup.

In 2005–06, they made it to the Stanley Cup Final again but lost

(clockwise) Wayne Gretzky, Blair MacDonald, Kevin Lowe, Ron Low

to the Carolina Hurricanes and have not been back to the postseason since. Now in a long rebuilding phase, they have had the first overall selection in the NHL Entry Draft for three years running from 2010 to 2012. It is only a matter of time before these youngsters help the Oilers become a success once again.

WAYNE GRETZKY

From the start, the hockey community touted Gretzky as a future superstar. His accomplishments on the ice as a youth helped the hype continually build, to the point where he turned pro as a 17-year-old with the WHA's Indianapolis Racers in 1978–79. He was an instant star, and the team traded him to the Oilers after just eight games. In a remarkable debut season, he finished third in the league's scoring race with 110 points and won the Lou Kaplan Trophy as Rookie of the Year.

"I remember seeing something on Wayne on television when I was younger," reflected Dave Semenko. "For a number of years, I didn't hear a lot, and when we went to play against them in Indianapolis it all came back to me. It was just one game and he did play well, but from the one meeting there was no way to predict what he would do. It didn't take him long to make us realize that he was something special. We spent a year in the WHA and he just excelled by leaps and bounds. I don't recall him talking about going into the NHL. I think he knew his ability and didn't have any doubts."

Not wanting to let the game's most prized prospect get away, the Oilers made him a priority selection before the expansion and entry drafts. Gretzky was not at all intimidated by heading to the NHL and showed a great deal of poise when dealing with doubters and critics.

"As the summer went on, I heard more talk about how it's going to be a different story this year," said Gretzky. "That I won't get 110 points like I did in the World Hockey Association in my first year of pro. Every year people have told me how I'm going to be in trouble at a higher level. I heard more of that talk this summer than I heard all my life. . . . Not that it's anything new. I knew I'd hear all that stuff again. Different guys told me how everybody is going to try and run me in the NHL.

One guy bragged that it took him 10 years to run Bobby Orr, but that he finally did it. Some of it was a psyche job, but most of it was serious. A lot of guys I met want me to be prepared."

From those who had seen him, however, the praise was often glowing. Bobby Orr himself commented on the youngster to the press at the time.

"He's good. I watched him in junior and I've heard so much about him that I know he's good. The puck follows him around."

Teammate Dave Dryden also had an honest appraisal of his abilities.

"Talent-wise, his biggest asset is his ability to control the puck and himself," he said. "He has that rare ability to wait for somebody to make a little mistake and take advantage of it for everything it's worth. Most players have preconceived notions of what they're going to do. I'm convinced he doesn't. You can't compare him to anybody else. He's unique, a delight to watch."

Part of Gretzky's preparation involved gaining weight as he moved from 158 to 170 pounds. He made his hotly anticipated debut on the road against the Chicago Black Hawks to open the 1979–80 season. He recorded an assist on Kevin Lowe's goal that night but did not personally score until the Oilers took on Vancouver four days later. His start was a bit slow in comparison to some of the years he would have later, but once he got warmed up, fans were in for a real treat.

Over his first 39 games, Gretzky racked up 58 points and was 25 points behind Marcel Dionne in the NHL's scoring race. He was selected to play for the Campbell Conference at the 1980 NHL All-Star Game on February 5, 1980, but did not get any points. Just 10 days later, he tied a league record by getting seven assists in a win over the Washington Capitals. He also made history as the youngest player at the time to get 100 points in a season when, on February 24, he assisted on a goal by Brett Callighen.

He closed the gap between himself and Dionne rather quickly.

"I don't know if I can catch up to Jesus [Dionne] or God [Lafleur]," he joked.

As the regular schedule wore down, Gretzky had a six-point

night against the Toronto Maple Leafs on March 29. He became the youngest player to record 50 goals in a season when he put the puck past Minnesota's Gary Edwards on April 2. Toronto's own superstar, Darryl Sittler, had some hefty praise for Gretzky and believed that he was the leading Hart Trophy candidate.

"For a 19-year-old to play on a new team in the league and to do as well as he has, well, it's unbelievable. To me, he's got to be the Most Valuable Player in the league."

The Oilers squeaked into the playoffs but were eliminated by the league-leading Philadelphia Flyers in three straight, but very close, games. Gretzky felt at the time that the team had met its goals and set the bar even higher for the next year.

"We made the playoffs and that was our number one goal. Next year, we'll try for 10th or 11th place in the regular season, then . . . who knows?"

Named to the NHL's Second All-Star Team, he finished the year tied for the league's scoring lead with Dionne but lost out on the Art Trophy as he had scored fewer goals. Because of his WHA experience, the NHL did not consider him a candidate for the Calder Trophy. Team owner Peter Pocklington publicly aired his displeasure through a guest column in *The Hockey News*.

"I'm, of course, emotionally and personally involved. But when I look at it from a point of view of what's good for hockey, I believe that Wayne should get the award. He's the upcoming player, certain to be a national hero in Canada in the next decade. . . . On the other hand, I don't suppose that whether or not he got the trophy is going to make any difference in how he is going to be accepted by the public.

"I guess I really don't understand why they won't give it to him. It doesn't make that much of a difference, even though Wayne certainly cares about it, as do an awful lot of people who have seen him play. It doesn't matter a damn one way or the other because the kid is great — Calder or no Calder."

There was some consolation, however, as he was awarded the Lady Byng Trophy for his gentlemanly play and then won the Hart Trophy, an award he did not surrender until 1987–88. Gretzky went on to establish numerous scoring records and win four Stanley Cup titles over the course of his career with the Oilers and beyond.

BLAIR MACDONALD

MacDonald was perhaps the first player who ever begged the question, "Does playing with Wayne Gretzky inflate your stats?" Long before the arrival of the Great One at the pro level, MacDonald was a proven performer with a nose for the net.

A junior standout who chose the WHA over the Los Angeles Kings, MacDonald scored 171 goals in over six seasons with the rival league's Oilers and Indianapolis Racers, but he never scored more than 34 goals or 71 points in a season before he made his NHL debut. The Oilers paid a hefty price to protect him when coming in, since they promised the Kings that they would take Larry Brown in the expansion draft and reportedly paid them $130,000 as well to keep the young winger.

The unfortunate reality was that they wouldn't have even needed to spend that money if they had protected him instead of Bengt-Ake Gustafsson. Despite these efforts to work out a deal with the young Swedish star's agent, general manager Larry Gordon made a crucial mistake and the Oilers ultimately lost Gustafsson after the NHL found them guilty of violating the terms of the merger. The end result was Gustafsson became a member of the Washington Capitals and Edmonton's wallet was considerably lighter.

All of the effort to keep MacDonald paid off for the Oilers during their first season, though, as he registered the best year of his professional career. He finished with an impressive 46 goals, good enough for second place on the club, and even ranked 10th overall among all scorers with 96 points. Perhaps his best performance of the year came in Edmonton's first victory, when he put three tallies and an assist on the board in a 6–3 decision over the Quebec Nordiques on October 19, 1979. Other hat tricks came against the Pittsburgh Penguins in a fight-filled game on January 19, 1980, and in an 8–3 romp over Toronto on January 26.

Coach Glen Sather had some lofty praise for the assistant captain and was pleased with his work on the ice.

"He's the most underestimated player in the NHL," said Sather at the time. "He's the one guy who has contributed to this hockey team every night he's had the uniform on. He's the example and the kids on the team are following him."

At mid-season, MacDonald received an opportunity to play for the Campbell Conference in the 1980 NHL All-Star Game and that marked the high point of his time with the Oilers.

STAN WEIR

Weir had already played three seasons in the Toronto Maple Leafs organization when he jumped to the WHA and signed with Edmonton as a free agent in June 1978. His new surroundings boosted his offensive output over the 30-goal mark for the first time, and he helped the club to an appearance in the AVCO Cup Final against Winnipeg.

As the Oilers prepared for arrival in the NHL, Toronto reclaimed Weir. But since Toronto wanted to protect veteran Ron Ellis from the expansion clubs, Edmonton picked Weir up off the waiver wire on July 4, 1979.

It proved a shrewd move on Glen Sather's part, as Weir responded with his best offensive year at the pro level. He was the club's most accurate shooter among regulars, as he scored on 31 of his 129 shots, and also finished third on the team in scoring.

Most important, Weir gained the respect of his teammates and the coaching staff. Sather offered his thoughts on the veteran to the press at the time.

"The mark of a good pro is somebody who comes to play every night," he said. "Well, almost every night. It's almost impossible over an 80-game schedule to not have a few off nights. But good pros keep them down to 10 or so. Stan Weir has been consistently good, night in and night out. On the road or at home."

One of Weir's most memorable moments occurred late in the season when he scored on a penalty shot granted against Toronto's Mike Palmateer on March 29, 1980. Before he was ready to skate toward the goal, arena staff needed to be called out on to the ice to scoop up several mice that had ventured out onto the playing surface at Maple Leaf Gardens.

BRETT CALLIGHEN

Glen Sather once remarked that, "If a coach had 20 Brett Callighens, the other team might not beat you. He's like a hummingbird, always buzzing, always darting. If anybody signifies the ethic of hard work, he does. I never have to worry about him punching the time clock."

That's some very lofty praise for a guy who actually stopped playing hockey as a teenager but returned to the game when he went to Centennial College in Toronto in 1973. From there, he played in the IHL and got a tryout with the New England Whalers in 1976. After that, he stayed in the pros — mostly with the Oilers, who acquired him in February 1977.

When Edmonton joined the NHL, the team retained Callighen's rights before the expansion draft and he became a part of the potent and youthful GMC Line with Blair MacDonald and Wayne Gretzky. Both of Gretzky's linemates often faced criticism from fans and the press for having inflated numbers thanks to the young lion's presence, but Sather had his own feelings on the negativity.

"People said Brett should have bought Gretzky a meal for making him a scorer, but really, that was a crack," he remarked. "Brett has always been able to skate and shoot. Now, he's got enough confidence to start putting the puck where it belongs. In the net."

Callighen's first NHL season was going remarkably well when a near tragedy struck during a game against the Boston Bruins on February 24, 1980. As he was charging for the puck against rookie Brad McCrimmon, he went down and sustained a serious injury to his left eye.

"It happened so quickly. I didn't know if it was a puck or a stick that hit me," said Callighen. "They tell me it was a stick. I was scared to death. I couldn't see."

Callighen ended up spending five days in hospital with dark patches over both eyes and needed to do exercises with hand weights to keep his sanity. About a week after the incident, he could make out images of colours and people but said that it felt like there was a film over his eye.

Sather weighed in on the incident. He believed that the injury had serious consequences on their quest for a playoff spot.

"Losing Brett is a terrible blow. Brett really makes the team go. I've never bought the theory that Gretzky has made Callighen."

RON CHIPPERFIELD

Chipperfield spent the last two seasons of the WHA in an Oilers uniform and was a dynamo for the club during their battle for the AVCO Cup with Winnipeg Jets, scoring nine goals and earning 10 assists over 13 postseason games. Even though he was drafted by the California Golden Seals and subsequently traded to the Philadelphia Flyers, Edmonton ended up retaining his rights when they joined the NHL.

Named the first captain of the team in their new league, Chipperfield was given the honour on October 9, 1979, as the team flew over the state of Minnesota. Three weeks later, he scored his first goal of the season against the St. Louis Blues. Then on November 30, he scored a pair in a 5–3 win over the New York Islanders.

After his offensive output greatly decreased, Chipperfield was traded to the Quebec Nordiques for Ron Low on March 11, 1980. Sadly, he was visiting his mother at the time and she passed away from leukemia the following day. Coach Glen Sather had to deliver the terrible news.

"It was the toughest thing I've had to do in years," he said. "To tell Chipperfield he was traded — what a terrible day for him with his mother so sick and the trade."

RISTO SILTANEN

Siltanen came to North America late in the 1978–79 season to play for the Oilers in the WHA and was a big part of the club's run to the AVCO Cup Final. Since the St. Louis Blues held his NHL rights, the team reclaimed him when Edmonton was set to come into the league. But the young defender known as the "Little Hulk" told them that they needed to trade him to the Alberta-based club or else he was heading back to Finland. Instead of losing him and getting nothing, the Blues granted his wish and sent him and Tom Roulston to Edmonton and got Joe Micheletti in return.

A puck-moving defender with the ability to generate well-timed hits, Siltanen reminded director of player personnel Bruce MacGregor of Pat Stapleton, and he appreciated his ability to stand his ground. Glen Sather was also impressed by the youngster's talent.

"He's the best I've seen at moving [the puck] forward. He has a knack for hitting the open man in flight. If he has a problem, it's that he sometimes moves it too fast . . . his teammates aren't anticipating the pass. Really, Risto is just like a first-round junior draft pick. People think he's older than he is, maybe because he was on the Finnish national team. But he's only 21 with a lot of good years ahead of him."

Had he been able to play a full season in 1979–80, Siltanen likely would have led Edmonton's defencemen in scoring. He still managed to generate his fair share of offence. His first two NHL goals came against Vancouver's Glen Hanlon in a 4–4 tie on October 14, 1979. He also registered a trio of assists while battling the Winnipeg Jets on February 1, 1980.

MARK MESSIER

Messier made the jump from Tier II junior to the pro ranks in 1978–79 as a 17-year-old when he signed with the WHA's Indianapolis Racers just three days after they sold Wayne Gretzky to Edmonton. The contract was just for a five-game tryout. But once the team folded, Messier was able to get regular work for the rest of the year with the Cincinnati Stingers. He managed only one goal and 10 assists over 47 games there but made a solid impression while skating on a line with fellow rookie and future Hall of Famer Mike Gartner.

In the 1979 NHL Entry Draft, the Oilers recognized Messier's potential and snagged him early in the third round. He had little difficulty making their roster out of training camp and scored his first goal with the team on October 13, 1979, against Rogie Vachon of the Detroit Red Wings. Soon after, he was sent down to Houston for a short spell as a disciplinary measure after missing a team flight to St. Louis.

"He was far and away the best player in the Central League when he was in Houston," said Sather. "He was too dominant to keep down there.

"I don't think there's a faster guy on the team," he continued. "When he's in full flight he just pulls away from guys . . . he catches defencemen a little flat-footed by his speed. The only thing he has to do is slow down a little inside the other team's blue line. He tends to go full out all the time. Inside the other team's end he could slow down a little and use his strength."

While he didn't set the league on fire that year, Messier garnered a lot of attention from other teams, and they were calling to see if they could pick him up in a trade. The Oilers held their ground, though, and he had some great outings, such as his two-goal effort while taking on the Minnesota North Stars on February 13, 1980. Opponents also took note of his physical play, and he tangled with some tough customers like Kim Clackson and Bert Wilson. In fact, he hit Dave Langevin of the Islanders with a left hook so hard he knocked Langevin's helmet straight off his head.

"He was young and you could see the raw talent in him," said Dave Semenko. "He could go from being the best player on the ice to being the worst. It was just a matter of time before he began to rein it in to become more consistent. He was a young guy learning the pro game. He wanted to do things and make a difference."

During the playoffs, Messier showed some glimpses of his potential as a clutch player when he scored in the third game of the opening-round series with the Philadelphia Flyers.

"My first impression was when he held out in training camp," said Cam Connor. "I knew he was 18 and I really liked Mark. I didn't think he'd have the career he had, but the raw potential was there. He had that complete package at 18, but Gretzky was around the same age and really rubbed off on him. If I knew those guys would do what they did, I'd have had them over for dinner more!"

KEVIN LOWE

As a junior, Lowe became the first English-speaking captain of the Quebec Remparts. The first player the Oilers selected in the NHL Entry Draft, he and the club have a long history that still lasts to this day. His accomplishments on and off the ice as a professional should one day earn him enshrinement in the Hockey Hall of Fame.

Lowe scored the first goal for Edmonton in their season opener against the Chicago Black Hawks when he flipped a backhand shot past sprawling legend Tony Esposito.

"I shot it and one of the Hawks, I think it was Bob Murray, deflected the puck. It kind of floated over Esposito," he said. "The first thing I thought of as I went to the bench was that I wished my mother had been here to see it. Then it dawned on me . . . it was [the] Oilers' first NHL goal. I guess I'm in the Oiler record book for good, now."

Early in the season, Lowe experienced ligament damage in his ankle and sat out for a month, but he earned accolades from Glen Sather.

"He's shown an amazing amount of poise, so early in his pro career," said Sather. "We turned down two picks from Atlanta to take Lowe. We could have traded our first pick to St. Louis and even obtained Garry Unger. I think Garry certainly has two or three good years in him, but Lowe could turn out to have 10 or 12 good years. It's better to go with kids. We'll never trade a first-round draft pick."

While Sather never lived up to his promise to never trade a first-round pick, Unger joined the Oilers late in the 1980–81 campaign. On March 21, 1980, Lowe earned three assists as the Oilers took on the Pittsburgh Penguins and he also had multi-point games against Colorado and Montreal during his rookie year.

Lowe also partnered up with wunderkind Wayne Gretzky off the ice and the pair shared an apartment for many years. The Great One was happy to be sharing his home with such a kindred spirit.

"Kevin is a super low-key kind of guy, too," he said. "He's dedicated to hockey. It was important to me to live with a guy who was similar to me."

CAM CONNOR

Connor is one of hockey's most unheralded tough guys from the 1970s. He was a force to be reckoned with during his time with the Phoenix Roadrunners and Houston Aeros of the WHA. Drafted by the Montreal Canadiens in the first round of the 1974 NHL Amateur Draft, he eventually joined the club for the 1978–79 season and was poised to help them to their fourth Stanley Cup in a row when he suffered what was initially thought to be food poisoning at a team meal during the semi-finals against the Boston Bruins.

"I think they mixed me up with Lafleur and gave me his plate," he joked.

The problem turned out to be more severe than anticipated and the virus stayed in his system for several days. As a result, he lost 20 pounds over the summer months and had to deal with being selected by Edmonton during the expansion draft. At training camp, he was sent by the team to see an old doctor who was in his early 80s and had seen the problem only once before. The actual cause for the problem wasn't determined until he underwent a five-hour bone scan.

"The combination of the virus and dysentery was weakening the muscles in his back. He couldn't skate full out or work out with us at camp. I really felt sorry for the guy," said Glen Sather.

In training camp, Connor was injured when he was knocked into the boards by Lee Fogolin, but he was able to get back to full strength during his time off. He also benefited from a short minor league stint in Houston before getting back to NHL action. He had his first goal of the season against the New York Rangers on January 11, 1980, and a little more than two weeks later, he had a goal and an assist against the Toronto Maple Leafs. During the February 13 game with Minnesota, he earned a pair of assists and also got into a scrap with Ron Zanussi.

Things seemed to be going well for Connor on March 9, when he got two more helpers against the Philadelphia Flyers, but his time with the Oilers drew to a close two days later.

"We were in Montreal on a stopover and it was the day of the trade deadline. It was 11:45 and I was about to go out on the ice, and I stop to listen to who had been moved. The first name I heard was Cam Connor. Dave Semenko said my jaw just dropped. I mean how many guys hear about that on the radio? They told me not to go out there. They gave me some of my equipment and that was the end of my time with the Oilers. Eventually, I got a call from John Short, and he apologized to me for not letting me know, but I had already left for the hotel."

Soon after, the Rangers signed him to a five-year deal, but he battled injuries and spent a lot of that time in the minor leagues before retiring. In 2011, he appeared on the television program *Wipeout Canada* and was the oldest competitor in the athletic division.

It should also be noted that Connor received some boxing training from a friend in order to compete in the WHA. That friend turned out to be professional wrestler "Rowdy" Roddy Piper.

DAVE SEMENKO

The Minnesota North Stars drafted Semenko in 1977, but he decided to try the WHA after starting the 1977–78 campaign with his junior club in Brandon. At the time, the Houston Aeros were also interested in him but declined after they got a negative scouting report.

"When I played for the Houston Aeros, we didn't have much of a farm team. Bill Dineen came up to me and asked if I knew Semenko," said Cam Connor. "He said the Oilers were interested and I agreed to call some friends. I called a guy named Riley Wilkinson and asked him to watch this guy. He called me back a week later and said, 'He's god-awful, they should trade this guy.' When I told Semenko this later, he said 'Some fucking guy who works for CN Rail determined my hockey future?' In the end, it worked out for him."

In two seasons with the WHA edition of the Oilers, Semenko gained a reputation as one of hockey's toughest young players. He holds a special place in the league's history books for scoring the last goal in their final game against Winnipeg. Since the North Stars held his rights, they reclaimed him.

"I got a call from Lou Nanne when all our rights converted to the teams we were drafted by," said Semenko. "Deep in my heart, I didn't really think I'd go there. Fortunately for me, things worked out the way they did."

The Oilers ended up making a deal to get him back, and it involved a swap of draft picks that eventually saw them take Mark Messier. Semenko started the season in Edmonton but did not drop the gloves until they faced the New York Islanders on October 23, 1979. That night, he took on two big opponents in Billy Smith and Garry Howatt during the same stop in play.

"Bugsy Watson warned me to watch out for Smitty, and I'm looking for some big defenceman or something and I saw this goalie skating around," he recalled. "I didn't think I had to worry about him. I went into the crease and got a butt end in my eye and I was bleeding. I went to punch him and I left an imprint on his mask and then Howatt jumped on my back. We've discussed it at length over the years and never got into each other's faces after that."

Semenko also participated in one of the wildest nights in team history on January 19, 1980, when they visited the Pittsburgh Penguins. He tangled with Russ Anderson and Kim Clackson in the second period and he recalled the craziness that ensued.

"I remember everything started after the initial fight. Once the brawl started, I thought, I'm not sitting in there! They were both trying to get me and haul me into the box. That was probably the last bench-clearing brawl we ever had in Edmonton."

He started the month of February by battling Winnipeg Jets rookie Jimmy Mann, who had nothing but praise for his opponent.

"I fought him a few times. Sammy was so big and strong. He didn't throw a lot, but he'd throw you. If he got a hold of you, it was tough."

It wasn't all fisticuffs for Semenko, however, as he had three points in an 8–2 win over Washington on February 15 and also had the game-winner against Chicago 12 days later. In just a short time, he would be regarded as Wayne Gretzky's protector and played a major role in the team's success.

JIM CORSI

Before beginning his big-league hockey career, Corsi played some pro soccer in the North American Soccer League in the early 1970s and attended Concordia University, where he graduated magna cum laude. After two strong seasons as a backup to Richard Brodeur for the WHA's Quebec Nordiques, he grew tired of waiting for confirmation that he was going to be re-signed and signed with the Oilers as a free agent.

"I always thought he was a pretty capable goalie when we played him," said Glen Sather. "He was available and I couldn't think of any reason why we shouldn't take him. He only had the best save percentage in the league last season."

There was one minor problem heading into training camp, however, as his equipment was still with the Nordiques and they weren't in a hurry to ship it out west. As a result, he ended up in the unique position of needing to hit the ice but not being able to play in goal, and so he got a chance to play up front.

"I ended up going to the Oiler camp with my gear still in Quebec, so I played forward for the first three days I believe. Right-hand shot, goalie skates . . . . I was small but slow," he exclaimed. "Good laughs but I did get to play exhibition games. I recall shutting down the Canucks for my second half of the game."

When the regular season started, Corsi was sent down to play in Houston but was recalled when the Oilers began to experience a goaltending crunch. He debuted against the Colorado Rockies on December 21, 1979, but the opporunity came at a most inopportune time, as he was quite ill. After he gave up five goals after two periods, Ed Mio relieved him in net.

"Ouch! Really not my best effort. Actually got sick between the second and third period . . . gastro-sick! Pulled and felt awful . . . unsure what was worse — pulled or up-chucking," he said.

After that, however, Corsi recovered and managed to see a fair deal of action over the next two months. He effectively played in games against the Los Angeles Kings, earning two wins and a tie against them. As Edmonton began to gear up for a playoff run, he was sold to the Minnesota North Stars, but they would only send him down to Oklahoma City to finish the year. The team had the option of getting him back for the next season.

"I felt I had arrived when we played against L.A. Kings and I stopped Marcel Dionne on a breakaway. It all started to come together," he said. "But of course, the natural progression wasn't enough. Good young talent came up . . . and the rest is history. Europe called and those exceptional kids won a series of Stanley Cups that changed the game!"

RON LOW

Low bounced between the Quebec Nordiques and their AHL farm club in Syracuse for most of the 1979–80 season, but the Oilers were on the hunt for some experienced goaltending in the march toward the postseason and they dealt away captain Ron Chipperfield to snag the veteran netminder. The Oilers were also well aware that he had won several honours with Kansas City of the CHL a year earlier, including Most Valuable Player.

Now with his third expansion club, Low knew how bleak things could be while playing for a first-year team, but at least Edmonton had several bright spots and a shot at the postseason. Down the stretch, he went an impressive 8–2–1, which included a 6–3 victory over his old club just a day after the trade was made.

"The way he competed, even in practice, he always worked hard. He played outstanding down the stretch and boosted our confidence. He was the main reason we got in there," said Dave Semenko.

Appearing in the playoffs for just the second time in his career, Low put up a valiant effort against the mighty Philadelphia Flyers. In Game 1, he made 47 saves in a 4–3 overtime loss that featured a tying goal by Rick MacLeish with 19 seconds left and a winning goal by Bobby Clarke. He was named the first star but the next game was a tough 5–1 defeat. The Oilers weren't about to give up, however. Game 3 went into double overtime and Low turned back 45 shots before Ken Linseman beat him to take the series.

DAVE DRYDEN

Once the WHA's Chicago Cougars ceased to exist, Edmonton claimed Dryden and made him the team's number one goaltender for the rest of their time in the rival league. During that period, he became the first goaltender to wear a modern fibreglass mask with a cage. In 1978–79, at the age of 37, he was at the top of his game and was named the loop's Top Goaltender as the Oilers went to the AVCO Cup Final.

After such a great season, he was reclaimed by his latest NHL club, the Buffalo Sabres. Not wanting to lose such a great talent, the Oilers made him a priority selection before the expansion draft. Although there was a glut of goalies at training camp, he had a new contract that had a clause that allowed him to become an assistant coach, so he was not too worried about his fortunes for the 1979–80 season.

"It wasn't extremely stressful. All of us knew there was competition there," he said. "In my case, I was 38 and I could look at it that way as having been through expansion with Buffalo before. It was going to be a great team, but I knew I wasn't going to be around. . . . I was motivated toward coaching at that point. I wanted to get on with my life."

In the early part of the year, when the young club was in the midst of a rough start, Dryden appeared in his last 14 professional games. His final appearance came on December 7, 1979, in an 8–3 loss to the Winnipeg Jets. A couple of weeks later, he approached Glen Sather while the team was in Colorado and told him that his playing days were over.

At that point the Oilers made him a goaltending consultant and he remained with them in that role until the end of the season. After that, he coached the Ontario Hockey League's Peterborough Petes and he now serves as the chair of Sleeping Children Around the World — a charity that was founded by his father and provides bed kits to children in the developing world.

EXPANSION YEAR RECORD: 27-34-19
(73 points — fourth in Norris Division)
COACH: Don Blackburn
GENERAL MANAGER: Jack Kelly
FIRST GAME: October 11, 1979 —
4-1 loss vs. Minnesota North Stars
FIRST GOAL: October 11, 1979 by Gordie Roberts

HARTFORD WHALERS

The New England Whalers were one of the original World Hockey Association franchises and became the first winners of the AVCO Cup in 1972–73. They played their first two seasons out of the Boston Garden but relocated to Hartford in 1974. While waiting for the Hartford Civic Center to be built, they played out of Springfield, Massachusetts, and continued to be a success on the ice and at the box office.

On January 18, 1978, the Whalers were thrown into temporary turmoil when the arena roof collapsed because of heavy snow, but fortunately they came back to Springfield until the problem was fixed. They spent their final two WHA seasons there and it became their home as they entered the NHL. As conditions of entry, the Boston Bruins asked that their name be changed to the Hartford Whalers to avoid any potential confusion, and the team also changed their colours to green, blue and white.

Most of the 1978–79 Whalers club remained with the team one way or another as they came into the NHL. Gordie Howe and his sons, Mark and Marty, stayed on the roster along with veterans Andre Lacroix, Al Smith and Dave Keon. They also held on to top young talents like Mike Rogers, Blaine Stoughton, John Garrett and Gordie Roberts as well. The only major losses were Brad Selwood, Warren Miller and George "Sparky" Lyle, who was the WHA's Rookie of the Year in 1976–77. The Toronto Maple Leafs reclaimed veteran defenceman Rick Ley, but they did not keep him and he quickly returned to the Whalers.

Hartford was not so lucky in their first NHL Entry Draft, though, as they did not end up with a major impact player. Their first-ever selection was Ray Allison of the Brandon Wheat Kings, who put up phenomenal numbers at the junior level but was unable to recapture that magic at the pro level. With the second-round pick, they got Ray Neufeld, who ended up playing nearly 600 regular-season games over his career.

Going into their first NHL season, the Whalers got a lot of recognition for having a strong defence corps and tons of pro experience. With Don Blackburn behind the bench, they had a teaching coach who was willing to work with young players. And fans were excited to see what Mark Howe was able to do. More than 40 players were invited to training camp, and some of those who did not make the big club were not going to be far away, since the team's AHL affiliate was also in Springfield.

The regular season began with a four-game road swing that started with a 4–1 loss to the Minnesota North Stars on October 11, 1979. Roberts scored their first goal that night. The Whalers did not earn a victory until their first home outing against the Los Angeles Kings, eight days later. Early on, Smith went down with an injury and Garrett had to take over since there was no experienced goaltender to back him up. The first month of action culminated with a visit to Toronto's Maple Leaf Gardens that was a homecoming for Keon. He had been cast away years earlier by Maple Leafs owner Harold Ballard, and the team worked together to ensure that his return resulted in a victory.

That victory kicked off a three-game winning streak, but their first half of the season proved a rough one with 27 games on the road. Lacroix announced his retirement early on. It was also apparent that the 1979–80 season was going to be the last for Gordie Howe, who received tremendous applause from the crowd on his return to Detroit on January 12, 1980. One thing that helped the Whalers out of the doldrums was the acquisition of Pat Boutette from Toronto, and as a result both Stoughton and Rogers began racking up points. The Hartford Civic Center finally re-opened on February 6, and that game ended in a 7–3 win over the Kings. The team was back in playoff contention.

Gordie Howe had some late-season problems, but he eventually scored his 800th career goal and finally got to play in an NHL game with both of his sons when Hartford came to Detroit for the second time on April 6 to close out the regular schedule.

At the end of the year, Stoughton tied for the league lead in goals with 56, and Rogers chipped in a whopping 105 points to rank among the NHL's best. Mark Howe was also phenomenal in the second half, as his shift from forward to defence proved to be a smart move and he scored 50 points over his last 38 games.

For their first playoff matchup, Hartford drew a formidable opponent in the previous year's Stanley Cup champs, the Montreal Canadiens. The first two games of the series were blowouts and a serious injury knocked Stoughton out of action early on. The third contest was a little closer, but Yvon Lambert ended up scoring in overtime.

The early 1980s were a terrible time to be a fan of the Whalers, as the team did not make the playoffs for five straight years. Numerous bad trades were part of the problem. The 1982–83 campaign proved one of the worst in franchise history as they surrendered more than 400 goals. By drafting well and hiring Emile Francis to serve as general manager, Hartford had a good run from 1985–86 to 1991–92, but they won only a single playoff series and there were many disastrous deals made — one of which sent Ron Francis to the Pittsburgh Penguins in 1991.

The Whalers ultimately were the victims of playing in a small market, and it was often rumoured that they would be sold to be relocated to a larger centre. Peter Karmanos took over as owner in 1994 and committed to four more seasons in Hartford, but because of a lack of ticket sales and financial support from both local business and state government, frustration quickly set in for the new ownership. The greatest fears of Whalers fans became a reality during the 1996–97 season and they were moved south to become the Carolina Hurricanes. Over their first decade in Carolina, the former Hartford club finally had some playoff success and won a Stanley Cup in 2005–06.

MIKE ROGERS

Considered small by some hockey executives, but huge on scoring talent, Rogers was an All-Star in the World Hockey Association who

(clockwise) Blaine Stoughton, Dave Keon, John Garrett

hit the 80-point mark on two occasions. He was originally drafted by the Vancouver Canucks in 1974, but the team unwisely chose not to reclaim him when the Whalers entered the NHL and he ended up staying with the rechristened Hartford club.

"As players, we looked at the WHA as a professional league," he said. "There were a lot of people who didn't think I was going to make it in the National Hockey League because I wasn't big enough. I had to sign a two-way contract for the first time in my career and really looked at keeping in shape for the first time as well."

During the season opener, Rogers assisted on the first goal in franchise history and then popped a backhand shot past Chicago's Tony Esposito for his first NHL tally on October 14, 1979. After that, he was a scoring machine with four-point nights against Toronto and Detroit in the first half of the year. A lot of that success had to do with being placed on a line with Blaine Stoughton and Pat Boutette, and the trio was dubbed "Bash, Dash and Stash."

"Don Blackburn put me on a line with Blaine and we just clicked. We added Patty Boutette from Toronto as well and everything came together."

Surprisingly, he was not selected to play in the NHL All-Star Game, but he went on to get a hat trick against the Boston Bruins on January 30, 1980.

"The biggest thing is that I went around Raymond Bourque for my hat trick goal. At the time, our biggest rivalry was with Boston, and to do it in Boston Garden was amazing."

Between February 18 and March 22, Rogers put together an incredible 18-game point streak, which was the best in the league in 1979–80. He made club history on April 4 with his 100th point of the year in a five-point night against the Quebec Nordiques. Once the playoffs hit, he led the club in scoring as they were swept by the Montreal Canadiens.

BLAINE STOUGHTON

A former first-round pick who jumped to the WHA in 1975–76, Stoughton was regarded by opponents as a dangerous man with the puck. He enjoyed a big 52-goal and 104-point season with the

Cincinnati Stingers in 1976–77. Dispatched to the Indianapolis Racers the following year after a slow start, he was sold to New England in December 1978 and quietly finished out the season with the club.

Since the Maple Leafs owned Stoughton's rights, they went to great lengths to reclaim him but puzzlingly let him go in the expansion draft. The move backfired on Toronto and he ended up back with Hartford. In the second game of the 1979–80 season, he had a goal and an assist in a 3–3 tie with Pittsburgh. Although Dave Keon's return to Toronto grabbed most of the headlines, Stoughton also got his fair share of revenge that night, too, as he scored the winning goal. He credited a lot of his early-season success to the presence of coach Don Blackburn.

"I started playing better when Blackie came last year," he told the press. "When Bill [Dineen] was here I was playing too much defence. That's not my game. Now I'm thinking offence and when the time comes, I pick up my man, that's all."

Over his first 50 games, Stoughton put up a very impressive 33 tallies, including hat tricks against Buffalo and Atlanta. On March 28, 1980, he became the first player from an expansion club to record 50 goals in a season, and the big moment came against Glen Hanlon of the Vancouver Canucks. In fact, he and then-teammate Bobby Hull are the only players to ever score 50 in a season in both the NHL and WHA. At the end of the year, he was tied with Buffalo's Danny Gare and Charlie Simmer of Los Angeles for the league lead with 56. His final point of the year was his 100th and it came on an assist when Pat Boutette scored an insurance goal against Detroit on April 6.

The Whalers finished first among the new imports from the WHA in 1979–80, but they drew a daunting playoff opponent in the form of the previous year's Stanley Cup champions, the Montreal Canadiens. At the end of the first period in Game 1, Stoughton fractured his right ankle and was out of action for the rest of the series.

MARK HOWE

Howe was a true superstar in the WHA with Houston and New England and he earned a great deal of recognition for his talent over the course of six seasons there. As the Whalers readied to join the NHL, the Boston Bruins attempted to reclaim his rights, but Hartford had an ace up their sleeve when they made him one of their priority selections. As a result, he was still able to play alongside his brother, Marty, and father, Gordie, in 1979–80.

"I was really looking forward to it," said Howe. "As much as I liked playing in the WHA, you grew up wanting to play in the NHL."

Unfortunately, Marty was a late cut in training camp and it had an immediate impact on the other members of the family.

"We played together pretty well every day since we were kids. It was different. I thought Marty deserved to be on the club as a seventh defenceman. It was really hard on me and really hard on Dad."

One of his early highlights in Hartford was a three-point night against Los Angeles on October 19, 1979, and it included the first game-winning goal in franchise history. The 1979–80 campaign also marked a shift for Howe, as he moved from left wing to defence. While it was a bit of a learning curve for him, he managed to excel and most of his point production came after the move.

"I knew I had the ability offensively, but I took a lot of pride in keeping the puck out of my net and got a lot more playing time."

Over the rest of the schedule, Mark Howe had some big games, including four-point outings against the Kings and Oilers, but he was really on fire facing the Bruins on January 30, 1980, when he racked up five assists in a wild 8–2 win. Boston general manager Harry Sinden had heavy praise for his abilities.

"The first time I saw Mark Howe play, I got goose bumps. Only five or six players have I felt that way about, and he's one of them. He's one of the best and most talented players in the league."

At the end of the season, he ranked as one of the NHL's top-scoring defenders and his future looked bright. He was one of the top blueliners in the sport over the rest of the decade and was enshrined in the Hockey Hall of Fame in 2011.

DAVE KEON

At the end of the 1974–75 season, Keon was embroiled in a nasty contract dispute with the Toronto Maple Leafs. The actions of then-team owner Harold Ballard forced his captain to choose to play in the WHA instead. Over the next four seasons, he still proved that he had lots of gas left in the tank and spent a good chunk of that time with the New England Whalers.

The club retained Keon's rights when they entered the NHL, and he had a fairly good start even though he was swiftly approaching his 40th birthday. His return to Maple Leaf Gardens on October 31, 1979, created reams of newspaper copy and was especially sweet, as he had a goal and an assist during the 4–2 victory to earn a first-star selection.

"Tonight was one of those nights that you hope for but doesn't happen very often," he said after the game.

Mike Rogers, who was taught by Keon how to play more defensively, recalled the significance of the contest.

"When you go back to a city where someone was traded, you always wanted to win for them. This was something different. The bizarre thing was that hundreds of people showed up for the morning skate just to see him."

Having reinvented himself as a defensive specialist, Keon was always on top of the top scorers for the opposition, so he saw a lot of action when the Whalers were shorthanded. Coach Don Blackburn was also very pleased by his play.

"Dave Keon has a bad habit of bottling up the other team's centremen. He's been doing it for 21 years. David doesn't know what it's like to play against anybody but Henri Richard, Beliveau, Mikita or Gretzky — people like that. It's always been Keon's job to match up with the top centremen in the game."

At the end of the year, the future Hall of Famer was the team's nominee for the Masterton Trophy. He continued to play until the end of the 1981–82 season. Teammate Mark Howe had tremendous praise for Keon as well.

"Any time you get a chance to play with an individual like that, it's a real pleasure to watch him work and play. He was a competitive guy and he demanded as much from others as he did from himself."

PAT BOUTETTE

Known in his playing days as one of hockey's best shadows, Boutette struggled with the Toronto Maple Leafs during his fifth NHL season in 1979–80 and he had only four assists to his credit after 32 games. The Leafs thought that they could offload him to the Whalers and get a solid prospect in Bob Stephenson, who had been tearing up the AHL, but Hartford had the last laugh when he put up nearly a point per game over the rest of the season.

Not long after the deal, Boutette recorded his first goal of the season against Gilles Meloche of the Minnesota North Stars. He earned a pair of assists in a battle with the Pittsburgh Penguins on January 17, 1980. The points kept on coming and he scored twice in a 5–5 tie with the Vancouver Canucks on February 12. The second of those tallies gave the Whalers the lead with less than three minutes to go, but Harold Snepsts scored with just 11 seconds left to force a deadlock.

GORDIE HOWE

The ageless wonder, Howe came out of retirement in 1973 and spent six seasons in the WHA with the Houston Aeros and New England Whalers, demonstrating that he had not lost a step as he headed into his 50s. Playing alongside his sons, Mark and Marty, certainly helped keep him young, but during the 1978–79 campaign, he battled injuries and had his lowest offensive totals in 30 years.

The Whalers retained his rights when they entered the NHL, and Howe scored a goal against Greg Millen of the Pittsburgh Penguins on October 13, 1979. That was his first tally since April 3, 1971, when he beat Tony Esposito of the Chicago Black Hawks. Once the game was over, he made the announcement that he would be retiring at the end of the season, but Pittsburgh coach Johnny Wilson was very impressed with his play at the age of 51.

"It's amazing the way Gordie Howe can still do the things he does at his age. He's got great peripheral vision. He just skates around and makes things happen."

When asked how he still kept playing, Howe was honest and upfront.

"It's not the how, it's the why. The dream of playing alongside my sons in the NHL hasn't been fulfilled yet. It'll come about, but they'd better hurry before these old legs give out."

Linemate Mike Rogers was awestruck, playing with a living legend along with another future Hall of Famer in Mark Howe.

"When you play with those two guys, you're bound to get scoring chances. Mark is one of the best skaters in all of hockey and to have him on the left side makes me skate a little bit harder and the thing about Gordie is that he opens the play up so much. He's not going to be streaking down the wing . . . but people are aware of him. And if you give him the puck inside the blue line, then he's going to make plays that pretty near nobody else can. If we are skating for Gordie, it's going to open up everything for us and that's what we've done ever since we've been together. Mark and I have done a lot of skating. Let Gordie take care of the other stuff — the passing, the work in their end."

On November 2, Gordie Howe scored twice and added an assist in a battle with the Toronto Maple Leafs. He put two more past Esposito when the Whalers earned a tie with Chicago nine days later. His strong play ensured that he received a spot at the 1980 NHL All-Star Game in his old stomping grounds of Detroit, and he set up the winning goal scored by Real Cloutier, which was met by thunderous applause.

Despite a rough second half of the season, Howe made history on February 29, 1980, when he became the first player in NHL history to score 800 career goals, beating Mike Liut of the St. Louis Blues. He did not bulge the twine again until the final contest of the regular schedule on April 6, when he scored for the final time, fittingly enough, against Red Wings goaltender Rogie Vachon. In the playoffs against Montreal, he chipped in a single goal during Game 2 of the opening-round series. He hung up the blades for good after the next game on April 11.

GREG CARROLL

Carroll split the 1978–79 season between the Washington Capitals and Detroit Red Wings and he chose to sign with the Whalers as a free agent after the next campaign began. At one time, he was a first-round pick and a top prospect, but junior success simply did not translate to big numbers in the WHA or NHL.

His new surroundings gave Carroll the spark he needed to prove that he was indeed NHL material. Used as a penalty killer, he was very effective on faceoffs, and he scored the winning goal against the Pittsburgh Penguins on November 30, 1979. What was appreciated most, however, was his passion for the game.

"The way I look at it, when Blackie opens the gate and says go, I just go wherever. If he says go here, that's where I go. I don't mind it," he revealed in *The Hockey News*.

At the end of the season, he was a free agent once again, but dark times were ahead, as he was arrested for the possession of narcotics for the purpose of trafficking in the summer of 1980. His career was essentially over at that point, but he had a brief stint with the Billings Marlboros club in the Continental Hockey League in 1985–86. Teammate Mike Rogers commented on Carroll's contributions to the Whalers.

"Immense talent but strange. Internally, his nickname was 'Bebop.' He was really out there and was carefree. I think he could have been a great player, but what he did out of the rink we had no idea."

NICK FOTIU

Before he became phenomenally popular as a member of the New York Rangers, Fotiu played for the New England Whalers in the WHA. He jumped at the chance to play for his hometown club in 1976–77. After three seasons in the Big Apple, he had a legion of fans and many of them were sad to see the team make his rights available in the expansion draft soon after their run to the Stanley Cup Final.

The second pick for Hartford, Fotiu surprised many by avoiding any major penalties during his first 25 games with the Whalers. His established reputation as one of the sport's toughest players ensured that no one wanted to tangle with him. His first goal of the season came on Tony Esposito of the Chicago Black Hawks on November 11, 1979, but he missed some action the following month because of a bruised heel. He still threw several pucks into the crowd during warmups, and his only fight of the season came against Scott Campbell of the Winnipeg Jets on January 21, 1980.

"Nicky played the game like crazy and played hard," said Mark Howe. "When you needed someone to stick up for you, he was there. He was playing on a line with my dad that year. They didn't get a lot of ice time but they still scored goals. You knew when you put him on the ice, he wasn't going to hurt your team."

Although Fotiu had a career-best 10 goals in his first year with the NHL edition of the Whalers, he was traded back to the Rangers for a draft pick.

BOBBY HULL

Hull's long association with the Winnipeg Jets drew to a close on February 27, 1980, when he was traded to the Whalers for future considerations. It was apparent to many that his days as an active player were numbered. Hartford was reportedly going to be his destination earlier in the year, but stalled contract talks and a shoulder injury delayed the trade process.

"I think he's going to help us. He's enthusiastic about playing and that's going to carry over to our team," said coach Don Blackburn. "If he can play anywhere near like he has in the past, that's a great bonus for us."

The trade was a bit controversial, since Hull was still a partial owner of the Jets and the league needed to determine if trading him created a conflict of interest, but he was eager to get back to action. His first goal with the Whalers came against Buffalo on March 6, and the final goal of his Hall of Fame career was in Gordie Howe's last visit to Detroit six days later. After nine regular-season contests and three more in the playoffs against Montreal, it was time to hang up the blades. After that, Hull tried once more to come back with the New York Rangers during training camp before the 1981–82 season.

"He wasn't there for very long but his presence made an impact," said Mike Rogers. "He went through a tough time and I didn't get to know him as much I would have liked to. You could still see that he could still be a dominant force at times. He was so strong and so ripped at that age and when I saw the shape he was in, there was a long way to go."

JOHN GARRETT

In his days in the WHA, Garrett was one of the league's premier net-minders. He spent the 1978–79 season with the New England Whalers after being acquired from the Birmingham Bulls and recorded his sixth 20-win campaign in a row. As the club got ready to head into the NHL, the Chicago Black Hawks attempted to reclaim him. The Hartford club nipped that move right away and made him one of their priority selections.

With Al Smith injured, Garrett had the heavy responsibility of being the team's starter for their first 13 games, and he went 4-5-4 during that time. On October 19, 1979, he recorded the first win in club history when they battled the Los Angeles Kings. He followed that by stringing together three wins in a row that included a pair against Toronto. Throughout the year, he continued to work on his stand-up game and earned a lot of praise from coach Don Blackburn.

"You can't fault Garrett. He's given us the chance to pick up points just about every night we've played, but we've got to start scoring some goals for him. We're putting a lot of pressure on him when he's sitting on a one-goal lead all the way along."

At the end of the season, the team's booster club named Garrett their Most Valuable Player.

MARTY HOWE

During his six seasons in the WHA, Marty Howe was practically inseparable from his brother and father, but that all changed once the trio came to the NHL with the Whalers in 1979–80. Typically, the Howe family was treated as a package deal, but team management felt the older sibling was prone to some defensive mistakes and needed to get his mojo back in the minors with Springfield.

Howe was not pleased by the demotion when the axe was brought down during training camp.

"When I first got the news I was a little upset about it. It was just that it was the first time it's happened to me and it was a little bit of a shock. It took me about half a day to get over that but it's working out okay."

He turned to his father for support and let the press know about the Hall of Famer's reaction.

"He didn't know what to say. He was having enough problems himself with all the press he'd been getting with his so-called 'dizzy spells'. . . . It was all my decision. I talked with [my parents] about it. I was interested in the different options that I had, but after considering the alternatives, I decided to go to Springfield. It's a living. It's a business and you've got to make business-like decisions."

With the Indians, Marty Howe broke his arm in two places and missed a good chunk of the season. He finally got a chance to make his NHL debut against the Boston Bruins on March 9, 1980, and, three days later, he skated on a line with Mark and Gordie when they took on the Detroit Red Wings. It was the only time in league history that a father and his two sons skated on the same line. A rib injury slightly hampered his return to big-league action, but he was back in time for the playoffs and he was on the ice when his father scored his final professional goal.

AL SMITH

"The Bear" came back to the NHL in 1979–80 and this time it was as a member of the Whalers, a club he had spent five of the previous seven seasons with in the WHA. A quirky veteran netminder, he missed the first part of the season thanks to a muscle pull in the back of his knee, but once he came back, he formed a solid tandem alongside John Garrett.

In his second game of the season, Smith earned a shutout in the team's first clash with the Edmonton Oilers on November 17, 1979. As Hartford's first year headed into the home stretch, he saw more regular duty and had his second shutout on February 29, 1980, with a 3-0 victory over the St. Louis Blues. In the playoffs, he was counted on in the opening round against Montreal but had rough outings in the first and third games, and the Whalers were swept in three straight.

EXPANSION YEAR RECORD: 25-44-11
(61 points — fifth in Adams Division)
COACH: Jacques Demers
GENERAL MANAGER: Maurice Filion
FIRST GAME: October 10, 1979 —
5-3 loss vs. Atlanta Flames
FIRST GOAL: October 10, 1979 by Real Cloutier

QUEBEC NORDIQUES

Had it not been for a collapse in funding for a proposed WHA club based out of San Francisco, the Quebec Nordiques might very well have never come into existence. However, the franchise was picked up by a group that owned the QMJHL's Quebec Remparts and they started play in 1972–73 with the legendary Maurice Richard as their coach.

"The Rocket" spent only two games behind the bench, but over the course of seven seasons, the Nordiques built themselves into one of the rival league's most powerful clubs. With prime talents like Real Cloutier, Marc Tardif, Serge Bernier, J.C. Tremblay and Richard Brodeur, they captured the AVCO Cup in 1976–77. During the final WHA season in 1978–79, they faced some internal strife, but were competitive enough to finish second overall. An early playoff exit ended their year, but at least they were able to look forward to entering the NHL and managed to hang on to most of their core talent, with the exception of Brodeur, who was shipped off to the New York Islanders.

The Nordiques did scoop up a new potential number one goalie through the WHA Dispersal Draft when they got Michel Dion from the Cincinnati Stingers. The 1979 NHL Expansion Draft was somewhat fruitful as well, the biggest prize being veteran defenceman Gerry Hart. The greatest success for the club came though the NHL Entry Draft, where they took future Hall of Famer Michel Goulet with their first-round pick and scooped up a tremendous prospect in Dale Hunter, who did not debut with the team until their second season.

Some pundits looked at the Nordiques as a wild card club, since they had held on to many WHA vets and added Hart and Robbie Ftorek but many of the new players in the lineup had never played together before. Goaltending was also a question at the start, since they had not decided on a number one goalie. The retirement of J.C. Tremblay and a rough pre-season certainly did not help, but management was adamant that they had a four-year plan in place that would take them to a division title.

"If we can get by just one of the other four in our division this year, then we will certainly have accomplished the first segment of our program," said coach Jacques Demers. "Don't ever forget, every NHL team and its coach, whether established or one of the 12 earlier expansion teams, has one thought in mind, collect eight points out of eight against us. And they're going to come out to get us every inch of the way. It's going to be dog eat dog."

General manager and director of hockey personnel Maurice Filion offered his thoughts about entering the NHL.

"With the World Hockey Association, it was not just survival on a year to year basis. We did not even know if we were going to exist for the next 24 hours. But, with the NHL, we know that 20 years from now, 40 years from now, the Nordiques of Quebec will still be young and thriving and though personally, we won't be there, our work today will determine the framework of the years to come.

"In the WHA, we had to go with everything we had, no matter the age of the player. Now, we can build, play the really young guys and two to three years from today they will be NHL stars. Why try for a seventh place overall our first year and fall flat in the future because our team is too old and we have nothing coming up?"

There was a ton of excitement in the air in Quebec as the Nordiques held a fan event that featured an open-air mass, disco, corn roast and an intra-squad game. The mood was loose and hopeful, unlike the previous year, when there were issues.

"I knew there were some deep problems breaking up our team," said Demers. "Every time I'd go into the dressing room I could feel the tensions. It hurt me very much, but I could not root the troubles out. We've only started into our exhibition season and already there is friendship and real camaraderie among all the guys with us this year. You cannot even imagine the wonderful feeling that it gives me. What a moral lift for everyone."

The regular season began for Quebec on October 10, 1979, as they hosted the Atlanta Flames. The crowd was packed into the Colisée, and Cloutier scored all three of the team's goals, but it was not enough to secure a victory. Their second outing three days later marked the beginning of the Battle of Quebec, and every hockey fan in the province was glued to the television. The Montreal Canadiens prevailed, but the Nords finally got a win in their third game with Colorado on October 18.

Montreal's first visit to Quebec came 10 days after that, and Quebec settled the score with a 5–4 triumph in front of an overflowing crowd of 12,000. It was the first time the Canadiens played a regular-season game in Quebec City in almost 60 years. Tremblay's number was retired that night as well. Since the contest was being shown on the CBC, arena workers were told to remove any advertising along the boards for O'Keefe Breweries and Coca-Cola, since the program had different sponsors.

The Nordiques had a fairly decent start, but injuries to most key players became a major problem, especially in the second half of the season. After 40 games, they placed 10th in the NHL and even hosted the touring Central Red Army club on January 6, 1980.

Controversy also arose when the team sent out a press release stating that all public address announcements were to be made in French and the national anthem would be done in French and English only if a visiting Canadian team observed the same practice. Even though the Nordiques felt justified since they claimed that 80 percent of their crowd was francophone, NHL president John Ziegler ordered them to go back to bilingual announcements for the time being. In a "spirit of cooperation," the team decided to take the matter to the NHL Board of Governors for consideration. They continued to have all announcements in French with the exception that goals were announced in both languages. The NHL eventually passed a motion allowing public announcements to be made in French only, with the provision that the visiting team's bench receive English announcements through a speaker behind the bench.

On February 27, the Islanders came into town and Brodeur was called up from the minors to get a 5–3 victory in his return to the Colisée. Remarkably, it was the first time a goalie other than Billy Smith or Chico Resch started a game for the Isles since Gerry Desjardins left the team in 1974.

"It was a special feeling for me coming back to play them," said Brodeur. "I was stunned when they told me I was going to play, especially because it was against Quebec. It's the greatest thrill of my life."

The relationship between Quebec's players and the local media, however, came to a head when a few days later they refused to conduct interviews as a result of what players called unprofessional behaviour following a series of articles about Marc Tardif and another about two players missing curfew.

As the team continued to battle the injury bug, they slipped further down the standings and finished the year in 19th place. Regardless, team executives were optimistic about their future in the NHL.

"We now definitely know that the Nordiques belong in the National Hockey League and that if we can stay healthy . . . we will have one helluva season next year," said Fillion. "The club's overall play completely dissipated the false ideas of a lot of hockey people who said when we came into the league that we would only be a hanger-on. I can't say enough about the players on our team; they have proved that we are a competitive team and that we will be even more so as years go by.

"We have some really good kids who are coming up in the organization, and who knows who we'll be able to pick up in the amateur draft in June. Take those factors and add in our promising attendance figures and we really don't have a lot to complain about. We are very happy about the outcome of this year and look forward to next season."

Fillion's statements proved true as the team helped Czechoslovakian stars Anton and Peter Stastny escape from behind the Iron Curtain, Jacques Richard exploded for 52 goals and Dan Bouchard was acquired from the Calgary Flames to help them to a playoff spot. Over the next few years, the Nordiques had tremendous success on the ice, and their rivalry with the Canadiens became one of the most intense in NHL

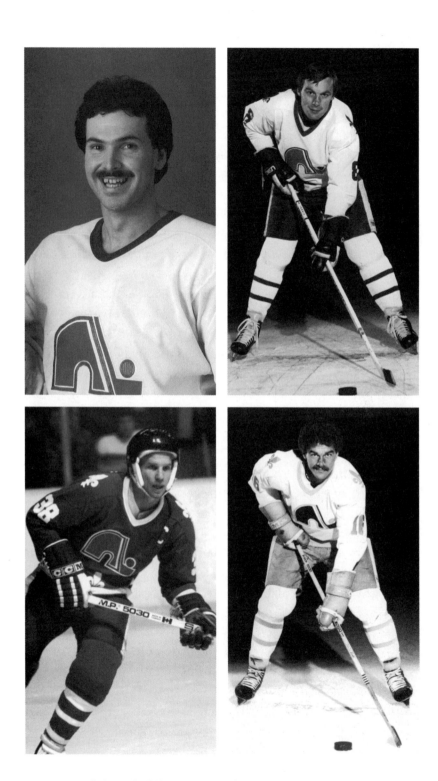

(clockwise) Real Cloutier, Marc Tardif, Michel Goulet, Robbie Ftorek

history, thanks in part to the creation of divisions based on geographic proximity.

Starting in the late 1980s, Quebec experienced several rough years, but as they built through the draft, they returned to contention. This process was aided when they traded away disgruntled first overall pick Eric Lindros to the Philadelphia Flyers and got a package of prospects and veterans in return. Following the 1994–95 season, however, financial losses caused in part by rising player salaries and a weak Canadian dollar did not bode well for NHL hockey in the league's smallest market. The provincial government was unwilling to provide a bailout, and team owner Marcel Aubut sold the Nordiques to investors based out of Denver, Colorado.

The Colorado Avalanche began play in 1995–96, and it was a bitter pill for Quebec's former fan base to see them finally win a Stanley Cup that year. Later on, the NHL implemented a revenue-sharing agreement for small-market Canadian clubs and that rubbed even more salt into the still-fresh wounds of the fans. A little more than 15 years later, there is some hope on the horizon as deep-pocketed business interests in Quebec are trying to bring NHL hockey back, with a new arena in the works as well.

REAL CLOUTIER

"Buddy" Cloutier, one of the greatest scorers in the history of the World Hockey Association, reached at least 50 goals in a season four times over five seasons with the Nordiques before they moved over to the NHL. In 1978–79, he led the league with an impressive 75 goals and 129 points, and Quebec had to basically bribe the Chicago Black Hawks with a first-round pick in the 1980 NHL Entry Draft to ensure they did not attempt to reclaim him. That selection turned out to be future Hall of Famer Denis Savard, so it was a tough blow, but not enough of a disappointment compared to the outrage they would have faced from fans had they not tried to keep the young star on their roster.

While making his debut against the Atlanta Flames on October 10, 1979, Cloutier tied an NHL record by scoring three goals in his first game, and all of them came during the first period against future teammate Dan Bouchard. Those tallies were also the first in franchise history.

"For the first two periods against Atlanta, I was always a step behind," he said after the game. "I was talking to myself. In the third, I got my rhythm. That's it."

Throughout the 1979–80 campaign, Cloutier had many solid outings and was excited to finally get a chance to play against the Montreal Canadiens and Guy Lafleur — a superstar he was often compared to in previous years, much to his frustration.

"I want to try the NHL for one season to see what I can do. I want to prove myself, to show my ability to play against the best players in hockey. I'm certain I'll be able to play well, but, now, I must prove it. . . . We're all looking forward to the game against Canadiens because it's going to be a tremendous rivalry," he predicted. "I met Guy Lafleur this summer and he told me that he planned to go all out in the games against Nordiques. He said that that they didn't want us cutting in on their territory — the province of Quebec. I told him that I planned to do the same thing against the Canadiens. We might just have a surprise for the Canadiens, who have had things all their own way down here for all those years."

During the second meeting between the two budding rivals on October 28, Cloutier scored a goal and added an assist in a big 5–4 victory. For the rest of the season, he racked up points at a very respectable pace considering the personnel losses the club had sustained. He was chosen to represent them at the 1980 NHL All-Star Game and scored the winning goal on a pass from one of his heroes — Gordie Howe. Needless to say, he kept the puck. Cloutier missed a little bit of time because of an ankle injury, but after his return, he had a hat trick and an assist while facing the New York Islanders. In the end, he flirted with scoring 50 goals and led his teammates in goals, assists and points during their first year.

MARC TARDIF

One of hockey's greatest players in the 1970s who rarely gets the respect he deserves for his massive success in the World Hockey

Association, Tardif was named the league's Most Valuable Player on two occasions and also won a pair of scoring titles. It was unbelievable that the Montreal Canadiens, the team he played for before jumping to the rival league, chose not to protect him during the expansion draft. The Nordiques were more than happy to welcome him back with a large multi-year contract — even if he never truly left.

Tardif opened the season with three assists on goals by Real Cloutier during the first game against Atlanta. He had a two-point night against the Colorado Rockies on October 18, 1979, scoring his first NHL goals since the 1972–73 season. Not content to rest, he earned another three points when they battled the Edmonton Oilers the following night.

Since he wasn't putting up points at the same pace as previous years, there were rumours circulating that he was going to be traded to the Philadelphia Flyers for Rick MacLeish. Getting benched by coach Jacques Demers one night also spurred some reported interest from the New York Rangers. He missed a few games because of knee issues, and the press in Quebec created problems when they reported that he and some other players had missed curfew. At that point, the team banded together and refused to conduct interviews with the press when the Minnesota North Stars came to town on February 5, 1980.

Michel Dion could relate to the pressure the media placed on Tardif, and both players eventually felt vindicated.

"The first year that I was with the Nordiques, the media was hard on him all the time, and it was the same the next year for me. The funny thing is that we both redeemed ourselves by the 1982 All-Star Game. We shook hands before the game and talked and I said to him that we both beat the media."

As the end of the season approached, Tardif had a hat trick in a 9–7 loss to the Detroit Red Wings on March 29. He finished the year with 68 points over 58 contests. He also made a solid impression on some of the team's younger players, including a future Hall of Famer.

"I had the chance to see Marc Tardif when I was younger and for me, the Quebec Nordiques and Winnipeg Jets were the best teams around," said rookie teammate Michel Goulet. "He was one of the most natural left wings in hockey and one of the best left wings to ever play. He was a guy that I admired and he knew how to play the game of hockey. He gave me tips on how to shoot the puck and how to get better. I had my eyes and ears wide open. I think at the end of the day, if Marc played in the NHL, I wouldn't be surprised if he was regarded as one of the greatest left wingers."

MICHEL GOULET

Goulet was one of several top junior hockey players who made the decision to jump to the WHA for the 1978–79 season, as one of the "Baby Bulls" in Birmingham. He did not speak any English during that first pro season and teammate Gaston Gingras served as his interpreter. Over the course of the year, he put up a respectable 58 points and was tabbed to come into the NHL through the 1979 NHL Entry Draft.

In a bold move, Goulet's agent went to court on the future Hall of Famer's behalf at the end of the season and received an order that blocked any other team besides the Nordiques from drafting him. When Quebec went to call out their first selection, it was no surprise when Goulet's name came up. He made his NHL debut against Atlanta when the 1979–80 campaign opened and earned his first point with an assist against the Hartford Whalers two weeks later.

Used primarily on the checking line for most of the season, Goulet did not score his first goal until November 10, when he put the puck by Doug Soetaert of the New York Rangers. He reflected on the historic moment.

"It's always the one I remember the most. The puck was dumped into the corner, and Pierre Plante fed it out to me and I was going to the net and tapped it in. It was a perfect pass. Scoring a goal there in Madison Square Garden was a big thrill. It took me 10 games, but after that it became a lot easier!"

Just eight days later, Goulet scored two goals, including the winner, in a battle with the Toronto Maple Leafs. His totals quickly began to pile up. He was placed on a line with Jacques Richard late in the year and he had a two-goal night against the Colorado Rockies on March 20, 1980; the second tally of the night was his 20th of the season.

"It was my first year in the NHL and I was just trying to do my best every single game," he reflected. "When you're 18 years old and playing against men, you can make mistakes, but it prepared you to be more conscientious."

ROBBIE FTOREK

Seemingly destined to become a professional hockey player, Ftorek was born shortly after his mother went straight to the hospital during a New Year's Day game between the Boston Bruins and the New York Rangers in the 1951–52 season. He was a member of the American Olympic team that won a silver medal in 1972, and he turned pro with the Detroit Red Wings soon after but found true success in the World Hockey Association as a member of the Phoenix Roadrunners and Cincinnati Stingers.

A free agent after the WHA closed shop, Ftorek signed a reported seven-year deal with the Nordiques. He scored his first goal of the season against Denis Herron of the Montreal Canadiens on October 13, 1979. Early on, he offered his opinion on the difference between playing in the NHL and the WHA.

"It's hockey," he said. "The NHL may have some better teams than we had, but we could have played with them. I play hard because that's the only way to play. I've learned how to get out of the way of a lot of hits, but I can take it if I'm hit and I can hit back. I'm not playing any harder here than I was there. Anyone who is was cheating himself, his team and the fans if he wasn't giving it all he had before. I'm not thrilled to be in this league or anything like that. I'm happy to be in hockey, period."

During his time in the lineup, Ftorek averaged nearly a point per game. He had a nice homecoming against the Bruins on November 22, when he scored a goal and added an assist in a 7–4 loss. In December, he had game-winning goals in consecutive home games against Los Angeles and Winnipeg. But his best outing of all was some wonderful revenge on the Red Wings when he put up five points in a game where the Nordiques lost by a score of 7–6. Not long after, he was put on the shelf with a knee injury that ended to his season.

"I liked Robbie," said Michel Goulet. "He was dedicated to hockey and to winning. When he came to Quebec, he didn't produce as much as everybody thought he would, but I thought he was an excellent guy to play with. He's passionate about hockey and it shows."

Curt Brackenbury also appreciated what Ftorek brought to the team.

"When you played against him before, he had a lot of intensity. He was 150 pounds soaking wet, but he played out there like he weighed 250. He came to win every shift and every practice. It was tough for him to come in as an American and explain things when you spoke another language. His word was his word."

JAMIE HISLOP

Hislop was a young star on the rise during his time in the WHA with the Cincinnati Stingers and he scored a career-best 70 points with the club in 1978–79. Since the team was not a part of the merger, he was claimed by the Winnipeg Jets, but he was packaged up along with Barry Legge in a trade with Quebec for Barry Melrose.

Hislop was arguably the heart and soul of the Nordiques during their first NHL campaign and the only player to appear in all 80 games. His contributions went well beyond offensive production. He was placed on a line with former Cincinnati teammates Robbie Ftorek and Reg Thomas and had several multi-point games throughout the year. Thanks to his dedication and perseverance, he was nominated for the Masterton Trophy. General manager Maurice Fillion had some kind praise for him.

"For me, the biggest surprise of the year had to be the play of Jamie Hislop," he said. "I really have to tip my hat to him; he played well in every game of the season for us and gave us so much more than we thought he could give. He never let up for one moment all season."

BOB FITCHNER

Fitchner spent six seasons in the WHA earning accolades for his work as a defensive forward and quietly put up decent numbers along the way. He joined the Nordiques late in the 1975–76 season and remained with the club when they became part of the NHL. Although the Pittsburgh Penguins had drafted him nearly a decade earlier, he was a free agent at the time he entered the WHA and they did not attempt to claim him.

"I was in Quebec City for the WHA years. We had two very good offensive lines and it was a luxury for us to have a line that focused on the defensive end of the game," he said. "We moved into the NHL with the same philosophy and had a really good start. I think the WHA teams surprised the status quo."

The team had originally tagged Fitchner for demotion to the AHL at the beginning of the year, but they quickly realized that his skill as a faceoff man was going to be missed. Over his first 18 outings, he had a very respectable five goals and seven assists. In November, he broke a bone behind his collarbone, and coach Jacques Demers let the press know how that was going to impact the club's on-ice fortunes.

"The Nordiques just can't keep up with Fitchner out of the lineup. He has done a fantastic job this season. He has got some goals, but his work on penalties has been the best I've seen in a long time. And when we have a crucial faceoff, Fitch comes up with it, anywhere, anytime. His value to the club cannot be replaced."

Appreciative of the praise he received, Fitchner commented on his former coach.

"My recollection of Jacques is if you put your best effort forth, it went a long way."

Near the end of the season, he had a pair of goals in a 6–2 victory over the Vancouver Canucks. He missed only 10 games that first NHL season, but 1980–81 saw him fall out of favour in Quebec and he appeared in only eight contests before finishing the year in the minors. In all, he was very pleased by his NHL experience.

"To play in those old rinks was a dream come true," he said. "But it was also an opportunity to come in and play against the big lines."

Long-time teammate Curt Brackenbury also had a lot of praise for Fitchner.

"He was a phenomenal faceoff guy and an excellent playmaker.

We played more of an aggressive style with more forechecking. Fitchy was very tough. He could really fight and had very long arms."

PIERRE PLANTE

Plante went to the Stanley Cup Final with the New York Rangers in 1978–79, and although he had a 31-point effort during the regular season, he made only minor contributions in the playoff run. So with four new teams coming into the league, he became expendable. The Nordiques were happy to bring another francophone player into the lineup and took him with their eighth pick in the expansion draft.

His ice time seemed reduced compared to the previous year, however, and his offensive totals plummeted. On October 28, 1979, he scored his first goal for Quebec on Bunny Larocque of the Montreal Canadiens, and on February 3, 1980, he fired in the winning goal while taking on his old club.

Frustrated by his experience with the Nordiques, Plante lashed out at the organization at the end of the year and told the press that they were the worst that he had ever played with. In particular, he directed a lot of venom toward coach Jacques Demers, who was, in his opinion, "only good enough to coach a bunch of cheerleaders," and said that assistant Andre Boudrias was "a man that you had to watch out for, because he was a hypocrite."

Needless to say, this outburst practically ensured that Plante never saw NHL action again.

"Pierre had to shoulder a lot of responsibility," said Curt Brackenbury. "Being a native of Quebec and playing in Quebec was a major responsibility. He came in from New York and playing in obscurity. He did not get that in Quebec. There was a lot more accountability there."

WALLY WEIR

Big and intimidating, Weir was a rock on defence for the Nordiques during their last three seasons in the WHA and served as one of the team's top policemen, protecting teammates from the opposition's tough guys. Since no NHL team had drafted him, Quebec retained his rights when they joined the NHL. His presence on the ice was going to be needed in 1979–80.

"On or off the ice, he was a pillar," said Curt Brackenbury. "He lived in Greenfield Park, which is a tough place. He went in and established himself and gave people courage and a sense of security. He didn't have to fight."

During the season opener, Weir took the first penalty in franchise history, and when the team met Atlanta again on November 2, 1979, he earned a pair of assists in the 4–4 tie. Just two nights later, he scored his first NHL goal on Detroit's Rogie Vachon. While like many of his teammates he missed some action, he did thrill the crowds with nine fights that included two in the November 20 game with Boston's Al Secord and Terry O'Reilly.

"That was wild. I must have been trying to make room for some guys on my team. O'Reilly I fought many, many times. He was a big guy and a tough guy. We usually fought face-to-face, where Al would come in from behind."

"There was no tougher guy than him," recalled Michel Dion. "Whenever you needed someone to shake things up, he was there. He never backed down from anybody and he hit clean. He didn't look for fights and he was smart about knowing what to do at the right time."

Weir was proud of his hard work.

"That was my dream come true to make it to the National Hockey League. I would show up in training camp already in shape and not a lot guys were doing that. They felt training camp was to get in shape. That was my edge."

CURT BRACKENBURY

Brackenbury was one of the most feared players in the WHA and led the league with 365 penalty minutes in 1975–76. That season, he came over to the Nordiques when the Minnesota Fighting Saints folded, and in subsequent years, he was allowed to focus more on his offensive play because of the respect he had earned from the opposition.

As Quebec prepared for admission into the NHL, Brackenbury fit into the club's plans, but changes were on the horizon.

"They told me that they wanted to play a different kind of style and not fight as much," he said. "The mood in hockey was changing with players like the Stastnys coming in."

His time in the sin bin decreased by nearly 100 minutes and he also missed some time as a result of an arm injury. On November 4, 1979, he got his first two assists of the season against Detroit and then 18 days later scored his first NHL goal on Boston's Gilles Gilbert. He was particularly up for games against Edmonton. He scored the game-winner against them on December 30, and less than two weeks later, he assisted on Rich Leduc's winning tally when the Oilers went down again by a score of 3–2.

Brackenbury truly enjoyed his experience in Quebec and made strides to adapt to the city's culture.

"I tried to speak French as much as I could and I think people appreciated it. I lived in an all-French neighbourhood when I was there. . . . I was very disappointed to leave Quebec City. The people there are very down to earth. They enjoyed life and enjoyed their team."

MICHEL DION

Dion was a promising prospect in both baseball and hockey, but he chose hockey in the early 1970s after having success in the WHA. He started with the Indianapolis Racers but spent the league's final two seasons in a Cincinnati Stingers uniform sharing the crease with Mike Liut. After seeing him in action on a regular basis, the Nordiques chose him in the dispersal draft to take over as their number one goalie for their first NHL campaign.

"My thought was that they wouldn't look at the ex-World Hockey Association players as equals," he said. "We almost felt like we had to prove to everybody that the other league was just as good. There was a lot of talent in the WHA and it wasn't fair to judge it as inferior."

Dion sat out for the season opener with Atlanta, but he made his NHL debut on October 13, 1979.

"I was told that I was being saved for the second game against the Montreal Canadiens. We had a great game. I played there in junior and I wondered if it was going to be different. It had been a few years, and everybody I had ever known seemed to be at that game and watching it on TV. Jacques Demers called me during the summer and really motivated me for that game. We ended up playing them twice in eight days and we beat them in front of our own fans and that kick-started the franchise."

The Nordiques also had a bit of a goaltending dilemma with three NHL-calibre starters vying for two positions. Ultimately, Dion got the majority of the work and recorded shutouts against Winnipeg and Pittsburgh.

"We pushed each other hard, but we all knew that we were trying to push each other out of a job," he said.

EXPANSION YEAR RECORD: 20-49-11
(51 points — fifth in Smythe Division)
COACHES: Tom McVie and Bill Sutherland
GENERAL MANAGER: John Ferguson
FIRST GAME: October 10, 1979 —
4-2 loss vs. Pittsburgh Penguins
FIRST GOAL: October 10, 1979 by Morris Lukowich

WINNIPEG JETS

Without the Winnipeg Jets and their landmark signing of Bobby Hull, the World Hockey Association may not have lasted the seven seasons that it did. Their success on the ice and at the box office ensured that the three-time AVCO World Trophy champions were to be part of the merger with the NHL in 1979.

In the early stages of the 1978–79 season, Winnipeg hired John Ferguson as their new general manager, and he brought in Tom McVie to serve as coach with fewer than 20 games to go in the regular schedule. The club had lost some of its high-octane offence with the departure of Anders Hedberg and Ulf Nilsson to the New York Rangers and Hull's retirement early in the year as well. To pick up the slack, they scooped up some talent from the Houston Aeros, including Morris Lukowich, who placed second in the league with 65 goals.

Winnipeg finished third in the league and defeated the Quebec Nordiques in the semi-final round of the playoffs before facing Wayne Gretzky and the Edmonton Oilers for the final AVCO Cup. They prevailed in six games, ending their WHA run on a high. The Jets and their fans probably weren't expecting a total demolition of their club, however, and the feeling was that their first season in the NHL was going to be a disaster before it began.

The losses for the Jets started with Terry Ruskowski and Rich Preston, who were reclaimed by the Chicago Black Hawks along with Hull. Other NHL clubs snatched back players like tough-guy Kim

Clackson, defenceman Barry Long and budding scorer Kent Nilsson, and what the team got in return wasn't nearly as good. They were able to get a promising blueliner in the WHA Dispersal Draft in Craig Norwich and their priority selections ended up being Lukowich, Scott Campbell and goalie Markus Mattsson.

In the expansion draft, the pickings were a bit slim, but the highlights included getting Hull back from Chicago and acquiring Peter Marsh and Pierre Hamel. A couple of weeks later, they traded to pick up bruising Barry Melrose and later re-signed free agent Willy Lindstrom. The 1979 NHL Entry Draft gave the club some prospects to look forward to when they made Jimmy Mann their first-round pick and also grabbed promising American Dave Christian.

Before the season began, Ferguson and the Jets were crowing in the media about needing to determine exactly where Preston's rights belonged. They wanted league president John Ziegler to take the matter to arbitration. His response to the matter was delivered to the press.

"I'm of the opinion that the Jets knew well ahead of time that Preston had signed last September with the Black Hawks and also realize that they might have no claim to him. But, upon receipt of their request for a ruling, I will review the facts and make a decision based on those facts."

Ziegler didn't end up taking that route, and Jets governor Barry Shenkarow responded accordingly in the press.

"I think it's just another case of being a new team in the league and the league is taking advantage of the situation and is jumping on us. I just don't know how he [Ziegler] can say, unilaterally, that we are not entitled to arbitration. It just doesn't make sense."

In the end, Preston stayed in Chicago for a few seasons, but there was at least some optimism with rumours that Hull was coming out of retirement. Coach Tom McVie took his ragtag group of players into training camp, realistic when asked if the team could challenge for a playoff spot.

"I suppose that's the number one goal for any expansion team, but it's not mine," he said. "As far as I'm concerned, my job this season is to prepare my hockey club as well as I can 80 times. If we have something to show for it at the end, then that's great. If I was to come out and say I expect so many wins, or so many goals, what happens when we get to a point in the season when we can't get there? Do we pack all the equipment away?

"There are going to be times when the players are going to say 'What's the use? Why bust my butt when it's hopeless?' But, we're just going to have to go out and perform our best for 80 games. . . . It's my job to keep the players enthused."

One forgotten footnote from this era is that equipment manufacturer Cooper Canada used Winnipeg's rookie camp as a test run for some new concepts in hockey equipment. This included the much-maligned Cooperall pants that came into use in 1982–83, which were 40 percent lighter and 20 percent more protective than conventional equipment. Interestingly, the Cooper model jersey that the rookies wore was visually similar to the Reebok Edge Ice jerseys NHL teams began wearing in 2007–08.

The Pittsburgh Penguins hosted the Jets for their first NHL game on October 11, 1979. Winnipeg was behind by three goals before Lukowich tallied for the first time at the 13:24 mark of the third period. Peter Sullivan got one less than three minutes later on the power play, but the team couldn't rally and lost by a score of 4–2. Their road swing continued the next night and they were shut out by the Boston Bruins. In that game, rookie Raymond Bourque scored his first professional goal.

Finally coming home on October 14, the Jets got their first NHL victory against the Colorado Rockies. During that first month they proved themselves one of the better new clubs with a 4–5–1 record. Some more good news was announced when after a long negotiation process Hull came to terms with the Jets on October 26, 1979.

McVie also made national news in November when he was suspended for three games and fined $500 for an incident during a game against Atlanta. He attempted to scale the partition between the benches to get at Atlanta coach Al MacNeil, and after removing his coat and tie and unbuttoning his shirt, he removed his upper plate and put it in his pocket. He received a game misconduct for his actions and NHL executive VP Brian O'Neill was not pleased.

"He has no explanation for his actions other than he became distraught at seeing his players involved in an altercation, which was taking place at the time. He expressed deep remorse for his conduct and vowed it would not happen again."

It was the second time McVie had been involved in such an incident that season and reportedly the first suspension ever handed down to an NHL coach.

"I've disappointed myself and my family and I was disappointed in doing that in front of my team," he said. "I've trained myself for 10 years to control myself and I have always told my teams to do the same. It was a mistake, but John Ziegler makes mistakes; Jimmy Carter makes mistakes. . . . I'll never do anything like this again. Never. I'm too good a coach to be doing that sort of thing. I'll tell you how strongly I feel about this. Don Cherry could punch me in the nose right now and his dog, Blue, could bite my son Denver in the leg and he wouldn't get a reaction out of me."

One of the most memorable events for Jets fans in their first NHL season was the first time they hosted the Montreal Canadiens, on December 15. It was dubbed "Black Tie Night," and fans were encouraged to show up to the game in tuxedos. Winnipeg got a big 6–2 win over the defending Stanley Cup champions in a nationally televised game. There was a big problem, though, as Hull showed up late and McVie told him that he was not playing that night. The aging superstar simply walked out and never played for the Jets again, as he was suspended by the team. Eventually, he was traded to the Hartford Whalers for future considerations.

A little more than two weeks later, Winnipeg hosted the touring Moscow Dynamo club in an exhibition and were destroyed 7–0. There was at least some positive news at this time, as Lukowich was given the chance to play in the 1980 NHL All-Star Game and the Jets were also getting some tremendous play from Ron Wilson, a high-scoring rookie they had picked up before the season began.

The Jets lost six straight in January, falling farther out of a playoff spot, and it just got worse later on when they did not taste victory during a 10-game stretch. It was around this time that they got an offensive boost with the arrival of Dave Christian following his gold medal win with the United States at the 1980 Winter Olympics, so they were at least able to play the role of spoilers in the last 10 games of the year as they went 5–5.

With one NHL campaign under their belts, the Jets still weren't ready to become contenders. In their second season they won only nine games and finished last overall. Their consolation prize, however, was the opportunity to take Dale Hawerchuk with the first overall pick in the 1981 NHL Entry Draft. As the team rebuilt with tons of top young-talent, they put together one of the greatest single-season turnarounds in league history and made the playoffs for the first time in 1981–82. For the rest of the decade, they regularly made the playoffs but only made it to the second round twice.

In the 1990s, Winnipeg remained competitive with talent like Keith Tkachuk, Alexei Zhamnov and Teemu Selanne carrying their fair share of the offensive load. But the team was having off-ice troubles that eventually forced them to relocate to Phoenix as the Coyotes. Fan support for the Jets was always high, yet factors like a weak Canadian dollar along with high operating costs and rising salaries were a deadly combination for the beloved team.

The Coyotes have had a rough time playing in the desert of Arizona, and many times in recent years have been rumoured to be on the move. The team finally went into bankruptcy in 2009 and the NHL took over the reins until a suitable owner could be found. Several candidates expressed interest, but when none of them panned, relocation rumours regularly went into overdrive. The city of Glendale, a suburb of Phoenix, battled back and forth with the league but the NHL eventually approved a 15-year lease agreement for new investors Renaissance Sports and Entertainment in 2013. There is a potential escape clause in place for the new owners, however, and they can move the club after five years or losing $50 million. Only time will tell if the Desert Dogs are to remain in Arizona.

(clockwise) Morris Lukowich, Dave Christian, Bobby Hull, Pierre Hamel

MORRIS LUKOWICH

After he scored 65 goals and racked up 99 points with the Jets in 1978–79, Lukowich was on the radar of the Pittsburgh Penguins as the team headed into the NHL ice wars, because they had drafted him back in 1976. They put in their claim, but team management in Winnipeg sought to protect their star player and made him a priority selection.

Although there was justified hype about his heading into the established league, Lukowich expressed some doubts regarding his readiness to coach Tom McVie, who praised his play.

"He's got just a tremendous shot coming in off the wing and you want to know the crazy part about it? Luke came to me the other day and said 'Do you think I have a good enough shot to play in the NHL?'"

Fittingly, Lukowich scored the club's first goal against Greg Millen of the Penguins in the team's first game and also had an assist later in the contest. In December, he had some strong outings, earning four points one night against the Edmonton Oilers and then, with a national audience watching, putting up three points in a 6–2 defeat of the Montreal Canadiens.

Since he was Winnipeg's top offensive producer, it was natural that Lukowich be selected to play in the 1980 NHL All-Star Game for the Campbell Conference. He finished the year with 15 more points than his closest teammate, Peter Sullivan. At the end of the year, he was awarded the Molson Cup for the most three-star selections on the club.

PETER SULLIVAN

Sullivan was originally drafted by the Montreal Canadiens in 1971 and, after tearing up the minor leagues, he chose to sign with the Winnipeg Jets. It was a smart move, as he won three AVCO Cup titles with the club and had a strong season in 1978–79 that saw him finish tied for third in the league with 46 goals alongside Edmonton's Wayne Gretzky.

When he finally made his NHL debut on October 10, 1979, Sullivan scored against Pittsburgh. He also scored the club's first goal at home four days later when they hosted Colorado. The firsts kept on coming as he took a penalty shot against Minnesota's Gary Edwards on October 19, but failed to put the puck in the net.

The son of Frank Sullivan, an early Canadian football star who also won a gold medal in hockey at the 1928 Winter Olympics, he felt that he had a lot to prove in the established league. He exacted some revenge on the team that drafted him as he scored the winner in addition to setting up four others against the Habs on December 15.

"I think I should have been here a long time ago," Sullivan said at the time. "I always believed I belonged, but there was a lot of politics involved. I don't want to say anything, though, because it would only sound like sour grapes. It would have been nice to play here with that C-H on my sweater, but I'm just as proud to be here wearing the Jets' crest. Probably more so."

At the end of the season, "Silky" was voted the Most Exciting Player on the team and he remained with Winnipeg for one more year.

RON WILSON

Yet another great prospect who was stuck on the farm with the Montreal Canadiens in the 1970s, Wilson was conditionally sold to the Jets just before the 1979–80 campaign began. If he made the team, he was going to be skating for Winnipeg, and if he was bound for the minors, he'd be back with the Nova Scotia Voyageurs. He worked hard and earned a spot with the new NHL club.

"There was more hope at this camp," Wilson said at the time. "At Montreal, you pretty well knew who was going to be on the team when you got there, so you didn't get your hopes up too high. That way you weren't disappointed when you were sent down."

General manager John Ferguson was very pleased by the acquisition, even if he had sustained a bruised heel during the season opener.

"In Ron Wilson, we got ourselves a hockey player who has gotten better each season," he said. "One of the good things about him is that he can play both centre and the wing positions."

On October 19, 1979, Wilson scored the first goal of his career on Gary Edwards of the Minnesota North Stars, and it gave the Jets the edge they needed in a 3–2 win. Just 12 days later, he scored another game-winner and chipped in two assists against the Quebec Nordiques. Over the course of the season, he produced at a good clip and was sixth among rookie scorers once the schedule was over. He remained with Winnipeg for many years after, and a decade later was the last member of the 1979–80 team to leave the club through a trade.

CRAIG NORWICH

Like many talented players drafted by the Montreal Canadiens in the 1970s, Norwich chose to play in the WHA to get some pro experience instead of spending time on their farm team in Halifax. Before he was drafted, he was a standout for the University of Wisconsin and had two very strong seasons with the Cincinnati Stingers before the rival league shut down.

After seeing him in action, the Jets made a play for him at the WHA Dispersal Draft. They saw him as the one who was going to be their primary offence provider from the blue line. For most of the year, he did exactly that. He had strong outings against the Edmonton Oilers on December 7, 1979, with two goals and an assist, and against the Los Angeles Kings a month later with a trio of power-play helpers.

The majority of his offence came in power-play situations, and he scored seven of his 10 goals with the man advantage.

"I consider myself a giver rather than a shooter," he explained. "I'd much rather feed it off to guys like Peter [Marsh] or Luke [Morris Lukowich] because both those guys have much better shots than I do . . . . Eventually, the other teams in this league are going to learn they can't take penalties against us."

By the end of the year, Norwich was regarded as the team's fifth defenceman, and his frustration was beginning to show — especially in his comments to the press.

"To tell you the truth, I don't know if I fit into this club's plans. I have somewhat of an understanding of what they're trying to do here, but I don't know if it includes me. . . . I plan to play out this contract and then quit," he said. "I've got two years left on my contract plus an option year, and it's up to me if I play out the option. I don't think anybody likes to get traded. It's sort of a demeaning thing. But, if something comes along that would help this club and help me . . ."

Management for the Jets didn't take these comments lightly and he was dealt to the St. Louis Blues soon after for Rick Bowness.

LARS-ERIK SJOBERG

The first captain of the Winnipeg Jets when they arrived in the NHL, Sjoberg had been a member of the club since 1974–75 and was an integral part of three AVCO World Trophy victories. In fact, his captaincy made history when he became the first European-trained player to wear the "C" on his chest. He also faced a wide array of challenges during their expansion season while coming back from an Achilles tendon injury that forced him out of most of the 1978–79 campaign.

A strong leader with the will to win, Sjoberg earned a pair of assists against the Colorado Rockies on October 14, 1979. He was particularly effective against the Los Angeles Kings with eight points over four games, including a three-assist effort on January 13, 1980.

As the end of the year approached, the frustration of playing for a losing team began to set in and he expressed his feelings in the press.

"I've only missed the playoffs once in my life and that was the 1974–75 season, my first with the Jets. But I think this year is worse," he said. "I haven't thought about it much, but losing bothers me. If I see someone on the team who I have faith in and he doesn't put out, then that really disappoints me. It makes losing harder to take. That's only happened once, but I was very disappointed to see it."

Goalie Pierre Hamel offered praise for the veteran blueliner's work.

"Any goaltender in the league would love to have Shoe in front of them. We used to get bombarded with shots in Winnipeg, so it was a good thing that he blocked so many shots for me."

At the end of the year, Sjoberg was set to become a free agent as well, but it looked as if retirement was looming.

"It's possible," he said. "It hasn't been that enjoyable this year. I don't like to lose, I don't know anybody who does. Many guys feel the way I do about losing, but I'm 35 now."

Ultimately, hanging up the blades was the option he took, but he went on to become a scout for the New York Rangers. He passed away on October 20, 1987, after battling cancer, and the Rangers chose to honour his memory by naming their team Rookie of the Year award after him.

DAVE CHRISTIAN

Christian's college career with the University of North Dakota drew the attention of the Jets, and they made him their second-round selection in the 1979 NHL Entry Draft. Instead of rushing him into pro duty, they allowed him some time to develop his skills with the United States National Team, and he was a big part of their run to a gold medal at the 1980 Winter Games in Lake Placid, New York. His father, Bill, had been a part of the original Miracle on Ice 20 years earlier, and the young star was given the key to his hometown of Warroad, Minnesota.

During that ceremony, Winnipeg's general manager, John Ferguson, came down to present him with his first professional contract and had glowing things to say about the team's new star.

"He is a very versatile hockey player and a most welcome addition to our club," he said. "The Christian name is associated with winning. We are obviously pleased that we will have one who will help us start that tradition in Winnipeg."

On March 2, 1980, he made his NHL debut against Chicago and scored his first goal against Mike Veisor mere seconds into his first shift. His biggest performance in the dwindling days of the 1979–80 campaign was a natural hat trick and an assist against the Hartford Whalers on March 26. He also lit up the Black Hawks once again with a four-point performance on April 2.

BOBBY HULL

Hull was the marquee superstar for the World Hockey Association and he gave the fledgling league instant credibility when he signed with the Winnipeg Jets in the summer of 1972. Over six full seasons with the Jets, he was a part of two AVCO Cup titles, but he chose to step away from the game early in the 1978–79 campaign.

With the merger between the NHL and WHA, the ownership of the

Chicago Black Hawks was salivating over the chance to bring one of hockey's greatest heroes back into the fold, even going to the lengths of holding a press conference announcing his return. Naturally, they reclaimed him, but then puzzlingly left him available in the expansion draft to protect Alain Daigle. This was great news for Jets fans — but there was one big problem — Hull wasn't ready to come back just yet and it didn't help that he didn't exactly see eye-to-eye with general manager John Ferguson.

The two sides ultimately came to an agreement in late October 1979, and Hull was pleased that the ordeal was finally over.

"It was no secret and I stated on more than one occasion that if I returned to the game as a player, I would have preferred an American-based team," he said. "Those feelings were expressed and based on personal matters. However, as a result of our meeting, these matters have now been resolved and I am very happy to say that I will be rejoining the Winnipeg Jets Hockey Club.

"It's been a long, drawn-out affair, although I wasn't too involved with it. We got together to hash things out. Had we both done this sooner maybe things would have been resolved sooner."

Ferguson was also pleased with the agreement.

"I am very pleased that Bobby has decided to make a comeback with the Winnipeg Jets. His return is a great bonus for the people of Canada and fans in the National Hockey League cities who will be able to see Bobby play again."

The return to Winnipeg lasted just 18 games. The best of those came against the Hartford Whalers on November 14, 1979, when he scored two goals, including the winner. He also had consecutive two-point nights in early December in matches with St. Louis and Detroit.

"Everybody was in awe of him," said Lindsay Middlebrook. "We didn't have a lot of superstars, but Bobby came in and had everybody on the team in awe. In practice, he would never shoot the puck. I asked him to shoot and once in a while he'd fire one in. As great a guy as he was, he didn't make a difference in whether we won or not. We struggled with him and without him."

Hull's last game with the Jets was a 5-0 loss to the Quebec Nordiques on December 12. He was expected to play three nights later in the nationally broadcast game against Montreal, but he showed up late to the arena and was told that he was not playing that night. Instantly, the tenuous relationship between Hull and team management soured, and he was suddenly on the disabled list with a shoulder injury. It was publicly announced that he was not practising with the club until his shoulder had healed.

Naturally, speculation began to grow and Hull asked to be traded to another team even though he was a partial owner of the one he was playing for. Ferguson blasted the star left-winger in the press in an effort to motivate his return.

"Hull does not fit into the Jets' style and hasn't been producing. He has to play more to get into the kind of condition he needs to be productive."

It took a few weeks, but Hull was eventually shipped off to the Whalers for future considerations, marking the end of an era for hockey in Winnipeg.

JIMMY MANN

Mann starred for the QMJHL's Sherbrooke Castors and established himself as a prime prospect heading into the 1979 NHL Entry Draft with 35 goals and 260 penalty minutes in his final campaign with the club. The Jets took him with their first-ever amateur selection, and that came as a surprise to the young prospect.

"My last year in junior I had a great year. I was really well known in the league at that time and they were terrified of me," he said. "All I wanted to do was play hockey and my goal was to get to a training camp. I worked my ass off. I got a call congratulating me for being a first-round pick and I thought they were joking."

John Ferguson was one of his idols growing up, and Mann quickly found a niche with the club, despite Winnipeg's exodus of talent that resulted from the merger.

"They dismantled that team . . . and they had a good team!

Personally, I didn't follow much of the WHA, but we didn't have an overly tough team. We had Scott Campbell and Dave Hoyda and I came in there all fired up. Fergie told me to take care of the team."

Mann recorded his first assist on a goal by Ron Wilson against the Colorado Rockies on October 20, 1979, and had his first two fights with Chicago's Doug Lecuyer four days later. On October 26, he served notice to the rest of the league when he battled three of the toughest members of the Boston Bruins, dropping the gloves with Terry O'Reilly, Al Secord and Stan Jonathan to spark the Jets to a 3–2 win.

"I pretty much won all three of them! I was 20 years old and ready to go," he said.

Mann got his first NHL goal while hosting the Vancouver Canucks on November 24. The goal was scored on Curt Ridley and it proved the game-winner.

"I remember getting the puck and shooting it in. It was exciting scoring goals — I only got 10! I wish a lot more came and if they let me play more, I might have got more."

Firmly positioned in the enforcer role, Mann continued to stand up for his teammates and ended up getting into 22 scraps over the course of his rookie season with other heavyweights like Willi Plett, Wally Weir and Dave Semenko. On March 16, 1980, he tangled twice with Dennis Polonich and received a game misconduct that resulted in a two-game suspension. At the end of the 1979–80 campaign, Mann led all players in penalty minutes.

PIERRE HAMEL

After years of toiling in the minors for the Maple Leafs organization, Hamel saw minimal NHL action, but he did benefit from the tutelage of Ed Johnston while playing for the AHL's New Brunswick Hawks in 1978–79. The recently retired goalie spoke with a couple of teams about getting the young netminder from Toronto, and John Ferguson listened, grabbing him in the expansion draft.

"I was kind of glad to get out of the Toronto organization because they had a pretty packed house," he said. "Going to an expansion team, there was less pressure and they weren't expecting the best. I went to training camp and I didn't know who was under contract. I knew that Smith and Mattsson had deals, and John Ferguson drafted Lindsay Middlebrook. I figured they brought me in for the minor league team. I always worked hard in training camp and I shuffled their deck a little bit."

After prevailing in the training camp dogfight for a backup position with the Jets, Hamel made his debut with the club during a 4-0 loss to the Boston Bruins on October 11, 1979. It took him a little while to earn his first victory, but he ended up prevailing over the Hartford Whalers on November 14. One of his favourite outings, however, was the 6-2 win on December 15 over the Canadiens, where he had a unique experience before the puck was dropped.

"We were playing Montreal in Winnipeg and the Stanley Cup was travelling with them. They brought it into the dressing room to stay safe," he said. "I was there and I figured it was going to be my only chance to grab it and hold it. A reporter was there and I told them not to write what I said or did. He was nice enough to never mention it and I let him know that I appreciated his silence."

Over the rest of the season, Hamel led the team with nine wins but did miss a little time with a cracked kneecap. He was back again in 1980–81, when the team experienced one of the worst seasons in NHL history.

"Personally, I enjoyed the first season better. You almost knew it was going to be a rough season. There was a lot of politics going on."

Fellow goaler Lindsay Middlebrook enjoyed playing alongside Hamel, and the pair shared the crease during the exhibition match against Moscow Dynamo.

"He was a funny, hilarious guy. He was very acrobatic. He'd look better letting in goals than I would stopping them. He had a flair and I was amazed by how he made things look so good."

BILL LESUK

After the shell shock of playing for the Washington Capitals for their first season in 1974–75, Lesuk jumped to the WHA's Winnipeg Jets and firmly re-established himself as one of the game's best penalty killers before going on to win three AVCO Cup championships.

"I wish I had more patience to stay in Los Angeles and Washington, but I look at my years in Winnipeg to be the best of them all," he said. "I always prided myself on being a hard-working player, but playing with guys like Hull, Hedberg, Nilsson and Sjoberg made me realize I had a long way to go to realize my potential."

Lesuk was a member of the team when they returned to the NHL but was used only on a limited basis. His lone assist came on a goal by Lyle Moffat when the Jets faced Edmonton on December 7, 1979. There were many nights where he was left off the lineup, but he never complained.

"Of all the guys in hockey, I respect him the most," said Jude Drouin. "He inspires the team. How many times have I seen him go through the pre-game warmup and come off the ice only to find that he isn't playing? Some guys would turn sour over that. But not Billy. As he would be taking his equipment off, he would be telling the guys to work hard, reminding them that they could win."

Because Lesuk appeared in only 49 games, he was excluded from being the team's nominee for the Masterton Trophy by just a single contest. Regardless, he was still positive about the team and the game itself.

"This team has a lot of character. We get paid to play 80 games a season and just because we're out of the playoffs doesn't mean we shouldn't put out," he remarked at the time. "Pride makes you play well. If we give anything less than our best, then we're not being fair to our fans."

Lesuk retired soon after and went on to have great success as a scout.

LINDSAY MIDDLEBROOK

A rising prospect, Middlebrook was property of the New York Rangers and spent the 1978–79 season with their AHL farm club in New Haven, where he won 29 games. The Jets took the former St. Louis University standout with their second pick in the expansion draft, and he battled seven other goaltenders at training camp for a spot with the team.

For most of the 1979–80 campaign, Middlebrook bounced between Winnipeg and Tulsa, but after sitting on the bench during one of his call-ups, he petitioned coach Tom McVie for an opportunity to finally get into his first NHL game. McVie responded to the inquiry when they were getting ready to take on the Quebec Nordiques.

"Have your parents ever been to Quebec City? No? Well, you better tell them to be there tomorrow night," he said.

Middlebrook was more than pleased to step into the crease even if he ended up being on the wrong end of a 5–0 shutout.

"It's something you grew up with in Canada, and it almost becomes unreal in some ways," he recalled. "The Nordiques were hard to play against at home. I was disappointed to let in five, but at the time, it didn't seem like a bad game."

Four days later, he got a second chance to see some action and was strong in a 4–3 win over the Edmonton Oilers. He admits to thoroughly enjoying his first season with the Jets and has many great memories.

"For me, every building I went into was the first time," he said. "I remember some of the goofy stuff like being able to go into a hotel room instead of waiting in line for a key."

Although he was sent back down to the minors toward the end of the year, Middlebrook had a strong finish with the Tulsa Oilers.

GARY SMITH

A veteran netminder who earned the nickname "Suitcase" for the number of times he switched teams during his career, Smith had split the 1978–79 campaign between Indianapolis and Winnipeg in the WHA and led the Jets to the final AVCO Cup championship that spring. The Jets retained his rights before the 1979 NHL Expansion Draft, and he was in net to make 18 saves during their first win against the Colorado Rockies on October 14.

The wins were few and far between after that, and the team had to make the difficult decision to send him down to Tulsa when the younger netminders under contract were all proving a bit more reliable in the crease. Smith discussed the demotion with the press at the time and expressed no anger.

"I'm not disappointed or bitter at all," he said. "The team isn't going anywhere right now and even if I was playing great, I wouldn't really be helping. Besides, now they've got the two goalies who should have been here all along."

Always one to march to a slightly different beat on the ice, he surprised fans and teammates by playing his last minor league game as a defenceman rather than staying in the familiar confines of the cage. While he sat on the bench most of the night, the crowd knew that he was dressed as a skater and the cheers grew louder throughout the game for him to take a shift. With 57 seconds left, he took to the ice but never fulfilled his dream of scoring a goal during a professional hockey game.

"Gary was a great guy," recalled fellow goalie Lindsay Middlebrook. "But off the ice he would strip down between periods and take a shower. He also wore about seven or eight pairs of socks at a time. We had some great times together in Tulsa."

MARKUS MATTSSON

Mattsson saw most of the regular-season action with the Jets during their final WHA campaign in 1978–79, but after the arrival of Gary Smith as the hot hand he spent his time on the bench during the team's run to the AVCO Cup. After selecting him in the 1977 NHL Amateur Draft, the New York Islanders held his NHL rights, but Winnipeg decided to make him a priority selection and retained his services for the 1979–80 season.

Following training camp, management made the tough decision to send Mattsson down to Tulsa to regain his confidence. He didn't let the demotion get him down.

"It was a bit disappointing to be sent to Tulsa at the start, but I'm happy with the way it ended," he said.

Team general manager John Ferguson also offered his thoughts at the time.

"We knew he would be exposed to a tremendous amount of work in Winnipeg. We thought he would lose his confidence if he stayed."

With the CHL's Oilers, Mattson ended up going 10-7-2 over 20 appearances, and his return allowed him to earn the first shutout in club history in a 0-0 tie with the Islanders on February 12, 1979. Another blanking followed on March 26 when Winnipeg let the shots fly during a 7-0 trouncing of the Hartford Whalers.

A NEW ERA OF
EXPANSION AND RELOCATION

Once the Colorado Rockies became the New Jersey Devils in 1982–83, the NHL experienced the calmest era of its post-expansion years, and there was no team movement of any kind for nearly a decade. It was a time that saw the end of the four-year stranglehold on the Stanley Cup by the New York Islanders and the rise of the Edmonton Oilers, who won five championships over a seven-season span.

Not long after the end of the 1987–88 season, the most significant trade in hockey history took place when Wayne Gretzky was sent to the Los Angeles Kings on August 9, 1988. The deal was regarded as the best thing for the NHL's hopes of expanding, as the Great One was exposed to a whole new audience in California and the game began to garner interest in non-traditional markets.

At the time, the NHL was drafting up some long-term plans to expand its membership from 21 teams to 30 by the end of the 1990s. While specific locations were not named, there were certainly hopes that some of these new clubs would come from warmer locales.

The first of these teams came out of a convoluted situation with the ownership of the Minnesota North Stars. The Gund brothers wanted to relocate the team to northern California, but there was a lot of pressure to keep the team in a traditional hockey market. As a result, an expansion team was set to start play in San Jose during the 1991–92 season and it drafted several players from the North Stars. Both teams then got some leftover players from the other 20 teams in the only NHL

Expansion Draft to bolster an existing club. The team, which became known as the Sharks, was a huge hit in the Bay Area, in stark contrast to the failure of the California Golden Seals 15 years earlier.

Around this time, the league decided to bring in two more clubs that hit the ice in 1992–93. Although many of the applicants seemed as if they were more financially stable, ownership groups in Ottawa and Tampa Bay were the only ones who did not balk at the $50-million entry fee required for a new franchise. Both clubs suffered a variety of problems from the start and were given their pick of the worst players available. On the ice, the Senators and Lightning were total disasters during their early years, and even a supplemental draft after their inaugural years provided little help.

Undaunted, the NHL was determined to get some serious corporate power behind its next round of expansion teams, but no one expected to see new clubs just one year later. Once Disney was on board with their Mighty Ducks of Anaheim, Florida businessman Wayne Huizenga was heavily courted and the Florida Panthers became a reality. The 1993–94 season also saw the Minnesota North Stars head south to become the Dallas Stars, much to the chagrin of fervent fans.

The shifting of franchises suddenly became a rather disturbing trend over the rest of the decade, as small-market owners were tempted by greater earning potential and in some cases, a stronger American dollar. The Quebec Nordiques were the next casualty. It was a bitter experience for their fans when a team that was finally on the rise found Stanley Cup glory as the Colorado Avalanche in 1995–96. One year later, the Winnipeg Jets were on the move to the desert climes of Phoenix and became the Coyotes. The fourth, and final, franchise shift of the decade belonged to the Hartford Whalers, who found new fans as the Carolina Hurricanes.

Even with such instability, the league made the rash decision to add four more teams over a three-year period from 1998–99 to 2000–01. The first of these new clubs was the Nashville Predators, and they were followed by the Atlanta Thrashers a year later in 1999–00. As strange as it was to see the NHL back in a city that two decades earlier could not support a team, it was believed at the time that strong ownership translated into long-term success.

The final two additions to the league hit the ice in 2000–01. The Columbus Blue Jackets and Minnesota Wild were big hits from the start, at least from a box office perspective. While hockey-mad Minnesotans were ready to support their team for the long haul, the same could not be said for the Blue Jackets, and their attendance has been in a steady decline, as the team is rarely seen as a contender.

With the league at 30 member clubs, a decade of franchise stability followed. Occasionally, there were rumours of teams being candidates for relocation and new ownership, but the league did its best to help its membership remain intact. When the 2004–05 season was cancelled, absence made the hearts of fans grow fonder, and the teams and players all benefited financially when action started up again the next year.

During the 2010–11 season, some serious stories were spreading about the financial troubles of the Coyotes and Thrashers while at the same time fans in Winnipeg were making noise about wanting a team back in their city. Although some fans preferred a return by the team that left, they really were not picky, and the former Atlanta team headed north. Called the Winnipeg Jets once again, they look to have a bright future and play in front of sold-out crowds.

The future for NHL expansion does not look tremendously bright at this time, and the league has no official plans to grow beyond 30 clubs. Relocation is a more realistic idea for several troubled teams. The New York Islanders will relocate to Brooklyn for the start of the 2015–16 season. There are plenty of markets interested in having an NHL team call their city home, including Kansas City, Quebec City, Seattle and Hamilton. In time, the league will certainly change one way or another, but the game itself will continue to be strong.

EXPANSION YEAR RECORD: 17-58-5
(39 points — sixth in Smythe Division)
COACH: George Kingston
GENERAL MANAGER: Jack Ferreira
FIRST GAME: October 4, 1991 —
4-3 loss vs. Vancouver Canucks
FIRST GOAL: October 4, 1991 by Craig Coxe

SAN JOSE SHARKS

While it is safe to say that the NHL's first experiment in the Bay Area proved quite a flop, the old California Golden Seals can be connected to the San Jose Sharks — a team that hit the ice a little more than 15 years later.

The ill-fated Golden Seals moved to Cleveland before the 1976–77 season, and after two disastrous years, they merged with another troubled franchise in the Minnesota North Stars. That fortified team rose from the bottom of the standings almost immediately, but toward the end of the next decade, there were rumours circulating that owners Gordon and George Gund III wanted to bring their team back to sunny California. In fact, they were once minority owners of the Seals and had a big part in their move to Cleveland, so the league wasn't too happy about the idea but changed its tune soon after as former Hartford Whalers owner Howard Baldwin and his associates were making a push to bring the NHL to San Jose.

In order to keep everyone happy, the NHL hammered out a compromise that saw the Gund brothers sell their North Stars shares to Baldwin and his group, and they received a Bay Area expansion team for their troubles. Interestingly, they were also allowed to take some members of the Minnesota club along with them, and the North Stars got a sweet deal as well by being allowed to participate in the 1991 NHL Expansion Draft.

After the deal was made official on May 5, 1990, a contest was held to determine the new team's name and more 5,000 entries were received. The winner was "Blades," but the Gunds vetoed that idea due to its association with weapons and went with "Sharks" instead. An interesting colour scheme for the uniforms was later unveiled along with an eye-catching logo of a shark biting into a hockey stick. It was a hit from the start throughout the hockey world, and their merchandise sales ranked among the top in the league before they even played a game.

The assembly of the Sharks began with the dispersal draft on May 30, 1991. There they focused a lot on younger prospects like Arturs Irbe, Neil Wilkinson and Rob Zettler, along with tough guys such as Link Gaetz and Kevin Evans. Later that day, they made their picks in the expansion draft and acquired more muscle in Bob McGill and Craig Coxe. If anything, the new team in San Jose was going to be tough, but it was not apparent that they would be scoring many goals.

At the 1991 NHL Entry Draft, they had the second overall pick and took promising Pat Falloon from the WHL's Spokane Chiefs, pegging him to be the face of the franchise. Perhaps an even better selection, though, was his junior teammate, Ray Whitney, who went on to have a lengthy career.

After signing a few more free agents, the Sharks got a leader in Doug Wilson in a trade with the Chicago Blackhawks. One of the best defencemen of the 1980s, Wilson was San Jose's first captain as they headed into training camp. Based out of the Cow Palace in Daly City near San Francisco, the team made its debut on the road against Vancouver on October 4, 1991, and lost by a 4–3 margin. The next night saw their home debut in a rematch with the Canucks and they were beaten soundly by a score of 5–2.

On October 8, the team won for the first time when the Calgary Flames came into town, but the honeymoon wasn't going to last long. They lost their next 13 outings, which included seven straight road defeats. That was fortunately their worst stretch during their expansion year, and they even managed back-to-back wins on a handful of occasions. With a weak offensive and porous defensive record that put them

(clockwise) Pat Falloon, Doug Wilson, Link Gaetz, Brian Hayward

last in the league, there was little doubt that they were destined to finish in the basement, but there was no consolation prize in the form of the first overall pick in the 1992 NHL Entry Draft since that privilege was reserved for the Tampa Bay Lightning.

Things didn't improve at all in 1992–93 when the team went through its worst year to date with a dismal 24 points. But they enjoyed a dramatic turnaround in 1993–94 and finished at .500, making it to the second round of the playoffs after defeating the top-seeded Detroit Red Wings. Since 1997–98, the Sharks have missed the postseason on only one occasion and have had consistent regular-season success, especially with Wilson as their general manager. Since they have yet to make the Stanley Cup Final, some fans and media members tend to feel that the team typically chokes under pressure, but there are many NHL cities that envy that kind of record.

PAT FALLOON

For decades, the sport of hockey has had its fair share of hyped prospects who don't necessarily meet the lofty expectations set out for them in the eyes of scouts, fans or team management. Falloon often gets unfairly placed in that group. After three seasons with the WHL's Spokane Chiefs where he won a Memorial Cup along with a gold medal at the 1991 IIHF World Junior Championship, the buzz around the young star was heavy, but it paled in comparison to the consensus first overall pick for the 1991 NHL Entry Draft — Eric Lindros.

Instead of going with a promising young defender like Scott Niedermayer, the Sharks made Falloon their first-ever amateur draftee. The results weren't so bad when you consider that he led the team in goals, assists and points during their expansion season. He registered his first career point with an assist during his NHL debut against the Vancouver Canucks on October 5, 1991, and followed it up with a goal and assist while playing the Calgary Flames three days later. His best outing as a rookie was part of a five-game point streak when he scored once and added three helpers in a battle with the Quebec Nordiques on February 26, 1992.

BRIAN MULLEN

Mullen was heading into his 10th NHL season in 1991–92 and he was one of the first players the Sharks ever traded for when they gave up aging power-play specialist Tim Kerr to get Mullen from the New York Rangers.

Often used as a penalty killer, Mullen was coming off three straight seasons of more than 60 points and had a strong start with 11 points in the month of October. His best single-game output of the year saw him earn three points in a win over the Quebec Nordiques on December 21, 1991, and he had a pair of two-goal games in February. At the end of the year, he was second on the team in scoring and shared the lead in shorthanded goals with Kelly Kisio.

DOUG WILSON

One of hockey's greatest defencemen in the 1980s, Wilson was approaching the twilight of his NHL career when the Chicago Blackhawks traded the dependable blueliner to San Jose for rough-and-tumble prospect Kerry Toporowski and a draft pick on September 6, 1991.

Wilson was named the first captain of the Sharks before the 1991–92 campaign. His leadership was sorely needed in the club's infancy and he represented the team at the 1992 NHL All-Star Game in Philadelphia. Among his best efforts that season were a two-goal outing against Los Angeles on January 14, 1992, and a three-assist night against Buffalo a month later.

Injuries cut his season short, but Wilson was the team's first nominee for the King Clancy Memorial Award for his extensive work in the community.

NEIL WILKINSON

A second-round pick by Minnesota in 1986, Wilkinson made his NHL debut in 1989–90 and saw semi-regular duty with the club, where he was praised for his defensive promise and mean streak. The Sharks must have coveted these skills when trying to get their initial roster going and took him away from the North Stars in the dispersal draft.

Following a steady start, Wilkinson took his play up a few notches in November and had nine points, which included a goal against the Los Angeles Kings and a three-assist effort while taking on the Edmonton Oilers. After missing a good chunk of action in February, he came back from injury in March and scored a power-play goal against the New York Islanders on March 26, 1992. Although his -11 rating looks bad to some, it was the best among Sharks blueliners who appeared in 40 or more games during the team's expansion year.

LINK GAETZ

Some players take a special place in the pantheon of hockey heroes regardless of their offensive accomplishments, since so many things they do on and off the ice generate incredible controversy and live on in the memories of fans everywhere. Gaetz is certainly one of those memorable skaters. There was little doubt that he was on the ice to protect his teammates at any cost.

Drafted by the Minnesota North Stars to serve as the eventual guardian of Mike Modano, Gaetz spent three seasons terrorizing the IHL before becoming an original member of the Sharks through the dispersal draft. He was an instant hit with fans and in his time at the NHL level that year, he got into 14 fights, which included a pair of battles on October 26, 1991, against Randy McKay and David Maley of the New Jersey Devils. A few weeks later, he took on the legendary Bob Probert and he eventually tussled with heavyweights like Gino Odjick and Kelly Buchberger. In fact, he was on pace to shatter the league record for penalty minutes in a single season, but he was forced to sit out his fair share of games as well.

On April 2, 1992, tragedy struck when Gaetz was tossed from the passenger seat of a car while driving with a friend who was under the influence of alcohol. He was semi-comatose for eight days and it was feared that he was near death. He sustained major injuries: his brain stem was damaged and he was partially paralyzed and had no memory of the accident. Many were shocked to see him return to action that fall, but he never appeared in another NHL game. His minor league odyssey was filled with crazy moments, and teams eventually grew tired of his antics. Many of those crazy moments are the subject of debate, but there is little doubt that hockey fans will ever forget "The Missing Link."

RAY WHITNEY

After a phenomenal 1990–91 season where he led the WHL with 185 points and helped take the Spokane Chiefs to a Memorial Cup championship, Whitney became the second junior player ever drafted by the Sharks. Because of his success playing with Falloon, he was a smart pick by the first-year club, but nobody could have predicted the amazing path his NHL career was going to take.

In 1991–92, Whitney was ready to make the jump to the pro level. He spent time playing for Canada's national team and had a brief stint with Kolner EC in Germany before trying his hand at playing in the IHL with the San Diego Gulls. His transition was very smooth, as he scored 90 points over 63 games, and he was ready to make his NHL debut toward the end of the season. On April 15, 1992, he took to the ice and recorded an assist against the Calgary Flames. The following night, he topped that performance with two more helpers in a loss to the Winnipeg Jets.

ARTURS IRBE

In the years that led to the fall of the Iron Curtain, the NHL held a couple of Super Series events where Soviet teams came over to play against their clubs. Irbe was one of the most intriguing young Soviet players showcasing his talents. A 10th-round pick of the Minnesota North Stars in the 1989 NHL Entry Draft, he starred for Dynamo Riga for several years before the Sharks took him during the dispersal draft.

Irbe started the 1991–92 season with San Jose's IHL affiliate in Kansas City but was called up to make his NHL debut against the Edmonton Oilers on November 8, 1991. He earned a victory that night and followed it with another the next day while hosting the New York Islanders. Those were only the second and third triumphs in franchise history, but also the only ones he earned over 13 games that year.

Sent back to the minors in mid-December, Irbe was recalled again briefly in the middle of February and end of March. His record with the Blades was rather impressive, though, as he went 24-7-1 over 32 regular-season games and then went 12-3 in the playoffs on the way to the Turner Cup.

BRIAN HAYWARD

In the late 1980s, Hayward was one of the strongest and most respected backup goaltenders in the game and he shared the Jennings Trophy with Patrick Roy on three occasions while playing for the Montreal Canadiens. In 1990-91, he was a part of the Minnesota North Stars club that made it to the Stanley Cup Final, but he knew ahead of time that he was destined to play in San Jose the following year.

The dispersal draft made the transaction official. Hayward was responsible for the first victory in franchise history when he made his Sharks debut on October 8, 1991, and turned back 36 shots in a 4-3 triumph. The rest of his season wasn't smooth sailing, however, as he was credited with a loss over his next two starts and then suffered a back injury. He attempted a brief comeback in December but had enough difficulties to end up back on the disabled list.

What most fans will recall about Hayward's short stint with the Sharks was the intimidating mask that he wore. While it didn't do much to faze opposing skaters, it does have a legacy all of its own.

EXPANSION YEAR RECORD: 10-70-4
(24 points — sixth in Adams Division)
COACH: Rick Bowness
GENERAL MANAGER: Mel Bridgman
FIRST GAME: October 8, 1992 —
5-3 win vs. Montreal Canadiens
FIRST GOAL: October 8, 1992 by Neil Brady

OTTAWA SENATORS

The deep roots of the original Ottawa Senators can be traced back to the days before hockey went professional, when the club won several Stanley Cup championships and featured some of the greatest early players, and before harsh economic realities forced them to shut down at the end of the 1933–34 season.

The death of that Senators club did not mean, however, that the sport was dead in Canada's capital, as several senior and junior clubs stepped in and filled the void for many years after. Ottawa was still loyal to the game and there were many fans who believed that it was only a matter of time and effort to bring the Sens back to the NHL. In the late 1980s, when it was rumoured that the league planned to expand by several teams during the next decade, an Ottawa-area real estate developer named Bruce Firestone decided to launch a local bid through a firm called Terrace Investments.

In order to make this vision a reality, the underfunded group planned to launch a mini-city project called West Terrace that included an NHL-ready arena. A promising site was found west of the city in Kanata and Terrace announced their intentions on June 22, 1989. They received permission from Tommy Gorman's descendants to use the old Senators name and kicked off a campaign that saw former team member Frank Finnigan presented with a new jersey with his old number, 8, on the back. It was expected that, as the only living member of the 1926–27 team that won the Stanley Cup, he was going to drop the puck when

347

they began play. Plans for a new arena called the Palladium were also announced, and they also had a logo that incorporated the Peace Tower into the city's name.

While the bid had tremendous support from fans, the reality was that it was considered a long shot by many hockey people, including then-NHLPA head Alan Eagleson. Undaunted, the Terrace executives made a presentation to the league, and in December 1990, it was announced that the NHL was coming back to town once again. The primary reason they got the okay was it was one of only two bids willing to put up the $50 million expansion fee the league was asking for without any debate.

At that point, the hunt was on to find someone to run the Senators. Respected hockey men Scotty Bowman and John Muckler turned down the opportunity to become general manager, and the team made a very unconventional move and hired former NHL player Mel Bridgman. He had no hockey management experience, but he had a decent academic background and was willing to take on the daunting task of putting together a serviceable roster. The coaching staff was to be headed by Rick Bowness, and he received support from prime talents in Alain Vigneault, E.J. Maguire and Chico Resch.

If there ever was a bad omen to start a team off, it was at the 1992 NHL Expansion Draft. The Senators were woefully unprepared when their laptop failed and they called out several ineligible names since they had no paper copies of their plan to refer to. As a result, the Ottawa club took a lot of journeymen and strong minor league players who were not regarded as prospects at that point. The roster was bolstered slightly through trades and, at the 1992 NHL Entry Draft, they chose Alexei Yashin second overall. Unfortunately, the young Russian was not coming over to North America for the 1992–93 season and they really did not have anyone who could be regarded as a franchise player.

On October 8, 1992, NHL hockey was officially back in Ottawa, and the crowd at the Civic Centre witnessed a pre-game spectacle that involved the retirement of Finnigan's sweater. Unfortunately, he had passed away less than a year earlier and did not get to witness the event. Alanis Morissette sang the national anthem that night and then-NHL president Gil Stein gave Firestone what was called a "certificate of reinstatement." The visiting Montreal Canadiens lost that night and hopes were high for Senators fans that the team might be competitive. Even the press joked that "maybe Rome was built in a day," but it was not to be.

Ottawa did not win another game until November 25, and after that it was bleak at even the best of times. The team's reliance on young talent was deadly, but Peter Sidorkiewicz deserved a purple heart for his play since he kept the scores much lower than they really deserved to be. He represented the team at the 1993 NHL All-Star Game, along with Brad Marsh, who was easily the team's most popular performer.

After winning three of five games between January 28 and February 8, 1993, the Sens went 3–24 over the rest of the schedule. They won their only road game of the year against the New York Islanders on April 10, but by that point, it was almost certain that they were going to finish last overall and earn the right to pick highly touted Alexandre Daigle in the 1993 NHL Entry Draft. They were in fact in a race to place at the bottom of the standings with the second-year San Jose Sharks and ended up with one less victory to claim what the press was calling the "Daigle Cup."

It was a horrible year all around for the Senators, but there was a ton of fallout coming. Bridgman was canned at the end of the season, and Firestone faced a lot of heat for making off-the-record comments to the press about the team deliberately losing games. The team was fined for his comments and the league later instituted a draft lottery to help avoid the problem in the future.

In time, the Senators built themselves into a competitor, but not without first experiencing some serious problems. The planned West Terrace development did not pan out, and financial strains forced Firestone to resign after missing payments. It was tough even to get proper financing for the Palladium, but it finally opened during the 1995–96 season. Shortly after, it was renamed the Corel Centre when naming rights were sold. Paying off the club's various debts became a big problem and they were forced to declare bankruptcy at one point before Eugene Melnyk bought the club in 2003.

(clockwise) Mike Peluso, Laurie Boschman, Brad Marsh, Peter Sidorkiewicz

On the ice, the Senators had three more difficult seasons before they finally became a playoff contender. With talent like Daniel Alfredsson and Wade Redden, they made the postseason for 11 straight years and even captured four division crowns. In 2006–07, they made it all the way to the Stanley Cup Final but lost out to the Anaheim Ducks. Their fortunes have declined somewhat since that time, but they are in the process of building themselves into contenders once again.

NORM MACIVER

Maciver had finally arrived as a regular with the Edmonton Oilers in 1991–92, after spending several years bouncing back and forth between the minors and the NHL. His 40 points over 57 games were fairly impressive since he missed a lot of action because of injury, and he led the club with a +20 rating. He was likely ready for another big year with the team, but the Senators claimed him in the waiver draft in the hope that adding him to the lineup would at least mitigate a few glaring weaknesses.

What fans in Ottawa were probably not expecting, though, was to see Maciver lead the first-year club in scoring. He started the season with back-to-back games in which he got two assists, and he had a five-game point streak between October 16 and 27, 1992. From an offensive perspective, he was certainly the club's most consistent contributor since he notched at least one point in 48 of the 80 games he appeared in. On February 8, 1993, he scored the game-winner against the Buffalo Sabres, and that gave the Sens their first back-to-back victories in franchise history. He also scored the difference-maker in a surprise win over the Pittsburgh Penguins 17 days later.

BRAD SHAW

After years in the minors, Shaw became a full-time blueliner for the Hartford Whalers in 1989–90 and was named to the NHL's All-Rookie Team. Over the next two seasons, he was a regular for the team, but his production dipped slightly and he was sold to the New Jersey Devils, so they did not end up losing him for nothing in the expansion draft. Instead, the Devils declined to protect him and were out of pocket when the Senators claimed him.

With Ottawa, Shaw got a lot more playing time and put up the best numbers of his career. He had his first multi-point game of the year against the Calgary Flames on November 5, 1992, and in a victory over the San Jose Sharks on January 10, 1993, he had a pair of assists on goals by Bob Kudelski. From March 22 to 30, he put up seven points over five games and then had a three-game assist streak in April before the season drew to its merciful close.

"I still have visions of watching Brad Shaw do drills," said Chris Luongo. "As I gained experience, it helped me understand the nature of hockey and other sports. He would do the same thing 20 or 30 times, and it had a lot to do later in my career in preparing to play and in coaching. It was interesting to watch him go about and do his business."

BOB KUDELSKI

Kudelski had his third straight 20-goal season with the Los Angeles Kings in 1991–92, but he struggled in the early part of the following season when he was traded to Ottawa as part of a deal for Marc Fortier and Jim Thomson. He had just three goals over his first 15 games, so his per-game average was a little below where it had been in previous years, but the Senators were certainly willing to give him a shot at a prime offensive role.

Kudelski's first goal with Ottawa did not come until they took on the Quebec Nordiques in his fourth game with the team on December 27, 1992. He was also responsible for one of the most exciting moments of the first season for the Sens when he scored all three goals, the franchise's first-ever hat trick, in a 3–2 victory over the San Jose Sharks on January 10, 1993. The March 4 matchup against his old club was a nice homecoming of sorts when he scored once and assisted on two other goals.

MIKE PELUSO

Peluso led the NHL with an incredible 408 penalty minutes in 1991–92, but his physical play was toned down greatly in the playoffs when the Chicago Blackhawks went all the way to the Stanley Cup Final. Chicago had plenty of tough players on the roster, so he became expendable in the expansion draft. The Senators picked him to ensure they had some toughness during their first year in the league.

Peluso surprised many when he took his offensive game to a new level with Ottawa, establishing career standards for goals and points. The majority of his points came before the All-Star break and he scored twice as many goals on the road than at home. He scored a goal against the Quebec Nordiques on October 10, 1992, and two days later scored a pair in a loss to the Boston Bruins. His lone game-winning goal was scored against the New Jersey Devils on November 25. Peluso had more than twice as many penalty minutes as any other player on the Senators at the end of the year.

LAURIE BOSCHMAN

Boschman had some of his best NHL seasons in a Winnipeg Jets uniform, but he was traded to the New Jersey Devils before the 1990–91 campaign. A veteran performer, he had 20 points in his first year in the Meadowlands, but he was even better in 1991–92, and it looked like he might stick around a little while longer — until he was unexpectedly left unprotected in the expansion draft.

"How it happened was I was with the Devils and I talked to Lou Lamoriello a couple of days before the expansion draft and he said that he thought I was going to be safe," he recalled. "My wife, my three kids and I were heading from New Jersey back to Winnipeg and we had to fly through the Minneapolis airport, and this is before cell phones, and I went on a pay phone to call one of my friends and I asked if he had heard about the expansion draft and he said 'I haven't heard your name, so I think you're fine.' When we got into Winnipeg, we got all our stuff and the security person said 'I see you're back for the summer. How do you feel about getting picked by the Ottawa Senators?' I said, 'What?' and that's how we found out! Needless to say, we were quite disappointed because we were really happy in New Jersey."

Named the first captain of the Senators before the start of the season, Boschman recalled coming into training camp and being surprised by the lack of big-league talent in the dressing room.

"My first thought was 'How come there are so many players on this roster whose names I don't recognize?' because so many of them had been with other teams and with the American Hockey League. So there really wasn't any current NHLers that I was aware of. I figured this was going to be a long year."

And what a long year it was in Ottawa. With just a few games left on the schedule, the team had just nine wins to their credit and all of them had come at home. The team battled the New York Islanders on April 10, 1993, and, with the captain's help, they finally got a road victory. In fact, he recorded a hat trick that included the game-winning goal and an empty-net insurance tally with just a second left on the clock.

"After I scored that third goal, I said to Jamie Baker 'We're going to Disneyland! We're going to Disneyland!' There was a lot of media there in Long Island, and after they left, the guys were waiting down by the bus and I came down and some of the guys were bowing down like they were in *Wayne's World* saying 'We're not worthy!'"

Just four days later, Boschman appeared in his final NHL game against the Boston Bruins and scored for the last time. While he did not particularly enjoy what happened on the ice in Ottawa during their first year, he is still active with the club as an alumni member to this day.

"It wasn't a positive end at all. It was very difficult way to end my career because we had a losing situation, but we loved the city. For what the Senators do for the community of Ottawa and how involved they are, we feel very pleased to be a part of that."

DOUG SMAIL

A fan favourite with the Winnipeg Jets for over a decade, Smail spent part of the 1990–91 season with the Minnesota North Stars club that went to the Stanley Cup Final before he signed on with the Quebec Nordiques as a free agent. Following a rough year that saw him put up points at a decent clip but miss time because of injury, he signed the dotted line with the Senators as they headed into the NHL ice wars.

"I was obviously winding down my career and had an injury in Quebec, but I would have liked to spend some more time with them," he said. "It was a little frustrating in Ottawa, but you knew that they were going to have to start building soon. I had been through the same thing in Winnipeg, but it was hard on some of the older guys."

From the start, fans in Ottawa were in for a treat, as Smail scored two goals in their opening game against the Montreal Canadiens.

"It was good. We had a lot of young guys on the team and they were pumped up. It was a legitimate win and Montreal was coming into a bee's nest."

The reality from that point on, however, was grim. And despite his experience, the club was not using him to his full potential.

"It was just a hard year for a lot of guys. You weren't getting the time on the ice you needed. I don't have a lot of fondness for that year. The first night was great, but it was difficult. There were guys who could play, but you needed more veterans in order for the young guys to develop."

Mercifully, Smail was released from his contract with about a month to go in the regular season, and his last NHL game came against the San Jose Sharks on March 2, 1993. From there, he joined the San Diego Gulls of the IHL for the remainder of the year. Part of the reason he went was because former NHL player Rick Dudley was looking to start a new league similar to the old World Hockey Association.

"They were planning on getting three or four NHL guys near the end of their career. It was going to be a nice fast-paced skating game. They were a decade ahead of their time. It might have evolved into something the NHL would have had to take a look at. It was kind of a hush-hush thing. If I recall, they had six commitments and needed eight. There was also the potential to get a television contract."

When that league never materialized, Smail headed over to Great Britain for three seasons to finish out his professional career.

BRAD MARSH

A defensive stalwart never known for generating a lot of offence, Marsh played it smart in his own end throughout his career and was extremely popular with fans wherever he went. In 1991–92, he hit the 1,000-game plateau in a Detroit Red Wings uniform but was sold back to Toronto at the end of the year. A little more than a month later, the Maple Leafs decided to move him to the Ottawa Senators.

In Ottawa, Marsh was named an assistant captain and was looked upon as a leader for their young blueline corps.

He caused some controversy in training camp, as the Sens wanted him to sign a waiver if he wanted to continue playing without a helmet. He initially refused, but he relented in time for the season opener. As a result of his popularity, a fan club was formed in Ottawa and he was a Commissioner's Selection for the 1993 NHL All-Star Game. In that contest, he scored his only goal of the season and the crowd in Montreal roared when it happened.

"I thought to have him and Boschman there was a good idea," said Doug Smail. "They were determined athletes and scared of nothing. I think John Ferguson might have had some influence in getting them and they could have been around for a few more years. They were heart-and-soul guys."

Late in the season, Marsh suffered from back spasms and missed some time, but he earned his last NHL point on March 7, 1993, with an assist on a goal by Mark Lamb against Chicago. His last big-league game took place against Boston on April 14.

Although he had signed with Ottawa in the hopes of getting an assistant coaching position with them, the team declined to offer him a job at the end of the year — even though they claimed to the public that Marsh had turned them down. Fans were naturally upset that the organization had cut him loose, and he was eventually offered any position he wanted in the front office. He remained with the Senators for several years and is still active with their alumni association.

PETER SIDORKIEWICZ

The only goaltender in NHL history to hail from Poland, Sidorkiewicz was a junior standout in the early 1980s before he got an extended apprenticeship in the AHL. In 1988–89, he finally had a shot at regular NHL work with the Hartford Whalers and was named to the league's

All-Rookie Team. Over the three seasons that followed, he saw a lot of work in net, but with the rise of prospect Kay Whitmore, his time with the club drew to an end as they failed to protect him in the expansion draft.

There was little doubt from the start that Sidorkiewicz was going to be Ottawa's top man in net, but nobody could have expected the grace he displayed for such a weak club. In the season opener against Montreal, he made 25 saves in the 5–3 win. But another victory did not come soon, as he went winless over his next 20 games.

"He was a horse for us," said Chris Luongo. "He was under the gun every night, but he didn't show frustration in my recollection. He went about his business and was able to move on to the next game."

By the time the All-Star Game rolled around, Sidorkiewicz had a record of 4–32–3 with a 4.40 goals-against average. Those numbers were often regarded with disdain, but nevertheless his dedication to the game was rewarded with a spot on the Wales Conference squad. Since he was in the net for the second period and present when the game-winning goal was scored, he was credited with the win. His workload was reduced over the second half of the season, but unfortunately he injured his shoulder during the last game of the year. He underwent surgery right away, but the Senators made the puzzling decision to trade him away to the New Jersey Devils soon after. He was supposed to take over as their number one goalie the next year but was still recovering. As a result a young goaltender named Martin Brodeur took over, and Sidorkiewicz spent most of his remaining playing days back in the minors.

EXPANSION YEAR RECORD: 23-54-7
(53 points — sixth in Norris Division)
COACH: Terry Crisp
GENERAL MANAGER: Phil Esposito
FIRST GAME: October 7, 1992 —
7-3 win vs. Chicago Blackhawks
FIRST GOAL: October 7, 1992 by Chris Kontos

TAMPA BAY LIGHTNING

Hockey in Florida? To most NHL fans a little more than 20 years ago, that seemed as unrealistic as anything could possibly be. With the league expanding into new territories in the 1990s, though, it became a reality that, for better or worse, has had an impact on the game.

In the late 1980s, the NHL wanted to expand, as their membership had been relatively stable in recent years. Two groups from the Tampa-St. Petersburg area were interested in having a club at the time. The one headed up by future Carolina Hurricanes owner Peter Karmanos and former goaltender Jim Rutherford had more financial stability, but they reportedly balked at the idea of paying the $50 million the league asked for up front. The other candidate, Phil and Tony Esposito's group, did what it took to get the full amount ready and had in place financing from a group of Japanese businesses that included golf course and resort Kokusai Green.

Wanting the big cash infusion, the NHL gave the green light to the Esposito brothers, and Phil served as president and general manager while Tony looked after scouting. Then they hired former Calgary Flames coach Terry Crisp to run the bench, and the Lightning were ready to start building a contender. The 1992 NHL Expansion Draft was not exactly favourable to the two new teams coming in, but Tampa Bay made the best of it by getting some minor-leaguers with offensive potential along with enforcer Basil McRae and experienced players like Brian Bradley and Rob Ramage.

It became apparent early on that goaltending could be a problem, so they made trades to get J.C. Bergeron and Pat Jablonski, and they added some free agent skaters like Marc Bergevin, Rob Zamuner and John Tucker to give the team a little more depth. They also had the first overall selection in the 1992 NHL Entry Draft and took a Czechoslovakian defenceman named Roman Hamrlik who was viewed as a potential All-Star.

Once training camp began, the Lightning made headlines the world over when they signed female goaltender Manon Rheaume as a free agent. She had previously played in a game for the QMJHL's Trois-Rivieres Draveurs and got her chance to make history during a pre-season contest against the St. Louis Blues. Appearing in one period, she surrendered just two goals and was later sent down to the minors to gain some pro experience.

The Lightning made their NHL debut on October 7, 1992, and sent more shockwaves through the hockey world when they defeated the previous year's Stanley Cup finalists, the Chicago Blackhawks, by a score of 7–3. Chris Kontos, known as a bit of a streaky scorer, potted four goals that night at the Expo Hall. In fact, Tampa Bay had a very good start for an expansion club and even won five of six games during a stretch in early November.

That momentum was not going to last long, though, as they had some killer road trips because of being placed in the Norris Division alongside Chicago, St. Louis and Minnesota. They were also prone to long winless streaks and had at least six of them that lasted a minimum of five games each. As a result, they finished the year with just 53 points. But for most fans, it was quite the consolation compared to what the Ottawa Senators went through during the 1992–93 season. The most pleasant surprise for the team had to have been Bradley's team-leading 42 goals, which stood as a club record for almost 15 years.

In 1993–94, the Lightning moved to the Florida Suncoast Dome for their home games and showed some improvement through the addition of goalie Daren Puppa. By 1995–96, they were playoff bound, but they lost in the first round. After that, five difficult seasons followed as a direct result of how the team was treated by Kokusai Green.

Throughout the team's early years, there were often rumours that the Tampa Bay club was headed for bankruptcy, since their operating budget was limited at the best of times. It was also no secret that the club was for sale at almost any price, but the convoluted ownership structure made it difficult to know who actually owned the team. Any of the money invested into it came from loans, and cash shortages were common. The principal owner was Takashi Okubo, and he was a man veiled in mystery. Not one person from the team or the league saw him at a game or in any situation until the spring of 1998, and the NHL was not pleased that the team was swimming in debt.

The Lightning were eventually sold to Art Williams, who removed the Esposito brothers early in the 1998–99 season, despite telling them that their jobs were safe. He also boldly stated that 1998 first overall draft pick Vincent Lacavalier was hockey's "new Michael Jordan" and was soundly humiliated in the press. The massive debt left behind by Kokusai Green was too much for him to handle, however, and he sold the team to Detroit Pistons owner William Davidson. After that, there were gradual changes made to the management team and prospects were allowed time to develop, and as a result the team eventually earned more respect from opponents. They won two straight Southeast Division crowns and captured the Stanley Cup in 2003–04.

In the years immediately after the lockout, Tampa Bay had limited postseason success and the team was up for sale once again. They finished last in the league in 2007–08, but were purchased by OK Hockey LLC, a group that included movie producer Oren Koules and former NHL player Len Barrie. The next season was even worse, despite the presence of star rookie Steven Stamkos, and they cleaned house once again in 2009–10 when the team was purchased by Jeffrey Vinik at the end of the campaign.

There was new hope for Lightning fans because the new owner hired Hall of Famer Steve Yzerman to take on the role of general manager. Guy Boucher was hired as coach and the team responded with a return to postseason glory. They made it to the seventh game of the Eastern Conference final before being eliminated by the Boston Bruins.

(clockwise) Brian Bradley, Chris Kontos, Roman Hamrlik, JC Bergeron

The 2011–12 and 2012–13 campaigns saw them miss the playoffs, but the future finally looks bright once again for hockey in Tampa Bay.

BRIAN BRADLEY

When you're getting only two minutes a game or playing almost exclusively on the power play, it can get a little frustrating for a player, so Bradley was able to breathe a sigh of relief when the Toronto Maple Leafs declined to protect him for the expansion draft.

"I just didn't get the ice time and didn't get to play much under coach Tom Watt," he said. "There were times where I would sit on the bench for a period and a half. When I heard that I got picked in the expansion draft, I was playing golf with Al MacInnis out in Calgary. I was hoping that it was going to be Tampa Bay instead of Ottawa because I was hoping to have a change and go down to the States."

His dream came true with a new home in Tampa Bay and scoring the first pre-season goal in franchise history. Despite the tremendous odds against first-year success, he recalls being optimistic at the time.

"We obviously knew that we were an expansion team, but when you looked around at the guys that were there, and we looked at our team and we felt that we were going to be able to compete every night and be competitive. We were in mostly all the games, and after the opening-night win over Chicago, we had the fans behind us. I think they appreciated the effort and that's how the game grew to the next level."

After going scoreless over the first two games of the season, Bradley put together a nine-game point streak that included a triumphant return to Toronto, where he had an assist in a losing effort on October 15, 1992. The next game was down the highway against the Sabres, but the Lightning encountered a bit of a problem when they got into town.

"We flew into Buffalo, and the ownership group never paid our hotel bill and the Hilton wouldn't let us stay there! We had to go somewhere else at two in the morning!"

As the season progressed, Bradley proved the club's top offensive weapon and he set league records for most goals and assists by a player on a non-WHA expansion club. He was also the first player to represent the Lightning at the NHL All-Star Game. It was a remarkable comeback and he ended up being regarded as one of the greatest players in franchise history.

"I played six or seven years down here and I don't think I ever met the ownership group. For the first two or three years, we didn't even know who owned the team. They were never at the games. That was really bizarre. In the end, it might have deterred some players from playing in Tampa, especially because we never had chartered flights. I know there's a few guys who wanted to play down here but didn't because of travel."

CHRIS KONTOS

A former first-round pick of the New York Rangers, Kontos spent much of his professional hockey career in the minors, but he occasionally demonstrated flashes of greatness when playing at the NHL level. This was particularly evident in the postseason in 1988–89 when he set a league record by scoring six power-play goals in a single series. For the 1991–92 campaign, he decided to spend part of the year with Canada's national team in pre-Olympic competition and then finished the year in Italy with the second-tier HC Courmaosta club.

A free agent, Kontos signed with the Lightning in an attempt to get back to the bigs and ended up winning a roster spot. Given a chance to finally be a key offensive performer, he made headlines on October 7, 1992, when he scored four goals for the debuting Tampa Bay club — one of them the first goal in franchise history. Four days later, he had two more in a rematch with the Blackhawks. He was one of the league's top offensive performers over the first two months of the schedule, as he had an incredible 20 goals and six assists over his first 27 games.

His goal production began to slowly dip, but he managed to set more up over the rest of the season. Because of a strained knee, his year drew to an early close and he last appeared in the March 12, 1993, contest against the Toronto Maple Leafs.

ROB ZAMUNER

Zamuner had a nine-game stint with the New York Rangers as a third-year pro in 1991–92, and although he had what seemed a respectable start to his NHL career, the club was not interested in extending their contract with him and he became a free agent at the end of the year.

Signed by the Lightning during the summer, Zamuner instantly doubled his career points total with three assists during the season opener against Chicago. He was one of Tampa Bay's top point producers in the early stages of the 1992–93 campaign and had 19 points to his credit before going cold in December and January. He began to warm up a little toward the end of February and scored twice in a 3–1 triumph over Montreal on March 3, 1993.

Most important, however, was that he began to carve out a niche as a budding defensive forward and earned praise from teammates.

"Robbie was a good two-way player," said Brian Bradley. "He played on a line with Johnny Tucker and that kick-started his career. I didn't know much about him at the time, but he worked hard."

ROMAN HAMRLIK

The Lightning had the pleasure of having the first overall selection in the 1992 NHL Entry Draft and they decided to go with Hamrlik, a young Czech defender who had made a great impression at the IIHF World Junior Championship earlier in the year.

Hamrlik was ready to start the season with Tampa Bay, and his first goal came during his sixth outing on October 20, 1992, when he put the puck by Bill Ranford of the Edmonton Oilers. A week later, he recorded a goal and an assist against the Quebec Nordiques, and on November 9, the New York Rangers fell victim to the first game-winning goal of his career.

ROB RAMAGE

A former first overall pick who turned out to be a solid All-Star defenceman, Ramage had a reputation for being a respected leader. After spending an injury-shortened 1991–92 season with the Minnesota North Stars, he was on the move again through the expansion draft.

Ramage's first offensive output of the 1992–93 season came on October 20, 1992, with two power-play goals and an assist in a clash with the Edmonton Oilers. Two nights later, he scored again while facing one of his old clubs, the Toronto Maple Leafs. As the Montreal Canadiens geared up for the playoffs, he was traded for some younger players, but he made some decent contributions on the way to a Stanley Cup championship.

"Rob was like our captain," said Brian Bradley. "I played with him in Calgary and Toronto. He was a good leader on our team and I can't say enough about Rob. He really took control of the team."

PAT JABLONSKI

On June 19, 1992, Jablonski came to the Lightning as part of a deal with the St. Louis Blues where he and three other players were picked up for future considerations. As a result, Tampa Bay now had a player in their fold who could potentially take over the role of starting goal-tender, since he had shown some promise in the minors.

After teammate Wendell Young started the team's first two games, Jablonski's debut was a 4–4 tie against Chicago on October 11. By November, it looked as if he was going to take over the starter's role and he put together a personal six-game undefeated streak that was capped by the first shutout in franchise history on November 13 — a 1–0 win over the Ottawa Senators. In spite of all the early success, he was struck with the kind of futility that often arises while playing for an expansion team, and he earned a victory in just two of his next 31 appearances.

EXPANSION YEAR RECORD: 33-34-17
(83 points — fifth in Atlantic Division)
COACH: Roger Neilson
GENERAL MANAGER: Bobby Clarke
FIRST GAME: October 6, 1993 —
4-4 tie vs. Chicago Blackhawks
FIRST GOAL: October 6, 1993 by Scott Mellanby

FLORIDA PANTHERS

The concept of hockey in Florida shocked the hockey world in the early 1990s. But with the NHL courting deep-pocketed potential owners and wanting to expand southward, it was only a matter of time before Miami got a chance to get a team of its own. After a chance encounter by Los Angeles Kings owner Bruce McNall and a follow-up meeting with then–league president Gil Stein, they landed a major player in H. Wayne Huizenga, who was the chairman of Blockbuster Entertainment and a budding south Florida sports magnate. He was awarded an expansion franchise on December 10, 1992, and was set to hit the ice for the 1993–94 season.

It was not the first attempt to bring big-league hockey to Miami, as the WHA tried to start a club there when the league opened for the 1972–73 season. The Screaming Eagles failed to take off, though, and ended up as the Philadelphia Blazers instead. There was also a bid for an NHL expansion club in 1990 by Godfrey Wood, but the deal fell through at the last minute when his group was not prepared to give the $50 million entry fee up front. That bid actually had one of the best chances among the candidates at the time, but the nod went to Tampa Bay and Ottawa instead.

On April 19, 1993, the new club was dubbed the Florida Panthers — much to the chagrin of many locals who were not pleased about the name. There was some consolation, however, in the fact that the Panthers and their expansion cousins in Anaheim were given a fairer shake when selecting players from the established teams. The Lightning and Senators were not able to get much for their initial rosters, so Florida could at least have a decent shot at being competitive in 1993–94.

Another thing that helped on the hockey operations side was that the Panthers could not have been better managed, with three Hall of Fame talents in team president Bill Torrey, general manager Bobby Clarke and coach Roger Neilson. Under Torrey's guidance, every attempt was made to emulate the success of the Stanley Cup–winning New York Islanders teams he built. Clarke had a great deal of success as GM of the Philadelphia Flyers and Minnesota North Stars, and Neilson ranked among the most respected coaches in the game.

One thing holding the Panthers back, at least financially, was a very unfavourable lease on the Miami Arena. The NBA's Miami Heat were the main tenants and they held on to such things as advertising and luxury box revenues and were not about to share any of that with Huizenga, since he had beat out their ownership in a bid for an NHL franchise. As a result, Florida ended up with a very poor lease and remained there until getting an arena of their own in 1998.

After much internal debate, the team unveiled its logo and uniform and it was a hit with local fans and received positive media attention. Soon after, the Panthers went into the 1993 NHL Expansion Draft with the goal of selecting character players. Clarke felt that the team's first few years in the league were going to be rough and he wanted men with the experience and ability to deal with adversity. The list of unprotected players was released on June 21, 1993, and three days later, they made their picks in Quebec City, where the 1993 NHL Entry Draft was also being held.

The Panthers won the coin toss to get the chance to select the first goaltender and they plucked John Vanbiesbrouck away from the Vancouver Canucks — a team that had picked him up from the New York Rangers to protect other netminders. "Beezer" proved their franchise player in the team's early years and he was to be backed up by Mark Fitzpatrick. Daren Puppa was also taken from the Toronto Maple Leafs, but the Tampa Bay Lightning claimed him soon after in the second phase of the expansion draft, which was meant to help out the previous year's new teams. Dominik Hasek of the Buffalo Sabres was also available, but Florida and Anaheim passed on him and, of course, he won the Vezina Trophy for the first time in 1993–94.

The first skater Florida picked was a bit of a head scratcher, as they took Milan Tichy from the Chicago Blackhawks. Their second selection, tough-as-nails Paul Laus from Pittsburgh, was much better. From there, they focused on getting defencemen, and while they were not exactly offensive stars, players like Joe Cirella and Gord Murphy were respected and knew how to keep the puck away from the net.

In the coin toss to see who was to take the first forward, Anaheim won, but the Panthers did not seem to mind as they began adding more gritty talent to their roster. They selected Tom Fitzgerald, who had played for Torrey on the Islanders, and went on to choose players like Dave Lowry, Brian Skrudland and Scott Mellanby instead of high-dollar veterans who were available, like Guy Carbonneau, Michel Goulet and Denis Savard.

When it came to the Entry Draft, the Panthers picked fifth overall and took Rob Niedermayer of the WHL's Medicine Hat Tigers in the hope that he could become a franchise player in time. Over the summer months, the Panthers added only a handful of free agents to their roster, but they started to make some big deals during training camp and brought in more defensive skill in Brent Severyn and Keith Brown.

On October 6, the Panthers made their first NHL appearance and skated to a 4–4 tie with the Chicago Blackhawks. Their first victory did not come until the third game of the year and it was hosted by their closest rivals, the Lightning. In front of a then-record 27,227 fans at the Thunderdome in St. Petersburg, Florida, they refused to back down and got a big 2–0 win. From there, they headed home and lost to the Pittsburgh Penguins in their debut at the Miami Arena by a score of 2–1.

What became apparent early in the 1993–94 season was that the Panthers were one of the most competitive teams in the NHL — even without a host of household names. After 21 games, they looked solid at the quarter-way mark with a record of 8–10–3 that included a three-game winning streak. Among the vanquished were the defending Stanley Cup champs, the Montreal Canadiens. Fans were kept cheering

(clockwise) Scott Mellanby, Brian Skrudland, Paul Laus, John Vanbiesbrouck

as the wins kept piling up and players like Stu Barnes and Bob Kudelski were acquired.

At the halfway point, the Panthers were at .500 with 42 points over 42 games and were in the midst of a nine-game undefeated streak that had opponents starting to take them seriously. Things looked grim for a while when Vanbiesbrouck sustained a major cut to his hand, forcing him to miss nearly a month of action during the race to the playoffs. Fitzpatrick played valiantly in his absence, but in the end, Vanbiesbrouck's rush to get back to the lineup had a serious impact on their postseason chances. Over the last 10 games of the year, Florida went 2–4–4 to finish just a win short of a playoff spot, but there were not too many disappointed fans or players, and the team had set a record for the best finish by an expansion club in NHL history.

In 1994–95, the Panthers were close to making the playoffs once again. They were surprisingly successful the following year, however, as they made it all the way to the Stanley Cup Final, only to lose to the Colorado Avalanche in four straight games. Over the next few seasons, the club made the postseason twice before missing the playoffs for a record 10 straight years from 2000–01 to 2010–11.

The fortunes of the Florida franchise began to turn around again once they hired Dale Tallon as general manager in 2010. He has helped the team rebuild and they finally made it back to the playoffs with a Southeast Division title in 2011–12 under new coach Kevin Dineen. The success was short lived, however, as they missed the playoffs once again the next year.

SCOTT MELLANBY

Mellanby had a disappointing season with the Edmonton Oilers in 1992-93, missing 15 games and putting up the lowest point totals of his career to that point, outside of his injury-shortened 1989-90 campaign. But he had started his NHL career in Philadelphia under the watchful eye of Bobby Clarke, and with an opportunity to pick up a known talent, the Panthers' GM made sure to acquire him through the expansion draft.

Given a chance to bounce back, Mellanby made club history on

October 11, 1993, when he scored Florida's first-ever goal on the power play against Chicago's Ed Belfour at 12:31 of the first period. From then on, he had his best season yet and he led the Panthers in goals and points during their first year in the league. Used extensively on the power play, he scored 17 goals with the man advantage and four of his tallies proved game-winners.

Over the course of the 1993–94 season, Mellanby had a dozen multi-point games. In one of them, an 8–3 drubbing of the Montreal Canadiens on January 24, 1994, he scored twice and added an assist. A little more than a week later, he was briefly forced out of action when a puck broke his nose and orbital bone on a clearing attempt by Pittsburgh's Larry Murphy. He missed only four games but had some trouble producing after the injury.

Mellanby remained in Florida until midway through 2000–01, but he was responsible for one of the most interesting chapters in franchise history when he killed a dressing room rat in the 1995–96 season and went out to score two goals that night. The phenomenon quickly became known as the "Rat Trick" and fans began showering the ice with rubber rats whenever a goal was scored during the team's run to the Stanley Cup Final that year. Unfortunately, the NHL swiftly nixed the practice and hockey was never the same for many fans in south Florida after that.

JESSE BELANGER

A free agent scoop by Montreal in 1990, Belanger was signed after two 100-point seasons with the QMJHL's Granby Bisons. He followed that up with three solid years in the AHL with the Fredericton Canadiens. Occasionally called up to the big club Habs, he saw limited action during the team's run to the Stanley Cup in 1992–93, but the presence of a bunch of talented centres in the organization forced them to leave him open in the expansion draft, where Florida was able to obtain his rights.

Over the first half of the season, Belanger was one of the league's top-scoring rookie performers and had 44 points to his credit by the end of January. One of his best games was against his old club on

January 24, 1994, when he scored once and threw in a couple of assists for good measure in a shocking 8–3 victory. His fast start was met with a dramatic crash, however, as he went scoreless in February before missing a month of action. Once he returned, his output was fairly limited until the final stretch of games, when he put up five points over his last seven.

BRIAN SKRUDLAND

Skrudland's reputation as a defensive forward was established in his days with the Montreal Canadiens, but the club dealt him away to the Calgary Flames for Gary Leeman during the 1992–93 season. He finished the year out west, but the Panthers took him in the expansion draft and named him their first captain soon after.

Not long after scoring a goal in the season opener, Skrudland put together a four-game point streak between October 26 and November 2, 1993, including multi-point efforts against Winnipeg and Philadelphia. On February 2, 1994, he scored the game-winning goal as the Panthers rolled past the dismal Ottawa Senators, but his greatest offensive output of the year came in March as the club strived to make it into the playoffs.

Skrudland's hard work in keeping the puck out of Florida's net was recognized by voters for the Selke Trophy, and he finished third behind Doug Gilmour and winner Sergei Fedorov.

STU BARNES

At one time, the Winnipeg Jets had high hopes for Barnes, the fourth overall pick in the 1989 NHL Entry Draft, but he got lost in the shuffle of youthful players as the team added talents like Teemu Selanne, Alexei Zhamnov and Keith Tkachuk to the lineup instead of making extensive use of his skills. In order to get him and a sixth-round draft pick, the Panthers had only to give up Randy Gilhen. They were excited to see if Barnes could live up to his potential.

It took a few games for him to adjust to playing for Florida, but Barnes was starting to produce in mid-December, scoring goals in back-to-back games against Montreal and Boston. His first of three game-winning tallies came in a 5–3 win over the Hartford Whalers on December 29, 1993, and he also assisted on Scott Mellanby's opening goal during the first period. His hottest month came in February, when he earned 12 points over 14 games and three of his five goals were scored in power-play situations.

ROB NIEDERMAYER

Niedermayer was the first amateur player ever selected by the Panthers when he was taken fifth overall in the 1993 NHL Entry Draft. He had just finished three solid seasons with the WHL's Medicine Hat Tigers and also wowed scouts as part of the gold medal–winning Canadian squad at the 1993 IIHF World Junior Championship.

After some tough contract negotiations, Niedermayer joined Florida in time for the season opener and that night he recorded an assist on the franchise's first goal by Scott Mellanby. His own first goal on October 14, 1993, came against Craig Billington of the Ottawa Senators and it gave the Panthers a 5–4 edge and the victory. Two weeks later, he scored on the power play against the New York Islanders and secured another win for the first-year club.

His hot start saw him rack up 14 points over his first 20 games, but Niedermayer battled injuries early on and sat out for several weeks before he returned to action on January 3, 1994, in a road game with the New York Rangers. For the rest of the season, his production was not the same, but he did manage a two-goal effort against Ottawa on February 2.

Over eight seasons with the Panthers, Niedermayer contributed strongly on the ice before he was traded to Calgary at the end of the 2000–01 campaign.

JOHN VANBIESBROUCK

The debacle known as the 1992 NHL Expansion Draft forced some serious changes the following year, when existing teams were only allowed to protect two goaltenders instead of three. As a result, a lot of teams scrambled in the weeks before the 1993 selections were to be made. The New York Rangers were in a position to deal away Vanbiesbrouck because of their depth in the crease, and the Vancouver Canucks grabbed him to protect their resources.

With "Beezer," the Panthers were able to draft a franchise goaltender. He was in net for their season opener before securing their first victory on October 9, 1993, in a 2–0 blanking of the Tampa Bay Lightning. From then on, he ensured Florida could contend for a playoff spot. Vanbiesbrouck was also named to the Eastern Conference squad at the 1994 NHL All-Star Game, where, taking to the ice for the third period, he became the second goalie in a row from a first-year club to earn a victory in the mid-season classic.

On February 1, 1994, he suffered a laceration on his hand in a loss to the Pittsburgh Penguins and did not return to action for another 17 days. With Florida in the hunt for a playoff spot, he gave a tremendous effort despite being embroiled in some public debate regarding a new contract. In his final 20 games, Vanbiesbrouck went 5–12–3 and the Panthers' fairy tale debut ended with them out of playoff contention. His efforts were recognized with a spot on the NHL's Second All-Star Team and he also finished third in voting for the Hart Trophy as the league MVP.

EXPANSION YEAR RECORD: 33–46–5
(71 points — fourth in Pacific Division)
COACH: Ron Wilson
GENERAL MANAGER: Jack Ferreira
FIRST GAME: October 8, 1993 —
7-2 loss vs. Detroit Red Wings
FIRST GOAL: October 8, 1993 by Sean Hill

MIGHTY DUCKS OF ANAHEIM

The genesis of the Mighty Ducks of Anaheim will forever irk hockey purists, as it came from a 1992 Disney movie called *The Mighty Ducks*. A story about a misfit group of kids coached by a ne'er-do-well attorney with a hockey background, it was a surprise hit that spawned some sequels, but it also gave the entertainment giant an opportunity to get on the NHL expansion bandwagon and extend its brand recognition.

Granted a franchise that was to begin play in 1993–94, the Anaheim club was the subject of many snickers and snorts of derision from hockey fans for their name, but they built a solid management team with general manager Jack Ferreira, who had a strong scouting background. Behind the bench, the Mighty Ducks were lucky enough to have Ron Wilson as coach, and it was to be his first time leading a team.

Set to play out of the newly constructed Arrowhead Pond of Anaheim, much of the team's initial lineup came from the 1993 NHL Expansion Draft. Their picks were an interesting mix of unproven young talent, tough guys, veteran leaders and blueliners who looked like they might not win a lot of games but had the potential to give a good effort every night. When it came to drafting junior players, they built for the future by taking Paul Kariya with their first selection, but he was not yet ready for NHL action. In the weeks and months leading up to their opening game, they barely dipped into the free agent market and kept trades to a minimum.

The Mighty Ducks made their NHL debut on October 8, 1993, and were trounced by the visiting Detroit Red Wings. Over their next four outings, the team looked much better as they managed one win and three ties. A tough six-game losing streak followed soon after, but they had four straight wins in November that showed they were not going to be pushovers for the established clubs. In the end, they exceeded the expectations of many by finishing the year with 71 points and even finished ahead of Edmonton and Los Angeles in the Pacific Division standings.

Once they got their expansion year out of the way with minimal problems, they endured their worst season in franchise history in 1994–95, but by 1996–97 they were on their way to playoff contention. The main reasons for this surge were the arrival of Kariya as a superstar and the acquisition of Teemu Selanne from the Winnipeg Jets, backed by a supporting cast that was determined to win. The early 2000s were a rough stretch for the team, but they made it to the Stanley Cup Final in 2002–03 and took the New Jersey Devils to a full seven games.

Disney sold the team to Henry and Susan Samueli in 2005 and they, after consulting their fan base and considering some of the Disney-owned trademarks, changed the name of the team to the Anaheim Ducks starting with the 2006–07 season. That year proved the greatest to date for the franchise as they defeated the Ottawa Senators for their first Stanley Cup — which was also the first time the legendary trophy was won by a California-based team.

TERRY YAKE

Over his first four pro seasons, Yake was a rising prospect in the Hartford Whalers organization, but he could not stick around the NHL for long before being sent back down to the minors. The 1992–93 campaign initially looked much of the same for him, but after he put up 22 points in 16 games with the AHL's Springfield Indians, he finally earned a long-term promotion and racked up 53 points over the rest of the schedule. Strangely, the Whalers declined to protect the centreman for the expansion draft, and Anaheim gave him a new rink to call home.

Yake had four points over the first three games for the Ducks and made history when he scored the team's first hat trick and added

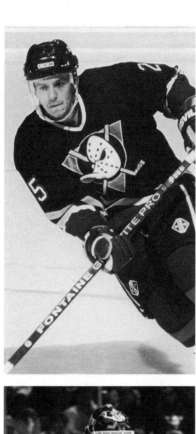

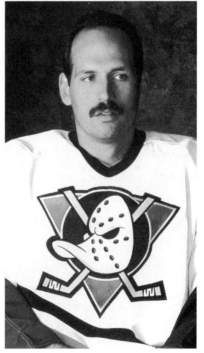

(clockwise) Terry Yake, Todd Ewen, Randy Ladouceur, Guy Hebert

an assist in a 4–3 triumph over the New York Rangers on October 19, 1993. He also had a strong outing against the Winnipeg Jets on December 20, scoring twice, one of those tallies the game-winner.

The speedy forward put up most of his offence before the All-Star break, but he earned two goals and an assist in a road win against Edmonton on February 13, 1994. He also had a three-game point streak in March.

BOB CORKUM

In 1992–93, Corkum caught on as a regular with Buffalo and produced 10 points over 68 games with the club. He did not get a ton of ice time, but the Sabres felt as if they had waited long enough for him to develop and they cast him aside when they put out their list of protected players for the expansion draft.

It was a move they must have ended up regretting, at least during the 1993–94 campaign, when he produced career numbers. Corkum led the Mighty Ducks with 23 goals, and 17 of those came in even-strength situations. His first of three shorthanded goals came against Chicago on January 6, 1994, a night when he notched an impressive four points. That month was one of the best of his career, as he racked up 17 points over 14 games. On March 11, he lit up the Blackhawks for two more goals, but Anaheim lost by a 3–2 margin.

BILL HOULDER

Before he went to the Mighty Ducks through the expansion draft, Houlder spent the previous six seasons bouncing between the NHL and the minors in the Washington and Buffalo organizations. Anaheim was certainly glad to get him under contract as he came off an All-Star season with the San Diego Gulls of the IHL, and he responded with his best year at the NHL level in 1993–94.

Offensively speaking, his best stretch came in November 1993, when he scored four times and contributed six assists over 13 games. He had only six career goals to his credit from his days before the Ducks and surpassed that total on January 6, 1994, when they defeated the Chicago Blackhawks. Two nights later, he popped in a couple more in another triumph — this time against St. Louis. By the end of the season, Houlder was Anaheim's leading scorer among blue-liners, but he was traded away before the beginning of their sopho-more campaign.

ALEXEI KASATONOV

Kasatonov was the first defenceman chosen by the Mighty Ducks during the 1993 NHL Expansion Draft, and his vast experience was exactly what the first-year club needed. The New Jersey Devils had left him available after a disappointing season in 1992–93, but a small comeback was in the works.

Kasatonov's second goal of the season was his biggest with Anaheim, as it secured a victory over the Calgary Flames on November 22, 1993. It was the team's third victory in a row and he continued to produce over the next few months. While playing against the Chicago Blackhawks on January 6, 1994, he put up three assists in a 6–2 victory. Just 16 days later, he had the honour of being the first member of the Mighty Ducks to skate in an NHL All-Star Game.

Despite all of the positive contributions Kasatonov made to the developing club, he was considered expendable later in the year when the St. Louis Blues gave up highly touted prospect Maxim Bets and a draft pick for him.

TROY LONEY

Loney was a member of the Pittsburgh Penguins for 10 seasons between 1983–84 and 1992–93. While he was part of two Stanley Cup champion-ship clubs, he also was the franchise's all-time leader in penalty minutes by the time he left for Anaheim through the expansion draft.

Loney was named the first captain in the history of the Mighty Ducks. He scored on the power play during the season opener against Detroit on October 8, 1993, and his first four tallies of the year came with the man advantage. On October 28, he suffered a bruised knee during a game with San Jose and, although he came back a little more than a week later, he re-aggravated it soon after and needed arthro-scopic surgery.

After Christmas, Loney was back in action and most of his offensive production came after the All-Star break. While facing the Vancouver Canucks on January 16, 1994, he scored during the close 4–3 loss and followed that up two days later with a pair of goals against Toronto that gave the Ducks a brief 3–0 lead later erased by the Maple Leafs.

TODD EWEN

Ewen was regarded as one of hockey's toughest customers in the early 1990s. His time with the Montreal Canadiens was interrupted by a series of serious injuries, but he managed to be a part of their Stanley Cup–winning squad in 1992–93, even though he only played in a single postseason game.

Taken by Anaheim in the expansion draft, Ewen was named an alternate captain before the start of the 1993–94 campaign. He missed just a single game after breaking his nose in a battle with the New York Rangers on October 19, 1993.

On December 5, Ewen had a pair of assists in a loss to the Tampa Bay Lightning, but his most significant statistic came from the whopping 24 fights he got into during the inaugural season for the Mighty Ducks — two of which came against Dean Kennedy of the Winnipeg Jets when the two teams met on January 26, 1994. As the end of the season approached, he injured his shoulder during a matchup with Toronto, but he still finished eighth in the NHL in penalty minutes.

GUY HEBERT

Hebert got into 24 games as a backup for Curtis Joseph with the St. Louis Blues in 1992–93. The Mighty Ducks made him their first pick in the expansion draft in the hope that he would be their number one goaltender in the long run.

After getting rocked in the season opener against Detroit, Hebert earned a tie with Calgary during his second appearance on October 17, 1993. He earned a victory at Madison Square Garden two days later in a battle with the New York Rangers. Over the first two months of the campaign, victories were scarce for him, but in mid-December, he won four straight, which included a 38-save shutout against Toronto.

On February 4, 1994, he earned his second whitewash of the year in a 3-0 victory over the Vancouver Canucks. By then, Hebert had asserted himself as the team's top man in net — a position he held for several years afterward.

EXPANSION YEAR RECORD: 28–47–7
(63 points — fourth in Central Division)
COACH: Barry Trotz
GENERAL MANAGER: David Poile
FIRST GAME: October 10, 1998 —
1-0 loss vs. Florida Panthers
FIRST GOAL: October 13, 1998 by Andrew Brunette

NASHVILLE PREDATORS

It may surprise some hockey fans, but the city of Nashville has a strong hockey tradition that goes back to the the 1960s and the days of the Dixie Flyers club. The success of East Coast Hockey League (ECHL) and CHL teams in the 1990s paved the way for the NHL to come in to town. In 1995, rumours spread that the New Jersey Devils would end up relocating to Tennessee because of the potential for a new building to play in and a lucrative $20 million relocation bonus, but after restructuring the lease on their own arena they ended up staying in the Meadowlands.

As a result of such a serious attempt to get an NHL club, however, the league at least considered the city in its planned expansion. Craig Leipold made a formal presentation to them in January 1997 and was granted a conditional franchise a few months later. The league would allow the team to start play in 1998–99 if they could reach the sales target of 12,000 season tickets and a finished arena before the three other potential teams did.

Soon after they reached their goals, the unnamed club hired former Washington Capitals general manager David Poile to undertake a similar role for them, and he then brought on Barry Trotz as coach on August 6. Both have remained with the club to this day.

Even before the team chose its nickname, they unveiled a sabretoothed cat as their logo, which paid tribute to the fact that a partial Smilodon skeleton had been found in downtown Nashville back in 1971. A public vote was held to determine the club's name, and Predators won out over Ice Tigers, Fury and Attack.

While the Predators geared up for their first season, it was reported in the press that there was a possibility the Edmonton Oilers would move to Nashville and the expansion franchise would be moved to Houston, Texas. Leipold shot down this idea quickly, and the team began signing free agents before getting a chance to poach opposing rosters through the 1998 NHL Expansion Draft. Their selections proved quite decent and they acquired some scoring punch with Andrew Brunette and Greg Johnson to go along with decent defenders such as Bob Boughner and the well-travelled J.J. Daigneault.

The player who was perhaps their best pick seems almost to have been an afterthought — Tomas Vokoun, who was a prospect with the Montreal Canadiens at the time. He eventually proved their franchise player during the early years and helped them become a playoff contender. They also made some trades that had a positive impact on their first-year roster, acquiring talent such as Darren Turcotte, Sebastien Bordeleau, Sergei Krivokrasov and Kimmo Timonen. During the 1998 NHL Entry Draft, the Predators had the second overall selection and took David Legwand from the Plymouth Whalers of the Ontario Hockey League (OHL). He was the last player from the 1998–99 season to remain with Nashville until he was traded to Detroit in 2014.

Before they were ready to officially hit the ice, the team added a few more players through trades and free agency. The signing of Tom Fitzgerald gave the Preds their first captain. On October 10, 1998, they opened the regular season at home and lost to the Florida Panthers in a tight 1–0 game, but three nights later they won against Carolina. Overall, their start was respectable for an expansion team, and they were 8–11–1 over the first 20 games of the year. Picking up veteran Cliff Ronning from the Phoenix Coyotes was a smart move, but as the year wore on, their inability to score or keep the puck out of the net caught up with them, and they finished at the bottom of the Central Division with a 28–47–7 record.

The Predators made all the right moves over the next few years and the patience of management allowed them to build into a playoff

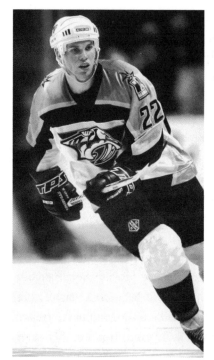

(clockwise) Greg Johnson, Kimmo Timonen, Mike Dunham

contender. They made it to the postseason for the first time in 2003–04 and have missed the playoffs only twice since then. The 2005–06 campaign saw them reach the 100-point plateau for the first time, but they were looking at potential relocation when they were purchased by Jim Balsillie, who intended to place them in southern Ontario. There was later another potential sale to a venture capitalist named William "Boots" Del Biaggio III that could have sent them to Kansas City, Missouri.

In short time, the team garnered the local support it needed and the group ended up including Del Biaggio. The next year, however, he ran into legal trouble, which resulted in a 97-month prison term that embarrassed the league, as they had not done their due diligence, much like when John Spano controlled the New York Islanders in the late 1990s.

Despite the uncertainty of the team's ownership situation, the Predators have been a dependable Western Conference force in recent years. In 2010–11, they finally won a playoff series but then narrowly lost out to the Vancouver Canucks. The success of the management team, combined with a hard-rock defence and sparkling goaltending, keeps the fans coming in and the catfish flying onto the ice. Perhaps in time, they can rise to even greater heights.

CLIFF RONNING

Ronning started the 1998-99 season with the Phoenix Coyotes, and all the diminutive playmaker and a prospect named Richard Lintner cost the Predators was some future considerations. His veteran experience made him an asset to the team, as did his abilities as a power-play specialist.

After going scoreless in his first three games with Nashville, Ronning registered points in his next six, including a pair of assists in a win over Los Angeles on November 12, 1998. Just five days later, he hit a personal milestone by scoring his 200th career goal against Mark Fitzpatrick of the Chicago Blackhawks. He earned his 600th point with an assist on Sergei Krivokrasov's game-winner when the team defeated the New York Islanders in a road game on February 12, 1999.

A frequent shooter, Ronning had 10 two-point outings with the Predators during their first year and led the club in assists and points.

GREG JOHNSON

After nearly four seasons in the Motor City, Johnson narrowly missed out on consecutive Stanley Cup championships with the Detroit Red Wings in the late 1990s and toiled for Pittsburgh and Chicago instead. Although he had a respectable 69-game stint with the Blackhawks, the team made the difficult choice to make him available in the 1998 NHL Expansion Draft.

He responded to his new surroundings with what proved his best offensive season but had some mixed emotions heading into the 1998–99 campaign.

"I was obviously excited on one hand but nervous on the other," he said. "It was an opportunity. I think everybody was excited about it. We wanted to go out and prove over 82 games that we belonged."

Johnson earned an assist on the first goal in franchise history on October 13, 1998, and also had another helper that night on J.J. Daigneault's winning goal to help put away the Carolina Hurricanes. Just eight days later, he scored his first goal in a Predators uniform against his old Detroit teammates and ended up with a team-best three shorthanded tallies on the year. That goal kicked off a six-game point streak, but he had a seven-game one as well from January 26 to February 9, 1999, which included goals in five straight contests.

Had he not missed nine games due to injury, it is likely that Johnson would have led Nashville in scoring, but he finished three points behind Cliff Ronning on the season.

"I had a good year. It was a good step forward and I felt my career was heading in the right direction," he said.

TOM FITZGERALD

With 10 NHL seasons under his belt, Fitzgerald had played for the first-year Florida Panthers in 1993–94 and signed with Nashville as a free agent. He was named the club's first captain, and his experience was going to be a definite asset for the Predators. His dependability became obvious, as he was the only skater to appear in at least 80 games in 1998–99.

"Tom was a great captain and a good leader from the start," said teammate Greg Johnson. "He was a hard-working guy and held everybody accountable."

Fitzgerald's first goal of the season came against the Vancouver Canucks on October 27 and he registered an assist while taking on Colorado in the next game four days later. When the Preds were deadlocked at three goals with the Calgary Flames, he potted an even-strength goal, which gave them the edge they needed for victory on November 25. His best month during the season came in March 1999, when he scored three goals and added six assists over 14 games.

KIMMO TIMONEN

At one time, Timonen was property of the Los Angeles Kings, but he wanted to remain in Finland and represented his country at the 1998 Winter Olympics. Since the Kings wanted to protect Garry Galley in the upcoming expansion draft, they cut a deal with the Predators and sent them the young defender and Roman Vopat in exchange for the assurance that they would not select the prized veteran.

Timonen started the season in Milwaukee and had 15 points over 29 games at the IHL level before he got the call-up to Nashville for their battle with Anaheim on December 16, 1998. A week later, he recorded his first NHL point with an assist against the Detroit Red Wings. Closer to the end of the year, he recorded a four-game point streak that included goals against Los Angeles, Chicago and New Jersey.

TOMAS VOKOUN

Many fans did not know what to expect when the Predators chose Vokoun in the 1998 NHL Expansion Draft, as his only previous action had been a disastrous single-period stint with the Montreal Canadiens during the 1996–97 season.

Vokoun bounced between Milwaukee and Nashville in the early months of the 1998–99 campaign and appeared in nine AHL contests with the Admirals. He debuted with the big club in a loss to Vancouver on November 7, 1998, and his first victory took place against the San Jose Sharks on December 10. Later that month, he strung together three consecutive wins and was in net for the franchise's first shutout on January 15, 1999, when the Phoenix Coyotes went down by a score of 2–0. In time, he became the team's number one man in net and he still holds several club records.

MIKE DUNHAM

Being the backup to Martin Brodeur in New Jersey has traditionally been an easy job in many ways thanks to his workhorse-like ways. Dunham spent two years as his apprentice, but they were drafted by the Devils in the same year, 1990. Dunham took a bit of a longer path to the NHL, but as a rookie in 1996–97, he got to share the Jennings Trophy, and the Predators took him in the expansion draft for his potential to be their number one goaltender.

Dunham played strong during Nashville's opener against the Florida Panthers, making 25 saves in the 1–0 loss on October 10, 1998, but three days later, he made sure the Preds notched their first win while taking on the Calgary Flames. His best stretch in the crease came between October 27 and November 12, when he won five of six games, but he later missed some time because of injury. On March 24, 1999, he was perfect in a tough clash with the Tampa Bay Lightning as he turned back every shot to earn a 3–0 shutout.

EXPANSION YEAR RECORD: 14-57-7-4
(39 points — fifth in Southeast Division)
COACH: Curt Fraser
GENERAL MANAGER: Don Waddell
FIRST GAME: October 2, 1999 —
4-1 loss vs. New Jersey Devils
FIRST GOAL: October 2, 1999 by Kelly Buchberger

ATLANTA THRASHERS

Nearly 20 years after the NHL's initial experiment in the southern United States failed, the pro hockey landscape had proven that the sport could sometimes work in warmer climates. The league made the somewhat controversial decision to grant a new franchise to Atlanta on June 25, 1997. Since there was some big money behind the club in the form of broadcasting mogul Ted Turner and Time Warner Inc., there was certainly optimism in the NHL's eyes, but some fans were still skeptical that big-league hockey could survive in Georgia.

The Thrashers, who were expected to begin play in the 1999–00 season, were named after the state bird. The Philips Arena — located at the same spot as the Omni, where the Flames had played years before — was to be their home. The club hired former Detroit Red Wings assistant general manager Don Waddell to serve as their first vice-president and general manager on June 23, 1998, and their colourful jerseys were unveiled a few months before they hit the ice.

Just one week before the 1999 NHL Expansion Draft took place, the team made a trade to get impending free agent goaltender Damian Rhodes away from the Ottawa Senators. On June 25, 1999, they selected many of the players that were part of their first lineup, but not all of them lasted the day as property of the team, though, as they made several other trades to bolster the lineup.

What fans were truly excited about, however, was the 1999 NHL Entry Draft, to see what young prospect the Thrashers were going to

389

take with their first overall pick. At the time, many hockey executives did not realize how weak the 1999 draft class would be. Atlanta could have taken one of the Sedin brothers, but twins Daniel and Henrik made it well-known beforehand that they only planned to go to a club that was going to select both of them. There was also some hype for Pavel Brendl from the Calgary Hitmen. Instead, the Thrashers selected Patrik Stefan, a teenager who had played professionally in 1998–99 with the Long Beach Ice Dogs of the IHL. In the end, Stefan proved to be somewhat of a bust, but he did skate in more than 400 games with the team that drafted him.

The next point of business was hiring a coach, and Atlanta went with former NHL player Curt Fraser, who had a great deal of success in previous years as the bench boss of minor league squads. He was brought up from the IHL's Orlando Solar Bears and ended up spending a rough three-and-a-half seasons with the Thrashers.

On September 11, the Thrashers won their first exhibition match against the previous year's expansion club, the Nashville Predators, by a score of 3–1. Their first real test, though, was their opening night game on October 2, when they fell to the New Jersey Devils by a 4–1 margin. Captain Kelly Buchberger scored their only goal in that contest, but they looked marginally better in their home debut a week later as they skated to a 5–5 tie with the Buffalo Sabres. Two days after that, they finally earned their first victory when Rhodes made 20 saves and chalked up a 2–0 shutout against the New York Islanders.

After that, the bright spots were few and far between during Atlanta's expansion year. Only twice did they string together two straight wins, and their second half was simply atrocious with four wins over their last 41 games. This period of futility also included a 16-game winless streak that ran from January 16 to February 22, 2000, when they got a surprise victory over the Colorado Avalanche.

With their first season mercifully finished, their record was a brutal 14–57–7–4 for a pathetic 39 points. It was not the worst finish ever by an expansion club, but it was the weakest since the 1992–93 Ottawa Senators. A glimmer of hope was around the corner, though, as they took Dany Heatley with the second overall pick in the 2000 NHL

Entry Draft and improved enough to win 23 games the next year. Soon after, they added Ilya Kovalchuk to the lineup and slowly began to build into contender that was on the cusp of finally making the playoffs.

Tragedy struck the team on September 29, 2003, when Heatley crashed his Ferrari and seriously injured himself along with passenger and teammate Dan Snyder, who died five days later due to septic shock. Heatley faced criminal charges that were ultimately dropped, but he was given three years of probation and community service.

Following the lockout, the team tried to build on its strong 2003–04 season and won 41 games in 2005–06 despite missing starting goaltender Kari Lehtonen for an extended period. They narrowly missed the postseason again, but they kept their momentum going the next year and finally made it to the playoffs as Southeast Division champs. When they were swept in four games by the New York Rangers, their lack of postseason experience was readily apparent, but there was some short-lived optimism in Atlanta at the time.

Over the next four seasons, things began to fall apart both on and off the ice for the Thrashers as they went through some coaching changes and were basically forced to trade Kovalchuk when it became obvious that he was not going to re-sign with the team. They still tried valiantly to make the playoffs and even hosted the 2008 NHL All-Star Game, but the situation looked bleak at best as a result of declining attendance and decreased revenues. Rick Dudley took over as their general manager in 2010–11 and the club made some last-ditch efforts to try to keep the Thrashers from relocating, attempting to find some local investors to keep the team around, but it was all in vain. At the time, the Atlanta Spirit Group owned the team and noted that they had lost $130 million over six seasons. Some of those losses were credited to an ongoing lawsuit with a former partner.

On May 16, 2011, it was reported that the Thrashers were being sold to Winnipeg-based True North Sports and Entertainment. Despite the NHL's denial, a deal was finalized four days later. The official announcement of the sale was made on May 31 and it, along with the relocation of the team, was formally approved on June 21. The Atlanta Spirit Group retained the rights and logos for the Thrashers, but True North

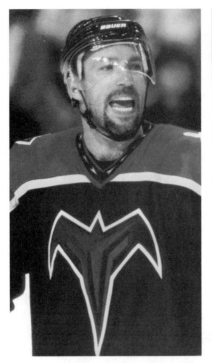

(clockwise) Ray Ferraro, Patrik Stefan, Damian Rhodes

eventually announced that the team was going to be called the Jets — a direct nod to the city's previous NHL team, which had been relocated to Phoenix in 1996. The new Winnipeg Jets have been a box office smash and came very close to reaching the playoffs in 2011–12.

ANDREW BRUNETTE

Brunette spent the 1998–99 season as a member of the first-year Nashville Predators and had the best season of his career to that point. Sent to Atlanta for a fifth-round draft pick, he was certainly motivated to prove his worth as an NHL performer with the Thrashers. There is little doubt that the Preds regretted making such a hasty move.

Although Brunette did not register a point in the first two games of the year, he had five points over his next three, which included the first game-winning goal in franchise history, when they shut out the New York Islanders on October 14, 1999. In fact, he had a very good start to the season with 32 points over his first 36 games.

His production cooled off a bit over the rest of the year, but Brunette hit the 20-goal mark for the first time on February 25, 2000, against the Edmonton Oilers. After that, he did not appear on the scoresheet for nine games and did not score another goal until March 18. He finished the year as Atlanta's leading scorer and finished up his career during the 2011–12 season as a member of the Chicago Blackhawks.

RAY FERRARO

After 15 seasons in the NHL, Ferraro had proved himself a solid performer and starred for four different clubs. After missing a good chunk of the 1997–98 campaign with an injury, he bounced back the following year, and that made him an appealing free agent in the summer months of 1999. When he signed on with the Thrashers, the hope was that there was still some gas left in the tank.

One of Atlanta's most exciting performers during their expansion season, Ferraro had more three-star selections than any other player on the club in 1999–00. Although he was held pointless over the first four games of the year, he notched a pair of assists in a tie with Tampa

Bay on October 16, 1999, and repeated the feat again 10 days later in a win over the Calgary Flames. A battle with the Buffalo Sabres saw him notch three points and that was part of a big 10-point month for the veteran forward.

YANNICK TREMBLAY

Fans in Toronto saw a lot of promise in Tremblay during the late 1990s, but the team itself was not necessarily convinced he was going to be a long-term fixture on the roster and he was made available in the NHL Expansion Draft.

It was a move they came to regret, as Tremblay remained healthy for most of the 1999–00 campaign with the Thrashers and led their defence corps in goals, assists and points by a country mile. Within the first month of play, he had recorded a pair of two-point games and ended up having five of them over the course of the season. Four of his 10 goals came on the power play and the first game-winning tally of his career came against the Florida Panthers on December 3, 1999.

While facing his old club on March 18, 2000, Tremblay scored the winner, one of three goals he had that month, in a 4–1 triumph. At the end of the season, he was selected to represent Canada at the 2000 IIHF World Championship.

PATRIK STEFAN

The 1999 NHL Entry Draft is often regarded as one of the worst in the history of the event, and often some that blame is placed on the shoulders of Stefan, who was taken first overall by the Thrashers. He chose to leave the Czech Republic during the 1997–98 season to play for the Long Beach Ice Dogs of the IHL and performed well enough against established professionals to move to the head of the draft pack. It also did not help that the Sedin brothers were insistent that they be drafted by the same club, since Atlanta might have taken one of them with the premier pick.

Making his big-league debut on October 2, 1999, against New Jersey, Stefan recorded his first point, which was an assist on Atlanta's only goal of the night by Kelly Buchberger. A week later, he scored twice and chipped in a helper in a 5–5 tie with the Buffalo Sabres. After a weak November, he picked up the pace in December and had 10 points over 13 games. From there, it was very much tough times for the rookie as he scored only seven points over the rest of the year. The highlight of that period was a two-point night in a win over the Colorado Avalanche on February 22, 2000.

KELLY BUCHBERGER

Edmonton's last link to their Stanley Cup dynasty, Buchberger played for the club until the end of the 1998–99 season and was their leader on and off the ice. A gritty and tough winger, he was picked up by the Thrashers in the expansion draft and was named captain for their first NHL season.

Because of his experience, he was given more opportunity to rack up ice time and his per-game average went up by slightly more than four minutes per game after switching teams. He scored his first goal of the season in the opener against the New Jersey Devils and followed it up with an assist against Detroit on October 7, 1999, and two more helpers two days later in a tie with the Buffalo Sabres.

Buchberger was also very busy stepping up for teammates and dropped the gloves nine times in a Thrashers uniform. During the first game of the year, he tangled with Lyle Odelein of the Devils and had subsequent scraps with heavyweights like Todd Simpson, Shayne Corson and Paul Laus. On December 23, 1999, he recorded three points against the Philadelphia Flyers, and all of his goals with Atlanta came in even-strength situations. As the trade deadline approached, he was shipped off to Los Angeles along with Nelson Emerson.

DAMIAN RHODES

Rhodes was coming off the best season of his career when the Ottawa Senators traded him to Atlanta for future considerations on June 18, 1999. Since he had been a big part of his former club's rise to playoff contention, the Thrashers felt that they had a potential number one netminder secured for their expansion season. He was the first player the club acquired.

Rhodes was in net for the club's first game on October 2, 1999, against the New Jersey Devils and made 26 saves in a 4–1 loss. Less than two weeks later, he made club history when they earned their first-ever victory and shutout in a 2–0 blanking of the New York Islanders on October 14. A sprained ankle derailed his season, however, and he missed a ton of action beginning in mid-November. Once he returned to action on March 10, he was back as the club's top goalie and won a pair of games down the stretch against Toronto and the Islanders.

EXPANSION YEAR RECORD: 28-39-9-6
(71 points — fifth in Central Division)
COACH: Dave King
GENERAL MANAGER: Doug MacLean
FIRST GAME: October 7, 2000 —
5-3 loss to Chicago Blackhawks
FIRST GOAL: October 7, 2000 by Bruce Gardiner

COLUMBUS
BLUE JACKETS

Before the arrival of the Columbus Blue Jackets, the NHL had made one foray into the state of Ohio, when the Cleveland Barons spent two seasons in the league in 1976–77 and 1977–78. The Barons had a rough time both on the ice and at the box office, but there were factors in play that assured their doom, such as an arena that was located far into the suburbs.

Nearly 20 years later, a group that included industrialist John H. McConnell decided to make a bid for a spot in the NHL's upcoming expansion plans. The city itself had not had a "big four" major league sports franchise at that point, but there was some pro hockey in Ohio's capital city with the ECHL's Columbus Chill that began play in 1991–92. The NHL expressed some concerns about the lack of a suitable arena, and the city itself held a referendum about the use of public funds to build one. If it failed, the city was not willing to put up funds, but McConnell promised the league that the arena would be built privately if necessary.

In the end, the referendum failed and the Nationwide Mutual Insurance Company declared that they were going to finance the new arena on May 31, 1997. Just 25 days later, the NHL announced that the new Columbus franchise was set to begin play in the 2000–01 season. They were called the Blue Jackets in honour of the state's Civil War history, although at the time some hockey fans were a bit confused by the team's name. They also released a preliminary logo that featured a

397

day-glow green bug named Stinger dressed up in Civil War regalia, and used that as their alternate logo from 2000–01 to 2004–05.

The team hired respected hockey executive Doug MacLean as their general manager on February 11, 1998, and right away he went to work putting the on-ice product together. Soon after, he was also given the responsibilities of club president. He was busy in the weeks leading up to the 2000 NHL Expansion Draft signing free agents and trading away some late draft picks for a few players that gave Columbus some depth early on. Two of his best pickups at this time were Espen Knutsen from Anaheim and David Vyborny, who went on to become one of the best players in franchise history.

Of all the players the Blue Jackets took in the expansion draft, just 12 of them suited up for the team during the 2000–01 season. They picked up several solid veterans like Geoff Sanderson, Kevin Dineen and Lyle Odelein before the 2000 NHL Entry Draft, when they took promising defender Rostislav Klesla in the first round.

Not long after the expansion draft, the Blue Jackets named Dave King their first coach. King had previous experience with the Calgary Flames and leading the Canadian National Team. They also signed some more free agents around this time, including veteran goaltender Ron Tugnutt and prospect Serge Aubin.

NHL hockey made its official return to Ohio on October 7 when the Jackets hosted the Chicago Blackhawks. Bruce Gardiner managed to score their first goal that evening, but they lost by a 5–3 margin. Their first victory came against the Calgary Flames five days later, and they put together an impressive four-game winning streak soon after. The club hit a major roadblock immediately after that, though, and lost eight games in a row before going .500 for the rest of the year.

For much of the 2000–01 season, the Blue Jackets remained competitive, but very streaky at times, and finished the year with 71 points. From a box office perspective, they were a success and sold out on 26 occasions — including their last 15 home dates. Tugnutt established a new record for most wins in a season by a modern expansion goalie with 22, and Sanderson bounced back to reach the 30-goal mark for the first time since 1996–97.

(clockwise) Lyle Odelein, Rostislav Klesla, Kevin Dineen, Ron Tugnutt

Since then, the Blue Jackets have been a bit of a hard-luck franchise. They have faced great tragedies such as the 2002 death of 13-year-old fan Brittanie Cecil, who was killed when she was struck in the head by a puck, after which the NHL made it mandatory for all of its arenas to install nylon mesh nets to protect spectators.

The club had the first overall pick in the 2002 NHL Entry Draft and selected Rick Nash, who is their all-time leader in most offensive categories. However, their draft record has some questionable picks like Nikolai Zherdev, Alexandre Picard and Nikita Filatov, who never panned out for them. After the lockout, the team still had trouble picking up momentum, and MacLean was eventually fired in 2007. Several months before he was dismissed, though, he hired the talented Ken Hitchcock as their coach, and he finally led them to the playoffs in 2008–09 with the strong play of rookie goalie Steve Mason. Unfortunately, they were swept by the Detroit Red Wings in the opening round. They have not been back to the postseason up to the end of the 2012–13 season.

In 2010–11, Columbus unveiled a new third jersey that players hated and briefly had a cannon-shaped mascot, which was quickly scrapped because of its phallic design and unpopularity with fans. In the summer of 2011, they signed Jeff Carter, who wouldn't last the season, and GM Scott Howson staged an ugly public battle with Nash, who had privately requested a trade.

The future of NHL hockey in Columbus often looks doubtful. Attendance has dropped to all-time lows in recent years and has actually slowly moved downward since the 2001–02 season. Since the death of McConnell, his family has taken over the team and doesn't seem exactly friendly toward the sport of hockey. In 2013–14, the club has begun play in the Eastern Conference and it is hoped that their years of futility may soon come to an end.

GEOFF SANDERSON

Between 1992-93 and 1996-97, Sanderson hit the 30-goal mark four times with the Hartford Whalers, but in the three seasons that followed, his numbers dipped greatly, and it seemed to many that his best days might be behind him. In reality, he simply wasn't being used enough and as a result, the Blue Jackets ended up with perhaps the biggest steal of the 2000 NHL Expansion Draft when they claimed him from the Buffalo Sabres.

In the early stages of the season, Sanderson was showing glimpses of a return to his old form, but after about 30 games he began scoring at a greater pace. On December 8, 2000, he recorded the first overtime game-winner for Columbus in a victory over the Boston Bruins and 15 days later had his first three-point game of the year against the New York Islanders.

The January 10, 2001, game against the Colorado Avalanche was the 700th of Sanderson's NHL career. He went on to record the first hat trick in franchise history one month later in a 3–2 win over the Nashville Predators. On March 9, he recorded his 30th goal of the season on Trevor Kidd of the Florida Panthers and became just the third player to reach that mark with an expansion team since 1991–92. That total might have been higher, but he suffered a knee injury against the Calgary Flames five days later to bring an end to a successful first season with the Blue Jackets.

ESPEN KNUTSEN

The man known to teammates as "Shampoo" returned to NHL action in 2000–01 after a two-year absence, and the Blue Jackets got a prime performer from the Mighty Ducks of Anaheim for a mere fourth-round draft pick.

A skilled playmaker who led Columbus in assists and shooting percentage during their inaugural NHL season, Knutsen was the heart and soul of the team's power play. He put up 25 of his assists while the other side was penalized. He sat out of the team's first eight games because of a broken finger sustained in the pre-season, but after a slight adjustment back to the North American game (he had played in the Swedish Elite League after his first brief NHL stint), he was one of the most reliable scorers for the Blue Jackets.

Interestingly, only one of his 11 goals in 2000–01 was scored at home. He recorded his first multi-goal game against his old teammates from Anaheim on February 25, 2001 — the first of which came just 17 seconds into the opening period. His best performance was saved for the Calgary Flames, however, when he set a club standard by earning five assists on March 24.

DAVID VYBORNY

Vyborny was on the radar of NHL scouts when he was a teenager and he was a second-round pick of the Edmonton Oilers in 1993. He tried the AHL on for size in 1994–95 with the Cape Breton Oilers but went back to the Czech Republic soon after to play for Sparta Praha. A regular on the international scene from that point forward, he helped take his country to three gold medal finishes at the IIHF World Championship between 1996 and 2000.

Vyborny was hot out of the gate and not only scored in the season opener, but also followed it up with goals in back-to-back games on October 14 and 15, 2000. In the latter contest, he scored on a penalty shot against Rob Tallas of the Chicago Blackhawks. On January 21, 2001, he recorded the first game-winning goal of his career just 27 seconds into the third period as the Blue Jackets downed the Tampa Bay Lightning by a score of 3–1.

After a rough stretch in February when Vyborny scored just a single point, he bounced back the next month with nine points. On March 19, he set an NHL rookie record by scoring his second penalty shot goal of the year on Tomas Vokoun of the Nashville Predators. Five days later, he had a goal and two assists in a 6–4 triumph over the Calgary Flames. At the end of the season, he suited up for the Czech Republic once again and won yet another gold medal at the Worlds.

LYLE ODELEIN

One of hockey's toughest customers in the 1990s, Odelein missed out on winning a second career Stanley Cup when he was traded to the Phoenix Coyotes by the New Jersey Devils late in the 1999–00 season. Despite a good showing down the stretch, he was exposed in the expansion draft and was taken by the Blue Jackets.

Odelein was given the honour of being the first captain in franchise history, and his leadership was certainly going to be needed during the team's debut season. He recorded an assist during the opening game against Chicago and his first goal of the season came on November 22, 2000, against Colorado. While facing the Avalanche again on January 10, 2001, he reached a career milestone by recording his 200th point with an assist on Bruce Gardiner's third period goal.

Perhaps an even greater milestone he reached during the 2000–01 campaign was the 2,000 career penalty minute plateau. He marked this record during the final outing of the year on April 8 when he went to the box on a roughing call at 16:49 of the first period. He was more than willing to drop the gloves for the Blue Jackets and got into 10 scraps with players who included Chris Dingman, Bob Probert and Georges Laraque.

RON TUGNUTT

Tugnutt played on his fair share of teams that faced big uphill challenges throughout much of his NHL career. The Blue Jackets made sure to sign him because of his grace under pressure, providing stability in net during their first season in the league. His two most recent teams at the time, Ottawa and Pittsburgh, did attempt to re-sign him but the contract offer from Columbus was impossible to refuse.

It was money well spent for the new club, as Tugnutt won his first game (which was also the initial win in franchise history) against Calgary on October 12, 2000, and had an impressive four-game winning streak during the early part of November. His first shutout of the year, which was also again the first for Columbus, came while playing one of his old clubs, the Montreal Canadiens, on December 18.

During the stretch toward the postseason, Tugnutt's play between the pipes kept the Jackets in contention as long as possible, as he went 8–4–1 over his last 13 appearances. By the end of the season, after 22 victories, he had established a new NHL record for most wins by a goalie during an expansion year and also finished ninth in the league in save percentage.

EXPANSION YEAR RECORD: 25-39-13-5
(68 points — fifth in Northwest Division)
COACH: Jacques Lemaire
GENERAL MANAGER: Doug Risebrough
FIRST GAME: October 6, 2000 —
3-1 loss vs. Mighty Ducks of Anaheim
FIRST GOAL: October 6, 2000 by Marian Gaborik

MINNESOTA WILD

The relocation of the Minnesota North Stars in 1993 caused great sadness among the state's hockey fans, and while high school and college hockey continued to thrive, there was still a ceaseless desire to bring back the NHL game.

On June 25, 1997, the Minnesota Hockey Ventures Group, headed up by Bob Naegele Jr., was granted an NHL franchise that was set to begin play during the 2000–01 campaign. A few months later, they announced several potential names for the team, and the official announcement that they were to be called the Wild came on January 22, 1998.

They were set to play in the all-new Xcel Energy Center in St. Paul, and the main architect for the club was to be former NHL player and Calgary Flames general manager Doug Risebrough. He hired former teammate Guy Lapointe to work in the scouting department, and on June 19, 2000, he scored a major coup by landing the celebrated Jacques Lemaire to act as their first coach.

A mere four days later, the team began to assemble a good part of its original lineup through the 2000 NHL Expansion Draft. Although few of the players had any name recognition, they certainly fell into the type of system that Lemaire wanted them to play. On June 24, the team had the third overall pick in the 2000 NHL Entry Draft and grabbed its first franchise player in the form of Marian Gaborik.

It was fitting that Gaborik scored the first-ever goal for the Wild during the season opener on October 6 in a 3–1 loss to the Mighty Ducks of Anaheim. Their start was a bit rough as they tied Philadelphia in their home opener five days later and finally registered their first win on October 18 in a 6–5 squeaker with the Tampa Bay Lightning.

The Wild had a rotating captaincy in their early years, but they later abandoned the idea to focus on having just one on-ice leader at a time.

The game that may have made the trials of that first season worthwhile, though, was when the Dallas Stars came to town on December 17. The former North Stars were shut down that night by a score of 6–0 and emotions ran high for the crowd. Over the course of the 2000–01 season, the Wild never won more than two games in a row, but their defensive record was impressive for an expansion team. They finished 12th in the NHL with 210 goals against, but their pitiful offence was dead last in the league with just 168 goals.

Finishing well out of a playoff spot, they did perform well at home and even had a nine-game unbeaten streak there at one point. The fans, realizing what they had missed over the previous seven years, came out in droves for every game, and the Wild set a record for largest attendance for an expansion team with more than 750,000 fans coming through the turnstiles.

Over the next few seasons, Minnesota continued to build on its success and showed steady improvement before making the playoffs for the first time in 2002–03. They went all the way to the Western Conference final that year but have made the postseason only twice since that time. In 2007–08, they won their first Northwest Division championship but have slid in the standings since then. Gaborik spent more time with the club than any other player in franchise history and holds several records, but he now plays for the Los Angeles Kings.

With stars like Mikko Koivu and Niklas Backstrom, the current club continues to be competitive and is owned by Minnesota Sports & Entertainment, which is headed by former Nashville Predators owner Craig Leipold. The fans continue to pack the Xcel Center, but the team's 409-game sellout streak ended in 2010. In 2011–12, the arena was not filled to capacity and the major factor for this decline is the fact that they have not made the playoffs in four years. Luckily, the club returned

(top) Marian Gaborik (bottom) Manny Fernandez

to playoff action during the shortened 2012–13 campaign. Should they continue to improve, hockey-mad Minnesotans are sure to be filling every seat once again.

SCOTT PELLERIN

By the late 1990s, Pellerin had established himself as a regular with the St. Louis Blues and he hit the 20-goal mark for the first and only time of his career in 1998–99. The following season saw his production drop by half, and the Wild were able to claim his rights during the expansion draft.

Given a new opportunity to get more ice time with the new club, Pellerin was able to regain some of his offensive momentum and was leading the team with 39 points after his first 58 appearances. He recorded assists in the team's first two outings and was brilliant with a goal and three assists against the Tampa Bay Lightning on October 18, 2000. Exactly one month later, he had another three helpers in a battle with the Boston Bruins.

Through December and January, he easily outpaced his teammates in scoring and had five two-point games in that span. The former Hobey Baker Award winner cooled off a bit in February, though, and was traded to the Carolina Hurricanes for two draft picks and an obscure prospect named Askhat Rakhmatullin who never made it beyond the ECHL.

MARIAN GABORIK

Gaborik was considered one of the most promising young talents in the world heading into the 2000 NHL Entry Draft, as he had helped Slovakia to a bronze medal at the 1999 IIHF World Junior Championship and averaged nearly a point per game with the Dukla Trencin club. The New York Islanders and Atlanta Thrashers passed on the chance to select him on draft day, but he was a perfect budding star for the Wild to build their team around.

During his NHL debut against the Mighty Ducks of Anaheim on October 6, 2000, Gaborik scored on veteran Guy Hebert, but it was not enough in a 3–1 loss. He helped Minnesota secure its first victory at home 12 days later with a pair of goals on the visiting Tampa Bay Lightning and during his first month in the league, made a very good impression. Because the Wild had such a defensive focus from the start, Gaborik did not rack up a ton of points as a freshman, but he finished second on the team in scoring and ranked among the league's rookie leaders. From January 17 to February 6, 2001, he recorded nine points over a seven-game span and part of that streak included a pair of goals against the Los Angeles Kings. He missed some time at the end of the season as a result of an abdominal strain, but his freshman campaign was deemed a success.

LUBOMIR SEKERAS

A hard-shooting defenceman who spent many years playing profes-sionally in his native Slovakia along with the Czech Republic, Sekeras helped take his countrymen to a memorable silver medal finish at the 2000 IIHF World Championship. The Wild took notice of his six points over seven tournament games and took a chance by selecting him in the eighth round of that summer's NHL Entry Draft.

It turned out to be one of the club's shrewdest moves, as Sekeras ended up being their top offensive power from the back end and was second in assists behind Scott Pellerin. On October 15, 2000, he scored his first NHL goal against Edmonton's Joaquin Gage and it was the first tally made by a Minnesota defender. A little less than a month later, he scored twice and added an assist in another loss to the Oilers. Six days after that, the Wild met the Boston Bruins and he scored twice, one of those tallies proving the game-winner.

Toward the end of the season, Sekeras put together a four-game point streak in early March and then joined his countrymen for the Worlds once again.

SEAN O'DONNELL

A solid pickup by the Wild in the 2000 NHL Expansion Draft, O'Donnell made a good impression with fans during his brief tenure with the club. Although he was selected from the scraps the Los Angeles Kings offered up to the new clubs, he was considered a dependable defender who could make some small offensive contributions when necessary.

His first goal of the 2000–01 campaign was one of the biggest for Minnesota's first season. The team's first captain, he scored the difference-maker in a 5–3 victory over the Detroit Red Wings on December 27, 2000. Another game-winner followed with his next tally and it helped his team to a win over Columbus on January 17, 2001.

Regarded as one of the team's best pieces of trade bait during the expansion year, O'Donnell was traded off to the New Jersey Devils on March 4 and helped his new team to an appearance in the Stanley Cup Final. His last NHL action came with Chicago during the 2011–12 season.

MANNY FERNANDEZ

The Wild did not need to give up a lot to get their hands on Fernandez. He had finally seen regular work with the Dallas Stars the year before as a backup to Ed Belfour, but the emergence of Marty Turco made him expendable. He became the franchise goaltender in the team's early years and was a hit with fans in Minnesota from the start.

After losing to Phoenix in Minnesota's second game of the year, Fernandez was given the honour of being the starter in their home opener against Philadelphia and made 36 saves in the 3–3 tie. Soon after, he missed three games because of an ankle injury, but the wins started piling up after his return to action. He had a three-game winning streak in November and earned a victory in five straight appearances over December and January. Over the course of the 2000–01 campaign, he racked up four shutouts and he ranked among the top 10 goaltenders in goals-against average and save percentage at the end of the year.

ACKNOWLEDGEMENTS

I would like to extend my most sincere thanks to the staff and management of ECW Press for supporting this project.

I also want to recognize the kindness of Dr. Brian Price, who graciously allowed me access to his hockey library, and Ken Whitmell, who was always willing to listen to a story and provide other support. Several friends also need to be recognized for their support as editors, including Jeffrey Griffith, John Pichette, Jon Waldman and Baron Bedesky.

I am indebted to the newspapermen who covered several of the expansion teams for local newspapers and *The Hockey News*. The work of writers such as Charley Barton, Spence Conley, Ed Conrad, Pat Doyle, Geoffrey Fisher, Jay Greenberg, Jim Huber, Harry Klaff, Bill Libby, Jim Matheson, Ken McKenzie, Buddy O'Connor, Lou Prato, Glenn Redmann, Hal Sigurdson and Wayne Warriner proved to be a tremendous resource for this work. I also relied on two key websites, Hockey-reference.com and the Hockey Summary Project (hsp.flyershistory.com), and scoured them almost daily to find relevant statistics.

Thank you also to the following players and coaches who took the time to discuss their roles in the grand history of NHL expansion: Paul Andrea, Andy Bathgate, Bill Bennett, Curt Bennett, Red Berenson, John Bethel, Laurie Boschman, Scotty Bowman, Curt Brackenbury, Brian Bradley, John Brenneman, Leo Boivin, Willie Brossart, Charlie Burns, Al Cameron, Wayne Connelly, Cam Connor, Jim Corsi, Bart Crashley, Terry Crisp, Ray Cullen, Joe Daley, Michel Dion, Dave

Dryden, Jack Egers, Doug Favell, Bob Fitchner, Val Fonteyne, Emile Francis, Ed Gilbert, Michel Goulet, Phil Goyette, Pierre Hamel, Denis Herron, Bruce Hood, Doug Horbul, Bronco Horvath, Mark Howe, Jim Hrycuik, Fred Hucul, Greg Johnson, Larry Keenan, Forbes Kennedy, Dave Kryskow, Jim Kyte, Gord Labossiere, Andre Lacroix, Bill Lesuk, Chris Luongo, Lowell MacDonald, Parker MacDonald, Randy Manery, Cesare Maniago, Jimmy Mann, Seth Martin, Ab McDonald, Peter McDuffe, Bob McGill, Lindsay Middlebrook, Bill Mikkelson, Tom Miller, Doug Mohns, Lew Morrison, Gerry Odrowski, J.P. Parise, Gilbert Perreault, Larry Popein, Poul Popiel, Lynn Powis, Noel Price, Jim Roberts, Leon Rochefort, Mike Rogers, Dale Rolfe, Randy Rota, Gary Sabourin, Ken Schinkel, Ron Schock, Bobby Schmautz, Dave Semenko, Doug Smail, Floyd Smith, John Smrke, Ted Snell, Ralph Stewart, Art Stratton, Red Sullivan, Bill Sutherland, George Swarbrick, Tom Thurlby, Gene Ubriaco, Gary Veneruzzo, Ed Westfall and Bill White. I am especially grateful to John Garrett for kindly agreeing to write the foreword for this book.

The photos in this book were graciously provided by Doug McLatchy and are available for purchase through his website (completehistoryofhockey.com).

Finally, a special thank you to my family for their support as I worked on this project. I could not have done this without you!

APPENDIX

TIMELINE OF NHL EXPANSION
AND FRANCHISE SHIFTS

1917–18

National Hockey League begins play with four clubs (Montreal Canadiens, Montreal Wanderers, Ottawa Senators and Toronto Arenas). After their rink burns down, the Wanderers cease operations after playing just four games. The Quebec Athletic Club (commonly known as the Bulldogs) are league members at this time and sit out this season and the one that follows because of financial woes.

1919–20

The Quebec Athletics (Bulldogs) finally join the NHL.

1920–21

The Quebec franchise is relocated to Hamilton and called the Tigers. The move is made to head off a potential rival league tied to Eddie Livingstone from heading into that city.

1924–25

The Boston Bruins and the Montreal Professional Hockey Club are the NHL's first expansion teams. The Montreal club is later called the Maroons for the colour of their sweaters. Also, the Hamilton Tigers stage a strike to protest the lack of increased pay for an increased number of games in the regular season.

1925–26

The New York Americans and Pittsburgh Pirates begin play. The Amerks are staffed with many players from Hamilton, but the franchise was actually granted before the Tigers ceased operations.

1926–27

After the death of western pro hockey, the NHL uses many of their players to make up the rosters of the Chicago Black Hawks, Detroit Cougars and New York Rangers.

1930–31

The Pittsburgh Pirates become the Philadelphia Quakers. After a disastrous first season, the franchise shuts down.

1931–32

As a result of the state of the economy, the Ottawa Senators take a year off from NHL play.

1932–33

The Senators return to action.

1934–35

After years of declining gate receipts, the Senators end their lengthy run in Canada's capital and relocate to St. Louis to become the Eagles. They last only a single season there because of high travel costs.

1938–39

The Montreal Maroons suspend operations for a year but do not return to action. The franchise is controlled for many years after by Len Peto, a director for the Montreal Canadiens, with the intention of moving it to Philadelphia. He cannot find a suitable arena by the 1946–47 season and the franchise is then removed.

1941–42

The New York Americans attempt to bring in bigger crowds by

renaming themselves the Brooklyn Americans for their first home game.

1942-43

The Original Six era begins when the Brooklyn franchise does not return to action. Despite the best efforts of Red Dutton to find them a new arena, the team is removed from the league in 1946.

1967-68

The NHL doubles in size with the addition of six new clubs. They are all part of the new West Division and include the California Seals, Los Angeles Kings, Minnesota North Stars, Philadelphia Flyers, Pittsburgh Penguins and St. Louis Blues. Within their first month of operation, the California Seals are rechristened the Oakland Seals.

1970-71

Two more franchises are added in Vancouver and Buffalo. The Oakland Seals are sold to Charles O. Finley and he dubs them the California Golden Seals.

1972-73

The formation of the World Hockey Association forces the NHL to expand. The Atlanta Flames and New York Islanders begin play.

1974-75

The NHL adds two more teams in the Kansas City Scouts and Washington Capitals.

1976-77

Although originally planning to grant expansion franchises to Denver and Seattle, the NHL decides to move the financially troubled Scouts to Colorado to become the Rockies, and the California Golden Seals relocate to become the Cleveland Barons.

1977–78
The Cleveland Barons finish their second season in dire financial straits and are merged with the troubled Minnesota North Stars.

1978–79
The WHA plays its final season before merging four of its six remaining franchises with the NHL.

1979–80
The Edmonton Oilers, Hartford Whalers, Quebec Nordiques and Winnipeg Jets begin play.

1980–81
The Atlanta Flames are relocated to Calgary.

1982–83
The Colorado Rockies head east to become the New Jersey Devils. Throughout the season, it is rumoured that the St. Louis Blues will move to Saskatoon, but the relocation never takes place.

1991–92
The San Jose Sharks are added to the league after splitting off from the Minnesota North Stars.

1992–93
The Ottawa Senators and Tampa Bay Lightning are added to the NHL's growing membership.

1993–94
The NHL wants to add more Sunbelt teams and seeks out owners with deep pockets. They welcome the Florida Panthers and Mighty Ducks of Anaheim. The Minnesota North Stars are moved to Texas and become the Dallas Stars.

1995–96

The Quebec Nordiques head west to become the Colorado Avalanche and win the Stanley Cup in their first season.

1996–97

Much to the chagrin of fans in Winnipeg, the Jets are sold and become the Phoenix Coyotes.

1997–98

The Hartford Whalers head south and are renamed the Carolina Hurricanes.

1998–99

The NHL's latest expansion program kicks off when the Nashville Predators begin play.

1999–00

Big-league hockey returns to Atlanta when the Thrashers hold their inaugural season.

2000–01

With the addition of the Columbus Blue Jackets and Minnesota Wild, the NHL's membership increases to 30 teams and a decade of relative franchise stability begins.

2011–12

Hockey in Atlanta is deemed a failure and the Thrashers are moved to Winnipeg, which warmly welcomes the club, and the Jets return to action.

2013–14 AND BEYOND . . .

The New York Islanders will be relocated to Brooklyn beginning with the 2015–16 season.

Financial instability for clubs could potentially lead to more franchise shifts. The often-rumoured locations for new teams include Quebec, Seattle and Kansas City.

At ECW Press, we want you to enjoy this book in whatever format you like, whenever you like. Leave your print book at home and take the eBook to go! Purchase the print edition and receive the eBook free. Just send an email to ebook@ecwpress.com and include:

- the book title
- the name of the store where you purchased it
- your receipt number
- your preference of file type: PDF or ePub?

A real person will respond to your email with your eBook attached. And thanks for supporting an independently owned Canadian publisher with your purchase!

Get the
eBook free!*
*proof of purchase
required